Few countries have had a more turbulent political history in the twentieth century than China. Although China's stability and prosperity in the 1980s offered hope that such turbulence was at an end, the crisis of Tiananmen Square, culminating in the massacre of June 4, 1989, demonstrated that the turbulence is continuing.

Here, eight distinguished China specialists provide broad-ranging, original essays that attempt to explain the dynamics of contemporary Chinese politics by analyzing the preceding patterns of development. Some of the essays focus on the most basic issues of the historical development of Chinese politics: the historical legacy and dilemmas of Deng Xiaoping's leadership, the problem of democracy in China from traditional times to the present, and similarities and differences between Chinese capitalism before the revolution and current reform trends. Other essays focus on developments in important policy areas since 1949: changes in political participation, in industrial policy, in the composition and capacities of the elite, and in China's understanding of its place in the world. The book concludes with a penetrating analysis of the Tiananmen events by Tang Tsou, professor emeritus of political science at the University of Chicago.

Together, the essays detail the weight of the past on Chinese politics, but also the long-term developments that prevent the simple recurrence of previous patterns.

CONTEMPORARY CHINESE POLITICS
IN HISTORICAL PERSPECTIVE

Contemporary Chinese Politics in Historical Perspective

Edited by
BRANTLY WOMACK

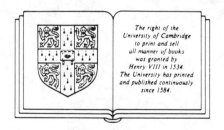

CAMBRIDGE UNIVERSITY PRESS

Cambridge
New York   Port Chester   Melbourne   Sydney

Published by the Press Syndicate of the University of Cambridge
The Pitt Building, Trumpington Street, Cambridge CB2 1RP
40 West 20th Street, New York, NY 10011, USA
10 Stamford Road, Oakleigh, Melbourne 3166, Australia

First published 1991

Printed in Canada

Library of Congress Cataloging-in-Publication Data
Contemporary Chinese politics in historical perspective / edited by
Brantly Womack.
p.   cm.
Includes bibliographical references and index.
ISBN 0-521-41099-1 (hardback). – ISBN 0-521-42282-5 (pbk).
1. China – Politics and government – 1949–   I. Womack, Brantly,
1947–
DS777.75.C66   1991
951.05 – dc20   91-13687
CIP

A catalog record for this book is available from the British Library.

ISBN 0-521-41099-1 hardback
ISBN 0-521-42282-5 paperback

To Yi-chuang Lu

Contents

Contents

Contributors

Marc Blecher is Chair and Professor of the Department of Government at Oberlin College, Oberlin, Ohio. He is the author of *China: Politics, Economy and Society – Iconoclasm and Innovation in a Revolutionary Socialist Country* and co-author of *Micropolitics in Contemporary China* and *The Tethered Deer: The Political Economy of Shulu County*. He has also written articles on Chinese politics, political economy, and political sociology that have appeared in *China Quarterly*, *Comparative Political Studies*, *Journal of Development Studies*, *Modern China*, *Pacific Affairs*, *Socialist Review*, and *World Development*.

Lowell Dittmer taught at the State University of New York at Buffalo and the University of Michigan before joining the Political Science Department of the University of California, Berkeley, in 1978. His principal works include *Liu Shao-ch'i and the Chinese Cultural Revolution*, *China's Continuous Revolution*, and *Sino-Soviet Normalization and Its International Implications*. He is now engaged in a study of Chinese reforms.

Joseph Fewsmith is Associate Professor of International Relations at Boston University. He is the author of *Party, State, and Local Elites in Republican China* and has published numerous articles on contemporary Chinese political and economic affairs. He is currently writing a book on economists and economic reform in the Dengist period.

Edmond Lee received his B.A. degree from Cornell University and is currently working on his doctorate in political science at the University of Chicago. From 1984 to 1987 he did research in Shanghai under a fellowship grant from the Committee on Scholarly Communication with the People's Republic of China. He has published articles in several Chinese academic journals and books. His interests include the politics of business in East Asia, the transitions to and from socialism, and the relationship between ethnicity and the state.

Hong Yung Lee is Professor of Political Science at the University of California, Berkeley, and Research Associate of the East-West Center in Hawaii. He is the author of *From Revolutionary Cadres to Party Technocrats in Socialist China, The Politics of the Chinese Cultural Revolution*, and *Research Guide to Red Guard Materials*.

Peter Nan-shong Lee is Head of the Department of Government and Public Administration at The Chinese University of Hong Kong, as well as Director of the Programme on China's Reform and Development of the Hong Kong Institute of Asia-Pacific Studies. He is the author of *Industrial Management and Economic Reform in China, 1949–1984* and has contributed many articles relating to China's industrial organization and policies in Chinese and Western academic journals.

Tang Tsou is Homer J. Livingston Professor Emeritus, Department of Political Science, University of Chicago. He is the author of *America's Failure in China* and *The Cultural Revolution and Post-Mao Reforms* and co-editor and co-author of *China in Crisis*. He has published articles in *American Political Science Review, World Politics, Political Science Quarterly, Orbis, Western Political Science Quarterly, China Quarterly*, and *Modern China*. He has also published in *Zhengzhi yanjiu* (Beijing), *Guowai zhengzhixue* (Beijing), *Shehui kexue* (Shanghai), and *Jingji shehui tizhi bijiao* (Beijing).

Brantly Womack is Professor of Political Science at Northern Illinois University, DeKalb, Illinois. He is the author of *The Foundations of Mao Zedong's Political Thought, 1917–1934*, co-author of *Politics in China* (3rd ed.), and editor of *Electoral Reform in China* and *Media and the Chinese Public*. He has contributed to *World Politics, China Quarterly, Journal of Asian Studies, Pacific Affairs, Asian Survey, Australian Journal of Chinese Affairs*, and other academic publications. His current research interests include democracy in China and Sino-Vietnamese relations.

Preface

This book began as an effort by some of Tang Tsou's students to honor him. Tang Tsou received his doctorate in political science from the University of Chicago in 1951 (his dissertation concerned the development of American political science), and he has been teaching there since 1959. As his seventieth birthday and retirement approached, Norman Nie, chair of the Political Science Department at the University of Chicago, suggested that his former students might organize a conference in his honor. Experienced academics reading this preface will know that, whether because of a deficit of filial piety among American academics or the lack of a thematic focus at such an occasion, such festschrift conferences and their written products often are diffuse and ephemeral. Former students and colleagues may want to participate out of nostalgia, but for outsiders they are like someone else's family album.

This project was different. First, Tsou's students' bond to their mentor is more than a historical bond. Tang Tsou is the most challenging and wide-ranging China scholar of our acquaintance, and so a conference honoring Tsou found us grappling with a current leader in the field, rather than engaging in retrospective reminiscences.

Second, it was fortunate that a number of Tsou's most active students are established experts in a quite comprehensive spread of important issue areas in Chinese politics. That diversity is due in part to Tsou's respect and support for the intellectual interests of his students. Credit also should be given to the Political Science Department at the University of Chicago, which has stressed intense intellectual activity over a wide range of substantive areas. Given these authors' range of expertise, every essay in this book has at least a monograph's measure of research behind it.

Third, the project had a successful model. Because of the importance of the Cultural Revolution, the University of Chicago sponsored a conference in 1967, called "China in Crisis," that attracted an exceptional collection of China scholars. The co-hosts were Ping-ti Ho of Chicago's History Department and Tang Tsou, and they subsequently edited and published the papers. The full set of *China in Crisis* was an important and popular contribution to the discipline. The first volume contained a general essay on the historical background of contemporary China, by Ho, and a general political analysis of the Cultural Revolution, by Tsou, that were intellectually formative for many in our academic generation. Those essays were rare syntheses of the practical task of coping with the present and the academic virtues of comprehensiveness and profundity. Following that model, each of us set out to write a major essay synthesizing the full range and depth of our various subjects for the present, producing thereby a generational sequel, after twenty-four years, to *China in Crisis.*

Potential participants were enthusiastic about the project, and the Political Science Department of the University of Chicago agreed to underwrite the expenses of a conference. Hong Yung Lee suggested the theme: "Contemporary Chinese Politics in Historical Perspective."

The conference honoring Tsou on the occasion of his seventieth birthday was held December 16, 1988, in the Common Room of Albert Pick Hall. Chris Achen, who had succeeded Norman Nie as chair, provided hospitable arrangements and co-chaired the conference, and Bernard Silberman and David Laitin chaired the two panels. Edward Friedman of the University of Wisconsin and Suzanne Rudolph provided excellent commentary for the panels. The essays were stimulating, and the audience was lively, asking incisive questions, but at the end Tang Tsou stole the show with an impromptu reminiscence that demonstrated how thorough was the blend between his life and his academic effort to understand Chinese politics. Later in the evening, in response to the department's request that he select a retirement gift, Tsou requested that each member give him a reading list of the best books in his or her particular area, because retirement had freed him to become a student again, and he intended to expand his horizons.

The demonstrations and ultimately the massacre of June 4, 1989, in Beijing were the most stirring and traumatic events in Chinese politics since the Cultural Revolution. They required a rethinking and reorientation of the oral presentations made five months earlier. It is testimony to the quality of the earlier work and to the underlying continuity of Chinese politics that the major task was that of reorientation toward the post-Tiananmen situation, rather than massive revisions of previous views. Indeed, Joseph Fewsmith's discussion of fundamental tensions in Deng Xiaoping's politics and Marc Blecher's critique of the antidemocratic features of the post-Mao era seemed prophetic in retrospect. But even the essays that established cumulative trends in various policy areas – the trend toward corporatism in industrial policy described by Peter Lee, and Lowell Dittmer's analysis of the maturing of China's international relations, for example – were borne out by the eventual policy parameters of China's new conservatism. The practical intellectual task of revising our essays, of asking how the events of Tiananmen related to our subjects and what was new and what was old after the massacre, helped pull us through the personal disorientation and depression of the summer of 1989. In retrospect, it is not surprising that an attempt to understand the preceding political phase in its full historical context was the best preparation for understanding the new phase.

Tang Tsou was most deeply affected by the events of Tiananmen. His plans for a relaxed retirement disengaged from Chinese politics may have been somewhat optimistic in any case, but China's tragedy riveted his attention and his emotions. His casual agreement to write a short, informal afterword to this book grew into a massive analytic essay focused on Tiananmen, but also suggesting the pitfalls and possibilities of post-Tiananmen politics. It is the most politically engaged of Tsou's writings, but at the same time the depth of scholarship and the dignity of the individual invested in the essay make it a classic response to a tragic historic event.

With the addition of Tsou's essay, what began as an effort to honor him has become somewhat more complex. Tsou has himself become a major contributor, and perhaps more people will pick up this book to read his essay than to read any other. It is Tsou's total dedication to understanding China that has made him an outstanding teacher and model, and it is fitting that in emulating him and honoring him his students have come to work alongside him.

It is a true pleasure to dedicate this volume to Yi-chuang Lu. Tang Tsou's first book, *America's Failure in China*, was dedicated "To my wife, whose unshakable faith in me has sustained me in my quest for identity." While pursuing her own scholarly career as a research psychologist, known especially for her work on schizophrenia and cross-cultural aspects of psychology, Yi-chuang always found time and energy for us. Tang Tsou joins us in dedicating this volume to her, and it is our heartfelt wish that they both enjoy *jiankang changshou* (health and long life).

Each essayist here acknowledges his own debts to colleagues, but the volume as a whole owes much to Emily Loose at Cambridge University Press. She has been unfailing in her enthusiasm and energy for the project. The external reviewers were helpful in their criticisms and even more helpful in their praise. Ilga Janouskovec of Manuscript Services, College of Liberal Arts at Northern Illinois University, put in countless hours of word processing. Our thanks to Xiaoshan Wang of Northern Illinois University for preparing the index.

This is the point at which the customary superfluous claim is made regarding responsibility for any errors. At the present moment, after Tiananmen and before the death of Deng Xiaoping, China experts are painfully aware of past mistakes and the dangers of anticipating the future. We can hope, however, that the more forgivable of our errors will have a certain historical authenticity in showing the way Chinese politics looked to observers in the aftermath of Tiananmen.

Introduction

BRANTLY WOMACK

The turbulence of Chinese politics in the twentieth century has given a peculiar twist to the utility of historical perspectives. Clearly, the projection of trends, the most obvious application of history, has been notoriously unreliable in Chinese politics. There have been times at which China has appeared to be threatened with national extinction, and it has variously been offered as proof of the international character of world communism, exemplar of a profoundly revolutionary and egalitarian societal model, and a confident pioneer in decentralizing political-economic reform. Each of those impressions was based on a particular course of events, and each proved misleading when projected into the indefinite future.

The most recent — and convincing — experience of the changeability of Chinese politics concerned the events now permanently associated with Tiananmen Square in Beijing. First, those demonstrations could not have been projected on the basis of previous events, although retrospectively we can make sense of them and figure out their origins. The death of Hu Yaobang played an important role in ensuring a sudden and protected beginning for the student movement, and the peculiarly dissonant situation within the top leadership raised hopes and mobilized forces on both sides. Second, the violence of the mass repression on June 4, 1989, was unprecedented. The deeper one's familiarity with Chinese politics, the more profound one's sense of shock and outrage at the massacre. Third, the chief feature of the postmassacre regime has been its unpredictability. It is unclear how long that regime will last, what might succeed it, and how it will attempt to resolve its contradictory commitments to repressive recentralization and to continuing modernization and "openness." By early 1991, anyone seeking to predict a trend is reduced to adding a dot each day to the line of the present.

But the utility of a historical perspective should not be reduced simply to the effectiveness of historical extrapolation. Precisely because of its

1

jagged course, Chinese politics often has been defined more by its historical dynamics than by static structures. The relationships of each phase of Chinese politics to preceding phases have been at least as important to the politics of that phase as have its own institutions and policies. To grasp the significance of major changes, one must step away from day-to-day events and consider the larger linear dynamics that have expressed themselves. Such historical perspectives do not take the surprises out of Chinese politics, but they should reduce the foolishness of interpretations.

The role of historical dynamics in Chinese politics is complex. The most easily demonstrable role is that of informing the actions of the participants. Such influence persists even if the predecessors are disowned. Despite the fact that Chinese modernizers rejected traditional China as a model, there were continuing influences of concepts and values. When the historical dynamics have been experienced personally by the political actors, the influence is, of course, much stronger. Given the rapidity of historical changes in China and the longevity of major political leaders, the role of lived history is undeniable and is ramified through personalities, friendships, and policy identifications.

But history as a subjective influence on actors – ingested history – does not exhaust its influence. Its objective, context-defining role can be distinguished from its effects on the intentions of actors. Here, also, the phases of Chinese politics lean heavily on one another. The magnitude of China's "total crisis" in the first half of the twentieth century can best be appreciated in contrast to the stability of the Chinese empire. Likewise, the centralization and harsh enforcement of orthodoxy in the People's Republic of China were responses to that nightmare of total crisis.

Each political phase leaves problems different from those it inherited. The need for a new phase might be dictated as much by the successes of the current phase as by its failures. For example, when the leftist phase of expansion of basic education began in the late 1950s, there were more college openings than there were senior-high-school graduates. Twenty years later, the rapid expansion of elementary and high-school education had made the need for expansion of the university system a burning issue. New policies and new political actors do not create their own starting points, and to some extent they are defined by what they negate.

If Chinese politics has been dependent on prior historical developments to an unusual degree and in complex ways, then a systematic understanding of such politics, especially by outsiders, requires a special effort to enter the dynamic contexts of Chinese politics and political actors. This does not preclude comparative perspectives and the use of more general concepts from social sciences, but it does subordinate those approaches to an effort to grasp from the inside what is going on in China. The effort to generalize beyond China and to explore the applicability

2

of concepts developed elsewhere are essential activities for the external observer, because one must assume that a more general framework of significance is possible (otherwise China would be solipsistic and impenetrable) and that a language is available for interpreting China to a foreign audience. But if the task of understanding the internal dynamic significance of Chinese politics is subordinated to a comparative or conceptual framework, then a multidimensional, thick reality will be skewed, fixed and flattened by whatever lens or standpoint the researcher assumes.

The approach suggested here requires the researcher to accompany Chinese politics on its linear, jagged course, because the actors, structures, and contexts of each moment depend on preceding developments for their significance. But this is not the same as a reduction of social-scientific interest in China to history. Paul Cohen takes a harsher view of general social-science approaches, but the idea of historical perspective that he puts forth is inadequate to the central research task described here.[1] His analysis of Deng Xiaoping's authoritarian modernization is based on comparisons with the dowager empress Ci Xi's reforms of 1898–1902, Yuan Shikai's reforms of 1911–1915, and Chiang Kai-shek's policies of the 1930s. The comparisons are refreshing in their counterintuitiveness and interesting in their analogies, but they bypass the unique gestalt of each situation. A historical perspective of Deng Xiaoping's reforms might well reach back to Ci Xi's time, but it should center on the dynamics inherent in that phase. Historical precedents, like cross-national models, are interesting, but secondary; the basic task of assessing the self-understanding of the moment should be displaced neither by model-shopping nor by precedent-shopping.

The paradigm for the approach to China taken here derives from the works and teaching of Tang Tsou. It is especially clear in Tsou's *The Cultural Revolution and Post-Mao Reforms*,[2] as well as in the final essay in this volume, that Tsou makes full use of historical analogies and concepts drawn from the social sciences, but at the same time the primary task remains that of understanding the structural dynamics of contemporary Chinese politics. He is an engaged observer whose attentions and energies are directed by the major problems facing Chinese politics, but whose status as an outside observer in the West sublimates engagement into an explication that is passionately careful and objective. In Tsou's hands the task of achieving an internal grasp of Chinese politics appears deceptively easy, because he is himself a member of the series of tragic and heroic generations that redefined China in the twentieth century, and since leaving China in 1947 he has accompanied Chinese politics through his research. He appears at times to expend great effort in finding and defining the social-science concepts with which he abstracts and generalizes his subject, but the conceptualization presupposes a confident un-

3

derstanding of the concrete situation in China. Because of his background and his research he is both a Western China scholar and native to his subject, and thus his insights are deeply appreciated both in the West and in China.

The contributors to this volume, all students of Tang Tsou, come from a wide variety of backgrounds, none, of course, as close to the core of twentieth-century Chinese politics as his own. Not only has he taught us the subject, but he himself has contributed a large part to our image of its subtleties and depth. For us, the effort to grasp the internal dynamics of Chinese politics is a more self-conscious endeavor. We lean more heavily on our concepts and our comparisons, and it is more of a challenge for us to attempt to present the specific areas of our expertise from a comprehensive, historical perspective.

The overall purpose here is to present a series of studies of major aspects of Chinese politics in which each contributor attempts to grasp and explicate the structural dynamic of his subject. These essays are the distillation of tremendous amounts of research and expertise; the seven essays are directly related to four books and two dissertations by the authors, as well as to countless articles. Through some design and much luck, the essays combine to form a remarkably comprehensive overview of Chinese politics, in terms of general patterns of development and also important policy areas.

The volume is structured into four parts. Part I, "Contemporary China and its prerevolutionary heritage," contains three chapters primarily concerned with the general pattern of modern Chinese politics. Fewsmith and Womack present overviews of the key problems of modernization and democracy, and Edmond Lee explores the problems of continuity and change through an in-depth examination of reformism in Shanghai. Part II, "Policy dynamics within the People's Republic of China," addresses the policy areas of local political participation, industrial policy, and cadre policy. As important as these topics are, the authors go beyond them to address more fundamental issues, such as the dynamics of grassroots politics during the Cultural Revolution and its fate in the Deng Xiaoping era, the restructuring of the state–society relationship, and the reciprocal effects of policy shifts and personnel recruitment within the Chinese Communist Party. Part III, "China's evolving world role," is composed of a major study by Lowell Dittmer of the emergence and shaping of China's national identity in a world context. He presents a comprehensive overview of China's self-presentation from 1949 to the present vis-à-vis its two major reference groups: the communist world and the Third World. In Part IV, "Tiananmen," Tang Tsou has contributed a major essay analyzing not only the crisis of 1989 but also the dangers and opportunities confronting post-Tiananmen Chinese politics.

4

Introduction

Joseph Fewsmith's essay, "The Dengist reforms in historical perspective," reaches back to the early twentieth century in order to understand present-day reforms, because, as he demonstrates, "although the Dengist reforms represent a reaction against the Cultural Revolution and the 'leftist' traditions within the CCP, they also are forced to confront the very dilemmas that produced the communist movement and revolution in the first place." Fewsmith's analysis emphasizes the resonance between traditional Chinese conceptions of politics and Leninism. A striking example is the underlying communitarian idea of the relationship of "public" and "private" (*gong* and *si*) in traditional thought, in the writings of the pioneer reformer Liang Qichao, and in Leninism. Although Liang criticized the traditional view, and the communists in turn criticized Liang's bourgeois view, each dissolved the individual into his social responsibilities, rather than, as in the modern West, constructing society from the interests and wills of individuals. Leninism succeeded in China not only because it fit the needs of a society in total crisis[3] but also because of the appeal of such "neo-traditional" aspects of its ideology.

Needless to say, a doctrine that is both revolutionary and neo-traditionalist, that expresses both China's resistance to external threat and its desire to be part of cosmopolitan progress, contains within itself deep contradictions. Its goal is modernization, but it is unwilling to acknowledge the unfolding of a society that is autonomous in its economic and political decision making. Hence, there is tension between the decentralizing reforms of the 1980s and the Leninist denial of privacy and citizenship. That tension has led to vacillation between periods of pragmatic suspension of orthodoxy (with everyone merely being encouraged to "get rich") and periods of crackdown and retrenchment.

China's relationship to the West manifests a similar tension, and here the tension has a geographical dimension as well as a historical dimension. A distinction is made between a coastal tradition that is more Westernized and commercially oriented and a hinterland that is agricultural and conservative. In between is a "self-strengthening" position that attempts to combine the values of both. The tension between those traditions has been a prominent thread in Chinese intellectual history, with many knots of controversy. The most recent is the controversy over the 1988 television documentary "River Elegy" (*He shang*), which portrayed China as an antimodern, riverine culture, and therefore implicitly an obstacle to its own modernization. Such a thoroughly critical view of one's own culture would elicit a powerful response in any country, and in 1989 the uproar led to a major campaign to discredit that documentary, coupled with presentations of new documentaries extolling China's historical grandeur.

The picture that Fewsmith paints of the Deng Xiaoping era looks quite

5

a bit different from the image that was common before June 1989: a modernizing leadership whose views differed only regarding the pace of modernization.[4] His is a darker picture of fundamental tensions not likely to wither away. It is remarkable that his essay was written before the upheavals of 1989, for its perspective rings even more true as a result of those unanticipated developments. Deng's claim that the demonstrators wanted to destroy the party is intelligible in terms of the contradiction between the Leninist state and the citizens' demands for rights that inevitably accompanied decentralization. The crisis and its outcome could not be foretold, but the major issues of that confrontation can be illuminated by a historical perspective.

The historical background for Brantly Womack's chapter, "In search of democracy: public authority and popular power in China," reaches to the foundations of Chinese civilization. It returns to the classics, because the relationship between popular power and public authority in China has followed a path quite different from that of Western parliamentary democracy, and so China's entire course of development must be considered. After contrasting the relationships between tradition and modernity in China and in the West, the essay explores the various attempts to adapt Western political ideologies, including Marxism, to Chinese conditions, concluding with an analysis of the political outcome of the Deng Xiaoping era.

The fundamental problem of democratization in China is that the period of total crisis early in the twentieth century created a situation in which Chinese political traditions came to be discredited, and Western political ideals were inappropriate. As a result, there was a series of adaptations, linked with the names of Sun Yat-sen, Mao Zedong, and Deng Xiaoping, that succeeded by linking aspects of modern politics with features of the existing political environment. As if in a series of Greek tragedies, the specific strengths of each of those innovative protagonists in time became their weaknesses, but in the process China moved beyond the ruins of a disintegrated traditional state to the edge of a modern political order.

Paradoxically, a serious consideration of democracy in China must begin with traditional China, because traditional China was conspicuously lacking in the rudiments of modern democratic ideology and institutions. Even the term for democracy, *minzhu*, was a neologism invented to describe European governments. In contrast to the West's slow, internal evolution of parliamentary democracy from aristocratic privilege, democratic reform in China was a radical, externally oriented attempt to vault directly from chaos to order and prosperity. Not only did the gulf between tradition and modernity in China define a political situation in which borrowed Western ideals would be inappropriate, but the cultural underpinning of the attempt to transform China was itself traditional.

Each of the three relatively successful ventures in modern Chinese politics sprang from a sobering reorientation mandated by failure. In the case of Sun Yat-sen, it was the failure of parliamentary institutions to redefine Chinese politics after the collapse of the empire in 1911. By the 1920s, Sun had decided that China was "a sheet of loose sand" that needed strong, pragmatic leadership before liberty. The compromise that Sun made with Chinese reality was to accommodate any real power, whether it be warlords, imperialists, Russians, or the Chinese Communist Party (CCP), in order to preserve and extend the influence of his Nationalist Party, the Guomindang (GMD), at the same time using the organizational strength of the GMD to maintain direction of the alliance. In other words, Sun settled for rearranging the top level of Chinese politics, for the moment giving up on restructuring the relationship of the people to the state. As a result, the GMD succeeded as a modern force, but not as a democratic one. Sun's realpolitik was based on the assumption that the people were not a power.

Mao Zedong's assumption was the opposite. The failure of the CCP in 1927 threw him into the countryside, and his survival depended on finding a way to organize peasant support for a party that had been created by urban intellectuals. His stroke of genius, which eventually made him a figure of millennial importance in Chinese history, was to reconstitute Chinese politics by organizing what had been its neglected periphery into an overwhelming revolutionary force. After twenty-two years of rural revolution, the CCP not only overthrew the GMD and its supporting rat's nest of elite accommodations but also formed the basis for a vastly more powerful state reaching into the social atoms of Chinese society.

In contrast to the program of Sun, Mao's method might be termed less modern but more democratic: The organizational center of gravity was dispersed in the villages; focus and unity were maintained through ideological study and a series of mass mobilizations, rather than through bureaucracy and professionalism. Although popular votes and deliberations did not control policy, the party had to be mass-regarding in its behavior because its only significant resource against a vastly more powerful enemy was popular support. The revolutionary base areas under the CCP had a "quasi-democratic system": Although the political structure was not democratic, the environment of competition with more powerful enemies required the party to pursue mass-regarding policies.

Victory in 1949 confirmed Mao's confidence in himself, the party, and the mass line, and it also established the party-state's monopoly of power. The party drifted toward Leninist bureaucratism, and Mao's attempts in the "Great Leap Forward" and the "Cultural Revolution" to renew the revolution by mobilizing the masses were disastrous. Instead of the quasi-democratic system of yore, Mao's dogmatic interventions created a quasi-totalitarian situation in which locally based anarchic groups fought each other over ideological, leadership-regarding issues. The negative effects of such leftist turbulence created a situation in which both the party leadership and the people recoiled from the dogmatic totalism of Mao's continuing revolution.

The reality to which Deng Xiaoping adjusted after the death of Mao was that of an overextended party-state, one that was too demanding and too penetrating. By pragmatically reorienting Chinese politics toward economic modernization and engaging in bold experiments with decentralization, Deng renewed the party's political leadership in a postrevolutionary environment. Although overshadowed by economic reforms, significant progress was made in legal reform and in political institutional reform. For almost a decade China appeared to have the most progressive leadership in the communist world.

The Achilles' heel of the Deng Xiaoping era was that the central leadership that patronized the reforms was itself unreformed. The bankruptcy of Cultural Revolution leftism gave the elite and the masses a common ground, but as the reforms progressed, the contradiction became sharper between an old vanguardist leadership and a society prospering because of its greater autonomy. Finally, in Tiananmen Square the new societal leadership demanded to be acknowledged as citizens rather than as masses, and in a tragic reassertion of the power of the past, the old guard threw out its reformist protégés and terrorized society into silence. For the moment, the future of Chinese politics lies uncertain in the battle zone between the organized power of the party-state and the dispersed power of society.

In sum, the relationship between public authority and the power of the people in China has taken a very different course from that of the liberal democratic West. The first modern government to follow the collapse of traditional China was a rather weak, aggregative authoritarian government. The second, based on revolutionary mobilization of the countryside, was truly innovative, opening a new chapter in popular revolutions, as well as in Chinese history. But it squandered its popular support in attempting to invoke revolutionary solutions for postrevolutionary problems. Finally, Deng Xiaoping achieved success and popularity by adjusting the policy of the party-state to the postrevolutionary environment, but ultimately he refused to adjust its structure and to leave the stage voluntarily.

Edmond Lee's chapter, "A bourgeois alternative? The Shanghai arguments for a Chinese capitalism: the 1920s and the 1980s," illustrates

8

the significance of historical and regional dynamics by comparing the reform ideology of contemporary Shanghai writers to that of their capitalist forerunners of the 1920s: the Shanghai General Chamber of Commerce. Lee then goes beyond comparison to a critical evaluation of the shared assumptions of the Shanghai perspective.

Lee's basic argument is that as much as the politics of China has changed in the past sixty years, reform in Shanghai is a new branch from an old root. The Shanghai of the 1980s was nostalgic about its past glory, resentful of its lack of progress in comparison with Tokyo and Hong Kong, and eager to "get rich first" through capitalistic modernization. The reformers of the 1980s shared the old assumptions that economic restructuring could solve all problems, that capitalism was patriotic, and that private property, market mechanisms, profits, and economic individualism were necessary for China's prosperity. Of course, Shanghai would be in a position to profit more from such reforms than would the areas that Fewsmith refers to as hinterland China, but Shanghai writers have always seen such uneven development as necessary for China's general prosperity. The major difference between the old and the new Shanghai positions was that the former advocated protectionism, whereas the latter supported free trade.

But what does the resilience of Shanghai's capitalist proclivities mean? Do continuities demonstrate the eternity of economic truth, or the narrow stubbornness of regionalistic interests? Edmond Lee finds not a little of the latter. After all, Shanghai capitalism in the 1920s may have benefited itself, but it did not elevate China. In the 1980s, the "Shanghai model" avoided the problem of accentuating the differences between the coast and hinterland, and among societal groups. Perhaps more fundamentally, the tendency of Shanghai to emphasize economics and to ignore politics did not work in the 1920s and may not work in the 1990s. The political structures in which economic reforms take place will influence even the economic outcomes, and "for every England and Japan, there are ten Polands and Burmas."

The general picture that Edmond Lee presents is disturbing to our stereotypes of the struggle over reform in the 1980s. The West favors Western-style reform in China and would like to see it as forward-looking and cosmopolitan, rather than localistic, as well as rational and coherent, in contrast to the self-interested habits of a conservative party-state. Although not hostile to the Shanghai approach, Lee's essay makes it clear that the Shanghai approach is not a thin, piercing ray of truth, but a thick subculture with local roots and internal tensions.

Part II of this volume concerns the evolution of major policy areas, and the lead essay is by Marc Blecher: "The contradictions of grass-roots participation and undemocratic statism in Maoist China and their fate."

On the basis of extensive interviews and research, Blecher presents a sophisticated and startling argument. He begins by contending that the democratic quality of village-level participation in China in the Maoist period has been ignored. There were impressive levels of spontaneity, expressions of divergent opinions, and access to leadership during that period. However, both the strength and the problem of local-level leadership derived from its relationship to the state. Initially, the unity of peasant and party interests in rural revolution and socialist construction encouraged lively local participation. However, the policies of the leftist period had contradictory effects. On the one hand, the state encouraged participation, and the redistributive character of local issues led to a radicalization of local politics. On the other hand, Blecher argues that local interest in participation was eventually alienated by the state's increasing monopolization of all significant issues. In effect, the state encouraged everyone to swim while it was draining the pool of issues. The Cultural Revolution was, as he puts it, "the fullest culmination of the contradiction between participatory local politics and undemocratic statism."

The post-Mao era, which usually is depicted as a period of democratization, appears quite different from Blecher's perspective. Local participation depended on the unity of politics and economics, and Deng's decollectivization policies dissolved that unity. The political structures of the team, brigade, and commune were simply no longer in charge of the vital economic decisions of daily life. Whereas the penetration of the leftist state had emasculated local politics, the retreat of the Dengist state depoliticized major areas of life, leaving local institutions in disoriented, caretaker roles. To be sure, Deng also strengthened the democratic institutions of the state, especially the people's congress system, but by and large the people ceased to be direct participants in politics – the politicized masses – and their new capacities as citizens in a representational system were but pale substitutes.

Far from creating dissatisfaction by diffusing mass politics, Deng created a depoliticized social base for the authoritarian state. Peasant energies were devoted to their private economic pursuits. As Blecher puts it, they had given up their revolutionary political role and had become politically dispersed and inert – the peasant potatoes despaired of by Marx in his pamphlet *The Eighteenth Brumaire*. And rural smallholders might well become the foundation of an authoritarian state in China, as they had for Napoleon III in France. The events of 1989 demonstrated the power and autonomy first of urban society and then of the state, and an authoritarian state may yet prevail as the guarantor of the newly created private worlds of the peasants.

Peter Nan-shong Lee's essay, "The Chinese industrial state in historical perspective: from totalitarianism to corporatism," breaks new ground by arguing for a corporatist interpretation of Chinese reforms in industrial policy from the 1950s to the present. The corporatist model, based on accommodation between the central leadership and the components of the economic system, reconciles the otherwise contradictory images of the all-powerful Chinese state and its incapacity to attain its economic objectives.

Peter Lee begins by distinguishing economic totalitarianism and political totalitarianism. Political totalitarianism is leadership based on revolutionary ideals, charisma, and mass mobilization. It was unusually strong in China and underwent unique postrevolutionary transformations in the Cultural Revolution. Economic totalitarianism is the subordination of the whole economy under central administrative rationality. In contrast to political totalitarianism, economic totalitarianism in China was more like Stalinism elsewhere, although weaker in its implementation. Tinkering with economic totalitarianism began in the mid–1950s, but experimentation was confounded and delayed by the failure of the Great Leap Forward and later by the ideological dogmatism of the Cultural Revolution.

As in the case of political totalitarianism, the reforms of the Deng Xiaoping era have marked a retreat from the presumption of unitary rational control of the economy. But a study of industrial policy reveals that economic totalitarianism is not simply decaying toward pluralistic incrementalism, as the direction of reform might suggest. Instead, the process has been one of granting limited autonomy in specific areas to individual enterprises in order to link the material interests of enterprises and workers with the modernization interests of the state. Totalitarianism's hard and arbitrary line of power gradually and partially softens into more flexible structures of mutual interest.

This complex and subtle development is explored in two areas: enterprise incentive and worker incentive. In the totalitarian model, both enterprise and worker are simply links in a command economy. But as the incapacities of mere power become apparent, policies are adopted by the central leadership to acknowledge the substantive interests of these subordinate levels in order to encourage their cooperation and initiative.

Mao Zedong first recognized the importance of a differentiated economic structure in his well-known essay "On the Ten Major Relationships," but attempts to decentralize industry in the Great Leap Forward were disastrous failures. The Cultural Revolution's hostility to material incentives had a stultifying influence on further corporatist reforms, but the post-Mao era blossomed with a series of decentralizing concessions. First, enterprises were allowed to retain a percentage of their profits; then, in 1983, they retained their profits and paid taxes on them; finally, large enterprises were permitted to experiment with a contractual system. Enterprise autonomy, however, has been constricted by two reservations on the part of the central leadership. First, the center has viewed the reforms as administrative adjustments, rather than as legal grants of authority that might restructure the center–enterprise relationship. As in politics, the Dengist regime has not let go of its end of the economic string. Second, the greater freedom allowed to enterprise initiative can be used only in the given environment of artificial prices and administratively allocated resources.

In the area of worker incentives, the initial concessions in the 1950s were those that created "work-unit (*danwei*) socialism": the provision of communal, nonwage benefits, including ironclad job security, that insulated state workers from the uncertainties and hardships of the general economy. Early experiments with bonus and piece-rate systems ran afoul of leftist egalitarianism. Deng Xiaoping has attempted to use wage policy to increase the individual worker's production incentives, but with mixed results. Six wage increases were granted between 1977 and 1983, and bonus systems have been instituted, but within the work unit there has been little differentiation according to output, and enterprises distribute windfall bonuses unrelated to or in excess of profits. On the more basic issue of the structure of employment, there has been some progress in expanding contractual employment, but it has yet to replace the lifetime security of work-unit socialism.

One might say that the importance of the corporatist model in China is demonstrated by the continuing difficulties as well as by the successes of corporatist reform. On the positive side, the remarkable economic success of the 1980s undoubtedly was founded on acknowledgment of the importance of material interests and a more complex structure of economic incentives. On the negative side, the regime's reluctance to restructure economic power and the tenacity of the workers in clinging to collective benefits demonstrate that the tensions of the economic structure have not been resolved by specific compromises, but only acknowledged. The future of the Chinese economy is likely to be one of further compromises, rather than either the return of economic totalitarianism or complete decontrol of the economy.

The evolution described in Hong Yung Lee's "From revolutionary cadres to bureaucratic technocrats" is not primarily a matter of institutional or policy development, but of the composition of officials and party members in the People's Republic of China (PRC). The question of the character of the political elite – their origins, capacities, outlook, and interests – is especially important in China because the party-state is both tremendously powerful and underinstitutionalized, a situation that gives enormous discretion to the political elite. As Hong Yung Lee observes, "the importance of the political elite is inversely related to the degree of institutionalization of political offices."

The political elite of China compose an especially complicated phenomenon: disciplined and yet non-Weberian, always touting youth and progress and yet ruled by seniority and the ghosts of earlier triumphs, revolutionary and yet reeking of feudalism, dispersed through every nook and cranny of society and yet not representative. The elite is a monolith, though clearly lined with different sedimentary strata of generational experience, and sharply fissured by cataclysms like the Cultural Revolution and Tiananmen. Even if the policy environment of China were placid, the tensions of such monumental contradictions would generate internal dynamics.

The party was already a composite when it came to power in 1949. On the one hand, its founding members and continuing top leadership were members of the urban, progressive intellectual class committed to the rebirth and modernization of China. On the other hand, the CCP had failed as an urban proletarian movement in 1927, but had succeeded in the following two decades by building an overwhelmingly rural, lower-class party. Although the party members were somewhat more literate and better educated than the population at large, the party had become a collection of village mobilizers rather than national modernizers.

The individual capacities and habits of that novel political elite determined, in large part, the aggregate capacity and style of the party-state. Many leftist and antiprofessional aspects of PRC policy normally attributed to Mao Zedong's personal proclivities are better interpreted as natural responses of an officialdom with only rural revolutionary expertise. They tried to handle tasks as an unstructured, personalistic "virtuocracy," in which the leaders of units were motivated more by uneasy anticipation of future rectification campaigns than by effective rules and regulations. To such a party, the Great Leap Forward was more congenial than Liu Shaoqi's attempts to Leninize and professionalize the party-state.

The Cultural Revolution created new divisions among the elite: initiators, beneficiaries, survivors, and victims. When the victims returned to power after the death of Mao, their personal experiences as victims, as well as their earlier preferences for bureaucratic modernization, led them to deemphasize ideology, to recruit intellectuals, and to raise educational standards for the elite. Those policies reshaped the party and state bureaucracies in the 1980s, but the principle of seniority has allowed the old guard to maintain its grasp on central leadership. Moreover, the new technocrats are divided into two camps: the more conservative, who, like Li Peng, favor cautious, centrally controlled modernization, and the more liberal, who want to progress by limiting the party and promoting decentralized initiative. Undoubtedly, these differences are now being compounded by the government's current policies, which are pitting the two interest groups against each other. Although the power of the state remains impressive, Hong Yung Lee believes that an essentially retrogressive effort to return to the Leninist state, like Mao's effort to return to Yanan in the Cultural Revolution, will eventually fail, leaving new fissures and new structural challenges for succeeding leaders.

Part III of this volume, "China's evolving world role," is composed of a single essay: Lowell Dittmer's "China's search for its place in the world." By analyzing China's relationships with its two most important reference groups, the communist bloc and the Third World, from 1949 to the present, Dittmer explores the structural dynamics of China's national (or international) identity.

The national identity of the PRC was originally based on complete repudiation of the preceding regime and its international relationships, as well as the assumption of a community of interest with two large and somewhat overlapping groups of countries: the communist world, and the more amorphous collection of colonies, former colonies, and poorer countries that came to be called the Third World. In general, China's behavior toward both groups developed from (1) a certain naive and friendly intensity in the 1950s to (2) an erratic "crazy behavior" from 1957 to the 1970s, costing China standing with both those reference groups, to (3) a gradual resumption of more distant and complex relations in the 1980s.

Although China's relations with the members of the communist world have always been determined largely by its relationship with the Soviet Union, Dittmer shows that they are by no means reducible solely to that pattern. China's initial assumption that the bloc represented an intimate community can be seen in the apparent contradiction between its tolerance for the Polish party in 1956 and its eventual harshness toward Hungary later in the year. The Polish developments were treated as non-threatening, fraternal diversity, a reflection of China's self-understanding of its own relationship to the bloc and to Soviet leadership. The Hungarian situation, however, quickly developed into a challenge that was perceived as hostile and external, an antagonistic contradiction. Similarly, China at first insisted on Soviet leadership of the bloc, turning down Khrushchev's power-sharing proposal, until it decided that Khrushchev was taking the revisionist road.

The events of 1957 posed a crisis for China's national identity, as well as for its domestic politics, and its external identity crisis was linked to but not identical with the swings of domestic policy. The China-induced crisis in bloc politics reached its most dangerous point as China was recovering from the Great Leap Forward, and its return to less ideological international relations began in the early 1970s, considerably before

Mao's death, and with his active participation. The bloc wounds were slow to heal, in part because "normalization" with the West was defined in terms of a united front against Soviet "hegemonism." Following normalization with the United States in early 1979, and Deng Xiaoping's general ideological mellowing, the CCP rapidly expanded its relations with other parties, not only with eighty communist parties but also with 150 other parties, culminating in Mikhail Gorbachev's upstaged visit to Beijing in May 1989. China is not as heavily invested in these relationships as it had been in the 1950s, nor are they as exclusive.

The PRC's affinity for the Third World is a different peer relationship, although the broad pattern of development is similar to that of its relationships with fellow communist countries. China's successful revolution was, of course, a model and inspiration to others suffering imperialist domination, and the dimension of encouragement to revolution underlies and entangles China's relationships with a number of countries, such as Malaysia, Indonesia, and Thailand. But China's major success in the 1950s was as a proponent of peaceful coexistence and Third World solidarity, symbolized by China's role at the Bandung conference in 1955.

With the radicalization of Chinese domestic politics in 1957, China became more discriminating and critical in its Third World relations, shunning bourgeois nationalist regimes. Dittmer speculates that in part that may have been due to competition with India for Third World leadership and to a difference with the Soviet Union regarding the likely American response to low-level conflict. During the Cultural Revolution, relations with the Third World deteriorated, and when China moved to a less ideologically bound standard for diplomacy in the 1970s (and improved its relations with the patrons of some states) it achieved nearly universal diplomatic recognition. The "theory of three worlds," attributed to Mao, but given its most complete statement by Deng Xiaoping in 1974, again lodged a claim for Chinese prominence in the Third World, and China has since actively pursued an advocacy of the interests of less-developed countries (LDCs) in many world forums. However, China is now also a competitor with other LDCs for concessionary benefits from the World Bank and other organizations, having sharply curtailed its own aid programs. In a number of important areas it has interests more closely associated with the interests of the developed countries. Here, too, China's relationships are more extensive, less intimate, and perhaps more stable than ever before.

The general implication of Dittmer's analysis for the present period is that a general maturation of China's national identity has taken place, and the restoration of old ties as well as the development of new ones toward the West do not mean a return to the old, tight relationship between China's sense of domestic mission and its international role. As the paths of China and European communist countries begin to diverge sharply this analysis will be tested.

The final essay in this volume, Tang Tsou's "The Tiananmen tragedy: the state–society relationship, choices, and mechanisms in historical perspective," is dramatically different from the others in that it is rooted in the vivid present of the post-Tiananmen world and the political choices now facing Chinese inside and outside of China. The essay is the most vigorous and gripping of Tsou's works; the nexus between political engagement and political analysis that is implicit in almost all of his writings here lies just below the surface.

The structure of the essay is un-Tsouist. Rather than beginning with a conceptual framework or at the beginning of a historical sequence (as his faithful students tend to do in this volume), he begins with the post-Tiananmen political crisis defined by a repressive regime in power and a radicalized intelligentsia in exile. Neither can unseat the other, and the confrontation seems desperate on the part of both antagonists, as well as fraught with danger for China. Stepping back, he sketches some general trends that led to the confrontation between the party-state and civil society, as well as the context of communication and leadership that constrained the party-state's responsiveness. Tsou then gives an analytical narration of Tiananmen developments from the standpoint of the "rejected options" and "inaccessible alternatives" of Zhao Ziyang and the demonstrators, detailing the prerequisites for a compromise, where opportunities apparently existed, and how the party discipline of the reformers, the radical spontaneity of the students, and disjunctive communications contributed to the failure to seize those opportunities. The concluding question, whether or not a reform option exists in the wake of the June 4 massacre, returns the essay to its beginning, but with a difference: The stalemate, the inability of either state or society to defeat the other, becomes the prerequisite for a possible politics of reconciliation.

To return to the beginning, the reality of post-Tiananmen politics is a polarization between a regime stigmatized by its use of repressive measures and a profoundly alienated urban society whose vocal spokesmen are in exile abroad. The power of each is considerable, and beyond the reach of the other: The government controls state power, while the exiles attempt to sway world opinion and affect China's international image and relations. The government's successes in repression, on the one hand, and the successes of the exiles in isolating China, on the other, do not end the hostile stalemate, but rather make the prospect of a peaceful and prosperous future for China seem more distant.

The confrontation between state and society that emerged so explosively in 1989 can be understood only in terms of the real but incomplete changes in the party-state that developed in the 1980s. The most basic of those developments was the recession of state penetration into society. As Deng Xiaoping ruefully noted in his speech of June 9, 1989, the party gradually lost its hegemony in ideology, culture, literature, and art during the 1980s, with the intellectual interests and tastes of China being set by renewed exposure to the West. New "public spaces" emerged in which heterodox views could be expressed or implied as long as they did not directly confront and challenge the party. Even the party's central role of providing political leadership was subtly undermined by its own research institutes, which designed public policy on the basis of expertise and innovation. Those changes, in conjunction with the massive societal effects of economic decentralization and decontrol, gave rise to an expectation and a momentum for continuing liberalization.

However, the prospects for a smooth development from liberalization to democratization were impeded by the official communications structure and the monistic structure of party leadership. The official communications structure tends to restrict the availability of reliable information to the party leadership and to provide for public consumption only information that supports the leadership's current agenda. The public's desire for credible, nonofficial information is supplied by rumor and by foreign news sources, especially the Voice of America, the BBC World Service, and the Hong Kong media. This results in two disjunctive communications worlds, the official and the unofficial, and the danger of miscommunication is especially acute and dangerous in a crisis situation. When martial law was declared, even the regime's dire threats were not credible, because they were contradicted by the occasional rumor or opinion.

Tsou goes into great detail in discussing the monistic structure of party leadership and its consequences, because it is a defining characteristic of the CCP "rules of the game," and it was the chief constraint on Zhao Ziyang's behavior toward the demonstrators. The leadership core ultimately reduces to one person, and party discipline prohibits any behavior other than unconditional compliance. Tsou uses newly available sources to explore the especially lurid case of Peng Dehuai's removal at the Lushan conference in 1959, but the critique of Zhao Ziyang's behavior during May 1989 betrays the same party norms. Zhao was caught in a fatal contradiction between the demands of his position as subordinate to Deng Xiaoping and the demands of his policy commitment to reform. Ultimately he upheld his reform convictions, but in doing so he lost his power and was castigated for violating the norms of monistic leadership.

With the structural and historical background that Tsou provides, the developments in Tiananmen look quite different from the television portrayal at the time. From the point of view of the central leadership, recognition of the autonomous student associations and repudiation of the April 26 editorial were options that had to be rejected. Deng perceived the challenge to the party-state implicit in granting autonomy, and Zhao could not challenge Deng's core leadership role. Zhao's "inaccessible alternative" was to temporize with the students, providing practical acknowledgments of their legitimacy and organizations, as well as guarantees against retribution, in the hope that the confrontation would end peacefully. The students, however, were in the opposite situation. Inconclusive withdrawal was their rejected option, in part because of their idealism and immaturity, in part because the spontaneity of the movement favored whoever promised to be the most radical leader and promptly discarded leaders who favored compromise. There were many messengers offering compromises to the students at various times, and the most promising was a statement issued on May 14 by twelve leading intellectuals that backed the major demands of the students but asked them to withdraw from the square. But the students were unwilling and organizationally unable to yield their tactical and moral advantage of occupation for a limited strategic and political gain. Their "inaccessible alternative" was a formal retreat by the government prior to their withdrawal from Tiananmen Square, precisely what Zhao Ziyang could not deliver. The all-or-nothing approach of both Deng Xiaoping and the students locked them into irreconcilable struggle.

The tragic results of the conflict are well known, and they produced an unprecedented polarization of state and society. But Tsou finds hope for reconciliation in the very situation of stalemate that both the regime and the exiled radicals find so frustrating. Because neither side can decisively eliminate the other, the mentality of total victory is inappropriate. Needless to say, the existence of a theoretical possibility of reconciliation is a far cry from practical prospects, and the worst-case scenario of each side pursuing its own situational advantage to the detriment of China continues to prevail. Perhaps Tsou's ultimate "hope against hope" is that the analytical power of this essay will contribute to political reasonableness and prudent leadership for China.

A multifaceted sense of China's historical individuality emerges from these essays. The authors have taken seriously the task of understanding the dynamics of Chinese politics, and though the picture that emerges is claimed to be neither complete nor univocal, it conveys the impression of a four-dimensional political reality, a thick polity in the process of formation through its own experiences. Although the confidence of China-watchers and Chinese in the predictability of Chinese politics was profoundly shaken by the events of 1989, it can be expected that the tensions, tendencies, and ideas described here will help shape the near future, and the near future's future as well.

These essays also attempt to make more general contributions to comparative politics. The notions of participation, democracy, corporatism, elite theory, and so forth that are discussed and applied here are not only useful in understanding China. The application to China becomes a test and an extension of these concepts. The unarticulated ecology of elite theory, for example, born of the late-nineteenth-century European experience of the co-optation of the leadership of mass socialist parties by bourgeois systems, is shaken like a rag doll in applying it to a revolutionary lower-class, peasant elite. What remains intellectually useful in this utterly alien context must be a truly profound insight into modern politics. In this application, elite theory makes a contribution to understanding China, and China begins to make a small part of its potential contribution to the general understanding of world politics. That is the purpose of academic study of Chinese politics, and it is exemplified for his students by the teaching and writings of Tang Tsou.

NOTES

1. Paul Cohen, "The Post-Mao Reforms in Historical Perspective," *Journal of Asian Studies* 47, no. 3 (August 1988): 518–540.
2. Tang Tsou, *The Cultural Revolution and Post-Mao Reforms: A Historical Perspective* (Chicago: University of Chicago Press, 1986).
3. This is Tang Tsou's argument in "Reflections on the Formation and Foundations of the Communist Party-State in China," in *Cultural Revolution*, pp. 259–334.
4. This is, for instance, the view suggested by Harry Harding's discussion of "moderate" and "radical" reformers in *China's Second Revolution* (Washington, D.C.: Brookings Institution, 1987).

PART I

Contemporary China and its prerevolutionary heritage

1

The Dengist reforms in historical perspective

JOSEPH FEWSMITH

The events of June 4, 1989, in a very real sense brought the Dengist period to a close. What defined the Dengist period more than anything else were three interrelated premises: the subordination of ideological struggle to economic development, the adoption of a "middle course," and the recognition of the "relative autonomy" of specific fields of knowledge. The crackdown on June 4 severely compromised each of those.

The Third Plenum of the Eleventh Central Committee, in December 1978 – the meeting that marked the inauguration of the Dengist period – called for shifting the emphasis of work to economic development. The importance of that decision lay in its reversal of the relationship that had existed between ideology and economic policy in the preceding three decades of the People's Republic of China (PRC). Previously, ideology had been the linchpin around which economic policy revolved. At the Third Plenum, the effort to integrate the party and nation around a common ideology, which had resulted in violent ideological struggle rather than unity, was abandoned in favor of an agreement on the primacy of economic development. The presumption was that with economic development, both the urgency and the divisiveness of ideological questions would be reduced.

Ideology thus changed from an organizing principle to a boundary. As expressed by the "Four Cardinal Principles" – which affirmed the leading position of the Chinese Communist Party (CCP), the role of Marxism-Leninism and Mao Zedong Thought, the people's democratic dictatorship, and the socialist road – ideology became a marker beyond which the expression of ideas was not to go, a barrier against "bourgeois liberalization." The Four Cardinal Principles were thus the counterpoint of the Third Plenum's emphasis on fighting "leftist" ideas, a thrust that

I would like to thank A. Doak Barnett, Paul Cohen, and Brantly Womack for their comments on an earlier draft of this chapter.

found expression in such pragmatic slogans as "emancipate the mind," "seeking truth from practice," and "practice is the sole criterion of truth." The opposition to "leftist" ideas, on the one hand, and bourgeois liberalization, on the other, thus defined, as Tang Tsou has pointed out, a "middle course" that struggled *against two fronts*. That middle course, then, attempted to build political consensus by rejecting the Cultural Revolution's emphasis on struggle *between two lines*.[1]

That focus on economic development and the demarcation of a middle course were accompanied by a recognition of the "relative autonomy" of specific fields of knowledge and the limits of state control. That recognition was based on an acceptance of what Tang Tsou calls the "sociological postulate" that "every sphere of social life and its activities has its special characteristics (*tedian*) and is governed by special laws" and the corresponding injunction that the "political leadership can and should create the general conditions favorable to the operation of these laws to promote development, but it cannot violate these laws without suffering serious consequences."[2]

For most of the decade that followed 1978 those premises underlay a gradual, though not uninterrupted, depoliticization of the Chinese economy, polity, and culture. That trend was challenged at several points – most notably in the campaign to criticize the writer Bai Hua in 1981, the campaign against "spiritual pollution" in 1983, and the campaign against "bourgeois liberalization" in 1987 – but, overall, the "center of gravity" of Chinese politics continued to shift toward greater depoliticization of society, greater use of market forces, and more recognition of societal diversity – until the use of force to suppress the democracy movement in 1989.

That shift was most apparent in the area of economic reform, with which the Dengist regime was so closely identified – the implementation of the rural responsibility system, the rapid development of rural enterprises, the adoption of various forms of the contract responsibility system, the experiments with shareholding, and the development of a significant individual and service economy. It also permitted greater decentralization of the economy and development of regional economies as local governments were given greater financial power and political latitude to guide their own developments.

Although the changes were most notable and most remarked upon in the area of economic reform and development, they were also apparent in the cultural and political realms. The "Resolution on Building Socialist Spiritual Civilization" adopted by the Sixth Plenum in 1986, for instance, was notable for its recognition of the diversity of Chinese society and the "immaturity" of the socialist system. It dropped the demand of the Twelfth Party Congress, held in 1982, that "spiritual civilization" be built "with Communist ideology as the core," calling instead for building spiritual civilization "with Marxism-Leninism as guidance." That less restrictive formulation allowed for greater stress on the development of a "common ideal" that could encompass "party members and nonparty people, Marxists and non-Marxists, atheists and believers, citizens at home and those living abroad."[3] The Thirteenth Party Congress in 1987 developed those ideas by expanding on the thesis that China was in the "primary stage of socialism" and by explicitly accepting limitations on the role of the party, acknowledging the "diverse interests and contradictions" in society.[4]

As the Dengist regime pursued reforms in the economic, political, and cultural spheres, it adopted policies that built upon and reflected long-standing trends in Chinese history. That was most striking, of course, in the manner in which the rural reforms tapped China's long and vigorous commercial tradition. Those reforms were characterized by a retreat of state authority from the local level, allowing peasant households greater freedom in their choices of crop selection and marketing outlets. Rural markets were restored and expanded, and far greater levels of intraregional and interregional trade were permitted.

In allowing such markets to develop, the Dengist reforms yielded to the imperatives of China's economic geography. A large nation with poor transportation, China has traditionally been divided into economic macroregions, within each of which a hierarchical network of marketing structures has existed.[5] By permitting greater trade, the Dengist reforms revived those marketing structures and built on the natural economic structures of China. The rapid expansion of rural industry and the growth of small cities in recent years have similarly been built on those traditional structures. In a sense, then, the Dengist reforms revived the commercial structure and commercial orientations that had developed so vigorously throughout late imperial China, and particularly in the late nineteenth and early twentieth centuries.

At the same time, the Dengist reforms moved to correct the imbalance between "public" and "private" so manifest during the Cultural Revolution and the period of the PRC in general. As epitomized by the slogan *dagong wusi* – literally, "all public and no private" – the Cultural Revolution was the culmination of a fifty-year trend toward the politicization of increasingly greater areas of life. By depoliticizing large areas of social life, the Dengist reforms moved to rectify that imbalance, creating a "zone of indifference" in which "private" activities were permitted far greater scope.[6] In doing so, the Dengist reforms seemed much more in harmony with China's tradition of "totalistic" but noninvasive political power.

Along with the rectification of the balance between public and private, the acceptance of the sociological postulate that various areas of human endeavor are subject to their own laws implied an acknowledgment of the limits of ideology. That recognition contributed greatly to the relative depoliticization of wide areas of social and intellectual life and to a rapid expansion in the role of intellectuals in Chinese life. Though obvious restrictions remained on the expression of ideas, it was also true that intellectuals – prior to June 4, 1989 – were generally given greater latitude to express themselves than at any time in the history of the PRC. The role of intellectuals in shaping public policy, particularly in the area of economic reform, was unprecedented in the history of the PRC.[7] Clearly, the denigration of intellectuals (which reached an extreme in the Cultural Revolution slogan that the more one reads the more stupid one becomes) was substantially altered. Although China's traditional society by no means guaranteed individual freedom of speech – as the literary inquisition of the eighteenth century showed – the status of intellectuals as a class was secure. Given the long and vibrant intellectual tradition of China, restoration of intellectuals to a higher status seems both inevitable and in keeping with China's past.

Finally, one might add, though with a lesser degree of certainty, that the Dengist policy of "opening to the outside world" also corrected an imbalance toward national seclusion that reached an extreme during the Cultural Revolution. Though China has historically been an ethnocentric society, its modern history in particular has been marked by the rapid absorption of a wide variety of foreign influences – economic, political, and cultural. The seclusion of the Maoist era stood in contrast to the openness of the preceding period, and the decision of the Dengist regime to reopen China to a wide-ranging interaction with other countries seems more in keeping with the development of modern Chinese history.

This seemingly felicitous convergence between the Dengist reform strategy and the broad trends of China's historical development in the modern period might be taken as suggesting that the shift in the regime's goals from mobilization to development has brought about a reconciliation between the CCP and China's past.[8] The events of June 1989, however, suggest that such has not happened. On the contrary, the reforms generated a series of tensions that have made such a reconciliation neither easy nor certain. On another level, however, it is apparent that the reforms have brought about a number of unintended consequences (particularly the changing relationships between Beijing and the provinces and the tentative emergence or, better, reemergence of a "public sphere") that lead one to believe that China is facing a series of problems and tensions not altogether unlike those that confronted earlier generations. These developments will be seen as the lasting historical legacies of the Dengist period, and it is these developments that indeed suggest a convergence between the current period and the broad trends of the past. And it is this convergence that is making the Maoist period look increasingly like an interregnum, rather than the historical solution to the dilemmas facing China that it was once thought to be.[9]

In looking at the relationship between the Dengist reforms and the Chinese past, it is apparent that the reforms stand in a Janus-faced relationship to the specific history of the CCP, on the one hand, and the broader trends of Chinese history, on the other. That is to say, although the Dengist reforms represent a reaction against the Cultural Revolution and the "leftist" traditions within the CCP, they also are forced to confront the very dilemmas that produced the communist movement and revolution in the first place. By opening up fundamental questions about the communist response to the dilemmas of modernization, the reformers themselves have been forced to confront the dilemmas that faced earlier generations of intellectuals, reformers, and revolutionaries of different stripes – questions about the relationships between state and society, the polity and the economy, and ideology and knowledge. Thus, there is a palpable feeling of déjà vu in reformers' efforts to come to grips with China's past.

LENINISM AND TRADITION

In retracing the intellectual footsteps of preceding generations, contemporary reformers must do so within the structure of a Leninist system that is itself a product of the historical, social, and intellectual pressures of an earlier period. Leninism, as Jowitt has persuasively argued, is a unique structure of authority that is able to combine the fundamentally conflicting orientations of "status" and "class" societies – the former based on the personalistic norms of corporate groups, the latter based on the impersonal norms of economic relations. It unifies these conflicting orientations through the creation of a party that is an exclusive, "status" organization and also the enforcer of impersonal authority – a party characterized by "charismatic impersonalism."[10] The importance of this concept lies in its ability to capture the interrelatedness of the exclusive orientation of the Leninist party as a corporate group, the society to which it is a response, and the authority relationship that links party and society, namely, neotraditional authority.

The Leninist response, then, is a particular response to a particular set of historical circumstances. That set of circumstances includes the continued domination of status orientations over class orientations and a considerable overlap between the public sphere – that is, an independent realm of public life, including public opinion and public expression – and public authority, the legitimate exercise of state functions. Despite the extensive commercialization of China in the late imperial period,

27

particularly in the "core" economic regions, there was never a "great transformation" comparable to that in early modern Western Europe.[11] Mercantile activities, despite their often close relationship with official-dom, continued to occupy an ambivalent status in China's Confucian order. Prescriptions granting trade a legitimate role in society – urging that the "people be made secure and trade facilitated" (*anmin tongshang*) – coexisted with a denigration of the profit-making sphere (*li*). As Susan Mann has recently put it, state policies protecting and fostering traders' activities were "aimed not at improving the status of merchants, but at preserving the agrarian social order."[12]

As the traditional order crumbled and new commercial and industrial activities expanded in the late nineteenth and early twentieth centuries, a nascent bourgeoisie did develop, particularly in the coastal cities. Freed from the restrictions of the traditional order, by the 1920s such bus-inessmen had developed a sense of themselves as belonging to an in-dependent class and as the purveyors of values essential to China's modernization. Merchants saw an emerging business ethic as containing both a dynamism that would break with the cultural conservatism of the past and a need for continuity and predictability that could provide the basis for both social stability and expansion of business. That newfound conviction that the values of the business community could and should become the basis for the nation underlay the oft-invoked phrase *yi shang jiu guo* – save the nation through business.[13]

That middle-class business ethic, however, remained too peripheral to Chinese society to provide the basis for a new political order. Having emerged in the context of both domestic political disarray and imperi-alism, such trends were soon overwhelmed by the nationalistic and na-tivistic impulses of first the Guomindang (GMD) and then the CCP. Both of those revolutionary movements, harking back to the status orientation of traditional society, imposed a form of "neotraditional" authority – a type of authority that, on the one hand, views economics as an extension of politics and, on the other hand, makes no legitimate distinction be-tween public and private.

As the research of such scholars as Keith Schoppa, Mary Backus Ran-kin, William Rowe, and David Strand has shown, the great commercial expansion in late imperial China led to an important expansion of the public sphere that paralleled in interesting ways similar developments in early modern Europe. In particular, Rankin has used a tripartite division of *guan*, *gong*, and *si* (state, public, and private, respectively) to delineate the growth of "elite activism" that emerged in the gray area between state and society, particularly in the post-Taiping period. Following Ran-kin, David Strand has extended this concern with the public sphere into the 1920s in his recent study of Beijing society. Strand documents the important roles that legal groups (*fatuan*) played in the governance of local society and in the articulation of public interest.[14]

In a recent stimulating article, William Rowe has explored the comparability of these developments to Habermas's analysis of the emergence of the public sphere in Europe in the seventeenth and eighteenth centuries. In the European case, the emergence of bourgeois society led, in time, from the claim to a right to engage in free debate with the public authority to the right to regulate that authority, in short, to the right of the bourgeois reading public "to compel public authority to legitimate itself before public opinion."[15]

There are, as Rowe points out, ambiguities in the meaning of "public" in both the European and Chinese cases. In both instances, the term "public" is used to refer to functions that are undertaken by the state on behalf of society (public education, public welfare, public defense), as well as activities that are unique to society (public opinion, public charity). In the European case, however, there was, at least in an earlier period of time, a clear-cut distinction between state and society, a sense in which public opinion was directed *against* the state, and that indeed "compelled" public authority to legitimate itself (the apparent loss of a clear-cut distinction between state and society in the current age is a major concern of Habermas, but one that we need not take up). That opposition of the public sphere to the state rested on the emergence of bourgeois society, which in turn rested on notions of the legitimacy of private activities, particularly private property.[16]

In the Chinese case, the term *gong* ("public") shared the ambiguity of the European term "public" in that it could be applied to actions undertaken by either state or society, but it never developed the sense of independence and opposition to the state that typified the revolution described by Habermas. One might suggest that many of the public activities undertaken by the social elite were understood as being on behalf of the state, that such public activities, as described by Rankin, Rowe, and Strand, were understood as being more of a bridge between society and state than as an opposition between the two.[17]

The ambiguous relationship existing between the public sphere and the public authority (the state) was mirrored by the ambiguous relationship between the public sphere and private activities. The term "private" (*si*) in China carries a variety of connotations. On the one hand, "private" is viewed in morally negative terms, as the equivalent of selfish, and hence is viewed as the opposite of "public" (*gong*). As Rowe points out, the *Shuo wen*, the dictionary dating to the first century A.D., analyzes *gong* etymologically as a compound of two simpler characters that together mean "turning one's back on the private."[18] Another tradition, which had its roots in the Confucian classic, *The Great Learning*, saw the individual and society as existing on a continuum; thus, the way to bring tranquillity to "all under heaven" was first to make sincere one's thought and rectify one's heart. Rowe argues that by the time of late imperial China, the "traditional dichotomy between private and public came to be muted by a growing belief that private interest, if sufficiently enlightened, could simultaneously serve the interests of society." That view, which appears to have gone hand in hand with the growth of the public sphere in that period, did not imply, as Strand says, that "profits themselves are righteous or that private points of view or interests have a privileged claim on public discourse."[19] Both the relationship between private interests and the public sphere and that between the public sphere and public authority remained ambiguous.

The writings of Liang Qichao can be used to illustrate the complex interrelations between the concepts "public" and "private" and between the public sphere and public authority in late Qing China. Liang, who more than anyone else of his generation scathingly critiqued the old order, used the popular opposition of public and private to attack the legitimacy of the monarchy as an institution. Fundamentally challenging the traditional assumption that the monarch represented the public welfare, Liang argued that the monarch ruled the nation as his own private property. Rather than seeing the monarchy as the institutional expression of *gong*, Liang saw it as the institutionalized pursuit of *si*.[20]

This critique of the monarchy as not representing the public interest appears very much in line with Habermas's analysis of the emergence of a public sphere in Europe; in fact, it is a clear expression of an emerging public opinion engaging in debate with public authority. But that emerging debate never led in China, as it did in Europe, to the point that public opinion could "compel public authority to legitimate itself before public opinion." Nor did Liang Qichao try to push the argument along those lines. In part driven by the late-nineteenth-century desire to *strengthen* the state (unlike the development of European civil society, which emerged *against* the state), and in part drawing on deeply ingrained notions of how state and society should relate, Liang developed his notion of popular sovereignty in terms that were, ironically, very much compatible with the patterns of elite activism so well described by Rankin, Strand, and others.

In contrast to Western notions of popular sovereignty that rest on the assumptions of individualism and the free interplay of competing – and private – interests, Liang viewed popular sovereignty as a coming together of like-minded (and public-minded) individuals. For Liang, each individual should develop within himself or herself the qualities necessary to create the nation. That is what Liang meant in drawing an analogy between the nation and a pile of salt – just as the quality of saltiness inheres in each grain of salt, the quality of "nationhood" must be present in each individual of the nation. Similarly, Liang liked to say that "a group of blind men cannot become a Li-hou [a man famous for his eyesight], a group of deaf persons cannot become a Shi-kuang [a man famous for his hearing], and a group of cowards cannot become a Wuhu [a man famous for his courage]."[21] Thus, if the qualities needed for the nation were not present in the individuals of the society, then it would be impossible to construct a strong nation.

It was his belief that the qualities of nationhood inhered in individuals rather than in individualism that led Liang to be more concerned with defining the content of citizenship (public virtue) than with designing the structural arrangements of the state. Unwilling to trust the affairs of the state to the subjective interests of individuals, Liang sought to train a citizenry that would, collectively and individually, embody *gong*. Thus, Liang's conception of popular sovereignty was double-edged. It held the state responsible to an abstract notion of the public good, but at the same time it held that society should live up to the same ideal; it was not an assertion of the public interest against the state. When Liang tried to redefine *gong* as inhering in society rather than in the monarchy, he looked not to "the people," but to the "new people." Rather than asserting that private interests had a "privileged claim" on public discourse, Liang continued to view state and society as existing along a continuum in which the value of *gong* ran the entire length.

That concept of popular sovereignty is why Liang's concept of "grouping" (*qun*) bore no relationship to interest-group pluralism. "Grouping" was a means by which the new people, infused with public virtue, could be brought together in such organizations as study associations and chambers of commerce to transmit their proposals and knowledge to the state. Groups were to be the transmission belts by which the state could be infused with the energy released by mobilizing the new people.

The congruence between that view of citizenship and grouping and the patterns of elite activism described by Rankin, Strand, and others is apparent. Liang, who was very much a product of the culture that generated elite activism, viewed groups neither as being based on private interests nor as antagonistic to the state. They were viewed as expressions of the public interest, compatible with the interests of society as well as those of the state.

Thus, despite the emergence of a public sphere in late imperial and early Republican China, there was no ideology that defined that sphere as resting on the private interests of society or as being independent of the state. One might argue that the sort of *fatuan* that Strand has studied might have, over time, laid a foundation for the public sphere emerging as independent of public authority, but such trends were cut short by a rising tide of nationalism that viewed such nascent autonomy as hostile to efforts to create a strong state. Organizationally, the Nationalists employed a combination of co-optation and coercion in the late 1920s and 1930s to extend the control of the state over society, and ideologically they promoted an image of organic unity that denied a legitimate distinction between public authority and the public sphere.[22] The CCP's ideological hostility toward any sphere of private activity accompanied its organizational penetration of society, and the curtailment of societal autonomy begun under the Nationalists was radically extended.

The emergence of neotraditional authority, then, can be seen as a response to a situation in which there was an emergent public sphere, but it was not based on a highly developed economic foundation (a bourgeois class), nor did it have a coherent or persuasive ideology defining itself against the state. When nationalist demands found effective organizational expression, first with the GMD, and then to a much greater extent with the CCP, the nascent public sphere was crushed under demands for a strong state. The irony is that now the CCP must deal with the consequences of its own success. Reform not only engendered the implicit recognition of semi-autonomous realms of knowledge but also fostered economic forces that have provided a basis for a tentative re-emergence of a public sphere. These developments have revived many of the questions that faced Chinese intellectuals and politicians alike in the early twentieth century – such as the relationship between state and society, the tension between Chinese culture and modernization, and the relationship between China and the outside world – and at the same time they threaten the authority structure on which the CCP, as a Leninist party, has based its rule.

LENINISM AND REFORM

If the unique characteristics of Leninist authority facilitate the quest for power and the initial mobilization of resources for modernization, they also present obstacles, and perhaps limits, to efforts to reform the system. For a party whose position in society is defined by its heroic orientation, the process of transformation from an "exclusive" party that accentuated its differentiation from society to an "inclusive" party that attempts to incorporate societal elements is tenuous at best.[23] Although willing to increase their responsiveness to societal demands in order to gain public support for regime goals, Leninist parties find it difficult to suppress demands that they be "representative."

The difference between being "responsive" and "representative" was dramatically highlighted by the debate between Fang Lizhi, then vice-president of the Science and Technology University in Hefei, Anhui province, and Politburo member Wan Li, who traveled to Hefei in November 1986 to try to reduce the tensions that were soon to erupt in the largest student demonstration that China had seen up to that time. Wan Li apparently tried to persuade Fang that the views of people like Fang could be reflected within the party. Fang replied that "democracy is not something that can be given to lower levels from those above," but is something that must be "struggled for." Otherwise, said Fang, "what is given to you can be taken away."[24]

Moreover, as a party system based on neotraditional authority, the Leninist system is more compatible with planned economies than with market economies. Planned economies do not undermine the heroic ethos of the Leninist party. On the contrary, they often manifest that ethos, as in the heroic efforts required to build such projects as the Great Hall of the People, the bridge over the Yangzi River at Nanjing, and the Red Flag Canal (in addition to less successful undertakings such as the backyard furnaces of the Great Leap Forward). The tension inherent in this conflict between the heroic orientation of the party and the requirements of economic modernization were vividly reflected in the fall of 1988 – as the tensions that would result in the open division of the party the following spring were becoming severe – when party conservatives, in clear opposition to the reformist agenda, aired a highly nationalist television program chronicling the dedication and sacrifices of those who had developed China's nuclear weapons.[25] The results of such efforts are viewed not as the outcome of rational economic activity but as expressions of the party's political wisdom and leadership.

In contrast, market economies are distinctly unheroic. It is precisely the day-to-day economic calculations of millions of independent individuals that underlie the constant flow of factor resources to the areas of greatest return. It is the essence of class-oriented societies that such decisions are made by individuals without regard to their positions in society. If there is a "hero" in a market economy, it is the successful entrepreneur, but the success of such people is distinctly individualistic; usually the attainment of such success comes not from relying on one's status but rather in defiance of society's norms. Nothing could be more foreign to the notion of "comradeship" – a concept that implies a disciplined acceptance of a hierarchically based order harnessed to the party-state – than entrepreneurship.[26]

Socialist reform, which is initiated in large part because of the inefficiencies of centrally organized economies, inevitably involves an effort to bring market forces to bear and a consequent deemphasis of planning. Socialist theoreticians have expended much effort trying to find formulas for integrating plan and market, but without success.[27] Chinese efforts to bridge the gap between plan and market culminated in the concept of a "planned commodity economy," which was given theoretical sanction in the 1984 "Decision on Reform of the Economic Structure." Although that decision marked a theoretical breakthrough at the time, allowing reformers to pursue market-oriented reforms more vigorously, the notion of a "planned commodity economy" was more compromise than concept. As senior economist Liu Guoguang wrote, although everyone could agree with those words, some emphasized the "planned" part of the formula, whereas others stressed the "commodity" part.[28]

The debate whether to give primary emphasis to the "planned" economy or to the "commodity" (market) economy reflected not simply an economic problem – though the difficulties in that regard were certainly formidable – but also a very real struggle between two conflicting principles of authority. As Jowitt has suggested, the incompatible orientations of class and status societies can coexist only under coercive auspices. A status society can have pockets containing modernized economies if they are "compartmented" and therefore do not threaten the larger society, or if they are so weak that they can be co-opted and thereby used to extend the power and scope of the stronger type.[29]

The relationship between guilds and the state in the status society of traditional China manifested that latter strategy. Guilds, as Susan Mann has pointed out, drew "strength from the government's sanction of their liturgical function, while at the same time depending on the state for their *raison d'être*."[30] In Dengist China, where the status orientation predominates, both strategies have been pursued. The creation of Special Economic Zones (SEZs) is a clear instance of compartmentalization (even if the intention behind their creation was to introduce new relations to the rest of society), and the rural reforms and the emergence of small-scale private entrepreneurship exemplify the latter approach. The state-owned economy remained so dominant, at least at first, that the more market-oriented sectors did not pose any real threat to the larger society.

This conflict between planning and market activities – and between status and class orientations – is reflected in the ambivalent attitude the Dengist regime has taken toward wealth. At various times, in order to promote economic reform and give ideological backing to the use of material incentives, the regime has urged people to "get rich." This theme, which became prominent in 1983, perhaps reached its apogee during the 1984 Spring Festival, when the party paper *Renmin ribao* touted the virtues of "getting rich" in uncompromising terms. Later that year, Ren Zhongyi, then the reform-minded party secretary of Guangdong province, declared that "the more revolution you make, the richer you should become."[31]

At other times – including the present – the Dengist regime has sought to dampen materialist urges. For instance, a 1981 *Renmin ribao* Commentator article said that whereas material incentives are important, "it would be utterly wrong to think that in stressing material incentives we can ignore the importance of moral values to the extent of using the bourgeois attitude that 'money is all powerful' and egoism as a guide to all our actions." In 1985, in response to the assertion of materialist incentives the previous year, there was a campaign to oppose the idea that "money is above everything" (*yi qie wei qian kan*). Similarly, in 1987, Guan Guangmei became famous for earning a sizable income from the state-owned retail stores she had leased, thereby becoming both a symbol for those who sought to tout the value of entrepreneurship and a target for those who thought that she, and China, were going down the "capitalist road."[32] Since the crackdown on June 4, 1989, the new general secretary, Jiang Zemin, has declared that admitting millionaires into the party, which was proposed in 1988, is incompatible with the communist ethic that party members are expected to uphold.

The same conflation of politics and economics posed a serious obstacle to reformist efforts to sort out relations of ownership and property rights. Reform-minded economists were aware of the need to redefine China's enterprises as independent (not "relatively independent") commodity producers restrained by market forces, but such hopes cut across four decades of socialist practice, during which, as Andrew Walder has observed, "employment [was] not primarily a market relationship, nor [was] the firm an economic enterprise in the capitalist sense."[33] The political obstacles to bringing about a fundamental change in that situation proved too great, and are likely to remain so for the indefinite future. As a result, economic reform could do little more than give enterprises greater autonomy, a change that was not sufficient to guide them toward economically rational behavior. Thus, China's economic reform followed the well-worn path of reform in Eastern Europe, where soft budget restraints led enterprises to "bear responsibility for profits but not for losses." Even in the countryside, where the results of reform were impressive in the first half of the 1980s, the failure to draw clear definitions of property relationships obviously has undermined the peasants' faith in reform and made them less willing to invest in agricultural production.[34]

Finally, as suggested earlier, the lack of differentiation between public and private finds expression in the relationship between ideology and knowledge. Despite the recognition of specialized areas of knowledge as separate from party ideology, all areas of intellectual inquiry, including the natural sciences, remained subject to party intervention when they seemed to violate important ideological tenets. Such intervention was most visible in areas where the distinction between professional norms and party ideology was less clear. For instance, the demands of journalists to have greater editorial control over newspapers, while consistent with journalists' growing conception of themselves as an independent profession, led to periodic crackdowns on the press, including Hu Yaobang's well-known speech in 1986 in which he reiterated the party's position that newspapers must be the "mouthpiece" of the party, as well as the sharp curtailment of journalistic freedom that followed the June 1989 crackdown.

OPENNESS, LENINISM, AND NATIONALISM

Although the policy of "opening to the outside world" has played a major role in China's reform program, it is clear that such openness has provoked opposition, thus raising questions about the degree and type of openness that China will be able to sustain over the long term. Such opposition has been apparent on three levels.

First, just as the inherent incompatibility between the status orientation of Leninist systems and the class orientation of market economies surfaces when market principles are introduced into the planned economies, there is a similar incompatibility between the basically autarkic economy traditionally practiced by socialist countries and the reforms intended to open them to the world economy. Becoming integrated into the world economy ultimately means establishing a convertible currency and accepting the inevitable disruptions of the domestic economy and the loss of party control over the economy that such moves imply. It is precisely because of that threat that Leninist systems have traditionally "compartmentalized" their external economic activities through the use of nonconvertible currencies and state trading companies. Integration into the world economy implies acceptance of the market rules that prevail there, and, just as with the development of a domestic market economy, such acceptance undermines the "heroic" orientation of the party.

Second, on an ideological level, openness undermines the antagonistic relationship presumed to exist between socialism and capitalism. To the extent that a policy of opening up is pursued, it is necessary to revise ideological tenets about both capitalism and socialism to show that whatever differences exist between the two systems, there are also underlying similarities. In China, that process started in the natural sciences, which were declared to have no class nature. Later, in order to extend market-oriented reforms, theoreticians argued that the concept of a "commodity economy" was not unique to capitalism (it was said that commodity exchange had existed long before the advent of capitalism) and so could be adopted by socialist systems. In 1988, as reformers tried to press the gains they had made at the Thirteenth Party Congress, an effort was launched to "reunderstand" the natures of both socialism and capitalism.

That endeavor sought to underline the commonalities between the two systems.

To the extent that capitalism and socialism are no longer seen as locked in a life-and-death struggle, but as being subject to common laws, there is an implicit convergence between the two systems. Just such a convergence was implicit in the use of the concept of the "new technological revolution." Thus, when Zhao Ziyang endorsed the concept of the new technological revolution, or the so-called third wave, in October 1983, he was not simply making an evaluation of the implications of new technology for China's modernization, but also was making an ideological statement about the relationship between superstructure and base: If socialism and capitalism are subject to the same laws of development, then the distinction between the two is attenuated at best.[35]

Precisely that implication was brought out in the summer of 1987 by an article in the party's theoretical journal *Hongqi* that appeared to criticize Zhao's impending selection as party general secretary. That article, written as a review of Alvin Toffler's *The Third Wave*, argued that Toffler's views "differ vastly from Marxist ones and we must not agree to them." Toffler's views were antagonistic to Marxism, the article said, because Toffler "preaches that scientific and technological progress can resolve various contradictions of the capitalist system and can even make the capitalist and socialist systems 'converge'." As a result, "the question of 'which triumphs over the other' will disappear and give way to the unification of the two."[36] The subsequent meeting between Zhao Ziyang and Alvin Toffler in September 1988 marked a vivid – but ultimately unsuccessful – rejection of such views.[37]

On a third level, China's open policy is intertwined with deep visceral feelings about interaction with the outside world – feelings that historically helped bring about the downfall of the Qing dynasty and fueled the Nationalist and Communist revolutions. Inevitably, Chinese nationalism developed in the context of foreign imperialism. That was the case in 1874 when the authorities of the French Concession in Shanghai attempted to build roads through the cemetery of the local Ningbo Guild, touching off a protest now regarded as China's first political boycott against foreign imperialism. More virulent and more populist nationalist upsurges occurred in response to later events: the Sino-Japanese War of 1894–1895; the decision of the Versailles Conference in 1919 to grant Germany's concessions in China to Japan; the May 30, 1925, shooting of Chinese protestors, which led to the nationalist upsurge that culminated in the Northern Expedition and establishment of Nationalist rule; and the Sino-Japanese War of 1937–1945 that paved the way for the CCP's takeover in 1949.

Whereas that history of conflict with imperialism produced virulent nationalistic – and xenophobic – responses, such as the Boxer Rebellion of 1900 and the extreme anti-foreignism of the Cultural Revolution, one can distinguish three other types of nationalistic responses that seem more likely to have a lasting impact on China's interaction with the world. Two of these traditions are suggested by the distinction that Paul Cohen makes between the "littoral" areas most exposed to Western influence and the "hinterland" most associated with both cultural conservatism and radical nativism.

The culture of the littoral areas was, in Cohen's words, "more commercialized than agricultural in its economic foundations, more modern than traditional in its administrative and social arrangements, more Western (Christian) than Chinese (Confucian) in its intellectual outlook, and more outward- than inward-looking in its general global orientation and involvement."[38] Although the distinction between hinterland and littoral is by no means absolute – there was much interaction between the two areas, and the hinterland was not always as agricultural or inward-looking as this dichotomy would suggest – it nevertheless provides a useful heuristic framework that highlights important differences in the ways in which Chinese reacted to the West.[39]

The littoral tradition of nationalism, associated with Chinese "liberalism," can be traced from such nineteenth-century reformers as Wang Tao, Ma Jianzhong, and Zheng Guanying, then to leaders of the 1898 reform movement such as Kang Youwei and Liang Qichao, and finally to Western-educated intellectuals such as Hu Shi and Ding Wenjiang in the 1920s and 1930s. In contrast, the hinterland tradition can be traced from such late-Qing cultural conservatives as Wo-ren, then to the later Liang Qichao (who turned away from his earlier infatuation with the Western model), and to promoters of the "national essence" such as Liu Shipei, neo-Confucian scholars such as Liang Shuming and Xiong Shili, and Sinocentric nationalists such as Tao Xisheng and Sa Mengwu.[40] In its radical nativist guise, the hinterland tradition found expression in the thought of Communist leaders such as Li Dazhao and Mao Zedong.

In between these two traditions, one can distinguish a third approach, that of "self-strengthening." Rooted in the Confucian tradition of "statecraft," the self-strengthening approach shares with the littoral tradition a concern for involvement in the world, yet remains, like the hinterland tradition, firmly embedded in China's cultural traditions. Finding its origins in late-Qing reformers such as Li Hongzhang and Zhang Zhidong, the self-strengthening approach tried to reinvigorate the Qing by blending Confucian traditions with the importation of Western technology. Summed up in Zhang Zhidong's famous aphorism, "Chinese learning as the essence, and Western learning for use" (*Zhongxue weiti, xixue weiyong*), that tradition finds contemporary expression in the pragmatic approach of the Dengist regime, which is why the Dengist reforms bear such an uncanny resemblance to the self-strengthening efforts of a century ago.

The contrast between the hinterland and littoral traditions was reflected in a well-known debate – one that had clear echoes in the polemics of the late 1980s – involving Sa Mengwu, He Bingsong, Tao Xisheng, and other intellectuals on one side, with Hu Shi and others opposing them. In 1935, a group of ten professors, including Sa, He, and Tao, concerned that traditional Chinese values were being eroded by various modern influences, issued a manifesto declaring that Chinese cultural values must be preserved in the course of economic, political, and cultural modernization. They recommended that the Chinese should "adopt a critical attitude" and "absorb what should be absorbed" and reject the rest.[41]

In response, Hu Shi condemned the manifesto as a "fashionable reflection of the general reactionary atmosphere of the present." In contrast to the manifesto's expression of concern that "China's characteristics" were being lost, Hu said that "what is most worrying in China today is that the political form, social organization, and content and form of thought everywhere preserve all the sins that China has always had," and he recommended letting world culture "freely and fully come into contact with our old culture."[42] What China needed was not to preserve its traditional values but "complete Westernization."[43]

The different nationalistic responses reflected in that debate resonate with similar debates, both intellectual and policy-oriented, in contemporary China. One expression of this conflict has come in the course of building the SEZs, themselves an expression of a self-strengthening approach to modernization. During one period of heightened controversy over the SEZs, the conservative party theoretician Hu Qiaomu gave voice to the hinterland tradition when he evoked the similarities between the SEZs and the foreign concessions in China's nineteenth-century treaty ports. Hu suggested that the Chinese government had given in to the "inordinate demands" of foreigners, and he charged that foreign businessmen "show no respect" for Chinese laws when they come to the SEZs.[44]

Precisely the same sort of conflict between different nationalistic traditions found echoes in the writings and speeches of the astrophysicist and human-rights activist Fang Lizhi and in the salvoes of the two campaigns (1987, and 1989 to the present) against "bourgeois liberalization." According to Fang, China needs "complete Westernization," which he, like Hu Shi, defines as a "complete and total openness." Fang argues that China is backward not in one or two respects but "in all respects," so its opening cannot be preconditioned on the upholding of some aspects or the defining of some things as "the essence" (*wei ti*). It was on the basis of that belief that Fang went so far as to ridicule Deng Xiaoping's notion of "building socialism with Chinese characteristics." For Fang, the idea of "Chinese modernization" sets a prior limit on modernization, but what China needs is "complete" modernization.

Fang's fervent embrace of "complete Westernization" was sharply opposed by those whose intellectual and emotional roots lay in the hinterland tradition of nationalism. Shortly before the campaign against bourgeois liberalization that was launched at the end of 1986, the conservative party elders Bo Yibo, Wang Zhen, Hu Qiaomu, Deng Liqun, and Song Renqiong expressed their anger at the student movement then growing throughout the country, as well as with the liberalizing trends that had been developing in recent years, by meeting with a traditional storyteller known for his rendering of the Chinese classic *Romance of the Three Kingdoms*. Wang praised the storyteller for "raising our national dignity and sense of pride," contrasting his efforts favorably with "some people" who "advocate national nihilism, debase and negate China, and call for the complete Westernization of China." Similarly, Bo warned that the policy of opening to the outside world and studying the advanced science and technology of foreign nations should not cause Chinese to "belittle" themselves or to "consider all things foreign to be better than in China." "We must not think," he said, "that 'the moon in foreign countries is fuller than in China'."[45]

There is, perhaps predictably, a close connection between these different nationalistic traditions and the ideological conflicts over the relationship between socialism and capitalism described earlier. The same *Hongqi* article that criticized Toffler's ideas went on to say that "we must never regard all foreign things as the correct standards to follow and blindly imitate them, and thus prostrate ourselves before Toffler's *The Third Wave*. Worshipping foreign things and inappropriately negating ourselves are like twins."[46] It was, after all, the hinterland tradition of nationalism that was the primary impulse underlying China's acceptance of Marxism and its understanding of socialism; it is not surprising that ideological conflict and different nationalistic impulses have become intertwined as China has struggled with redefining its ideology and opening to the outside world.

CHINESE CULTURE AND MODERNIZATION

Closely connected with these divergent strains of nationalism are contemporary reflections on Chinese culture, which similarly resonate with earlier periods of cultural introspection, such as the late Qing, the May Fourth period, and the 1930s. The continuity of such basic questions as the relationship between China and the West, and that between Chinese culture and Western culture, provides strong testimony to the continuing tension between China's cultural traditions and the task of modernization. Among other things, the evident and continuing force of this tension lays to rest Joseph Levenson's hypothesis that Communist ideology had found a way out of the dilemmas that had entrapped earlier generations of intellectuals and had "museumified" Chinese history by rendering it irrelevant.[47]

What has resurrected these debates is the self-evident failure of the communist authorities, particularly during the Cultural Revolution, to modernize China economically, culturally, or politically. Emerging from the Cultural Revolution, Chinese intellectuals of all sorts, whether in literature, history, philosophy, natural science, or social science, have had to ask themselves, What went wrong? Was the Cultural Revolution an aberration that will not be repeated once the "good traditions" of the party are reestablished? Or is there something in Chinese social structure and culture that supported the various manifestations of "leftism" throughout the history of Chinese Communism and led, perhaps inexorably, to the Cultural Revolution?

Inevitably intellectuals find part of the answer lying in China's "feudal" history. They find that although the CCP has continually criticized both "feudalism" and "capitalism," the emphasis in practice has been on expunging every manifestation of capitalism, thus leaving feudal influences free to grow and develop. Thus, such intellectuals find the negative influences of feudalism strongly reflected in the practices of the CCP: overconcentration of power, rule by man rather than rule by law, one-man say, and the politicization of intellectual life.

Having found such feudal influences reflected in China's political life, intellectuals have naturally embarked on a search for the sources of those influences, and in doing so, they inevitably have found themselves retracing the steps of late-Qing intellectuals such as Liang Qichao and May Fourth intellectuals such as Hu Shi, Chen Duxiu, and Lu Xun.

Like their predecessors in earlier generations, Chinese intellectuals remain divided over the essential characteristics and value of Chinese tradition. One group of scholars, known as the "new Confucians," believe that it is necessary to find the seeds of modernization within Chinese tradition itself – though ironically they base that belief in no small measure on conclusions drawn from Western social science and philosophy. Building on the work of philosophers such as Liang Shuming, Xiong Shili, and Feng Youlan, this group has been strongly influenced by such non-PRC scholars as Mou Tsung-san and Tu Wei-ming. Such scholars emphasize that "modernization is not the same as Westernization" and argue that unless China finds the sources of modernization within its own tradition, it will become detached from its "roots" and continue to

41

face a "crisis of identity." This approach, which has contributed greatly to a revival of interest in and understanding of traditional Chinese culture, after being criticized for so many years, finds powerful support in the developmental experiences of such Confucian-shaped societies as South Korea, Japan, Taiwan, Singapore, and Hong Kong. For those who take this approach, Confucianism, like the Protestant ethic, can provide a basis for rapid economic development. Moreover, they argue, such "Confucian capitalism" can avoid the moral pitfalls of Western capitalist development. In this sense, a "third wave" of Confucian development not only can pave the way for economic development of China but also can provide a powerful corrective for Western nations.[48] Expressing this point of view, philosopher Tang Yijie concludes that "if a people lose the traditions of their national culture, then it is impossible for them to fully absorb foreign thought and culture much less to make their own thought and culture go to the forefront of other peoples."[49]

In response, philosophers such as Bao Zunxin have argued that even though modernization is not the same as Westernization, absorbing the experiences of Western nations is an inevitable part of modernization and nothing to worry about. In Bao's view, "using the excuse that 'modernization is not the same as Westernization' to refuse to absorb the fruits of other nations and to refuse to consult their modernization experiences is the same as erecting a stop sign on the way to modernization. The 'modernization is not the same as Westernization' that the new Confucians talk about is precisely such a sign."[50]

Those who, like Bao, espouse Westernization as a necessary component of modernization do so in large part because they see China's traditional culture as the problem rather than the solution. Like their predecessors in the May Fourth period, such intellectuals see the deep-rooted intellectual, social, and cultural habits of China's traditional culture as having been obstacles to China's modernization in the late nineteenth and early twentieth centuries and as continuing to retard modernization today. Although such intellectuals are willing to agree that there are many aspects of traditional culture worthy of praise and even cultivation, they see the "deep structure" of China's traditional culture as having formed an organic whole that is fundamentally antagonistic to the requisites of the modern world. For such intellectuals, the pressing intellectual task is to build on the tradition of the May Fourth Movement by continuing, and deepening, the critique of China's traditional culture.

One attempt to view current political, economic, and cultural problems as stemming from weaknesses inherent in China's traditional culture is that by the literary critic Liu Zaifu and the historian Lin Gang. Not unlike many other critics, Liu and Lin see the relationship between traditional moral values and political power as corrupting of both and believe that contemporary China has been unable to escape the moral–political paradigm that shaped traditional China.[51]

Their critique is based on the belief that China's traditional culture was "pan-moralistic" (*fan daode zhuyi*). Their contention is that Confucian morality, rather than remaining confined to a specific moral sphere, was infused throughout all spheres, particularly the political, thereby undermining both morality and the political system. Thus, they argue that "when good and evil are made the center of life and the foundation of the nation's organization, they are no longer a matter of conscience but attached to force." As a result, they become the haunting, dominating forces that Lu Xun described as "man-eating."

In the political realm, the fusion of morality and government brought about rule by man rather than rule by law. What counted in traditional rule was not an objective standard of legality but moral judgments of "right" and "wrong." On the other hand, that fusion of morality and political rule made the scope of government theoretically unlimited. Because the central concern of government was moral propriety, there was no area of life that could not become a legitimate subject of government interference. Thus, there was no sense of "privacy" in traditional culture.

Moreover, that fusion of morality and government, Liu and Lin argue, prevented improvement of the political system over time. When dynasties declined and fell, the influence of China's traditional moral system was such that people blamed political failings on the decline of morality, rather than looking to specific problems in the political system. That tendency only strengthened the grip of morality on politics, making it ever more difficult for China to work its way out of its dilemmas.

At the same time that the fusion of morality and government corrupted the method of rule and gave unlimited scope to the authority of the state, it undermined the very moral values it was designed to cultivate. Thus, Liu and Lin argue that because moral values were central to success in traditional society, that could only lead to hypocrisy and manipulation of moral values to achieve political success.

Finally, traditional moral concepts were always group-centered, stifling individualism. The individual who rebelled against the system not only would be rejected by family and friends but also could find the whole weight of the system thrown against him or her. Thus, pan-moralism led politically to totalism, on the one hand, and to a lack of privacy and individual vitality, on the other; morally it led to hypocrisy and selfishness, as well as withdrawal from society. Both public virtue and private virtue suffered accordingly. Such characteristics of China's traditional culture, then, stand in contrast to the "Faustian" spirit, the pluralist values, the emphasis on logic, and the action-oriented pragmatism said to characterize the West.

43

One of the most powerful intellectual frameworks for dealing with the cultural dilemmas described by such scholars as Liu and Lin has been developed by the philosopher Li Zehou.[52] Li has put forth the slogan "Western essence and Chinese use" (*xiti zhongyong*) – a deliberate play on Zhang Zhidong's famous aphorism – not only to be provocative but also to underscore his belief that China's difficulty in modernizing over the past century and a half has resulted from the age-old tendency of Chinese society to "Sinocize" foreign ideas, rendering them devoid of their original content. In sharp contrast to those, either in the past or in the present, who see Western ideas and culture as a threat to Chinese values, Li focuses on the way China has repeatedly taken foreign ideas, stripped them of their foreign essence (*xiti*), and turned them into supports for China's essence (*zhongti*) – a critique that he applies widely (e.g., the importation of Buddhism from India, the adoption of Christianity by the leaders of the Taiping Rebellion, and the use of Marxism in modern China).

What gives the "Chinese essence" its strength, Li argues, is the combination of its economic structure, particularly its basis in "feudal," small-scale production, and an ideological consciousness that corresponds to that base. That essence can be changed, he believes, only with the development of a "commodity economy"; only then will "Western learning" be able to take root.[53] Despite his materialist conception of "essence," Li, like his forerunners in the May Fourth period, believes that changes in the economic base can be accelerated by appropriate changes in the "superstructure," particularly the spheres of culture and political organization. Hence his critique not only of traditional Chinese culture but also of the "new Confucians," who, he believes, are indirectly supporting the old economic base.

The tensions implicit in the different traditions of nationalism and the arguments over the compatibility between Chinese culture and the requirements for modernization dramatically entered the realm of elite politics with the broadcast of the television program "River Elegy" (*He shang*) in the summer of 1988. Employing the contrasting metaphors of the Yellow River, the cradle of Chinese civilization, and the blue sea, connoting openness to the West, the program sharply criticized the conservatism of Chinese culture, viewing it as antithetical to modernization. The party's general secretary, Zhao Ziyang, endorsed the film by presenting a copy to the Singapore prime minister, Lee Kuan Yew, during his visit to China. Meanwhile, conservatives, led by Vice President Wang Zhen, vehemently denounced the film. Since the student demonstrations of April–May 1989 and Zhao's ouster as party head, the hard-line government in Beijing has repeatedly denounced "River Elegy," and democratic activists abroad have appropriated its symbolism.[54]

The entire debate over the merits of Chinese culture and the way in which the debate became politicized marked a significant shift in the history of the Chinese Communist movement. The debate between proponents of the new Confucianism and those critical of traditional Chinese culture has been carried on almost entirely without reference to Marxist thought. That reflects not only the essential irrelevance of Marxist categories to contemporary intellectuals but also the reemergence of intellectuals as a partially autonomous interest group. That is to say, Chinese intellectuals, prior to June 4, were beginning to resume the position they had held in Chinese society in the late Qing and early Republican periods as the articulators of a "public interest." This suggests that, however tentatively and problematically, a "public sphere" is beginning to re-emerge in China. It seems premature, however, to talk in terms of an emergent "civil society," not simply because of the events of June 4 (which can only retard these trends, not stop them), but more importantly because of the continuing weakness of intellectuals as a group, because their relationship with government remains one of dependence, and because of the weight of tradition in which many (perhaps most) intellectuals continue to perceive their role not as representatives of an independent civil society but as the articulators of a public interest within the scope of state authority.[55] The remarkable thing about the events of May–June 1989, as Tang Tsou points out in this volume, was the degree to which intellectuals for a very brief time articulated the interests of an independent civil society. The possibility of that becoming a long-term trend, however, seems remote.

The other thing that strikes one as remarkable about this debate is the posture of the party. Fifteen years ago, when Michel Oksenberg and Steven Goldstein surveyed the political spectrum of the party leadership, they could find no one supportive of traditional Chinese culture.[56] Rather, the Chinese Communist movement based its nationalism and nativism on the "little" tradition of the peasants and criticized the "big" tradition of Confucianism (the "four olds"). Today, however, no matter how uneasy some leaders may be about it, the party has come to terms with Chinese tradition and Confucianism and even views them as bastions of support against those who criticize Chinese culture from a perspective of "wholesale Westernization." The effort to transform society in the name of Marxism is over, and with it the "exclusive" orientation of the party has been lost.

CONCLUSION

Placing the Dengist reforms in historical perspective not only highlights important continuities between pre-PRC China and the current period but also underscores the tensions involving China's historical traditions, Leninism as a unique form of authority, and the demands of reform. The dilemmas that Liang Qichao faced in trying to deal with relations between state and society and between public and private are very much the dilemmas of modern China. On the one hand, because Liang's critique of the traditional monarchy was rooted in nationalism, his denial that the monarchy represented *gong* (the public interest) was not accompanied, as it was in Europe, by a concomitant assertion that an emergent public sphere could legitimately articulate a conception of *gong* against the state. On the other hand, as the bearer of a cultural tradition that viewed the scholarly class as upholding the general interest, his concept of *gong* was not rooted in notions of private interest or the interplay of private groups. Thus, his critique of the traditional monarchy was more savage than thorough. He argued neither against totalism per se nor against the absence of an autonomous public sphere in Chinese life, and his concept of the "new people" was not a concept of citizenship, but rather a delineation of the moral values Liang thought necessary for the creation of a modern, and stronger, state. Here, Liu Zaifu and Lin Gang's critique of China's traditional continuum between individual morality and political power rings true.

Liang's intellectual failure to adequately sort out the relationships between public and private and between state and society was "resolved" by the political imposition of neotraditional authority, first by the GMD, and then, more thoroughly and successfully, by the CCP. *Gong* was to be embodied in neither state nor society, but in the party. In that view, a strong state could be created without statism, and society could be mobilized without the interplay of private interests. The seamless web between public authority and private interest would be maintained by the party's supervision of both state and society. Thereby the basic assumptions of a status society could be harnessed to the goal of a modernizing state.

The Dengist reforms have called into question the basic assumptions of that "solution." Economic reform has challenged it by setting the class orientation of the market economy against the status orientation of the party. Ideological reform has questioned it by setting autonomous realms of knowledge against party claims of scientific truth. And the opening to the outside world has challenged it both ways – threatening both to integrate the Chinese economy into the world economy and to undermine ideological assumptions about the relationship between socialism and capitalism. At the same time, the opening revives old questions about the relationship between China and the outside world, thus provoking different strains of nationalist response.

The most significant long-term development brought about by the reforms, however, has been the reemergence of "society" as a meaningful participant in political life. This development, stimulated by the devolution of economic authority to local governments, makes the continuities between the pre-PRC period and the present all the more clear, while highlighting the very real sense in which the Maoist period has come to appear as an interregnum. This reemergence of society means that the questions that preoccupied earlier generations – defining the relationship between public and private and working out ways of relating local government to central government (possibly including some notions of a new federalist arrangement) – have once again appeared on the political agenda.

As the foregoing discussion suggests, however, one must be cautious about viewing this revival of society in terms of an emerging (or reemerging) "civil society." Going back to Habermas's description of the emergence of the public sphere in the West, it should be apparent that there exists little basis in China – culturally, sociologically, intellectually, or economically – for the emergence of civil society in the Western sense, that is, for an independent "public opinion" to establish the legitimate right to supervise the state. It seems more likely that a variety of intermediary entities (one cannot call them associations because they are neither voluntary nor, in most instances, nongovernmental) will emerge, but that they themselves will be of both state and society.

If such trends continue, then it seems possible to conceive of a future in which greater authority might be delegated to officially recognized entities – including local governments, interregional organizations, enterprises, and even intellectuals affiliated with research institutions – that would simultaneously articulate the interests of their constituents and enforce state policy. Such a development would certainly be in keeping with the many proposals made in recent years to establish a state asset-management bureau, free from direct state intervention, that would manage state assets, as well as with the many discussions of "trade management."[57]

Such trends seem to point to the possibility of creating a type of state corporatist structure that could draw on China's guild tradition as well as its traditional preference for a limited, but not delimited, state. Such a structure would balance centralism and decentralism, providing for local autonomy as well as state control. It would suppress and limit the scope of interest representation, yet allow the expression of interests within a certain scope. Such a decentralized system would necessarily be less ideologically rigid, permitting the expression of a wide, but not unlimited, range of ideas. It would open to the outside world, and perhaps integrated in part into the world economy, but it would retain a degree of central control over foreign-trade activities. Such a development might provide a means of reconciling China's past with its present, its diversity with its need for unity, its ideology with the expression of divergent views, and its nationalism with a continuing opening to the outside world.

Such an outcome seems conceivable whether or not China remains a Marxist system. The revival of regional economies, the failure of Marxism as an integrating ideology, the increasing scope of the state's "zone of indifference," and the tentative reemergence of a public sphere over the past decade all suggest that trends strengthening society vis-à-vis the state are likely to continue. At the same time, however, the absence of a tradition legitimating the role of an independent public sphere suggests that the relations between public and private and between state and society will continue to be foci of intellectual and political contention. It seems that China's century-long effort to reconcile its past with its postrevolutionary present will remain problematic.

NOTES

1. Tang Tsou, "Political Change and Reform: The Middle Course," in *The Cultural Revolution and Post-Mao Reforms: A Historical Perspective* (Chicago: University of Chicago Press, 1986), pp. 219–258.
2. Tang Tsou, "Political Change and Reform," p. 220.
3. "Communiqué of the Sixth Plenary Session of the Twelfth Central Committee of the Communist Party of China," Xinhua, September 28, 1986, trans. Foreign Broadcast Information Service (hereafter FBIS), September 29, 1986, pp. K1–K15.
4. "Continue Along the Road of Socialism with Chinese Characteristics," Beijing Domestic Service, October 25, 1987, trans. FBIS, October 25, 1987, pp. 10–34.
5. G. William Skinner, "Marketing and Social Structure in Rural China" (parts 1–2), *Journal of Asian Studies* 24, no. 1–2 (1964–1965); G. William Skinner, "Cities and the Hierarchy of Local Systems," in G. William Skinner, ed., *The City in Late Imperial China* (Stanford: Stanford University Press, 1977), pp. 275–351.
6. Tang Tsou, "Introduction," in *Cultural Revolution*, p. xxiv.
7. See, for instance, Nina Halperin, "Information Flows and Policy Coordination in the Chinese Bureaucracy" (paper presented at the conference on "The Structure of Authority and Bureaucratic Behavior in China," Tucson, Arizona, June 19–23, 1988).
8. The classic statement of that shift in regime goals is by Richard Lowenthal: "Development vs. Utopia in Communist Policy," in Chalmers Johnson, ed., *Change in Communist Systems* (Stanford: Stanford University Press, 1970), pp. 33–116.
9. Suggestive in this regard is Arthur Waldron's article, "Warlordism Versus Federalism: The Revival of a Debate?" *China Quarterly*, no. 121 (March 1990): 116–128.
10. Kenneth Jowitt, *The Leninist Response to National Dependency* (Berkeley: Institute of International Studies, University of California Press, 1978), p. 36.

11. The term "great transformation" is borrowed from the title of Karl Polanyi's book *The Great Transformation: The Political and Economic Conditions of Our Time* (Boston: Beacon Press, 1944).
12. Susan Mann, *Local Merchants and the Chinese Bureaucracy, 1750–1950* (Stanford: Stanford University Press, 1987).
13. See, for instance, "Shang xiguan yu shangye" (Business customs and business) and "Shangye yu zhengfu" (Business and government), *Shanghai zongshanghui yuebao* (Journal of the General Chamber of Commerce of Shanghai) 3, no. 12 (December 1923), and 6, no. 5 (May 1926).
14. See Keith R. Schoppa, *Chinese Elites and Political Change: Zhejiang Province in the Early Twentieth Century* (Cambridge: Harvard University Press, 1982); William T. Rowe, *Hankow: Conflict and Community in a Chinese City, 1796–1985* (Stanford: Stanford University Press, 1989); Mary Backus Rankin, *Elite Activism and Political Transformation in China: Zhejiang Province, 1865–1911* (Stanford: Stanford University Press, 1986); and David Strand, *Rickshaw Beijing: City People and Politics in 1920s China* (Berkeley: University of California Press, 1989).
15. William T. Rowe, "The Public Sphere in Modern China," *Modern China* 16, no. 3 (July 1990): 309–329; Jürgen Habermas, *The Structural Transformation of the Public Sphere*, trans. Thomas Burger, with the assistance of Frederick Lawrence (Cambridge: MIT Press, 1989).
16. Habermas, *Structural Transformation,* pp. 79–85; Rowe, "The Public Sphere in Modern China," pp. 311–312.
17. The parallel with conceptions of regionalism are suggestive in this regard. Diana Lary argues that regional leaders in the early twentieth century envisioned regionalism as a "bridging phenomenon" that would give way as the center reasserted itself. See *Region and Nation: The Kwangsi Clique in Chinese Politics, 1925–1927* (Cambridge University Press, 1974), pp. 8–9.
18. Rowe, "The Public Sphere in Modern China," p. 316.
19. David Strand, "Protest in Beijing: Civil Society and Public Sphere in China," *Problems of Communism* (May/June 1990): 5.
20. Hao Chang, *Liang Ch'i-ch'ao and the Intellectual Transition in China, 1890–1907* (Cambridge: Harvard University Press, 1971), p. 103.
21. Liang Qichao, "Xinmin shuo" (On the new people), in *Yingbingshi quanji* (Essays from the ice-drinker's studio) (Taipei: Wenhua tushu gongci, 1967), pp. 2–3.
22. On the imposition of Nationalist control over society, see Joseph Fewsmith, *Party, State, and Local Elites in Republican China* (Honolulu: University of Hawaii Press, 1985).
23. Kenneth Jowitt makes the distinction between inclusion and exclusion in his article "Inclusion and Mobilization in European Leninist Regimes," *World Politics* 28, no. 1 (October 1975): 69–96.
24. Fang Lizhi, "Minzhu bu shi ziyu de" (Democracy is not something given), in *Women zhengzai xie lishi* (We are writing history) (Taipei: Commonwealth Publishing Co., 1987), pp. 132–133.
25. A seminar lauding the television program "The Motherland Cannot Be Forgotten" was reported in *Guangming ribao*, November 1, 1988, p. 1. Synopses of the four-part program appeared in the same paper on November 3, 6, 8, and 9. That show clearly was intended as a rejoinder to *He shang* ("River Elegy"), the controversial program highly critical of China's traditional culture that had been broadcast the previous summer, as discussed later.

26. The classic discussion of comradeship is by Ezra Vogel: "From Friendship to Comradeship: The Change in Personal Relations in Communist China," *China Quarterly*, no. 21 (January–March 1965): 46–60.

27. In his most recent book, Janos Kornai states baldly that "the basic idea of market socialism simply fizzled out. Yugoslavia, Hungary, China, the Soviet Union, and Poland bear witness to its fiasco." See *The Road to a Free Economy* (New York: Norton, 1990), p. 58.

28. Liu Guoguang, "Guenyu woguo jingji tizhi gaige de mubiao moshi ji moshi zhuanhuan de ruogan wenti" (The target model of China's economic structural reform and some problems in changing the model), in Liu Guoguang, ed., *Zhongguo jingji tizhi gaige de moshi yanjiu* (Studies on the model of China's economic structural reform) (Beijing: Shehui kexue chubanshe, 1988), p. 3.

29. Jowitt, *The Leninist Response to National Dependency*, p. 15.

30. Mann, *Local Merchants and the Chinese Bureaucracy*, p. 24.

31. Guangdong provincial radio, September 23, 1984.

32. See the fascinating description of contention over Guan Guangmei's activities in Li Honglin's "Yi jiu ba qi, Zhongguo di wu hao xinwen renwu – Guan Guangmei jishi" (1987, China's Number 5 newsmaker – an account of Guan Guangmei), *Dangdai*, no. 2 (February 1988). See also the recent controversy over whether a millionaire should be permitted to join the CCP. Xinhua, September 6, 1988, trans. FBIS, September 7, 1988, p. 27.

33. Andrew G. Walder, *Communist Neo-Traditionalism: Work and Authority in Chinese Industry* (Berkeley: University of California Press, 1986), p. 11.

34. Joseph Fewsmith, "Agricultural Crisis in the PRC," *Problems of Communism* 37 (November–December 1988): 78–93.

35. As Carol Hamrin brings out, Zhao's endorsement of the concept of a new technological revolution was also very much a part of the ideological struggles then taking place among the leadership. See *China and the Challenge of the Future* (Boulder: Westview Press, 1990), pp. 75–78.

36. Tian Sen, "Jottings Written After Reading 'The Third Wave' – Also Commenting on 'Comments on "The Third Wave"' and 'A Big Lever'," *Hongqi*, no. 12 (June 16, 1987): 30–34, trans. Join Publications Research Service, JPRS-CRF–87–006 (August 20, 1987): 49–55. Tian was the general editor of the *Contemporary Sociology* (*Dangdai shehuixue*) book series. His article was based on remarks made at a December 1986 meeting to discuss Toffler's book. See Gao Fang, ed., *Ping "Di san ce chaolang"* (Evaluating "The Third Wave") (Beijing: Guangming ribao chubanshe, 1988), pp. 207–212.

37. On Zhao's meeting, see Xinhua, September 13, 1988, trans. FBIS, September 21, 1988, p. 5.

38. Paul Cohen, *Between Tradition and Modernity: Wang T'ao and Reform in Late Ch'ing China* (Cambridge: Harvard University Press, 1974), pp. 241–242.

39. The use of the hinterland/littoral distinction is not meant to imply geographical determinism, although it is true, as Paul Cohen points out, that many Western ideas took root first in the coastal areas and that a majority of pioneering reformers grew up in or had extensive exposure to the culture of the coastal areas. Particularly as time went on, the geographical dimension of this distinction became less pronounced. Inland areas such as Changsha were notable for their cosmopolitanism, and coastal cities such as Shanghai also bred rejection of Western values. In borrowing this concept to describe

different nationalistic traditions, my intention is to focus not on geographical differences (though they are not negligible) but on the relative openness of different people to foreign ideas. Paul Cohen has suggested the continued usefulness of the hinterland/littoral distinction in the preface to the paperback edition of his book *Between Tradition and Modernity*.

40. The thoughts of many of these conservative intellectuals have been explored: Charlotte Furth, ed., *The Limits of Change: Essays on Conservative Alternatives in Republican China* (Cambridge: Harvard University Press, 1976).

41. "Zhongguo benwei de wenhua jianshe xuanyan" (Manifesto on the construction of a China-based culture), *Wenhua jianshe* (Shanghai), October 1, 1935.

42. Hu Shi, "Shiping suowei 'Zhongguo benwei de wenhua jianshe' " (Critique of the so-called 'construction of a China-based culture'), in *Hu Shi wencun* (Collected essays of Hu Shi) (Taipei: Yuandong tushu gongci, 1953), 4:535–540.

43. Hu did not actually use the term "complete Westernization" in his critique of the ten-professor manifesto, but he did in his essay on cultural conflict in contemporary China that appeared in the 1929 *Christian Year-book*. He later expressed a preference for the term "fully cosmopolitan" rather than "complete Westernization." See his essay "Chongfen shijiehua yu quanpan xihua" (Fully cosmopolitan and complete Westernization), in *Hu Shi wencun*, 4:541–544.

44. "Hu Qiaomu Warns in Xiamen that Foreign Investment Enterprises Are Not Concessions; Their Inordinate Demands Cannot Be Given Tacit Consent," *Ming pao*, June 22, 1985, trans. FBIS, June 24, 1885, p. W8; "Special Economic Zones Are Not Special Political Zones; China's Laws Must Be Upheld, Says Hu Qiaomu," *Zhongguo fazhi bao*, June 28, 1985, trans. FBIS, July 8, 1985, pp. K19–20.

45. Xinhua, December 28, 1986, trans. FBIS, December 30, 1986, pp. K6-K8.

46. Tian Sen, "Jottings Written After Reading 'The Third Wave,' " p. 55.

47. Joseph R. Levenson, "The Problem of Historical Significance," in *Confucian China and Its Modern Fate: A Trilogy* (Berkeley: University of California Press, 1972).

48. See, for instance, the interview with Tu Wei-ming in *Dushu*, October 1985, pp. 118–128.

49. Tang Yijie, "Zhongguo xin wenhua de chuangjian" (Creating a new Chinese culture), *Dushu*, July 1988, pp. 6–10.

50. Bao Zunxin, "Xiandaihua he xihua" (Modernization and Westernization), *Wenhui bao*, September 23, 1986, p. 2.

51. The description of the views of Liu and Lin that follows is based on their two-part essay "Chuantong daode de kunjing" (The poverty of traditional morality), *Shehui kexue zhanxian*, no. 2–3 (1988). For a more complete statement of their argument, see Liu Zaifu and Lin Gang, *Chuantong yu Zhongguo ren* (Tradition and the Chinese people) (Hong Kong: Sanlian shudian, 1988).

52. See Li Zehou, *Zhongguo jindai sixiangshi lun* (History of modern Chinese thought) (Beijing: Renmin chubanshe, 1979); Li Zehou, *Zhongguo xiandai sixiangshi lun* (History of contemporary Chinese thought) (Beijing: Dongfang chubanshe, 1987).

53. See Li Zehou, "Man shuo 'xiti zhongyong' " (Discussing "Western learning as essence, Chinese learning for use"), in *Zhongguo xiandai sixiangshi lun*,

especially pp. 331–333. It seems ironic that while Li can hardly be considered a Marxist philosopher, his conception of "essence" is heavily influenced by Marxism.

54. Su Xiaokang and Wang Luxiang, *He shang* ("River Elegy") (Hong Kong: China Books Press, 1988). The literature for and against *He shang* has become voluminous. An early description of the political battle over it is provided by Liu Yen-ying, "Dien-shih cheng-lun ju 'He shang' chen-ching chungnanhai" (The controversial television drama "River Elegy" shakes Zhongnanhai), *Ching pao*, August 1988, pp. 40–42.

55. This discussion has benefited from conversations with Corinna-Barbara Francis.

56. Michel Oksenberg and Steven Goldstein, "The Chinese Political Spectrum," *Problems of Communism* 23 (March–April 1974): 1–13.

57. Senior economist Xue Muqiao is one of those who have advocated reviving the federations of trade and commerce as guild-type organizations to provide indirect management over various trades. See his article "Establish and Develop Non-Governmental Self-Management Organizations in Various Trades," *Renmin ribao*, October 10, 1988, p. 5, trans. FBIS, October 18, 1988, pp. 33–35.

2

In search of democracy:
public authority and popular power in China

BRANTLY WOMACK

The zigzag and sometimes tragic search for democracy has been a central theme of modern Chinese politics. Often the searchers have been torn between the intellectual attraction of the modern ideals of democracy, based on foreign ideologies, and the practical necessity of adapting to Chinese conditions. Democracy in China has remained elusive both as an ideal and as a reality; at no time in the twentieth century has there been general satisfaction with the prevailing relationship between people and state.

The most successful political leaders of modern China – Sun Yat-sen, Mao Zedong, and Deng Xiaoping – have self-consciously pursued "Chinese paths" that have included limited commitments to popular power. It could be said that the successes of those leaders and the ensuing shape of Chinese politics have been based to some extent on their correct perceptions of the existing possibilities for feasible relationships between public authority and popular power, and their failures have been due to misjudgments of those relationships.

Since the summer of 1989, the post-Mao period has taken an especially tragic turn with regard to democracy. After ten years of unparalleled progress in democratizing reforms, Deng Xiaoping and the party leaders are attempting to reimpose unquestioned and unlimited control over society. Can the party really effect such a dramatic, authoritarian turn? Or will the societal forces already set in motion render such an attempt a very harmful but temporary atavism? The practical contradiction between the current policies of control and repression and the earlier policies of modernization through decontrol and openness has made the question of the relationship between popular power and public authority central to any prognostic analysis of current events.

By Western standards, the relationship between people and state in China has had little to do with democracy. Although the West has been the primary inspiration for Chinese democratic thought, the direct influence of Western democratic institutions may seem vestigial. Individual freedom of speech and conscience, effective legislatures and legal systems, free and competitive elections – the hallmarks of mature legislative democracy – do not and have never played key roles in modern Chinese politics. Such issues have not been totally lacking (they were more relevant to political reforms in the 1980s than they had ever been in the past), but for the most part they have provided and continue to provide a vulnerable and tragic foil to the main course of Chinese politics.

It would be a mistake, however, to dismiss the search for democracy in China as merely unsuccessful, or to assume that Chinese politics in the twentieth century has no lessons to teach the West regarding democracy. Both the successes and failures of popular power in China (the most sweeping popular revolution in history, followed by the self-consumption of a strong state in the Cultural Revolution) have been experiences of the relationship between popular power and public authority that have approached the fringes of human societal capacity. There are lessons here regarding what can and cannot be done in politics that are most directly relevant to contemporary China, but they also have more general significance waiting to be explored.

But why use the term "democracy"? Why not reserve this term for the more familiar domain of citizen-based legislative systems? There are two parts to my answer. The first is necessary, but too simple in itself, namely, that the term "democracy" (*minzhu*) is used by the Chinese themselves. A serious attempt to understand Chinese politics must take seriously its internal framework of significance. To assume that the Chinese do not know what they are talking about would be arrogant and would leave the researcher and the object of research with incompatible vocabularies. The linguistic prolegomenon of serious comparative research must begin by understanding the internal system of significance for the object and then interpret it into the researcher's own language. To assume that "I know what democracy is, and they don't" would presume a special access to truth on the part of the researcher, a claim to objectivity that would be only a product of the researcher's relative indifference and disinterest. Although one is not obliged to accept a usage uncritically, one is obliged to understand it before criticizing or dismissing it.

A second reason for taking seriously the role that the idea of democracy has played in China is that if democracy retains its philological meaning of the power of the people, then democracy in China must be understood and judged in terms of the desires, interests, and situations of the Chinese people. In other words, the question of democracy, of popular power, is an endogenous question, one of *this* people's power. To the extent that political institutions are shaped by history and culture, the institutions that evolved during the development of modern democracy in the West

54

cannot be generalized into an abstract standard of democracy. If that were the case, then "the power of the people" would mean no more than "the power of the (Western) people." If culture is a significant variable, and if Chinese democracy implies the power of the Chinese people, then one must expect that it would differ from Western democracy.

The attempt to understand China's self-understanding of its search for democracy has the potential to be far more fruitful for a cosmopolitan political science than would a search for Western democratic traits in Chinese politics. The radically different context of modern Chinese politics skews and frustrates any attempt to find institutional similarities to the West, but at the same time it provides, as Tang Tsou pointed out,[1] a good testing ground for the general significance of Western political science. Precisely because of the vast situational differences between Chinese and Western politics, any generalizations about democracy that can span both of these cultures will mark progress toward a general theory of modern democracy.

The bulk of this chapter will be devoted to an analysis of the development, in theory and in practice, of the role of the people in modern Chinese politics. It begins with a brief consideration of the differences between the institutional heritage of China and that of the West, as well as the role of the people in classical Chinese political thought. The borrowings and adaptations from two Western ideologies are then considered: first, the attraction of the liberal democratic state and its sinification by Sun Yat-sen and the Guomindang (GMD, Nationalist party); second, the attempt to apply Marxism-Leninism in China. The development of a rural, mass-regarding, revolutionary politics by Mao Zedong receives special attention. Several phases of subsequent politics in the People's Republic of China (PRC) are analyzed: the modified Stalinist structure of the 1950s, the "leftist" transformation, the experience with mass movements in the Cultural Revolution, and finally the situation of democratic reform in the post-Mao period.

DEMOCRACY AND CHINA'S TRADITIONAL HERITAGE

One could make a plausible argument that China's traditional political heritage is irrelevant to its modern search for democracy. Contemporary Chinese discussions of democracy usually trace the word to its Greek roots. Indeed, although the Chinese word for democracy, *minzhu* (literally, "people rule"), is found in classical texts, there it has the rather antidemocratic meaning of governance over the people, *min zhi zhu* ("the ruling of the people"). *Minzhu* in its modern sense of democracy was first introduced in the 1860s in translations and descriptions of Western politics. Moreover, in the period before Sun Yat-sen, even Chinese reformers considered the antimonarchical implications of *minzhu* too radical for China, and they argued instead for the milder term *minquan* ("people's rights"), a notion that could coexist with the hereditary empire.[2] It could be said, therefore, not only that democracy was missing from the Chinese tradition but also that its acceptance in China was delayed because democracy's spearhead was pointed unequivocally at the heart of traditional political institutions. Democracy was emphatically modern, and modernity in China arrayed itself against China's past.

Nevertheless, it would be a mistake to ignore traditional China in the study of Chinese democracy. Modern China pushed off from traditional China and was guided by alien ideologies, but its initial context was set by its past. Moreover, as the writings of Mao Zedong richly illustrate, traditional China continued to supply a common cultural vocabulary and menu of examples. Most important, between traditional China and modern China there has remained a common ground of basic assumptions about politics. These assumptions are difficult to specify because they were not consciously adopted by reformers, but rather formed their basic schematic for viewing politics. At this depth of continuity, even the condemnation of traditional China and the reorientation toward the West can be related to a continuity in the Chinese view of relationship between people and state.

Subtlety is prized in the study of traditional China because a sense of texture can easily be lost in sweeping generalizations and stark contrasts with the West. Unfortunately, in this essay I can do no more than touch upon some major features of traditional Chinese institutions and thought. So let me warn those unfamiliar with traditional China that what will be said will be thin simplifications of a vastly more complex reality, and let me ask those more knowledgeable to focus their critical attention not on the exceptions to my simplifications but on whether a more accurate simplification could be made.

The relationship between tradition and modernity was fundamentally different in China than in the West. What for the West was a relatively gradual transformation was for China a cataclysm. Chinese civilization was more cohesive, more centralized, and more cumulative, and the forces of modernity suddenly struck China from the outside in the nineteenth century. It was an experience of national humiliation and weakness, and it led to an abrupt repudiation of old China and a reorientation toward the West. The "Chinese renaissance," to use Hu Shi's phrase,[3] was more a baptism of China into a modern and Western world than a rebirth and rediscovery of things Chinese. By contrast, modernity emerged more slowly in the West and from a more disparate background, and it empowered an expanding world hegemony. As traumatic as the modern experience sometimes was in the West, it lacked the additional crisis dimensions of external imposition, defeat, subjugation, and abruptness experienced in China and in many other non-Western countries.

Feudal representative institutions in the West provided a uniquely advantageous context for the emergence of legislative democracy. The German historian Otto Hintze has argued that representative institutions developed in the West because of the confluence of three factors: feudal privilege, the tension between church and state, and international rivalries within Europe.[4] Privilege, a "private law" (*lex privatus*) between sovereign and subject, defined the limits of state power. Privileges provided the prototype for rights, and the privileged estates composed the feudal assemblies. The existence of separate hierarchies for church and state also delimited the realm of state power, and the church, as a major privileged group, supported the assemblies. Rivalries among the European states strengthened representative institutions by putting a premium on state effectiveness and by forcing sovereigns to depend on the cooperation of their assembled estates. The modern Western democratic state developed from the weakness of its feudal precursor, rather than from its strength.

The general picture of the European feudal state is one limited by the privileges it had granted and by its competition with its siblings and the church. The institutional structure of imperial China could not have been more different. The Chinese empire was a centralized power unrestricted by privilege, religious power, or rivals of equal stature, and served by a scholar bureaucracy recruited by merit rather than by birth.[5] The longevity, administrative articulation, and efficiency of the empire were wonders of the premodern world. Not only was the empire not burdened by representative assemblies; absent also were territorial constituencies, spheres of immunity from public involvement, and the concept of protection against the sovereign. The state was not externally limited, nor was there an incipient, autonomous civil society.

A Westerner would expect such a society to have been arbitrary and autocratic, because it did not have the institutions that in the West limited the abuse of prerogative. Of course, abuses occurred (as they did in the West), but the discipline of the system was different from that of the West. Instead of the discipline of external delimitation, in which the subjects possessed their bounded rights and the sovereigns possessed their bounded power, the Chinese emperor and his officials were bound by ideology, ritual, and tradition. Confucianism, especially, provided a well-developed ethic of rule, and mastery of that ethic was a major requirement of bureaucratic recruitment. It was an orthodoxy not of revealed truth but of ritual and ethical standards – the soul of a civilized pyramid of virtue. The responsibility of the emperor, as well as the official, was to act according to the ideal, moral obligations of office. So the hard lines of power in the imperial system were encumbered by a soft but strong web of ethical expectations.

In contrast to the formidably centralized imperial institutions, traditional Chinese political thought shows a very active concern for the welfare of the people, though there is no concept of the people as participants in politics. The concern for popular welfare can be illustrated by a passage from Confucius's disciple Mencius:

King Hui of Liang said, "I wish quietly to receive your instructions."

Mencius replied, "Is there any difference between killing a man with a stick and with a sword?" The King said, "There is no difference."

"Is there any difference between doing it with a sword and with the style of government?" "There is no difference," was the reply. Mencius then said, "In your kitchen there is fat meat; in your stables there are fat horses. But your people have the look of hunger, and on the wilds there are those who have died of famine.... When a prince, being the parent of his people, administers his government so as to be chargeable with leading on beasts to devour men, where is his parental relationship to his people?"[6]

Classical Chinese political thought assumed that the welfare of the people was the root of the prosperous state. The ruler who was a bad shepherd of his people risked losing heaven's mandate to rule, and in any case he weakened his state. Even military strategists such as Sunzi considered popular support of primary importance. But that did not imply popular participation in government. Rather, the people were more like a natural force influenced by and influencing in turn the behavior of the king.

Undergirding the apparent contradiction between the importance of the people and their lack of political rights was a familial paradigm of society. That paradigm assumed a natural givenness of unequal status relations at the same time as it exhorted everyone to live up to their specific responsibilities. It is quite interesting that in various portraits by Chinese thinkers of the "state of nature" and the origin of government, the Western question of why the rational individual should obey is not raised. Instead, the importance of political order to group survival is stressed. Although a sense of personal moral responsibility is exquisitely developed in classical Chinese thought, the ultimate ground of rational action lies in a naturally structured society, rather than in abstract rational individualism.

By its own standard of communal strength and prosperity, traditional China became a failure in the nineteenth century. As early as the 1860s, according to Mary Wright, the attempts to restore imperial order after the Taiping Rebellion "demonstrated with a rare clarity that even in the most favorable circumstances there is no way in which an effective modern state can be grafted onto a Confucian society."[7] The sinocentric cosmopolitanism of the empire gradually became a narrow, empty provincialism, and the new cosmopolitans rejected the dead hand of Confucianism and turned toward the West.[8] To be sure, there were Confucian revivals in the twentieth century. But when Liang Shuming, "the last Confucian," fulfilled his moral duty of criticizing collectivization at a meeting of the Central People's Government Council in 1953, he appeared to Mao Zedong as absurdly out of place and reactionary, as if he had worn traditional court robes.[9]

Clearly, however, modern China's rejection of its past did not change its parentage. I shall mention only a few of the most important continuities. The first is the cluster of political values whereby the moral obligation is to serve the community, and the test of regime legitimacy is the welfare of the people. That was traditional China's own standard, and in confrontation with the West, China was found wanting. The Western orientation and radicalism of twentieth-century reformers transformed the content of Chinese politics, but those reformers had been pressured to do so by an ethic that dated back to the Zhou dynasty. The Qing dynasty lost its mandate to a new era. Just as Confucianism was not conquered by Buddhism in the later Han dynasty, but rather withdrew into itself because of a sense of its own failure,[10] so the deepest levels of the Confucian ethic could carry and even force a total reorientation toward new principles of wealth and power.

The second continuity is the assumption that the Chinese government should be unitary and centralized, and that disunity means unacceptable chaos and disorder. The four decades of Chinese unity under the PRC make it easy to forget how extraordinary the commitment to unity was during the period of total crisis. Even in the "warring-states period" there was no legitimating ideology of separatism, and that helped to preclude the legitimation of China's disunity in the twentieth century. Oddly enough, that assumption rested rather more lightly on Mao Zedong: At one time he supported independence for the province of Hunan, and after 1927 he was quick to perceive the opportunities of scattered base areas under communist control. By contrast, one of Deng Xiaoping's most powerful arguments for repression is the threat of chaos from spontaneous societal forces.

A third continuity is the assumption of a governing mission for the intellectuals. Here the particular Chinese heritage of the scholar bureaucracy must be differentiated from more common patterns. As Eric Wolf observes in his general study of modern peasant revolutions, modern professionals in developing countries – teachers, doctors, lawyers – tend to become radicalized by their contacts with developed countries, their professional frustrations, and their exclusion from the traditional power structure. These "marginal moderns," who have little continuity with traditional culture, then supply the necessary leadership skills for more broad-based popular movements.[11] In China, the tradition of the scholar bureaucracy as the political class incorporated by an orthodoxy provided a special continuity between traditional and modern intellectuals. There was the assumption of a responsibility to govern, an unselfconscious elitism of service. This is in special contrast to the Russian *intelligentsia* (originally a Russian word), which had a problematic relationship to Russian culture – at times Westernizing, at times romantically Russian – and defined itself against the tsarist system and the aristocracy. It is not implausible that the greater factionalism of Russian radicals is related to a more critical and individualist intellectual posture. If we consider Lenin and Mao as culturally representative revolutionaries, Lenin was more polemical and radically critical, whereas Mao was more pragmatic and governance-oriented.

A fourth continuity is the assumption that government can be controlled through self-discipline and moral education, rather than through institutions of external control. This is particularly clear in Sun Yat-sen's idea of a tutelary elite who would guide China to democracy. This continuity created a predisposition toward Leninism, although it tended to shift the basis of authority away from the scientific grasp of doctrine (as with Lenin) to more personal qualities of leadership (e.g., Chen Duxiu before 1927). In any case, the ideas of democratic centralism within the party and indefinite party-state power after the revolution were less of a cultural shock in China than they would have been in England.

Finally, and summarizing the other continuities, the starting point of modern Chinese political thought remains community rationality, rather than the abstract rational individual. The concepts of order and of ethical behavior were founded on a direct relationship to the public good, and that justified the primacy of politics as the most legitimate concern. The orientation toward communal rationality can be seen in the skew of Yan Fu's transmission of the classics of Western thought,[12] and it reached its most destructive point in the Cultural Revolution's slogan of "all public and no private" (*da gong wu si*). This continuity is well illustrated by Joseph Fewsmith's analysis of *gong* and *si*, public and private, in Chapter 1 of this volume. I certainly would not argue, as Etienne Balazs has done,[13] that communist totalitarianism has its roots in traditional totalitarianism. Both are more complicated than that. But the reception and shaping of Marxism-Leninism in China, and the horizons of the party-state, are clearly related to common assumptions that were already present in Chinese political culture.

It is ironic that the very strength and longevity of the traditional empire in China contributed to the trauma of modernity. The weaker and more limited governments of the West had no choice but to acknowledge the societal complexity that incubated bourgeois civil society, and to permit the rise of institutions that could evolve into a legislative state. The Chinese state was sufficiently strong that its only restrictions were self-restrictions, and its corporate orthodoxy was publicly oriented and flexible enough to preserve its power until that power was smashed from the outside by the maturing modernity of the West. Although the crisis that then confronted China was unprecedented, Chinese political culture was deep enough to provide a transition and to shape the reception of foreign models. The old pyramid of virtue was abandoned and vilified, but the obligation was quietly shouldered to create a new one.

THE FAILED SINIFICATION OF THE LIMITED STATE

Traditional China was not overthrown by John Locke and John Stuart Mill, but by the gunboats of liberal democratic imperialism. It should not be surprising, therefore, that the primary motive for studying the West was to create a new, prosperous China, as powerful as its adversaries. Nevertheless, democracy – with regular, popular elections of leadership as a key feature – was seen as essential to the power of the West. Democracy, according to Chen Duxiu in a famous essay, was one of the two Western gentlemen with whom China must become acquainted.[14] In the early twentieth century, China learned from the West at a speed befitting a culture of scholars; indeed, the very rate of appropriation of Western ideas – what I call "compressed intellectual modernization"[15] – deeply affected Chinese reception. Learning from the West also entailed the transfer of Western institutions to China, an effort that proved continually frustrating. Finally, Sun Yat-sen set in motion an effective "sinification of the liberal democratic state." Like the limited Western state, China acknowledged and compromised with the forces existing in society: the warlords, imperialists, and communists. The Guomindang (GMD) state that emerged was successful because it adapted its politics to its weakness. It was neither liberal nor democratic, and eventually it lost to an uncompromising revolutionary strength based directly on popular mobilization.

From the failure of the "Hundred Days Reform" in 1898 to the "Northern Expedition" of 1927, the intellectual life of China underwent a complete transformation. In 1898, few Western books had been translated into Chinese; by 1920, Bertrand Russell and John Dewey were making extended lecture tours in China at the invitation of their returned Chinese students. Their talks were immediately translated and appeared in the newspapers. Within three decades, China had appropriated three hundred years of Western cultural development.

The rate of change in political ideology can be illustrated by the fate of Kang Youwei: In 1898 his reform program had been scandalously revolutionary; in 1916 he embarrassed his students and admirers by participating in a scheme to restore the empire. Yet he was proud of the fact that his views had not changed; what appeared to be his movement from extreme left to extreme right was in reality a measure of the change in China's field of political discourse. Such rapid intellectual change meant that there had been no time for maturation or institutional articulation of specific viewpoints. Kang Youwei was called "China's Luther" at the turn of the century, but there was no time for a Confucian protestantism to unfold.

Intellectual modernization necessarily produced an urban and youthful orientation, because the schools and the cities were the contact points for the outside world. City and countryside rapidly became different worlds, one not daring to look beyond the local gentry, and the other choosing among Wilson, Kropotkin, and Marx. In some respects that was a golden age for youth. Six years after Mao Zedong read his first newspaper, he published an article in China's leading progressive journal. It took little apprenticeship to participate in attempting to lead China; the examinations, the old ladder to success, had been discontinued in 1905.

The basic problem of compressed intellectual modernization was that ideas vastly outran realities. As the empire fell and China degenerated into warlord rule, urban progressives moved further into the borrowed intellectual world of Western politics and emerged with ever more radical prescriptions for China's happiness. For the communists and the left GMD, that culminated in the tragedy of betrayal and defeat in 1927.

The transfer of Western political institutions into China began with an improbable patron: the Empress Dowager.[16] After the debacle of the Boxer uprising, she decided that reform was necessary and that Western models of government should be studied. In 1905, official delegations were sent to Japan, Europe, and the United States to study their institutions, and a nine-year reform program for instituting constitutional government (*xian zheng*) was devised according to their suggestions. The reforms included a declaration of constitutional principles, as well as elections of provincial and ultimately national assemblies. The scope of the reforms impressed some contemporary observers and later scholars,[17] but progressives viewed them as insincere attempts to delay truly democratic change. One incident well expressed the tension between imperial reform and the demands of progressives: The train carrying the first official delegation to study Western politics was blown up by an anarchist's bomb.

The constitutional history of the Republic of China is quite complex, and it included some serious efforts to impose a structure of legislative government.[18] But the impotence of such efforts was their most striking feature. During the warlord period, the machinations of the "legislators" often provided a comic foreground to the serious business of warlord factionalism. Under GMD rule after 1927, parliamentary and constitutional questions occasionally became major political issues, but at no time was the country's political direction under the control of the legislature, or the officials under control of the electorate, or indeed politics in general under the control of constitution and laws. Despite modified Western trappings, the Republic of China was neither liberal nor democratic.

Just as it would be a mistake to judge the contribution of the PRC to popular power in terms of constitutional democracy, it would be a mistake to judge Sun Yat-sen's political heritage in terms of the effectiveness of borrowed Western institutions. To be sure, a good part of Sun's historic role was to symbolize the modernization of China in a Western sense, and republican political institutions were an important part of that. In that respect, Sun contributed to the political myth of the GMD, but the myth shadowed the actual ineffectiveness of the borrowings. So Sun's mission, in large part, was a failure. But the failure did not occur in 1949, or even in 1927. It had already begun in 1913, and it reached its nadir in 1918, and Sun's later politics, including his *Three Principles of the People,*[19] included adjustments to his earlier naiveté. The success of the GMD in 1927 was based on Sun's accommodation of his failed Westernizing ideals to the realities of Chinese politics.

Sun's sinification of the liberal democratic state involved an acknowledgment of the limitations imposed by existing Chinese conditions and a determination to pursue political effectiveness – in a word, it was based on compromise. In his political theory, the compromise was most clear in the idea that a situation of political tutelage was necessary before democracy could be implemented. In his political practice, it was expressed in accommodations with a variety of warlords and foreign powers, as well as in the alliance from 1923 to 1927 with the Chinese Communist Party (CCP). Consider the following passage, in which Sun tried to show the perfidy of one of his erstwhile warlord patrons:

Why did Chen Jiongming lead a revolt against us in Guangzhou year before last? Many people said that he only wanted to seize Guangdong and Guangxi for himself, but that is far from true....I thought that perhaps...our northern expedition might seem to be interfering with his domain, so on the last day of our conferences, I said to him with utter frankness, "If our punitive expedition against the North succeeds, our government will be moved to either Wuhan or Nanjing and will certainly not come back here, in which case we will entrust the two Guang provinces to you and ask you to be our rear guard. If the northern expedition should unfortunately fail, we will have no face to come back here and . . . you will certainly be able to preserve your sphere of influence."[20]

Clearly, Sun was willing to make the compromises necessary for survival and victory and to develop an agglomerative hegemony based on arrangements with various "real powers." Doubtless Sun would have provided a unique style of leadership had he lived long enough to rule, but Chiang Kai-shek's politics of accommodation did not differ in principle.

Compromises with existing forces enabled the GMD to come to national power in a chaotic environment in which no existing power was sufficiently strong to compel obedience. This can be called a sinification of Westernism, because the GMD government played the game of a weak government vis-à-vis other social forces, a game common enough in the West, but against the Chinese imperial tradition. By building on arrangements with other social forces, the GMD government approximated the situation of the feudal governments in the West: a sovereignty with a negotiated relationship with society. Unfortunately, the chief negotiations were with warlords and foreign powers, so the limits of the GMD state were not liberal democratic limits.

As Sun's willingness to compromise implied, by 1920 he had little faith left in the revolutionary power of the people or in the transformative power of Western democratic institutions. Dedication to democratic ideals remained important, but democracy was not an effective answer to China's current problems. China was disorganized – a "sheet of loose sand" – with too much democracy, rather than too little. A tutelary GMD elite would first have to establish its political control before the process of democratization could begin.

The Republic of China as a weak authoritarian state was similar to many others in developing countries and to those in the earlier history of the West. Obviously such states are not democratic; neither popular interests nor popular institutions control public authority. Indeed, to the extent that the gaming table of government is open only to elite powers, the power of the people threatens the entire game. As Mao Zedong observed from a dangerous angle, the one matter on which the warlords and the GMD all agreed was opposition to popular revolution. Nevertheless, various institutional characteristics of Western states can thrive in such an environment: Parliaments, cabinets, constitutions, and even elections can become the rules and counters of an elite game, because all players except the most powerful want rules. It is impossible to know how the politics of the GMD would have developed; Chiang Kai-shek seemed more committed to consolidating strength than to accepting and respecting limits. But the remarkable

GMD experiments with democratization in Taiwan since 1987 can be understood as a compromise in an entirely new context of social forces and political horizons.

There is little direct continuity between Western liberal democracy and the PRC, but such democracy appears to have a certain attractiveness in the post-Mao period. Various reforms, such as elections with more candidates than positions, suggest that the current leadership is recalling arguments from an earlier time concerning the nature of democracy. Perhaps this is because of their personal sufferings under the tyranny of the masses during the Cultural Revolution. Perhaps the focus on modernization has reawakened the linked images of Western power and liberal democratic politics. One could also argue that the goal of modernization, because of its reliance on expertise and entrepreneurship, puts societal forces that are largely outside the party in a position of some strength. In any case, the reforms within the Marxist-Leninist party-state have in general been in a liberal direction, although no redefinition of state legitimacy has occurred.

COMMUNISM AS A WESTERN INFLUENCE ON CHINA

In the West (and in this essay), the term "Western" usually refers to the countries of industrialized capitalism, but it is important for our understanding of the communist influence in China to recall that communism's initial appeal in China was as the latest and most radical Western influence. It provided a Western critique of the West as China had experienced it: imperialist and exploitative. It claimed to advance beyond the historical phase of capitalism, and it provided a model for radical political organization. The young intellectuals who joined the CCP in the 1920s composed the last and most cosmopolitan of the waves of compressed intellectual modernization; that was also the wave most out of touch with the gray realities of China, and it broke upon the rocks of warlordism and compromise in 1927. As a Western influence, communism failed. It eventually triumphed as the ideological and organizational paradigm of a rural revolution.

The uniqueness of the appeal of Marxism-Leninism lay in its relationship to the Russian Revolution. The October Revolution demonstrated that ideologically directed political transformation was possible in a way that transcended Japan's copying from the West. The evil aspects of traditional China – "feudalism" – and of capitalism could both be overcome, and Chinese radicals could be at the vanguard of national salvation and at the same time active, conscious participants in world revolution. Marxism-Leninism provided a proven model. In the terminology of Clifford Geertz, it provided an ideology that could replace the discarded cultural system of traditional China.[21] Class struggle became the analytical key to sorting out domestic and international phenomena.

Just as important as the intellectual orientation provided by communism was the organizational model of the disciplined, revolutionary party. The idea of a dedicated party core leading mass groups and occasionally forming united fronts with other groups for specific goals was quite compatible with the capacity of the intellectuals for dedicated effort and with the opportunities afforded by the chaos of Chinese society. It provided a practical starting point for effective action that would be directly linked to national and even world transformation. Just as Marxist ideology provided a comprehensive response to the disorientation of total crisis, so the party provided a tough, flexible framework for action in a chaotic society.

Communism had a more direct relationship to the power of the people than had the GMD in the 1920s. Indeed, within the GMD-CCP alliance of 1924 to 1927, the CCP specialized in mass organization. In line with Marxist theory and Bolshevik practice, the CCP concentrated on organizing urban workers. Originally it had hoped to lead an autonomous proletarian revolution, but after railway workers were slaughtered by a warlord on February 7, 1923, the CCP decided to follow Comintern advice and join a united front with the GMD against warlordism and imperialism. But the basis of its organizational strength remained its union activities.

Of course, worker organization did not imply a commitment to democracy in a "Western" sense. Marxism-Leninism emerged in Europe as a radical critique of Western, capitalist politics and therefore considered itself superior to bourgeois democracy. Because all states were organs of class rule, the only significant political question was which class would be in power. The masses were a natural historic force; the details of their political participation were insignificant. This is reminiscent of the role of the people in traditional China, except that communism encouraged the revolutionary activity of the masses. They were mobilized rather than shepherded; class struggle and striving for the future replaced the "five bonds" and respect for the past. Nevertheless, the revolutionary elite was neither controlled by the masses nor limited by institutions; its popular legitimation depended on a self-proclaimed service to popular welfare.

The CCP in the 1920s was an organization of urban intellectuals with an organizational base among urban workers and allied with the GMD and the peasantry against China's semi-colonial, semi-feudal status. It was confident of victory because of its ideology and the guidance of the Comintern. The GMD had been building military and political strength around Guangzhou (Canton) since 1923, and at the end of 1926 it initiated the pattern of alliance with some warlords and confrontation with others that led to the success of the Northern Expedition and to national power in 1927. The GMD alliance with the CCP was inconvenient to its acquisition of new partners, and so the CCP was crushed. Remnants of the CCP escaped to various isolated spots in the countryside. In the cities, Marxism became an academic interest rather than a political interest.

The reasons for the failure of the CCP in 1927 look rather obvious in hindsight. It was uncompromising with the real powers in China, and its own power base was small and vulnerable in a military confrontation. The GMD's broad-mindedness in compromising with the communists made predictable its treachery when confronted with better offers from the right. But the CCP was blind to its impending fate. The leadership was bitterly divided in early 1927 over how much support to give to the peasant associations or whether the alliance with the GMD should be upheld to the end, but both factions were terribly wrong in their anticipations. It was foolish for Chen Duxiu to imagine that the alliance could be preserved, but Mao was just as wrong in his prediction that the peasants would arise "like a hurricane, a force so swift and violent that no power, however great, will be able to hold it back."[22]

The CCP that reemerged after 1927 and succeeded in 1949 was not the same as its predecessor. It was based in the countryside, and it knew that "political power grows from the barrel of a gun." It had developed a rural revolutionary strategy that was suited to Chinese conditions. The continuity between the successful, peasant-based CCP and its urban, intellectual predecessor lay primarily in party organization and also in general ideological orientation. The disciplined party structure worked well in chaos, even the chaos of its own defeat. It turned out to be well adapted to survival, and its pattern of forming a political base by mobilizing the masses was applicable to the new situation. Ideological adaptation was more complex. A proletarian revolution was out of the question, but the analytical tool of class struggle could be applied to the village, and the overall confidence in the science of Marxism-Leninism was an even more necessary consolation. The rural reformation of Chinese communism after the defeat of 1927 could thus be described as a creative adaptation to Chinese conditions, a sinification of Marxism-Leninism.

MAO ZEDONG AND THE MASS LINE

The Cultural Revolution and its aftermath have made it difficult to appreciate Mao Zedong's primary contribution to Chinese history. Mao's development of a strategy of rural revolution not only eventuated in victory in 1949 but also brought the Chinese masses into Chinese politics for the first time in modern history. The village, which had been at the periphery of elite politics, became the center of revolutionary politics. The mobilized power of the people was the party's primary resource, and it became the basis of a very strong party-state. Despite the CCP's success in mass mobilization, however, the political structure of the CCP was not democratic.

The relationship between the party and the masses was called "the mass line" (*qunzhong luxian*), a process of consultation and continual adjustment of policy. Democratic mechanisms such as elections and citizen rights played only a marginal role in this process, and yet the party responded seriously to mass criticisms, demands, apathy, and so forth. The reason that the party was mass-regarding in its politics, despite its authoritarian political structure, was that its survival depended on mass support. Superiority in every other resource lay incontestably in the hands of the government. In competition with a more powerful enemy, the CCP had to remain close to the interests and capacities of the masses in order to optimize its chances for survival and victory. I call this a "quasi-democratic system": an authoritarian political structure systematically tending toward mass-regarding politics because of a competitive environment.[23] We shall first consider the origins of the mass line and its organizational characteristics, and then compare its democratic components to Western concepts.

From the beginning of his political career, Mao Zedong had been concerned with mass-oriented policies and with political effectiveness. Those concerns brought him into the CCP after the failure of the May Fourth movement of 1919. In early 1927 Mao's populism brought him into conflict with Chen Duxiu's cautious attitude toward peasant associations; according to Mao, a "true revolutionary" could not be afraid of mass mobilization. After he was forced into the countryside, Mao, as a matter of survival, had to pay close attention to local conditions and adjust his policies in a process of trial and error. From 1927 to 1930 he developed his basic tactics of guerrilla warfare and his land-reform policy. More important, he saw that popular mobilization would depend on the party's closeness to the masses. The most dangerous sin for the party and for individual cadres would be *tuoli qunzhong*, estrangement from the masses, because distance in the party–mass relationship would increase the strain and friction of mobilization. As head of government for the Jiangxi Soviet from 1931 to 1934, Mao innovated the technique of mass campaigns, and after the "Long March," when he became the most powerful leader in the CCP, Mao systematized his approach and applied it throughout the CCP. The mass line and its techniques remained revered principles in the PRC, but the change in context from struggle with the

GMD to party-state monopoly of power fundamentally affected its democratic character.

The basic outlines of political organization remained the same as they had been before 1927: The party organization was the disciplined minority core of larger mass organizations, and policy direction was dictated by revolutionary strategy. The larger organizations amplified and applied core policy, but their reactions to policy also served as a constraint on the party's policy-making. Outer organizations were useful not only for their service to party policy but also for the encouragement of activists (potential party members) and for reflecting mass opinion. Especially when one adds the specific features of mass-line organization discussed later, it is more accurately thought of as an organization of concentric circles than as a vertical hierarchy.[24]

First, the mass line was base-oriented. Its broadest circles reached out to almost every inhabitant of a village, and its core was kept to a minimum. There was little hierarchy and professionalization of roles. That was reflected in the Red Army's guerrilla style and in every other form of management as well. All cadres were expected to minimize their cost to the movement by raising their own food and avoiding waste. Second, there was considerable cadre discretion. Cadres were, of course, bound by party discipline, and there was much emphasis on correct ideology, but there was broad discretion for territorial leadership at each level. Weberian measures of organizational discipline – rules, reports, sanctions, clear demarcations of responsibility, professional recruitment – were minimized. Mao encouraged originality; cadres were supposed to behave like general commanders. Mao said that in disputes between local and outside authorities, the presumption of correctness should lie with the local leadership.[25] Each cadre was responsible to the center, and sometimes to the masses, for the objective results of their leadership, and they were exhorted to investigate local conditions and avoid bureaucratism.

The key to the organizational focus in the base areas was the third characteristic: the campaign cycle. Campaigns directed general attention toward urgent goals – food production, army recruitment, land reform, cadre rectification – and associated other policy goals with those main targets. Everyone would participate in the campaign, regardless of their normal tasks. The typical campaign went through a cycle of experimentation with models and cadre orientation, a high tide of mobilization, and then consolidation, including reports and corrections of mistakes. Official guidelines tended to be collections of slogans and models at high tide, with detailed official policy only in the consolidation phase. The targets of mass campaigns were matters of obvious mass interest: survival, land, food, good leadership. There were election campaigns, but like the others they were considered successful when everyone was enthusiastic and targets were achieved. Elections did not control or directly affect leadership or policy. The influence of the masses rested in the fact that the party needed their enthusiasm.

Fourth, the mass line favored an alliance-maximizing principle of reaching decisions. The decision-making style was consensual rather than adversarial, an approach that advantaged the agenda-setting role of the party and responsible cadres. When consensus was a problem, the party's strategy was to maximize the alliance rather than simply to allow the majority to dominate, because the basic mobilizational problem was that of having maximum support against minimum opposition. That meant that policy was determined by the interests of the most marginal member of the coalition, though it also had to include the interests of the majority. For example, during the war against Japan, patriotic landlords were encouraged to join the struggle, and therefore a policy of reduction of rent and interest replaced the policy of redistribution of landlord holdings.

Clearly, popular support was essential to the mass line, and the close relationship between party and masses in the revolutionary period was later recalled with nostalgia. But there were fundamental differences between the mass line as a democratic ideology and Western notions. For Mao, the mass line provided a self-correcting, mass-oriented executive structure. Policy-making was a practical problem of leadership, but it was not a political problem to be resolved by popular sovereignty. The unity of party policy and mass interests was absolutely unproblematic in theory and was the key tenet of correct, situationally appropriate leadership in practice. Thus, in principle, there could be no division between control and spontaneity, or between legislative and executive functions. The popular electoral structure was pseudo-legislative. Its function was to reflect the opinions of the masses within the current horizons of party policy. If the horizons were narrow, the range of public discussion was narrow.

This is totally different from Rousseau's idea of the general will. Rousseau starts from the assumption of absolute individual spontaneity and then argues that it is rational to submit only to an authority that is all-powerful and is based on equal, universal citizenship. The general will thus created is a fantasy of collective spontaneity: It cannot be in error; it is not an aggregation of factions or representatives; it is the true common denominator of the participants. It is an overwhelmingly legislative system; the executive merely applies the general will. Marxism-Leninism preserves the myth of supreme popular power, but rejects the abstract, free individual as its base. The Marxist base is the concrete historical actor, the proletarian class. The content of the general will is correspondingly concrete – revolution – and so the macro-political problem of Marxism-Leninism is an executive problem of realization and execution.

Mao's attention to the problem of maintaining closeness to the masses was a significant deviation from Marxist-Leninist assumptions, but he did not return to popular sovereignty as the aggregate of individual wills. Mao turned the communist assumption of party correctness into the key problem area for leadership. His goal of closeness to the masses implied and recognized the problem of distance between the party and the masses: In a concrete, practical sense, the party must serve the masses. However, its mass-regarding political style occurred within the assumption that that was not in conflict with the party's service to history. There was no chance that popular style and flexible policy would evolve into citizen and legislative control.

The success of the mass line in mobilizing rural support led eventually to a massive popular revolution that crushed the entire framework of previous elite politics and brought to an end the general situation of weakness, disunity, and chaos that had characterized modern China. In twenty-two years of revolutionary experimentation and construction in the countryside, the CCP had built a new power base through attention to the welfare of the overwhelming majority of the Chinese population. As Hong Yung Lee describes in Chapter 6 of this volume, the personnel, policies, and values of the revolution became the heritage of the PRC. But the competitive context of the quasi-democratic system was changed by victory, and neither the party in general nor the individual cadres remained as dependent on the goodwill of the masses.

DEMOCRACY AND THE TRANSITION TO SOCIALISM

The founding of the PRC on October 1, 1949, set an entirely new framework for the relationship between popular power and public authority. In contrast to traditional Chinese politics, a government was founded that promoted social and economic change, that had led a class struggle of peasants against landlords, and that had a dual, party-state political system. The PRC was vastly more powerful than the empire had been. Not only did it have the technologies of modern government at its disposal, but also, because of its rural origins, it reached down to and inside of every village in China.

The contrast between the PRC and the Republic of China was even more striking, because the PRC ended the situation of total crisis to which the GMD had accommodated itself. It was not a weak, aggregated government of established elite forces, but a successful challenge to the entire

71

elite structure, based on the power of the masses it had brought into the revolutionary struggle. It rejected the GMD and proclaimed that it was establishing a people's democratic dictatorship.

From the communist perspective, China had passed into a new historical era in which its politics would be guided by the true interests of the vast majority. Just as a state serving a minority ruling class could not be democratic, so a state serving the majority was necessarily democratic, and bourgeois limits to its authority could only hamper its service to the people. The PRC was a democracy toward the people, and a dictatorship toward their enemies. The total crisis that had beset modern China had been resolved with an equally total solution.

Party-state formation in the 1949–1956 period was determined by three factors. First, revolutionary success had confirmed the CCP's confidence in Marxism-Leninism and had opened new vistas and new tasks, so the natural course was to learn from the advanced experience of the Soviet Union in instituting state power. Second, success with two decades of base-area governance confirmed the political habits and values of the CCP, so new institutions and goals tended to be filled with familiar content. Third, the specific historical task of the 1949 to 1956 period was to make the transition to socialism. That task set the policy direction and political structures of the PRC, and when the task was accomplished in 1956, that opened the question of what the general political line should be for the new historical period. We shall briefly consider each of these factors.

The formal structures and the main policy targets of the PRC were determined almost entirely by the model for postrevolutionary government pioneered by the Soviet Union. Even the term "people's republic" was an approved innovation: The first people's republic had been Mongolia in 1924, and "people's republic" (Hungary, Bulgaria, Poland) or "democratic republic" (East Germany) became popular after World War II to suggest governments based on a coalition of political parties. In the case of China, the term highlighted the role of the broad array of political and social forces symbolized by the Chinese People's Political Consultative Conference in determining the provisional constitution and writing the 1954 constitution. As in the other people's republics, the CCP moved rapidly to consolidate its power in the state and other public organizations and to secure control over the news media, finance, and commerce. The party continued to be flexible and broad-based in its recruitment, and it monopolized political leadership. It had been a vanguard party in pursuit of revolution, and it continued to be a vanguard party in pursuit of socialist transformation. In agrarian policy, where China's methods differed most significantly from the experience of the Soviet Union, the three

72

broad stages of land reform, basic cooperatization, and higher-level cooperatization were shared with other communist countries.[26]

Despite the strong similarities between the political systems and policy orientations of the PRC and other communist countries, it should be emphasized that the CCP brought to these structures a very different political experience. Victory had convinced the CCP of its own correctness as much as of the correctness of Marxism-Leninism, and the massive scale of its popular revolutionary victory gave the CCP some unique advantages. The CCP began its rule with a large membership well dispersed and rooted in rural areas. It had thoroughly defeated its enemy, and neither foreign threats nor foreign friends overshadowed it. Within the centralized party-state framework, the CCP could operate with enviable confidence and power.

The political style of the revolutionary period, of course, remained a major influence, as Hong Yung Lee details in Chapter 6. The new leaders were experienced governmental leaders in the primitive and informal context of mass-line politics. Such political traits as mobilization campaigns, a general ambiguity of control and responsibility, the importance of access and connections, and the undercutting of formal institutions by personal power can all be related to the base-area pattern of governance. To be sure, some of those traits reinforced traditional authority patterns, and some were fostered by characteristics of the party-state system, but such habits were natural to people who had been socialized into their leadership style before 1949. However, the situation of real dependence on the people because of competition with a hostile government was necessarily lost. The high value placed on party–mass relations remained, but with only moral pressure and organizational sanction – not self-interest – to keep the cadre close to the people. The cadre became an official rather than a mobilizer of the masses. The success of the party diminished the clout of the people, and without constitutional provisions establishing citizen rights, popular influence faded.

The 1949 to 1956 period was defined as one of transition to socialism. That provided the CCP with clear goals: instituting the party-state, centralization and socialization of the economy, the cooperatization of agriculture. It was a phase in which continued alliance with nonworkers was justified, and so the united front that had emerged in the civil war remained. The 1954 constitution was explicitly a constitution of the transition period; its procedural guarantees and the legal codification movement of which it was the centerpiece had the Achilles' heel of being specific to the pre-socialist stage. Unfortunately, that phase was much briefer than the fifteen or twenty years first envisioned, and a new reorientation for the tasks of socialism became necessary.

AT THE EDGE OF HISTORY

With the completion of the transition to socialism in 1956, Chinese communism had reached a point where there were no clear models or practical policy guidelines. The Soviet Union could no longer be a guide, in part because it was itself still in the socialist stage, and in part because Khrushchev's criticisms of Stalin had raised serious questions about Soviet leadership. China still faced the obvious tasks of economic development, but it was not clear whether such problems should delay political progress toward the ultimate goal of communism or whether a political leap forward could pull the economy along with it. Recalling the power of mass mobilization in the base areas, Mao and most of the leadership believed that a Chinese way to communism would be to rely on the masses in an all-out campaign for comprehensive political-economic transformation – the infamous "Great Leap Forward" of 1958. The failure of the Great Leap Forward led to the restoration and tightening of a more routinized party hegemony identified with Liu Shaoqi. The inherent conflict between the left Leninism of Mao Zedong and the right Leninism of Liu Shaoqi definitely involved different conceptions of the relationship between popular power and public authority, and Mao asserted his idea in the Cultural Revolution.

The leftist period of Chinese politics, 1957 to 1976, was characterized by dogmatism and a self-deluding, authoritarian optimism. It is correctly associated with Mao Zedong, but it is odd that his previous politics had been more prudent and practical, and yet his beliefs had not undergone a major change in the 1950s. I have argued elsewhere[27] that by 1957 Mao had run beyond the practical targets set by goals such as victory and socialist transformation and had begun to orient his politics according to the vision of the communist future alluded to by Marx and Lenin. Policy was judged by insatiable standards of equality: the elimination of societal differences, government through mass participation, the replacement of private incentives by public incentives, and maximum communalization of ownership and productive activity. Mao knew that realization of those goals would involve difficult experimentation, and he assumed that individuals who hindered, questioned, or opposed the socialist road favored the capitalist road.

There was a profoundly contradictory relationship between the power of the people and public authority during that period. On the one hand, the great engine of China's transformation was to be mass mobilization. At the beginning of each campaign there was great optimism that the party and the people thought in the same way, and so the problem was how to unleash the enthusiasm of the masses. On the other hand, individuals and groups could not participate in their own right and for their own interest, but only as members of the masses and for officially defined public interests. If their conceptions deviated from the current orthodoxy, that was proof that they were enemies of socialism – rightists or "capitalist-roaders." The more the losing faction proclaimed their devotion and commitment to socialism, the more strongly they were denounced as "waving the red flag to oppose the red flag."

The first mass mobilization to display the contradiction of mobilization and control through orthodoxy was the "Hundred Flowers movement" of 1956 to 1957. All were encouraged to contribute their ideas for building socialism. A Mao Zedong speech from that period, "On the Correct Handling of Contradictions Among the People," seemed to be a virtual Areopagitic. He said that truth is often with the minority, that Marxism cannot flourish as a hothouse plant protected from other ideas and criticism, and so forth. But when criticism suggested that there were tensions between the party leadership and the people, the "Anti-Rightist Campaign" of 1957 was launched, and the critics were denounced and punished as "poisonous weeds."

Because the Great Leap Forward followed on the heels of the Anti-Rightist Campaign, it did not have a problem with ideological conformity. Everyone tried to be more left than the next person. Partly as a result of such hyperleftism, the Great Leap crashed into unperceived realities of objective limits of productivity and organizational effectiveness. Production shortfalls and the inability of the new communes to function effectively were inadmissible, and so China was plunged into famine. Only a government that had been built from the countryside and had the self-confidence of popular support could have been strong enough to cause a disaster of such magnitude.

In the aftermath of the Great Leap, a clear difference began to emerge between Mao Zedong's tendency to rely on mass campaigns and ideological appeals and Liu Shaoqi's reliance on improving the organization and discipline of the party structure. Mao's position might be called "left Leninism," because it emphasized the interactive relationship of party and masses and an openness to experimentation and volatility in the campaign cycle. It contained the potential for a radical, mass critique of the party as an elite. Liu's position was "right Leninism": a more Stalinist assumption of the correctness of the party and of the party's bureaucratic responsibility to administer the revolution on the people's behalf. Their underlying Leninist similarity lay in the assumption that mass and party interests could be identical. Both Mao's radical critique of the party and Liu's confidence in the party's self-discipline were based on that assumption. If that assumption was questioned, then the institutional relationship of the party and the masses would have to be reconsidered.

THE CULTURAL REVOLUTION

The Cultural Revolution, like any revolution, was a vivid swirl of noble ideals and human tragedy, heroic action and the collapse of social order. Unlike any other revolution, it was called forth to do battle with a political hegemony by the founder of that hegemony. The Cultural Revolution was effective because of the strength of the party-state, and because it was effective, it irreparably undermined that strength. Because it was an official revolution, only its positive aspects were highlighted while it was going on, but that has been reversed since its termination. Without suggesting that there is a "proper balance," both need to be appreciated.

From the vantage point of the relationship between popular power and public authority, the Cultural Revolution was nightmarish for all concerned, including, I think, for Mao himself. But from a more detached perspective it was an endlessly fascinating event that has not begun to be sufficiently analyzed. There were three broad aspects that deserve our attention: the ideological dimension of interpreting Mao's actions, the political dimension of mass activities, and the question of the effects of the Cultural Revolution on subsequent Chinese politics.

By the 1960s, the revolution that Mao had led seemed to be in grave danger of derailment and decay. Of course, the failure of the Great Leap was a cause of great disorganization and disillusionment, but the problem was more general. Khrushchev's Soviet Union showed that it was possible for revisionism to triumph in a socialist state. The negative example of Soviet revisionism not only sharpened policy debates but also highlighted the urgency of providing for revolutionary successors. Meanwhile, the resistance to and misinterpretation of Mao's initiatives by the CCP organization, and the contrary spirit of its own initiatives, began to focus Mao's attention on the possibility that the party's own leadership might be the chief danger to the revolution. That would be an unthinkable thought for a Leninist, and Mao was not prepared to face the possibility head-on. He first concentrated on the problem of work style, and then criticized persons in authority as capitalist-roaders, but he never went so far as to call into question the system of authority itself. Mao never intended that his call to "bombard the headquarters" would lead to destruction of the structure of party authority and a free-for-all among the masses. When it did, he sided with party order: He brought in the army, suppressed mass organizations, and restored party hegemony.

Although the Cultural Revolution was intended by Mao to be a reliance on the masses, on the model of the mass-line politics of revolutionary days, it had the opposite effect. Indeed, the mass mobilization of the Cultural Revolution was a complete inversion of mobilization in the base area. The primary difference was that the new mobilization was ideologically derived, rather than being connected to the practical necessities and material interests of everyday life.[28] An untenable contradiction was posited between the public good, on the one hand, and particular and private interests, on the other, though, of course, the actual pattern of group formation reflected such interests.[29] Although mass spontaneity was encouraged, it was encouraged only as support for Chairman Mao. The "truly red" masses were in direct communion with Chairman Mao; to raise concerns over individual rights, procedures, or elections would seem hopelessly (and dangerously) bourgeois. Instead of the united-front, alliance logic of the base areas, which had tried to maximize friends and minimize enemies in pursuit of a common goal, the driving principle was to draw a sharp line between "ourselves" and any possible contamination by the enemy. Therefore, factionalism predominated, rather than the overwhelming coalition, producing fissured and destructive competition. That was in the name of selfless idealism, though factionalism is actually the lowest form of common interest.

In contrast to the quasi-democratic system of the 1927–1949 period, we might call the mass politics of the Cultural Revolution a quasi-totalitarian system. It was characterized by competing factions that were mass-controlled, rather than shepherded by the party's authoritarian structure. But the mass-regarding policies of the quasi-democratic system were replaced by a total submission to the deified will of Mao. The terrorism of the Cultural Revolution was to a great extent self-imposed at the basic level, rather than being the work of a centralized organization. In the context of a strong state's call for an ideologically derived mass mobilization, even decentralized, competing mass organizations could be expected to be leadership-regarding in their actions.

Although the Cultural Revolution cannot be said to have had constructive effects in Chinese politics or to have accomplished any of its goals, some of its destructive effects have defined the context of post-Mao politics. First, it ended the ideological appeal of leftism in China. Its failure to establish a new, viable ethos of socialism provided conclusive proof of the bankruptcy of leftist idealism. The "Gang of Four" – especially Jiang Qing, Mao's wife – became seedy symbols of the feudal opportunist reality behind the slogans, whereas the targets of the revolution were returned to power or were vindicated posthumously. Leftism had hanged itself on a ten-year-long rope; a succeeding regime stressing material interest and social order was bound to be popular. Any person, policy, or practice associated with the Cultural Revolution became vulnerable.

Second, the vicissitudes of the Cultural Revolution destroyed the political innocence of the public. One could no longer assume that the party's rule was a natural hegemony of virtue, or that the current orthodoxy had a given, objectively valid content. Following the removal of Liu Shaoqi and Deng Xiaoping, and then Lin Biao, and then the Gang of Four, and then Hua Guofeng, one could certainly doubt the quality and orthodoxy of even the highest levels of leadership. And people were disillusioned by their own experience of the quality, morality, and effectiveness of mass mobilization. The Cultural Revolution confirmed a distance between the party and the people, and therefore the post-Mao regime has been constrained to offer inducements to participate and to institutionalize public authority.

Third, the Cultural Revolution provided a unique political education for all concerned. For the elite, who were attacked but eventually returned to power, it was a personal experience of the tyranny of the masses. They returned with a visceral knowledge of the fallibility of the party and the danger of mass action. For almost everyone else, apparently, the experience gave rise to a general suspicion of ideology, of politics, and of the party. As a result, the political demands made by demonstrators in the 1970s and 1980s included constitutional specifications of citizen rights and party authority. Such demands were similar to suggestions made in the 1950s, but they were being made from vivid experience with the excesses of a strong party-state. Nevertheless, the demands were for structural reform of the party-state, rather than for its downfall or replacement.

In general, the Cultural Revolution failed as a millenarian effort to create a purely socialist society, but it succeeded in calling into question the assumptions concerning the legitimacy of an absolute party and the mass base of party authority. It was an attempt to preserve the revolutionary spirit beyond its natural life, and its failure ended the revolutionary period of Chinese politics that had been defined by total crisis. In the Cultural Revolution, a crisis had been caused by totalism, by an "all-round dictatorship." The reaction to the Cultural Revolution, therefore, was to pursue a postrevolutionary politics of security and material welfare for both the establishment and the masses.

REFORM AND REACTION IN POST-MAO CHINA

The relationship between state and people in China was profoundly shaken and disoriented in 1989, first by the spectacular demonstrations of April and May, and then by the declaration of martial law and the bloody repression of the demonstrations on June 4. Both the demonstrations and the repression were surprising to participants as well as to observers. In my opinion, neither was a "necessary" event, an unavoidable outcome of trends, but it is possible in retrospect to see the characteristics of the post-Mao situation that led to confrontation between the forces of reform and those of reaction. This section will analyze the overall situation, and then separately consider Deng Xiaoping's politics, structural reform, and the reassertion of orthodoxy and central control.

Because of the failure of the Cultural Revolution and the generally acknowledged bankruptcy of leftism, the post-Mao regime could be content with a negative ideological definition – opposition to the Cultural Revolution. Reaction to the Cultural Revolution explains the major policy guidelines of the 1980s: the precedence of economics over ideological politics, the utilization of material incentives, and the acknowledgments of the need for expertise and of the importance of societal complexity. Criticism of the Cultural Revolution created a pleasant but peculiar ideological situation for the leadership: By rejecting dogmatic purism, the regime backed into a naturally more permissive and relaxed intellectual environment.

Tang Tsou has well described the resulting "middle course" of Chinese politics: Rather than seeing itself as waging a "two-line struggle" between the forces of good and evil, the Chinese leadership, headed by Deng Xiaoping, has pursued an essentially pragmatic "struggle on two fronts," occupying a broad middle ground between two unacceptable extremes.[30] Although Chinese policies have undergone tremendous development, the boundaries remained remarkably clear and stable until 1989. On the one hand, it has been unacceptably leftist to criticize the priority of economic development. Any critique of current policy is suspect if it is ideologically derived and indifferent to considerations of material welfare. At the Thirteenth Party Congress in 1987, Zhao Ziyang defined that edge of the field of discussion as the acceptance of the policies of modernization and openness.[31] On the other hand, challenges to the party's leadership and its orthodoxy have been ruled out. In 1979, Deng defined this as the obligation to uphold the "four fundamental principles": the socialist road, the leadership of the CCP, the dictatorship of the proletariat, and Marxism-Leninism and "Mao Zedong thought." It was already clear from the failure of various reform initiatives prior to 1989 that the right boundary of the political field was the political and ideological hegemony of the party. That also was reaffirmed at the Thirteenth Party Congress. Officially, at least, these boundaries remain in place. The demonstrations in Tiananmen generally avoided openly challenging party hegemony until martial law was declared, and Deng Xiaoping claims to be pursuing modernization and openness even more strongly since declaring martial law. But in fact, the demonstrations and ensuing repression broke the boundaries, and politics has begun to spill into new terrain.

The "struggle on two fronts" allowed reformers and the party's orthodox conservatives to cohabit an ambiguous middle ground. It was not a peaceful cohabitation; each tried to gain control of policy, and part of the struggle was the effort by the reformers to extend the definition of modernization, countered by conservative alarms concerning alleged violations of the four principles. The reformers would push forward when their economic policies were doing well, and the conservatives would push back when the top leadership was scandalized by a particularly adventurous literary piece, the spread of pornography, or economic difficulties related to reform. Some issues were interpreted by the two sides to fit their respective causes. Corruption, for instance, was condemned as a remnant of feudalism by the reformers, but the conservatives saw it as a product of bourgeois influence.

The differences between the reform and conservative policy camps became more and more clear and personally acrimonious throughout the 1980s, and the two camps were confirmed by the removal of Hu Yaobang by the conservatives in January 1987. But the divisions in the leadership were officially denied, and policy-making at the center continued to be controlled by a process of consensus. That was demonstrated, for instance, when Hu was succeeded by Zhao Ziyang, a fellow reformer. The process of consensus, however, was a highly pressured and dynamic matter. On a spectrum of policy options from A to E, policy would tend to move from B to A, and then, as difficulties mounted with that extreme, to D, and then to E. The A-to-D movement would be the result of a coalition shift (but in terms of a change in Deng Xiaoping's position, not in terms of a majoritarian vote count), and the B-to-A and D-to-E movements would be the results of consolidations of initial victories. Consensus, therefore, was not a negotiated process of finding the middle position. It involved forbearance in not removing the losing side from leadership circles, but there was tremendous pressure on the losers to conform. Discipline was as important as real agreement in building a consensus.

Reformers and conservatives had asymmetric advantages in that power environment. Reformers benefited from the negative ideological definition, that is, opposition to the Cultural Revolution, because it provided less control over innovation. More important, the overall characteristic of the reform program was decontrol, and decontrol is much easier to initiate than to terminate. So any system that allowed policy oscillation would favor reform in the long term. The actual structure of power, however, benefited the conservatives. It was an informal, highly centralized configuration of personalities in which age was the sine qua non of influence. Deng Xiaoping was the authoritative swing vote on major decisions, and his world was that of the "court politics" of the elderly. Because the conservatives could not be removed, and oscillation would favor reform, the decentralizing and societally liberating effects of policy in effect crowded and cornered the center's political structure.

China's economic problems of inflation and lower grain production weakened the reform leadership of Zhao Ziyang in 1988, and by early 1989 the reformers were anxious, and the conservatives aggressive. The sudden emergence of massive political demonstrations by Beijing students on the occasion of Hu Yaobang's death more than turned the situation around. Besides showing the societal strength of reform, the demonstrations challenged the center's control over the pace of reform, as well as the party's control of political articulation. The conservatives tried to regain the initiative with the April 26 editorial condemning the demonstrations as disturbances.[32] The editorial infuriated the students, and it prompted Zhao Ziyang to present his own official view, not condemning the students, in a speech to the Asian Development Bank on May 4. Zhao's apparent approval and the visit of Mikhail Gorbachev encouraged much larger demonstrations. As Premier Li Peng described it, "more than one million people took part in the demonstrations on May 17 and May 18. The Central Committee immediately decided to impose martial law."[33] From May 19 onward the conservatives were in total control. When the initial implementation of martial law was frustrated by Beijing citizens and evoked opposition within the army to the conservative course of action, the center decided to act harshly, leading to the massacre of June 4 and further repressive measures.

It is clear that the April 26 editorial, and then Zhao's May 4 speech, broke the rule of consensus and made it impossible for the reformers and conservatives to continue to cohabit at the center. It was as if two people in a small boat were moving farther and farther apart, and finally one fell out. As the reformers were excluded, the actions and rhetoric of the center lurched back into the terminology of class struggle dating from the Cultural Revolution. The boat is now so out of balance that the possibility of the reformers climbing back in is less likely than is a fall of the current factional victors.

With this general situation in mind, we can now return to a closer analysis of the positions of the conservatives, Deng Xiaoping, and the reformers with regard to democratization.

Although the conservatives of the 1980s often are called "leftists" by their opponents, they have little in common with Cultural Revolution leftism. Indeed, their efforts might more aptly be viewed as a re-Stalinization, in that their chief concerns initially were to restore Marxist-

81

Leninist orthodoxy and central control over politics and economics after the intellectual and social turmoil of the Cultural Revolution. Similarly, they defended central control and ideological orthodoxy against the innovations of the reformers in the 1980s. Because the conservative position reflected the unquestioned orthodoxy of the party in the 1950s and early 1960s – the high tide of the careers of the current top leaders – their arguments and values seem intuitively obvious to party elders, while appearing opaque and atavistic to students. It is probably more than coincidental that this viewpoint also serves the convenience and interests of the party elders.

The key to the relationship between state and people in conservative thought is the party's role as the vanguard of the proletariat. Attempts at democratization are unnecessary and suspect because they imply that the current relationship between party and people is institutionally inadequate. Political problems are to be overcome by strengthening the party, not by limiting it. Any external challenge to the party, whether from individuals or from demonstrations, threatens the party's vanguard role and thus is counterrevolutionary. Such a threat cannot be from the people, of course, but must result from a small number of agitators who mislead the people.

The problem with upholding the old idea of the vanguard party is that even the conservatives do not now maintain that there is a historical goal that is the special domain of the party. In the 1950s the party believed in the future historical stage of communism, but the Cultural Revolution shook Marxist millenarianism out of the party. The conservatives have the residual orthodoxy of the vanguard party, but without any justifying dynamic. The ideological, political, and practical conveniences for the central establishment explain the orthodoxy, not any active, future-oriented function. The orthodoxy of the vanguard party is in fact used to cover the reality of a rearguard party fighting the historical necessity of succession.

Deng Xiaoping's politics certainly appears to be inconsistent. Had he died before May 1989, he would have been considered a hero of reform; but since the summer of 1989, many believe that China cannot return to a reform path until after Deng is gone. The key to Deng Xiaoping's politics is his pragmatism. His spirit is captured in his most famous theoretical statement: "black cat, white cat, it doesn't matter as long as they catch mice." His approach was exactly antithetical to the dogmatic factionalism of the Cultural Revolution and well suited the mood of the people and the leadership after Mao's death. Economics prevailed over ideological politics, material interest over moral appeals and collectivism, expertise over "redness."

The role of the people in Deng's politics was more tricky than complex.

In the struggle against leftist inertia in the party, the popularity of Deng's policies made the people a natural ally. In the heyday of "Democracy Wall" in November and December 1978, when Deng was deep in the final struggle with the leftists, he was even allied with demonstrators. But his support for democratizing reform was always predicated on the assumption that the people would support the party and his policies. That had two implications: first, that power was not really yielded in reform; second, that if reform led to a confrontation with the party, reform would yield. Within the party-state structure, Deng acknowledged the need for structural reforms in order to reduce bureaucratism, but that did not imply a lessening of party hegemony or a redefinition of the party's relationship to the people.

Essentially, Deng's political thought adjusted for the predicament in which the party found itself after the Cultural Revolution, as well as for reorientation of policy toward economic modernization, but it remained uncritical concerning the basic relationships of party to state and of state to people. Reform was a process of self-limitation and self-control by the party. The party retained its political monopoly. Despite new rules and new directions, it remained a vanguard party.

Deng's commitment to old values of party hegemony and to new policy content made him the perfect arbiter of the "struggle on two fronts." The flexibility of that position suited his pragmatism. He could be either conservative or reformer, depending on the circumstances. However, as the gap between the conservative and reform positions widened, his flexibility and discretion were reduced. With the ejection of Zhao Ziyang, the uniqueness and power of Deng's position as arbiter collapsed. Deng has attempted to rebuild his middle position by sponsoring as his successor Jiang Zemin, who is not tainted with the blood of Tiananmen. But the continual concern with health, retirement, and succession in the central leadership proves the transitional nature of current arrangements. Regardless of how long Deng continues to live, the era of Chinese politics that he defined is over.

The reform position is, of course, much more difficult to define, because its supporters have ranged from those at Democracy Wall and Tiananmen Square to the highest levels of the party, and policy content has changed during the decade. What I would use as the defining feature of reform was the attempt to provide an external, institutional definition to the relationship between state and people – in effect, to constitutionalize the party-state. From the point of view of the reform leadership, that was a challenge of structural reform and political modernization. Each level of the cascade of power – the party center, party leadership within the state, and the state's penetration of society – should be brought under a rule of law and institutional definition, and also under popular control. From the point of view of the intellectuals and of concerned people in general, the objective was citizen rights, including both rights of control over officials (articulated as criticism of corruption) and individual rights against the state.

Significant progress was made in every area except structural reform of the party center. Constitutional and legal activities flourished, with the high points of new state and party constitutions in 1982. The state became less intrusive into the personal lives of citizens, and electoral mechanisms were strengthened in the party and workplace, as well as in the people's congress system. Although they were far from acting as a parliament, the people's congresses expanded their roles of overseeing officials and policies at the national and local levels. The changes in China's political life in the 1980s were not as dramatic as those in economics and society, but if one compares the political activity of early 1989 with that of early 1979, innovations that had once seemed radical were becoming routine.

The Achilles' heel of the reform program was that it was fostered by and depended upon an unreformed central leadership structure. Deng Xiaoping was the hero and patron of reform, much as Mao had been for leftism. The power of reform did not depend on the support of its beneficiaries, but on the support of its ultimate target. Political reform was acceptable as long as it provided an orderly accompaniment to economic reform and made difficulties for the midlevel bureaucrats remaining from the Cultural Revolution. But when societal forces became self-confident enough to challenge the party's political monopoly and to criticize the center leadership, Deng abandoned and attacked his clients.

Was Deng correct in saying that the conflict was inevitable? Are democratizing reforms ultimately incompatible with the party-state? Both conservative communists and anticommunist observers would say yes. In my opinion, which is elaborated elsewhere,[34] democratizing reforms do not simply evolve into a democratic party-state, but party-state democracy is possible. The key threshold for party-state democracy is that crises of political leadership be resolved by recourse to institutionalized, democratic procedures rather than by a retreat into the assertion of central authority. In other words, in order to become democratic, the party-state must put itself at risk to the people through public institutions. The demonstrators confronted the party center at this threshold. Zhao Ziyang, probably like most of the younger leadership, was willing to accept the challenge of democratization in order to relegitimize the party as a postrevolutionary, popular party, just as Gorbachev was willing to do in the Soviet Union. But the octogenarians still in charge of the party center were not.

CONCLUSION

The historical course of the people–state relationship in China does not dictate a course for the current crisis of the Chinese state. Indeed, according to my analysis, China stood at a crossroads in the spring of 1989 between a decisive move toward party-state democracy or a fall back into party authoritarianism, either of which would have been a significant change from the ambiguity of the Deng Xiaoping era. Moreover, the age and frailty of the top leadership, its lack of ideological credibility, and the contradiction between repression and modernization all suggest an instability in the current situation. It seems likely that the leadership's failure to resolve the succession problem has brought China to a period of unpredictable crises and crossroads.

One utility of the historical perspective developed here is that it enables us to perceive the resonances of the current situation with the past. It is clear, for instance, that the conservative orthodoxy rests not only on a Stalinist interpretation of Marxism-Leninism but also on the assumptions of a natural hierarchy and order that go to the roots of traditional Chinese political culture. Democracy, *minzhu*, in its general, modern sense of institutional control of authority, is as foreign to the current old guard as it was to imperial China. Care for the people is a status obligation of those in power; the vanguard party shepherds the people, but it does not represent them.

Perhaps the most important historical resonance of the conservative position is with the fear of chaos and the drive for order in the twentieth century. The postulate that the interests of the parts should be subordinate to the interests of the whole becomes salient when the existence of the whole political order is threatened. The historic achievement of the CCP was meeting the challenge of total crisis presented by imperialism and internal disintegration, and the conservative viewpoint is defined by that experience. Every crisis is seen as one of life or death, and every challenge appears to lead ineluctably to a crisis. Any demonstrator calls for the overthrow of the party and the socialist system, no matter what that demonstrator actually says.[35] The overriding concern for order reinforces the traditionalist and Marxist predilection to deny legitimacy to pluralization, institutional and procedural structure, and citizen rights. Even if the leadership does not really believe itself to be mortally threatened, it is to the interest of its complacency of power to sound the alarm. Crisis justifies dictatorship, even if the party produces the crisis.

The reformist position also has ancient and modern resonances. The traditional notion of the people as the root of the state was not simply the hypocritical convenience of those in power; it was grounded in the perception that the survival as well as the justification of the state de-

85

pended on its service to the material interests of its inhabitants. And from the time of Confucius, scholar-officials have acknowledged the possibility of misrule and the advantages of rational government over the convenience and unreflective inclinations of power-holders. Clearly, the June 4 massacre drew a line between the power-holders and the scholars. History will show the power-holders in the wrong, if for no other reason than that the scholars write the histories.

A key concept of reform is modernization, and it possesses today the overtones of support for diversity, openness to Western influences, and criticism of established power first voiced at the beginning of the century. But I think that the primary modern root of reform in the 1980s is the post-1949 experience of the PRC. Political structural reform is based on the perception that postrevolutionary crises of government in China have been caused primarily by the amount of unstructured power cascading from the center of the system. Instead of total crisis, the problem has been numerous crises of totalism, in which the diversifying society has been especially vulnerable. "Order" is not the monistic prevention of chaos, but a differentiated texture of laws and institutions to which a complex society can relate. This approach will require the restructuring of the vanguard party-state into a constitutional party-state dependent on the citizenry.

The Deng Xiaoping era pragmatically combined conservative habits of power with reform policies, and as a result its political direction oscillated as it struggled on the two fronts of defending the existing orthodoxy while promoting modernization. But the declaration of martial law introduced a qualitatively new level of uncertainty. By once again preventing the transfer of power from the old guard to designated successors, it put the center of Chinese politics at the mercy of a handful of very old biological clocks. Moreover, the regime is fully committed to a repressive consolidation of its own power that threatens ever-widening circles of people and policies. Its declarations of support for modernization and openness merely demonstrate that, in contrast to the idealistic turbulence of the Cultural Revolution, repression now serves no higher end than the preservation of power. Clearly, there is a practical contradiction between the tightening of central party control and the premises of decontrol and diversification inherent in modernization and openness.

Recent events have demonstrated to my satisfaction that the future of Chinese politics is difficult to predict, but it seems to me that the old-guard regime is a transitional phase to a basic question, namely: Is China heading toward a new total crisis or is it merely working out the last painful throes of the party-state vanguardism? The new total crisis would be the end of the party-state. If repression so radicalizes the forces of reform that they reject the possibility of reform within the party-state

86

system, then future politics will be defined by a chaotic struggle between new forces of revolutionary radicalism and establishment forces defending public order. The vanguard party will relegitimate itself as an unideological authoritarian party, and reform politics will be radicalized into antiregime activities reminiscent of opposition to the late empire. The advantage will be with the establishment, which might in time feel secure enough to tolerate a new cycle of reform efforts.

The other possibility is that the intervention of the old guard into the general trend toward modernization and democratization will prove temporary. If vanguardism is interred with the last of the revolutionary vanguard, and a new regime condemns the Tiananmen massacre, much of the political optimism of the 1980s could be rescued. The triumphal return of reformers and their policies, strengthened in their popular support by their mistreatment, would be reassuring. But the trauma of the June 4 massacre probably would require that a returning reform leadership provide institutional guarantees of popular control of authority. Constitutional reform would be a high priority, and the task would be to structure a modern democratic regime with Chinese characteristics. At that point, China's search for democracy would not be over, but perhaps its path could be expected to be less tortuous.

NOTES

1. Tang Tsou, "Twentieth-Century Chinese Politics and Western Political Science," *PS* 20, no. 2 (Spring 1987): 327–332.
2. Xiong Yuezhi, *Zhongguo jindai minzhu sixiang shi* (A history of modern Chinese democratic thought) (Shanghai: Renmin chubanshe, 1986), pp. 10–15.
3. Hu Shi, *The Chinese Renaissance* (Chicago: University of Chicago Press, 1934).
4. Otto Hintze, "The Preconditions of Representative Government in the Context of World History," in Felix Gilbert, ed., *The Historical Essays of Otto Hintze* (London: Oxford University Press, 1975), pp. 302–353.
5. For an overview, see Charles O. Hucker, *The Traditional State in Ming Times (1368–1644)* (Tucson: University of Arizona Press, 1961). For a negative evaluation, see Etienne Balazs, "China as a Permanently Bureaucratic Society," in his *Chinese Civilization and Bureaucracy*, ed. Arthur F. Wright, trans. H. M. Wright (New Haven: Yale University Press, 1964), pp. 12–27.
6. *Mencius*, trans. James Legge (1895; reprint, New York: Dover, 1970), p. 133.
7. Mary C. Wright, *The Last Stand of Chinese Conservatism: The T'ung-chih Restoration, 1862–1874* (New York: Atheneum, 1966), p. 300.
8. Joseph Levenson, *Revolution and Cosmopolitanism* (Berkeley: University of California Press, 1971), p. 5.
9. For more on Liang, see Guy Alitto, *The Last Confucian* (Berkeley: University of California Press, 1979). For Mao's reaction, see *Selected Works of Mao Tse-tung* (Beijing: Foreign Languages Press, 1977), 5:121–129.

10. Arthur Wright, *Buddhism in Chinese History* (Stanford: Stanford University Press, 1959), pp. 21–64.
11. Eric Wolf, *Peasant Wars in the Twentieth Century* (New York: Harper & Row, 1969), pp. 287–289.
12. Benjamin Schwartz, *In Search of Wealth and Power* (Cambridge: Harvard University Press, 1964).
13. Balazs, "China as a Permanently Bureaucratic Society."
14. The other was science. See Chen Duxiu, "*Xin Qingnian* zui'an zhi dabian-shu" (A rebuttal to the crimes of *New Youth*), in *Zhongguo xiandai sixiang shi ziliao jianbian* (An anthology of materials for modern Chinese intellectual history) (Hangzhou: Zhejiang Renmin chubanshe, 1986), vol. 1; originally in *Xin qingnian* 6, no. 1 (January 15, 1919).
15. Brantly Womack, "The Phases of Chinese Modernization," in Steve S. K. Chin, ed., *Modernization in China* (Hong Kong: University of Hong Kong Centre of Asian Studies, 1979), pp. 1–16.
16. Norbert Meierberger, *The Emergence of Constitutional Government in China (1905–1908)*, Schweizer Asiatische Studien no. 1 (Bern: Peter Lang, 1980).
17. For a sympathetic and informed contemporary account, see Paul Reinsch, *Intellectual Trends and Political Currents in the Far East* (1911; reprinted, Freeport, N.Y.: Books for Libraries Press, 1971), pp. 225–271; the imperial reforms have been evaluated positively by Meierberger, *The Emergence of Constitutional Government in China*; and by John Fincher, *Chinese Democracy* (New York: St. Martin, 1981).
18. Ch'ien Tuan-sheng [Qian Duansheng], *The Government and Politics of China 1912–1949* (Stanford: Stanford University Press, 1950).
19. Sun Yat-sen, *San Min Chu I: The Three Principles of the People*, trans. Frank W. Price (Shanghai: China Committee, Institute of Pacific Relations, 1927).
20. Sun, *San Min Chu I*, p. 185.
21. Clifford Geertz, "Ideology as a Cultural System," in *Ideology and Discontent*, ed. David Apter (New York: Free Press of Glencoe, 1964), pp. 47–71.
22. Mao Zedong, "Report on an Investigation of the Peasant Movement in Hunan (March 1927)," in *Selected Works of Mao Tse-tung* (Beijing: Foreign Languages Press, 1965), 1:23.
23. This concept is developed further by Brantly Womack: "The Party and the People: Revolutionary and Post-Revolutionary Politics in China and Vietnam," *World Politics* 39, no. 4 (July 1987): 479–507.
24. See Tang Tsou, "Reflections on the Formation and Foundations of the Communist Party-State in China," in his *The Cultural Revolution and Post-Mao Reforms: A Historical Perspective* (Chicago: University of Chicago Press, 1986), pp. 266–267.
25. Mao Zedong, "Rectify the Party's Style of Work [1942]," in his *Selected Works*, 3:45.
26. Eugen Wädekin, *Agrarian Policies in Eastern Europe* (The Hague: Martinus Nijhoff, 1982).
27. Brantly Womack, "Where Mao Went Wrong: Epistemology and Ideology in Mao's Leftist Politics," *Australian Journal of Chinese Affairs*, no. 16 (July 1986): 23–40.
28. As Marc Blecher points out in Chapter 4 in this volume, mass participation was much more benign when it remained focused on the material and economic problems facing basic-level units.

29. Hong Yung Lee, *The Politics of the Cultural Revolution* (Berkeley, University of California Press, 1978).
30. Tang Tsou, "Political Change and Reform: The Middle Course," in his *Cultural Revolution*, pp. 219–258.
31. Zhao Ziyang, "Advance Along the Road of Socialism with Chinese Characteristics," *Beijing Review* 30, no. 45 (November 9–15, 1987): 23–49.
32. That editorial was written and approved while Zhao was out of the country, clearly a manipulation by the conservatives. Yang Shangkun claimed that "a cable was sent to Comrade Ziyang, informing him of the Standing Committee's decision and Comrade Xiaoping's view," and that Zhao cabled back his support. Editorials are (or should be) authoritative, consensus positions agreed to by all members of the top leadership. See Yang Shangkun's speech of May 24, 1989, trans. Foreign Broadcast Information Service (FBIS), May 30, 1989, p. 17.
33. As quoted in the *South China Morning Post*, May 29, 1989, trans. FBIS May 30, 1989, p. 1.
34. Brantly Womack, "Party-State Democracy: A Theoretical Exploration," *Issues and Studies* 25, no. 3 (March 1989): 37–57.
35. See Deng Xiaoping's June 9 speech, *New York Times*, June 30, 1989.

3

A bourgeois alternative? The Shanghai arguments for a Chinese capitalism: the 1920s and the 1980s

EDMOND LEE

If capitalism can be said ever to have taken root in China, it was in Shanghai in the early 1920s. Fertile ground for modern banks and for new industries of all sorts, the city was the center of a budding bourgeois way of life.[1] And if anyone can be said to have tried to plant the seeds of capitalism wider in China, it was the old Shanghai General Chamber of Commerce (*Shanghai zongshanghui*).

Founded in the late Qing period, the Chamber of Commerce of the 1920s filled its ranks from the city's wealthiest and most prestigious Chinese guilds, trade associations, native-place associations, companies, and stores. The participation in its activities of such local luminaries as the comprador-merchant (and friend of Chiang Kai-shek) Yu Qiaqing, the highly respected banker and industrialist Fang Jiaobo, the political firebrand Feng Shaoshan, and the cagey tobacco tycoon Jian Zhaonan made it a power to be reckoned with, even by the French and British authorities in the great treaty port. Outspoken and public-spirited, it played a vital and controversial role in Shanghai's whirlwind politics of great anti-foreign boycotts and popular movements.[2]

In a China being ravaged by war and revolution, the Chamber of Commerce made no secret of its bourgeois ideals. Between 1921 and 1927 it celebrated capitalism in its house organ: the *Monthly Journal of the Shanghai General Chamber of Commerce (Shanghai zongshanghui yuebao)* (hereafter referred to as the *Journal*). Responding to China's "total crisis" when many thinking Chinese were seeing "dangers so imminent...as to raise the question of [national] survival,"[3] the *Journal* boldly predicted a great future for a capitalist Shanghai:

Take a look at London and New York. Have they not set the precedent for Shanghai? The prosperity of the industries in the two cities is several times greater than Shanghai's. Yet, they have more strikes, higher wages, and more expensive land. [Still,] London and New York remain the financial centers of the world. Their development is just unfolding. What, then, has Shanghai to fear?[4]

A bourgeois alternative?

Thus was born the "bourgeois alternative," which, as elaborated by the editors and writers of the new *Journal*, preached that a powerful native capitalism spreading outward from the treaty port could save all China from the abyss of eternal poverty and foreign subjugation.

The *Journal* thrived in one of the most vigorous and unsettled Chinese societies in history. The early 1920s were a time of intellectual frenzy, when the center no longer held and the Chinese state had cracked to the extent that it could no longer impose ideological orthodoxy on society, when there was a frantic "search for a solution [to China's crisis] in foreign ideologies and models,"[5] when many Western doctrines, from anarchism to liberalism to the various socialisms, were fighting for the loyalty of the Chinese people. In that great unrest, Shanghai found itself at the very heart of the storm. The city of some two millions was pluralistic, and its society animated, so much so that it spawned and sheltered groups as different from each other as the notorious "Green Gang" led by Du Yuesheng, the literary talents of the Creation Society (*Chuangzao she*), the young radicals of the Chinese Communist Party, and a new and energetic native bourgeoisie. Until the arrival of the "Northern Expedition," the *Journal*'s writers spoke out freely in a cosmopolitan city where Japan and the Western powers may have enjoyed extraterritorial privileges, but where also there was a truly unfettered debate on new ideas and ideologies.[6] We should not be surprised that the period was, as Marie-Claire Bergere says, the golden age of the Chinese bourgeoisie,[7] when some Chinese were speculating that the native capitalists of Shanghai held the future of the country in their hands. Even while the Chamber of Commerce was divided by bitter political infighting and rivalries,[8] the *Journal*'s writers threw themselves fully into the country's great debate, devoting themselves to winning converts to its pre-Keynesian brand of capitalist ideology. With the printed word in hand, and free from censorship by any Chinese government, its contributors taught the ideas of Adam Smith and the other classical economists and denounced China's Marxists, militarists, and militant workers. The *Journal* may have been published in Shanghai, but it claimed to be the voice of all the country's businessmen, and it announced to the world that it had taken on itself the mission of "guiding commerce and society" in a disintegrating China.[9]

The 1920s saw the *Journal* plea, using the time-honored logic of Adam Smith, for the right of capital to help rebuild the Chinese polity. The *Journal*'s editors and analysts sought the creation of a rejuvenated state that would wield just enough internal authority to help a young native capitalism mature and generate wealth and power for China. The new state was to put in place the infrastructure for promoting trade, enforcing law and ensuring order, supporting education, and seizing back China's customs sovereignty.[10] But after all that had been done, businessmen were to be left to their historical task of enriching China; "when the laws were complete, the system of trust prospered, and the morality of the nation was high," there would no longer be any need for state intervention.[11] Beijing was to help Shanghai realize its bourgeois destiny; in return, Shanghai would tutor Beijing in the ways of making money.

Free from having to answer to a state committed to a hostile ideology, the *Journal* of the 1920s was not at all reluctant to boast that private business was by far the most productive part of the economy and therefore of the nation:

There is never a time when a society does not have surplus resources . . . that are not being used. Ordinary people overlook them. But industrialists are engaged in using them, seeking economic development for society and creating progress in the livelihood of the people.[12]

The *Journal* was quick to remind its readers that these were men who belonged to civil society, not to the state. "Please take a look at all those enterprises in China run by officials," Nie Yuntai, a textile manufacturer and a grandson of Zeng Guofan, asked his readers, "which one is not corrupt?"[13] From the viewpoint of the *Journal*, all state enterprises were inherently corrupt and inefficient. On that point the *Journal* never equivocated or compromised.

The Shanghai argument of the 1920s never doubted the wisdom of taking Western capitalism as a model for China. In a Shanghai and a China that were hypersensitive to anything even hinting of imperialism, the *Journal* mentioned capitalism without any second thoughts, because its editors never entertained the popular notion, as Leninists did, that imperialism was the inevitable by-product of capitalism. The *Journal* writers were consumed with hatred for imperialism, and they condemned the great powers (*lieqiang*) as imperialists. The *Journal*'s analysts, for example, denounced the 1921 proposal to create an international consortium to make public loans to China as a plot to divide up (*guafen*) the country among the great capitalist powers.[14] But the *Journal* also declared that the link between capitalism and imperialism was not at all inevitable, that a capitalist Shanghai and China would be fighting only to be treated equally by Japan and the West, not for the power to exploit the poor nations as imperialists in their own right. Yu Qiaqing himself made this claim: "[The Chinese] love peace and friendship. We have never invaded and attacked weak and small nations."[15] In China, every contributor to the *Journal* preached that "each nation should receive the same treatment and have the same chances."[16] So it was only natural that the *Journal* writers felt no qualms whatsoever about presenting what they thought were bourgeois ways of business and thinking to their audience.

Yet, the *Journal*'s influence in the world of Chinese thought was slight. It was largely isolated from the mass of Shanghai's and China's intellectuals at a time when, as Tsou says, they were "the most important agents of change" in the country.[17] The intellectuals who did write for the *Journal*, such as the learned economist Ma Yinchu, were conspicuous because were so few. Those whose work did appear in its pages were well-informed individuals, often as well read in English and Japanese economics as they were in the Chinese classics. But few other Chinese intellectuals paid much attention to the virtues of making money or had a good word for those who did. The preference of such influential thinkers as Hu Shi for Western liberalism was hardly the same as an approval of capitalism.

Moreover, the *Journal*'s argument was presented in China at a time when there was widespread skepticism, but also much hope and excitement, about the promise of Marxism. In the 1920s, though not yet in the intellectual mainstream, that alternative still enjoyed far more prestige among Chinese intellectuals than the bourgeois option ever did.[18] It was Marxism, not capitalism, that eventually won the sympathies, if not always the total loyalty, of the great Shanghai writers such as Mao Dun and Lu Xun. The *Journal* editors were painfully aware of that imbalance on the ideological battlefield. Even while the *Journal* damned Marxism and praised capitalism, it printed numerous articles that insisted that China did not have any true native capitalists and that the Marxists were therefore wrong to agitate the workers against their employers. In a clever definitional sleight of hand, one prolific editorialist, Deng Zhibing, protested that Shanghai and China might have a young capitalist economy, but they did not yet have true capitalists like those in Europe and America.[19] His colleague, Lu Fuzhou, was anxious to make the same point:

If [China's so-called capitalists] are compared with foreign capitalists, I am afraid that we would only be able to sigh that ours are too inferior to bear comparison. Strictly speaking, it can only be said that China has industrialists.[20]

For all that, the *Journal* writers were convinced "it is unavoidable that, when workers have organized, they will oppose the bourgeoisie."[21] Those words were eloquent testimony of the degree to which the writers of the *Journal*, as the self-proclaimed defenders of Chinese capitalism, took the Marxist challenge seriously. Furthermore, they were correct, because in the end they did not win the hearts and minds of the Chinese people. The Chinese were indeed to find the siren calls of Marxism more compelling, even though its triumph would not be brought about by the working class. It would seem, then, that as ambitious as they were, the

93

editors of the *Journal* were, at the last, unable to find an audience other than among the businessmen for whom they professed to speak.

By the 1930s and 1940s, the Shanghai argument for the primacy of economics had been decisively refuted, falling victim to the epic struggle between the communists and the nationalists. After the communist victory of 1949, bourgeois Shanghai was stripped by the communists of its hope that it might supply the ideas that would guide the economic development of China.[22] By the time of the Cultural Revolution, radical Maoists were launching an all-out political attack on everything "bourgeois." The great historical irony was that that convulsive and wasteful campaign was first launched from, of all places, Shanghai.[23] Backed by such ultraleftist stalwarts as Zhang Chunqiao and Yao Wenyuan, a radical "Shanghai school" of Maoist economics emerged to justify the total primacy of politics.[24] It all climaxed in the feverish claim that Maoist politics could create a new socialist man and a truly unselfish form of economic collectivism. Paraphrasing Tang Tsou's words, we can say that the fundamental trend in China was toward the penetration of society and the economy by political power.[25] One might be forgiven, then, for thinking that any talk of a bourgeois alternative was hopelessly illusory.

Yet, as Tsou also notes, the Chinese perception that the Cultural Revolution was a catastrophe in every sense struck what might turn out to be a deathblow to the ultraleftist model of development.[26] Quite a few Western economists, including analysts from the World Bank, Joan Robinson, and even the usually skeptical John Kenneth Galbraith, believed that for all its ups and downs, communist China had not done so badly in building up its industry and feeding its people.[27] But that was not how a great many Chinese themselves saw things. Those Chinese were not interested in comparing their country with India, or Shanghai with Bombay. They wanted to compare China with its East Asian neighbors, and Shanghai with their booming metropolises. There is no doubt that Wu Tianming, the noted filmmaker, voiced the bitter and angry sentiments of countless numbers of Chinese:

From my youngest days, I lived in the revolutionary camp. I loved the revolution passionately. I suppose that, the more passionate is the love, the more extreme the disappointment.... In 1945, the "little Japs" had lost the war, their economy ruined and their morale destroyed. How could they in some 30-odd years build what they have now? They were a defeated nation. We were a victorious one. At the time, Japan's economic foundation was no stronger than ours. How has it been able to do all [that it has done]? ... and then there is Hong Kong. When the Chinese mainland was liberated, Shanghai was the greatest city in Asia. Hong Kong was nothing but a rag-tag city. Yet, in some 30-odd years, what has Hong Kong become? But Shanghai has stayed unchanged. Why?[28]

A bourgeois alternative?

The Cultural Revolution was more than just a political cataclysm. The total bankruptcy of its claims for ultraleftist politics and pure political will created an intellectual climate in which there was the danger that another "total crisis" would arise in China. There had arisen a ubiquitous and deep crisis of faith in the radical form of Chinese Marxism, and it became obvious to many intellectuals and politicians that the country had to find another path to prosperity.

During the 1980s, what were some of the perceived alternatives to the utopian Maoist model of economic development? There were, of course, the two that communist China had sometimes picked and that Dorothy Solinger has documented for us: the bureaucratic model, centered around the planned economy and championed by such men as Xue Muqiao; the marketeer model, reliant on the market to set production, and promoted by the likes of Deng Xiaoping.[29] We could argue that when Deng opened up China to the world economy, he had no intention of launching a transition to capitalism. In a sense, his plan was as much Chinese as it was communist; he was, we could say, simply trying to import methods and technology from the advanced capitalist economies so that he could build a "socialism with Chinese characteristics" (*you Zhongguo tese de shehuizhuyi*). Arif Dirlik, for example, believes that Dengist China chose Mao Zedong's old idea of "New Democracy" (*xin minzhuzhuyi*) to guide the building of a market economy driven by capitalist engines, but policed by a vigilant socialist state.[30] Yet, regardless of what Deng and those who were Dengists might have wanted, did all Chinese intellectuals follow their lead and ask for nothing more than New Democracy?

The Shanghai scholars of the 1980s did take pains to stress that they did not approve of capitalism itself, but only of those aspects of capitalism that could be used by China to develop a market socialism. We can see an example of that claim in one short piece on advertising in the journal *Shanghai Enterprise (Shanghai qiye)*. The literary formula used by the author, Xu Xiaoming, was typical of a multitude of those Shanghai articles that introduced capitalist methods to the Chinese:

What we need are stern and fresh advertisements. We must never depart from the demands of our socialist formation, to cater blindly to an unhealthy psychology of consumption. But we can look boldly to learning from and putting to our own use the scientific part of advertising in the capitalist countries.[31]

Many writers in the Shanghai journals and newspapers of the 1980s applauded and justified the partial withdrawal of the Chinese state from the economy. The turbulent history of Shanghai under communism had taught them the profound lesson that political power is a dangerous

95

weapon whose edges can cut both ways. Not a few implied that it was best for Shanghai to stay far from Beijing:

Since 1979, the road of reform which we have taken of strengthening the vitality of the enterprises...and of simplifying government and relinquishing authority has been proven by practice to be necessary and correct.[32]

Those writers, however, did not mean that civil society was to come before the state. Like their colleagues elsewhere in China, they had to pay homage to Marxism-Leninism and "Mao Zedong thought," for despite the crisis of belief in those doctrines, China's rulers still swore allegiance to them,[33] and the enforcement of that ideological hegemony by the party-state set limits on any argument for the merits of capitalism, limits that had not existed in the freewheeling debates of the early 1920s. It was not unusual to find, all in the same Shanghai articles, orthodox passages on the need to uphold Marxism and the four fundamental principles, while other sections rhapsodized on the wonders of an entrepreneurial economy. Elaborating on the place of private businesses in China, one Jiang Xuemo said that because

the proportion taken by the private economy is small, the production materials for industrial enterprises and the source of goods for commercial enterprises must mainly come from the socialist enterprises. If the managerial style of the socialist enterprises is proper, the private sector will find it very difficult to engage in profiteering and swindling.[34]

We are told, then, that the entrepreneurs in China's civil society, even in those places with a rich pre-1949 history of private enterprise, such as Shanghai, were supposed to subordinate themselves to politics after all.

Most important, those in Shanghai who argued for the infusion of certain capitalist practices into China's economy were less the voice of a resurgent civil society than they were part of a deliberate, if haphazard, effort by certain groups in the Chinese party-state to reform the country's socialist economy. The many historical studies of the old Shanghai bourgeoisie put out by the Shanghai Academy of Social Sciences (*Shanghai shehui kexue yuan*) and by the Shanghai People's Publishing House (*Shanghai renmin chubanshe*), the theoretical and empirical research aimed at justifying economic reform in such journals as *Shanghai Enterprise, Social Science* (*Shehui kexue*) (Shanghai edition), *Shanghai Economics* (*Shanghai jingji*), *Shanghai Economic Science* (*Shanghai jingji kexue*), and *Talent Exploitation* (*Rencai kaifa*), the daring editorials and articles of the *World Economic Herald* (*Shijie jingji daobao*), which was informally called China's *Wall Street Journal* – all those forums were within the boundaries of the party-state, supported by state funds, and ultimately subject to state and party supervision and control. As such, the journalists, writers, and scholars who were published there were participating in a proposed project of reform that was going from the top to the bottom. In short, they were state intellectuals. They enjoyed the patronage of the state, even though not all their ideas were accepted by their political patrons, and even though there were many in the state who opposed their views.

Yet, I would argue that the party's clarion call for building a "commodity economy" (*shangbin jingji*) finally encouraged some Chinese to go beyond the marketeer model. Everywhere in China, scholars and politicians looked closely at the iconoclastic market socialisms of Eastern Europe, particularly those of Hungary and Yugoslavia,[35] and they tried to absorb what they supposed were the lessons of economic success in Asia's new "gang of four" – South Korea, Singapore, Hong Kong, and Taiwan. In short, the whole process and rhetoric of economic reform opened the floodgates to many exciting alternatives that had once seemed closed to China.[36] Among the most vivid illustrations of that was that Shanghai, for yet a second time, came up with its answer to China's crisis of faith: the bourgeois alternative.

After decades of communist rule, there emerged, centered around Shanghai, a good number of editors, historians, economists, and journalists who constructed an argument rich in parallels to the Shanghai General Chamber of Commerce's old defense of capitalism. They may not have intended to do that, but they did so all the same. With full knowledge and often with no little pride that the history of pre-communist Shanghai had been in many ways the history of Chinese capitalism, they (let us call them Shanghai writers) responded to the party's call for fresh economic ideas by eagerly resurrecting much of the Chamber of Commerce argument for a bourgeois alternative. Those Shanghai writers were careful to take their cues from the party on the general line to be followed in their writings, but they also laced their work with a pungent Shanghainese flavor.[37] Their argument was not taken up by every writer in Shanghai. Neither were they necessarily all Shanghainese. Nor were they all agreed on every detail of analysis. But they and their intellectual fellow travelers did share an understanding of history that took the pre-communist, capitalist past of Shanghai to be the key to the present and to the future of China.

Moreover, their obsession with Chinese capitalism in general and Shanghai capitalism in particular distinguished them from their colleagues in the other parts of the country. There were other proposed alternatives that also sought to assert the primacy of economics. But most social scientists in Guangdong, for instance, did not respond to Beijing's call for economic reform by probing the past. They did not mine eighteenth- and nineteenth-century Cantonese history for insights into Guangzhou's old merchant capitalism. Instead, they chose to answer the call to build a commodity economy by contemplating the concrete day-to-day practice of integrating Guangdong's and Hong Kong's economies.[38] The Fujianese also began to rebuild their economy not so much by turning to the past for ideas as by trading with Taiwan and by soliciting investments from their compatriots abroad and from businessmen in Taiwan. And the famous Wenzhou model evolved far more through local innovation and, rumor had it, indirect Taiwanese investment than through the inspiration of formal and official theories of history.

In contrast, while Shanghai was widely perceived both in China and abroad as falling badly behind in all areas of economic reform,[39] many of its scholars and writers were busily rehabilitating the city's history under capitalism when it had been the industrial and commercial colossus of the country. They developed a general theory of economic development drawn from a study of Shanghainese history, and they concluded from both theory and history that Shanghai would be able to draw on its capitalist heritage and participate again as a major actor in the world economy.

Here, we might ask the academic question, Was that theoretical reading of Shanghainese history "correct"? But we would be missing the point. In a very important sense, the question is irrelevant. What mattered was that Shanghai writers did believe that they had hit on a true understanding of Chinese history and universal economic laws. They really did think that they had the solution to China's crisis, and they fully expected that "the Shanghai spirit" (*Shanghai jingshen*), which was said to have inspired the old Shanghai capitalists, would revitalize the material life of the whole country. Knowing this, can we be surprised that Rhoads Murphey's seminal study of the pre-1949 history of the city, entitled *Shanghai, Key to Modern China*, was translated into Chinese and published in Shanghai, with a ringing endorsement of its theme by its translators?[40]

Did Chinese history truly come full circle in the 1980s? Was the Shanghai argument for capitalism reborn? Did communist China really face a bourgeois alternative?

Let me make a few comments about the word "capitalism" here. An army of careful scholars has never tired of reminding us that its meaning is notoriously elusive, because it has been used to describe economies with prodigious philosophical diversity, ranging all the way from those founded on laissez-faire doctrines, such as Jay Gould's America and British-run Hong Kong, to those justified by corporatist rhetoric, such as Salazar's Portugal and fascist Italy. But as Andrew Shonfield argues — and rightly so — it is indispensable because "there has not been a better word to put in its place."[41] It reminds us that there is surely a crucial threshold in the ideological balance between private and public economic power that separates, for example, the welfare capitalisms of Sweden and Canada from the goulash communism of Hungary and the heterodox market socialism of Titoist Yugoslavia.

How, then, should we understand an argument, born of crisis in a Marxist party-state, that proposed to look for the salvation of socialism in capitalism? I suggest that part of the usefulness of the word "capitalism" for understanding the Shanghai arguments for the bourgeois alternative is that many Shanghai writers, of the 1980s as well as of the 1920s, deliberately contrasted capitalism with socialism, in particular with existing state socialisms, and found capitalism enticing enough to argue for its virtues. The impression one has after reading their writings is that they did not think about gradations from socialism to capitalism or about the subtle tensions between the public and the private in mixed economies. Instead, correct or not, most Shanghai writers preferred to speak about "Capitalism" and about "Socialism."

The *Journal* of the 1920s juxtaposed capitalism to the Bolshevik form of state socialism and concluded that Bolshevism's superiority was hardly so self-evident that capitalism had to be rejected out of hand as an alternative for China. Nie Yuntai, for one, passed a scathing judgment on communism:

Communism is very appealing to the ears. But once it has been put into practice, one discovers [that it has] many harmful effects. So Russia itself has repeatedly retreated to using private capital and a system of private commerce.[42]

Many Shanghai writers of the 1980s, for all their Marxist-Leninist training and convictions, were no less critical of socialism as it had been practiced in China. These were the words of Yong Wenyuan, a prize-winning scholar, who sought to justify economic reform both theoretically and empirically:

During the 20th century we were impatient to realize communism at one leap in full disregard of the situation of the development of the productive forces. This is not only wrong as far as economics is concerned, but also constitutes a blunder in world history.[43]

It was not just scholars in Shanghai circles who believed that. Throughout the 1980s, everywhere, Marxism-Leninism was put more and more on the ideological defensive by the widespread perception that the economic performances of state socialisms had been disappointing, even disastrous. In China, the quest for reform spurred on the questioning of almost everything in the socialist economy, from the system of factory management, to financing, to the setting of prices, to even the ownership of the means of production. Shanghai writers took full part in that historic reexamination of what had once been thought to be eternal ideological truths. A look at the 1987 index for *Shanghai Enterprise*, for instance, shows an outpouring of theoretical articles on the urgent need to carry out massive reforms in Shanghai's factories. By the mid-1980s, one would have been hard pressed to find in the city's publications, by anyone other than party propagandists, more smug slogans regarding the "superiority of socialism" (*shehuizhuyi de youyuexing*).

It may turn out that years from now, historians will look back and judge that the new economic ideologies of the 1980s succeeded in accommodating into a revised Chinese socialism ideas that had once been attacked as bourgeois. But I do not think the only possible outcome was accommodation. Whatever their defenders may have thought, at least one set of ideas – those embodied in the Shanghai alternative – had the potential to lead China down another path, one by which economic reforms, if thought through and carried out to their logical ends, could have justified and brought about a transition from socialism to some form of capitalism, suggesting that what Tsou calls the "refunctionalization" of Chinese socialist ideology, the process of bringing it closer to reality,[44] held the potential to take China where even the most liberal of party reformers had never intended it to go. For all the loud and indignant protests of Shanghai writers that they were Marxists and that they were not trying to revive Chinese capitalism, there simply were too many powerful similarities in substance and reasoning between the arguments of the 1920s and 1980s for their protests to be convincing. What were some of those similarities?

1. The old Shanghai argument claimed that not only economic problems but also many social and cultural problems could be solved by capitalist practices. So, too, did the new argument. The ideological implication was that capitalism could heal not only the body of China but also its soul. Economics could solve everything; politics was unnecessary. In this sense, both the old and new Shanghai arguments can be seen to be "total," though not totalitarian, responses to China's crises. In the 1920s, the *Journal* writers claimed in an almost Saint-Simonist way that good business ethics created high standards of morality in society. Like Hu Shi and Lu Xun in the 1920s and Bo Yang and Sun Longji in the 1980s, the periodical saw little worth preserving in Chinese traditions. Its writers delighted in the idea that the old ways of doing business would be replaced by the bourgeois culture of honesty and efficiency that was coming in from the West to Shanghai and, through Shanghai, to the rest of China:

Who [in China knows] that business stresses morality above all else, that is, what is called the use of good faith to carry out business? . . . Foreign businessmen stress morality, but Chinese businessmen have always been deceitful.[45]

"Chinese love to spout empty theories," one iconoclastic commentator named Hu Jingxiu added, "But if we wish to develop our industry, it is natural that we will have to abandon the philosophical ideas which have been bequeathed us by our ancestors."[46] The *Journal* downplayed any possible ill effects of building capitalism in China and the social conflicts that might create in society. Instead, editors and writers insisted that it was precisely the absence of capitalism that made economic and cultural life so backward in China:

The businessmen of our nation have always known only about abiding by past experience. They have earnestly advocated a spirit of conservative practice. In contrast, the businessmen of Europe and America try their utmost to study and seek practical knowledge, and they are rich in the spirit of making great discoveries.[47]

The *Journal* writers believed that social harmony was not incompatible with capitalism. On the contrary, they argued that workers did not have any grievance that was so serious that it could not be answered by increasing the mutual understanding between them and their employers. The *Journal* writers hotly disputed what they called the socialist view that the interests of capital and labor were incompatible, and they implored Shanghai's workers not to be misled by "ruffians" and communists.[48] The workers, it was said, could learn that the interests of their factories were indeed their own, and businessmen could be persuaded that good pay and investment in training workers would lower the costs of production: "One has to make it so that the workers share 'a common interest' with the company and retain 'a loving affection' for the management."[49] The workers and businessmen of Shanghai had to work together peacefully, to oppose their true enemies: imperialism, warlordism, poverty, and political radicalism.

In much the same way, many Shanghai writers of the 1980s claimed that a new and better, more harmonious, Chinese culture could be created by the importation of contemporary capitalist methods of business into the workplace. As one writer, Xu Kun, put it, "the establishment of professional ethics is the establishment of socialism with a Chinese face."[50] But that seemingly orthodox formula was injected with a new meaning in discussions on how to instill those professional ethics and on what those ethics might be in practice. No longer was the old, divisive Maoist call to wage class struggle invoked. One letter writer to *Talent Exploitation* spoke for many when he offered his views on the proper

101

behavior for managers and concluded that they ought "to take care of their subordinates, respect their dignity, and make them feel close to them."[51] Exploring that theme, familiar Marxist rhetoric often gave way to more concrete and unorthodox terms, such as "corporate culture" (an idea imported from the United States).[52] Chinese readers were urged to study the managerial methods of such capitalist firms as Honda, Sony, and Mary Kay Cosmetics.[53] And in the Shanghai style of uniting history and theory, more than a few historical studies rammed home the lesson that, in that respect, it was old capitalist Shanghai that had pioneered the way for all Chinese. Consider this passage from a lengthy article on the old national bourgeoisie by Qian Xiaoming, an economic historian at the Shanghai Academy of Social Sciences:

Respecting talent and knowing to appoint the right people: these are important conditions for entrepreneurial creativity. Before Liberation, particularly in the 20s and 30s, it was obvious that, in comparison, the technical and managerial talent in Shanghai was superior.[54]

2. The Shanghai argument of the 1920s never failed to insist that there were powerful bonds between capitalism and patriotism. Its advocates took special care to distinguish between what they called true business-men, that is, industrialists and entrepreneurs, on the one hand, and spec-ulators, rentiers, and traditional merchants, on the other. The *Journal* conceded that entrepreneurs always try to make profits for themselves. After all, Yu Qiaqing admitted, "it is human nature to benefit the self."[55] But in the true spirit of Adam Smith, the *Journal* writers also claimed that that selfish motive would have stupendously unselfish results. Know-ingly or not, the *Journal* editors reproduced much of the argument of the early European economists and philosophers that the satisfaction of private passions could create a public good.[56] "An industrialist has to be ambitious," the periodical taught.[57] But because that ambition would promote industrialization, it was surely in the interests of China as well. How could the businessmen of Shanghai be predators on their fellow Chinese? They were simply fulfilling their patriotic duty through their noble effort to modernize the Chinese economy.

So, too, did the new argument laud the patriotism of past and con-temporary entrepreneurs. A good illustration of that was how historians took a new look at the motives of the old Shanghai bourgeoisie and came up with a glowing assessment of their patriotism. Such prominent Shang-hai figures of the 1920s and 1930s as the match and cement tycoon Liu Hongsheng and the American-trained banker Chen Guangfu were gen-erously acclaimed for their love of China. They were admired for putting their industriousness and boldness in the service of their country when it had been facing enormous difficulties and dangers.[58] Ding Richu, a highly distinguished scholar at the Shanghai Academy of Social Sciences, minced no words in affirming the value of their work:

[Compared] with foreign capital in China, native capitalism was weak. But under certain conditions, it played a very important function. During the Sino-Japanese War, the amount of Shanghai's industry which had been moved to the rear area in the Southwest was equal to only about 10% of the city's installations in 1936. Yet, this laid the foundation for the industrial construction of the rear during the War.[59]

3. During the 1920s, the *Journal* defended private property as being indispensable in any economy: "The foundation of the principles in all economic phenomena is [private property]. The system of private property has existed for a long time. Today, we see it as a heaven-given right."[60] That was a view that obviously was quite different from the views of the Chinese anarchists and Marxists of the time. But it also departed from the beliefs of Sun Yat-sen and such Guomindang politicians as Hu Hanmin and Wang Jingwei, who basically rejected capitalism and believed that private property could be held only as long as it served the public good.[61] The *Journal* was willing to see some restrictions on the use of private property so that workers could become capitalists more easily, but they insisted that ultimately private property was sacred and that the state would do best to leave it untouched.

Similarly, many Shanghai writers and scholars of the 1980s did not shy from defending the idea of private property. They were keen to find theoretical and historical justifications for the partial privatization of a hitherto almost entirely socialized economy, and they eagerly adopted for their own use the party line that China was still in the primary stage of socialism. For example, Jiang Xuemo concluded that although the private sector had many shortcomings, it had the great virtue of being able to "invigorate production techniques, improve management, [and] decrease the cost of production."[62] Does it not make sense for us, then, to say that from this iconoclastic view, the many historical books and articles on the Shanghai bourgeoisie in fields as different as the match, rubber, machine, flour, textile, cotton, banking, cigarette, broadcasting, and pharmaceutical industries could be seen as, in effect, affirming the beneficial use of private property? As often as not, such studies, especially those compiled or written in the late 1980s, left the reader deeply impressed with how much the old capitalists had been able to achieve, in spite of the long odds they had faced in competing against imperialism in a "half-feudal, half-colonial" China.[63] By thus demonstrating again and again that much good could come and had come from the existence of private property, even while it did not dare to question outright the primacy of the party-state, the Shanghai argument of the 1980s suggested that the idea of private property was indispensable and that its realization was in fact necessary for the economic development of China. The subtle hint was that civil society, left to its own devices, could be far more innovative than the state and could do far more to enrich China. It is no mystery why so many Shanghai editors and writers became entranced by that idea. Anyone who visited the city during the 1980s would quickly have found out that its inhabitants believed that their economy had already stagnated and suffered for too long because of the overbearing attentions of the party-state.

4. The argument of the 1920s defended the use of the market and of market mechanisms to enrich China's economy. The *Journal* writers saw economic competition to be natural and desirable. Fang Jiaobo observed in one essay that competition was not necessarily destructive. Chinese factories could indeed "compete together and move ahead together."[64] The *Journal*'s wealth of articles on double-entry accounting, management, and advertising all taught the virtues of competitiveness in the marketplace. The periodical objected to the presence of foreign capitalists and goods in China not because its contributors were xenophobic but because they were convinced that the unequal treaties gave unfair advantages to foreign businesses in the Chinese economy. In issue after issue, *Journal* articles hammered away at the point that the goal of politics was to do away with that artificial inequality and to allow the economy to develop strong capitalist sinews. Once China had broken the chains of the unequal treaties, the logic went, the economy would be able to hold its own. There would be no need, then, for China to fear any nation, not even in the international market: "We will be able to expand our foreign trade gradually, and then we shall be able to wrestle with the other nations of the world."[65]

The new Shanghai argument, too, celebrated competition in the marketplace. In many theoretical and historical studies there was barely a word about the formerly sacred cow of central planning. Instead, it became far more common to find that the greatest possible stress was put on the need for competitiveness among enterprises. For instance, the Rong brothers, the greatest flour and cotton-textile magnates in old Shanghai, were acclaimed for their devotion to strengthening their businesses in the market by buying out their competitors and improving the quality of their products.[66] It was understandable that capitalists were expected by the proponents of the new argument to be competitive in the market. But workers, too, were asked to be competitive! Although some Shanghai writers insisted that "labor is not a commodity under [China's] socialist conditions,"[67] they explained that there was also an urgent need to create labor mobility and a labor market.[68] In sharp contrast to the extreme egalitarianism and proletarian sympathies of the radical Maoist model, there appeared an implicit willingness to tolerate different wages – and, by logical extension, even the once unthinkable prospect of unemployment – for workers according to their different abilities and marketability.[69] Just as important, that eagerness to embrace the market for both capital and labor was translated into a hearty endorsement of private enterprise. It was in that spirit that two Shanghai scholars, one an economist at the Shanghai Academy of Social Sciences and the other a social scientist at Tongji University, suggested that politics should serve society, not dominate it: "The existence and development of the private sector is the natural result of a commodity economy.... The government should protect and encourage its continued development."[70]

5. The *Journal* praised economic individualism, contending that it was individual initiative and innovation, rather than collectivism or the political dictates of the state, that promoted economic development. In a very Schumpeterian way, it extolled the virtues of entrepreneurship. The Shanghai argument of the 1920s portrayed Chinese businessmen as fledgling and intrepid industrial entrepreneurs who had to be cherished and protected. Many, if not all, of the *Journal*'s observations are familiar to anyone who has read the research and economic treatises of the 1920s and 1930s by contemporary scholars such as H. D. Fong, D. K. Lieu, and Akira Nagano.[71] Because most Chinese entrepreneurs were capital-poor, it was argued, they had to learn new methods of management and apply new technology to get the most out of what little capital was available to them. Indeed, Deng Zhibing went so far as to praise entrepreneurs for having superior judgment.[72] But the *Journal* did try to find a middle ground between the Western, particularly the American, celebration of unrestricted competition and the early Japanese ideal of social harmony among capitalists.[73] Hu Jingxiu, for instance, saw a need for both competition and cooperation among Chinese businessmen:

One does not manage business only for personal profit.... Today, industrial and commercial development is not something which one or two individuals can accomplish.... Thus, a division of labor should be treasured.[74]

The Shanghai argument of the 1980s spoke about entrepreneurship in much the same "Chinese" fashion, praising those who used their individual talents and initiative in both competition and cooperation with others and who worked not only for themselves but also for the good of society. Much was expected from those enterprising individuals, whether they worked in the public or private sector. A regular feature in *Shanghai Enterprise* was its numerous profiles of "outstanding managers" (*youxiu changzhang*) in state companies. For instance, in 1987 its July issue included a visit with the model manager of an import-export firm, and in November its reporters wrote on the innovative director of a coal loading and unloading company.[75] The theme that it was individual creativity, not Maoist collectivism or state planning, that would revive the economy found particularly frank expression in *Talent Exploitation*, which began publishing in 1986. Such journals provided public forums for entrepreneurs to present and defend their new ideas and put their individualism in the most favorable light possible. There was this blunt summary of one typical article on China's pressing need for entrepreneurs:

Markets which do not have entrepreneurs do not exist.... Entrepreneurs are not "state officials." Only when enterprises are separated from the state administration and only when entrepreneurial managers become independent of the government will there form a colony of entrepreneurs.[76]

Moreover, it was claimed, Shanghai enjoyed the unique advantage of having a great history and tradition of entrepreneurship: "the enterprising nature and entrepreneurial talent shown, under adverse conditions, by the businessmen of old Shanghai are still worth our studying and emulation."[77] If not for unfavorable "external conditions," it was explained, the Liu Hongshengs and the Chen Guangfus would have been able to unleash the full potential of their talents. An alert reader might have caught on that one powerful implication of that line of argument was that if China had not been invaded in 1937, Shanghai's private businessmen could indeed have done much to help the nation. Was it possible that it had not been Chiang Kai-shek and the Guomindang after all, but the Imperial Japanese Army that had dealt the deathblow to the Shanghai bourgeoisie and thereby to China's hopes?

Where entrepreneurial daring appeared in contemporary China, Shanghai writers were also quick to jump to its defense. So we should not be too surprised to read this passage from a sympathetic interview in *Talent Exploitation* with a private entrepreneur in Zhejiang who complained that society misunderstood his actions:

Speaking truthfully, before, I did not want others to know I was a private entrepreneur, because there is so much prejudice against private entrepreneurs from people who invariably say that we only think of making profits.... [But] I want to be an entrepreneur, a manager, an inventor.... My goal in running an enterprise is to have a top reputation, to produce top quality products...and to provide the finest benefits.[78]

6. The *Journal* celebrated profits and the profit motive. Its writers believed that profits were fairly earned when they had been made through investment in industry and were then reinvested in production. The *Journal* writers carefully differentiated between profit and interest, the former

a just reward for entrepreneurship, and the latter the monies received by rentiers, and usually wasted by them on luxuries. "Scholars have always accepted [the legitimacy of] all desires," one writer named Shu Gui argued in stern Veblenesque tones. "They see an increase in desires as the motive power behind economic prosperity. . . . But who does not know that this is wrong?"[79] The waste of capital on conspicuous consumption was condemned. It was that, Deng Zhibing insisted, that Marx should have attacked, but did not because he had not known about the difference between profit and interest.[80] Only if Chinese businessmen made profits would they be able to maintain and expand production and thus keep Chinese workers employed; the making of profits was not an exploitation of the proletariat. Anticipating what is today called trickle-down theory, a *Journal* writer said that capitalist profit-making would eventually increase everyone's standard of living: "The success of a minority can become the fertilizing rain for all."[81] Moreover, only businessmen could pave the way. If a capitalist did not work for even one day, Hu Jingxiu explained, his employees would lose out that day.[82] Proletarians, it was said, could not save China on their own. It was privately owned factories, set up to earn profits by competing successfully in the marketplace, that animated Shanghai and that would eventually enrich all of China. Indeed, using an American argument common then, the periodical suggested that through their social trusteeship of capital, businessmen could create prosperity for all.[83]

The new Shanghai argument, too, endorsed the idea that individual pursuit of profits could be good for all society. Consider, for example, the way it looked at the profits made by the entrepreneurs who had been conjured up by the reforms of the 1980s. One writer proposed that "to work solely for profits is the nature of the private economy," but that, under certain conditions, the private pursuit of high profits coincided with the interests of society.[84] Entrepreneurs had the right to expect high incomes. "This," one Jia Songqing concluded in an article in *Talent Exploitation*, "is the assessment of their special contributions of labor."[85] What could those contributions be? The answer, two historians argued, could be found by understanding the good that had been produced by the pursuit of profits in pre-1949 Shanghai. Customers, they said, had been offered a wealth of products by businessmen who had known that the best way to make profits was by pleasing their customers. The quality of service had been high, and the standards of management admirable.[86] But once profits had been made, to what good use could they be put? The new Shanghai argument answered that question by echoing the old claim of the *Journal* that true capitalists conscientiously reinvested their profits in their businesses and expanded production. Many of the old Shanghai industrialists, it was said, had been especially praiseworthy;

when China badly needed them, they had plowed back all their profits into their mills and factories, unlike so "many [other wealthy Chinese who] preferred to purchase land or collect interest on loans."[87] Once again, the history of Shanghai capitalism was no longer cited as an example of capitalist decadence and depredation, but rather as an inspiring illustration of bourgeois patriotism.

7. The Shanghai argument of the 1920s implicitly accepted that it was inevitable that the workings of the mechanisms and institutions of capitalism – private property, the market, entrepreneurship, and the pursuit of profit – would at first lead to economic development that would be geographically and sectorally unbalanced and to a distribution of income that would be highly unequal. But that initial cost, the *Journal* contended, was acceptable, because eventually all Chinese would be better off. Its writers insisted that if cities like Shanghai could build up profitable native industries, there could be no doubt that their businessmen would be able to compete both domestically and internationally with foreign capital. It was only natural that the prosperity they would create in Shanghai would then be shared with the rest of the country. Only industry in such cities as Shanghai, Hu Jingxiu pronounced, could save the peasant masses of the country: "In the economies and societies of this century, agricultural nations can no longer hold their own."[88]

The new Shanghai argument was even more direct in taking that view. Having been milked for decades by the party-state, Shanghai, as the 1980s unfolded, tried to reclaim the eminence it had once enjoyed. The Academy of Social Sciences, the municipality's most influential think tank, was especially zealous in trying to revive the old 1920s dream that the city could become the economic leader of China:

[It] is essential to adopt all kinds of flexible measures to successfully complete the strategic shift in Shanghai's economy and to enable the city not only to go on as an advanced industrial base of the country, but also to become the largest trade and marine transport centre as well as an important financial and information centre, and to play a more active part in achieving the modernization of China.[89]

To that end, the argument continued, it was only logical that a major network of cities and towns should be built up in the Yangtze River delta, with Shanghai as its center. That region, explained an urban economist at the Institute of Sectoral Economics (*Bumenjingji yanjiusuo*) at the academy, was to become the major junction in China's planned integration into the world economy: "Establishing the idea of the regional economy is the path to common prosperity."[90] If we keep in mind Zhao Ziyang's idea that the coastal areas should be allowed to become wealthy first so that they could later help the Chinese hinterland to become wealthy too, it is not difficult to see that the Shanghai argument of the 1980s, like that of the 1920s, was a grand version of trickle-down theory and that some of its propositions were not being advocated only by those in Shanghai.

What did that resurrection of the bourgeois alternative suggest about the ideological upheaval in the Shanghai and the China of the 1980s? For one thing, the strong similarities between the arguments of the 1920s and the 1980s implied that in spite of the massive politicization of the economy, in spite of the enormously costly efforts to transform the economy by using the capital of the coast to develop the interior, it was still perceived by many scholars and writers in and around Shanghai that the economic structure of the country had changed little, if at all. In other words, whether or not they realized the devastating implications of their ideas, the new advocates of the Shanghai argument in effect concluded that the past several decades of Chinese economic development had been a Maoist equivalent of the search for the Holy Grail.

It probably is not too farfetched to say that the implicit line of thinking went something like this: The old Shanghai argument was still valid, because nothing had really changed. All the Maoist diatribes against Western capitalism and the parasitism of such capitalist strongholds as Shanghai had led to nothing but foolishness, destruction, and lost chances. The practice of Marxism-Leninism and Maoist politics had not made China wealthy. Beijing had been wrong to deny Shanghai its destiny. The comparative advantage in the Chinese economy remained with places like Shanghai, where there were still to be found the greatest numbers of prospective entrepreneurs and the greatest hope for an economic takeoff. The bourgeois alternative had been China's greatest chance for salvation back in the 1920s. It was still so after six long decades, and Beijing ought to recognize that truth and let Shanghai go about its business of doing business. I do not think that it was a simple coincidence or a mere matter of academic curiosity that by the late 1980s, a number of historians at Fudan University and the Shanghai Academy of Social Sciences were studying and compiling materials on the General Chamber of Commerce.[91] In Shanghai, the crisis of Marxism led to the Phoenix-like rebirth of an old regionalist ideology of economic development. If that ideology implied anything at all, it was not that China was being haunted by the specter of communism, but rather by that of capitalism!

The similarities between the old and new Shanghai arguments also showed that not a few Chinese still longed to discover a single cure for their country's ills. There still was a powerful tendency among learned and sincere Chinese editors, writers, and scholars to find simple ideological answers to complex problems. There is no doubt the bourgeois alternative of the 1980s was a simple one. Basically, all it was saying was that if politics was downgraded and capitalist mechanisms were allowed to work in places with a rich bourgeois history, such as Shanghai, China would become wealthy. There also is no doubt that the argument was tremendously appealing to some, in part because it was so readily understandable and because the causality was so straightforward. Indeed, quite a number of Westerners thought that it was the only kind of argument that those who wanted China to prosper could really make. Milton Friedman, for instance, believed that.[92] Other Western analysts were even more outspoken, arguing that a decline in the primacy of politics and the triumphant rebirth of capitalism were in fact inevitable in the communist states:

[It is] significant [that there] has been [a] hesitant but unmistakable movement toward a greater reliance on the elements of capitalism in much of the Communist world: first in Hungary, then in China, and now even in the motherland of socialism, the Soviet Union. To be sure, this movement has been gradual and equivocal.... Yet it has already progressed beyond the early stages, when capitalist measures were adopted in a de-facto and almost surreptitious manner. Today, while maintaining verbal allegiance to the disembodied ideal of socialism, Chinese and Soviet officials are increasingly explicit in their criticisms of its institutional foundations.[93]

It may be that Alexander's answer to the riddle of the Gordian knot does apply here. Perhaps complex issues can be understood with a simple ideology, and complex problems solved with simple answers. But was the bourgeois alternative too simple? Did its very simplicity, its sweeping generalizations, obscure more of the great complexities of the ideological crisis in communist China than it exposed? I would say that the Shanghai argument did not address many vital and basic questions, and those questions had to be confronted if the new argument for a bourgeois alternative was to have a serious chance of converting those Chinese intellectuals and politicians who were not, by accident of birth or residence, committed to a Shanghai perspective on economic development.

Was the bourgeois alternative in its new form able to confront and answer those theoretical, ideological, and empirical questions that, when brought up during the 1920s, had made the old Shanghai argument seem at first absurd and finally irrelevant to most Chinese, regardless of their political loyalties? I would suggest that the Shanghai argument of the 1980s was unable to answer convincingly some basic questions about private passions and the public good, about the need for entrepreneurs, about the relationship between economics and politics, and about the likely results of trying to put the bourgeois alternative into practice in a China where many of its ruling elite were more likely to be obsessed with keeping political power for themselves than with the welfare of the people. That was a great intellectual weakness. The case for the bourgeois alternative, as presented by many of Shanghai's intellectuals and their sympathizers, was not cut-and-dried. It may have convinced many in the municipality and in the surrounding regions, but there was little proof that its special wedding of theory to history had won a wider geographic audience.

Tsou suggests that in the past, the Marxist-Leninist alternative converted many Chinese intellectuals because it could help them in "creating a new history."[94] But did non-Shanghainese feel that a bourgeois alternative extrapolated from Shanghainese history was what they should choose to create a new history and a new economy? Probably not. It is very likely, for instance, that the Chinese of Guangdong felt no need to learn from Shanghai when they already had a dynamic and far more contemporary capitalist model to study in neighboring Hong Kong.[95] And it may be doubted that the multitudes of poor and illiterate Chinese in the interior provinces, such as Guizhou, Gansu, and Shaanxi, saw Shanghainese history as telling their story, when so much of their own modern history had been distinguished more by struggles for bare physical survival than by great entrepreneurial adventures.[96]

In addition, like its predecessor in the 1920s, the argument of the 1980s suffered from serious lapses in logic. To have had more than the slightest chance of winning ideological support outside Shanghai, it would have had to remedy its shortcomings in argumentation. But it did not. Consider, for example, the idea that the private passions of entrepreneurs could be channeled into serving all of society. A perceptive Chinese could ask many embarrassing questions about the degree of truth in that idea. Was there a point at which private capitalist passions would no longer serve the public good? In Tsou's words, "who [was] going to decide what reciprocal relationship between the individual and the society [was] the correct one?"[97] The rulers of the party-state in Beijing? Or the entrepreneurs themselves in cities like Shanghai? What were the possible trade-offs between reaping the rewards of entrepreneurship and the chance that such entrepreneurship would create mass resentment of the successful? Might the unleashing of private passions in a socialist state lead to an entirely unintended and unexpected outcome in which China would have created the worse possible form of the mixed economy? Would China be risking what an ailing Poland was said by some to be facing?

In trying to gain the "best" of socialism and capitalism, the reformers [could] in reality end up with the worst of both worlds – combining economic inefficiency with high unemployment, a widening gap between a rich minority and an impoverished majority of the populace.[98]

111

And was it really true that most Chinese workers, even in a city with a capitalist heritage, such as Shanghai, would be willing to exchange guaranteed lifetime employment and the socialist "iron rice bowl" (*tiefanwan*) for uncertainty in a free labor market?

The new Shanghai argument, like the old, never clarified where the private passions of Chinese entrepreneurs fitted into a world capitalist system. What might be the implications of economic ties between foreign capitalists and native entrepreneurs in a communist China? Might not the rebirth of an entrepreneurial Shanghai with stronger ties to the world market than to the Chinese interior, as happened during the 1920s, excite angry accusations that the city was a hotbed of traitors and foreign exploiters?

In this regard, it is truly revealing that there was one issue on which the old and new Shanghai arguments did not agree. The argument of the 1920s had been philosophically committed to free trade, but it also had been fiercely protectionist in promoting a native-goods movement and in making its suggestions to fix what it saw as an unjust imbalance in China's foreign trade. Only after China's businessmen had matured, the *Journal* said, could they practice free trade and compete with the great capitalist economies. The periodical bitterly attacked any proposal that foreign capital could help native entrepreneurs develop the Chinese economy: "[When] foreigners set up factories – including Sino-foreign joint ventures – in our nation," Deng Zhibing suggested, "they become the bourgeoisie and we the proletariat."[99]

The Shanghai argument of the 1980s, however, was all for free trade and for working with foreign capitalists. It abandoned the inflammatory anti-imperialist rhetoric of Mao and revived the kind of hopeful language used by the Marx who had described capitalism as a positive and liberating force in the poor nations. Witnesses to the ills brought about by Mao's and the party's decisions to follow a policy of "self-reliance," many Shanghai writers were outspoken defenders of the Sino-foreign joint venture and direct foreign investment.[100] Harking back to Shanghai's heritage as the leading treaty port in pre-communist China, the city's economists singled it out as the great key to opening up the country to foreign capital:

[Shanghai] should be good at taking full advantage of the golden opportunities presented by the world situation today, to attract more foreign funds to help achieve the modernization of China, and should make itself a base for introducing, assimilating and spreading advanced technology from abroad.[101]

Thus, the new Shanghai argument claimed, in a way that even the old argument had not dared, that China could profit only if it integrated itself fully and immediately into the world capitalist economy. Needless to say, few, if any, in Shanghai circles suggested that China's new private entrepreneurs should be excluded from that proposed integration. It was perhaps the greatest ideological twist of all that self-professed Marxist writers of the 1980s were far less wary of the potential traps awaiting China in a capitalist world economy than the bourgeois advocates of capitalism had been in the 1920s. They feared far more the costs for China of being cut off from foreign capitalists than of being exploited by them! That was a view that argued for the primacy of economics with a vengeance.

Yet, were there really no conflicts between entrepreneurial passions, on the one hand, and patriotism as a ruling government might define it, on the other? One did not have to be a xenophobic Chinese or a rabid Maoist to be skeptical about that Shanghainese variation on a widespread notion that in the United States had been embodied in the claim that what was good for General Motors was good for America. To anyone who was just the slightest bit sensitive to the problematic relationship between transnational capitalists and the nation-state, the proposition would have seemed optimistic at best, and naive at worst.[102]

Even if the Chinese had overlooked the many problems of reasoning in the Shanghai argument, they still could have criticized its understanding of the entrepreneur's role in China's economic development. Were entrepreneurs truly indispensable for economic development, and could they thrive only in a privatized economy? Perhaps so. Yet, intellectually and ideologically there was much room for debate about the answer, and where there was still controversy, the criticisms of the intellectual and ideological opposition had to be answered. John Roemer, for example, asks an important question that no doubt could have been asked by those who still wanted to salvage Chinese Marxism: "Is [entrepreneurial ability] a factor that is necessarily scarce, or is it scarce because most people in a capitalist system do not have the opportunities to develop their entrepreneurial abilities?"[103] If the latter, it could then be asked, How really useful was it to study the history of entrepreneurship in the old capitalist Shanghai? The asking of a question like Roemer's would have begged further questions. Did the bourgeois alternative err in identifying the lack of economic vitality in China with a lack of capitalist entrepreneurship? In other words, was it actually the absence or scarcity of entrepreneurship and capitalist methods of management that was responsible for the relatively poor economic performance of communist China? Or could the source of that failure be found in China not having practiced what Alec Nove calls a "feasible socialism?"[104] Did the economy fail to develop because Shanghai had been prevented from spreading entrepreneurial capitalism throughout all of China, or was it because the party had practiced the wrong kind of socialism?

On the other side of the debate, even if one had accepted the Shanghai argument for capitalist entrepreneurship, one still might have presented this problem for thought: Such periodicals as *Shanghai Enterprise* and *Talent Exploitation* placed high hopes in the managers of public enterprises, as well as in the entrepreneurs of the private sector. The managers did, after all, supervise the great majority of Chinese factories, and it was assumed that, once liberated from the direct control of the state, those new "socialist entrepreneurs" would act like private businessmen. But would they? Might the logic of a socialist economy without a true market not prevent them from behaving like capitalists, and instead encourage them to continue to play the familiar game of expanding production with no heed to quality, rather than maximizing profits and efficiency?[105] If so, how could state managers be transformed into genuine businessmen? If the answer was, as the Shanghai argument implied, that such a transformation could come about only through the creation of a market for capitalist buying and selling, then one needed a theory on how such a market might emerge in a party-state economy like China's. In short, like it or not, if they were indeed convinced that only a revival of capitalism could save their country, Shanghai writers had to buttress their ideas with a theory on how the role of the private market could become decisive in the Chinese economy, in other words, a good theory of how China could carry out a transition from socialism to capitalism. But they did not.

Nor did the Shanghai argument in its old or new form offer any original insights into the price that China might have to pay for choosing the bourgeois alternative as the path to economic development. It was, however, a problem that was sure to worry the more orthodox Marxists in the party. Was the working out of economic laws in the marketplace enough to produce wealth for all Chinese? Were large coastal cities like Shanghai as integrated with the Chinese hinterland as the advocates of the Shanghai argument and some party reformers such as Zhao Ziyang implicitly claimed when they assumed that sooner or later the wealth of the coast would filter down into the interior? How could that assumption be squared with the other implicit proposition of the Shanghai argument that there was really a dual economy in China, one part in the interior and the other in the coastal regions, a division that had not changed these many decades? If the duality was structural and had survived decades of forced extractions of capital from the coast, what would guarantee that growing prosperity on the coast would not remain confined there, while the vast hinterland fell further and further behind? If that should turn out to be the case, it would surely discredit the idea that entrepreneurs in Shanghai and the other parts of the coast could bring prosperity to all of China. Why, then, should the party functionaries, the intellectuals, and the populace of the vast Chinese hinterland consent to give free rein to "the Shanghai spirit"? The new bourgeois alternative was silent on those crucial questions of inequity and unbalanced development, preferring instead to assume them away with wishful rhetoric.

That weakness of the Shanghai argument would have been especially glaring to many Chinese who had studied the recent history of developing capitalist economies. For instance, it might eventually have occurred to those who were unconvinced by the Shanghai form of the bourgeois alternative and who were familiar with economic development in other parts of Asia to ask this question, which would have been at once theoretical and empirical: Was Shanghai's the sole form of capitalism that the Chinese could adopt? In other words, was the Shanghai argument, with its particular mix of ideas and assumptions, the only kind of bourgeois alternative that could be considered by the Chinese? The Chinese of the 1920s could look only to Shanghai for a native model of capitalist development. But the Chinese of the 1980s had the laissez-faire model of Hong Kong as well. Perhaps even more important, they also had the model of Taiwan before them. And under its own form of capitalism, in which an interventionist state sought to create the conditions for the free play of market economics,[106] post-1949 Taiwan had achieved an impressive level of economic equity as well as a spectacular industrial takeoff – both "growth" and "equity."[107] In fact, by the early 1980s, its distribution of income ranked among the most equitable in the world.[108] Taiwan's record on equity had been better than Hong Kong's, and it maintained that high standard even as it moved to the very brink of joining the ranks of the developed economies.

Party reformers did not adopt the Shanghai argument in full. Yet, as watered down and erratic as the economic reforms of the 1980s were, they did echo some of its most important ideas about the market and entrepreneurship, so much so that many foreigners were seduced into concluding that communist China was on its way to becoming a capitalist country. Who can forget that after visiting a free market during his visit to China, President Reagan referred to China as a "so-called" communist country? But if it was true that the ideas of the Shanghai argument could save the nation, why was their implementation spawning a growing and, some Chinese feared, possibly irreversible disparity not only between the coast and the hinterland but also between the entrepreneur and the worker on the coast? If the old division between the two Chinas was already hardening under the impact of what were still limited economic reforms, might not the situation be even worse under the bourgeois alternative? If it was true China had to practice some form of capitalism as the only way out of its self-perceived economic trap, did it make more sense to search for theoretical and historical lessons in old Shanghai capitalism than in modern Taiwanese capitalism? It was Shanghai's great captains of industry, such as the Rong brothers, Liu Hongsheng, and Jian Zhaonan, who were the heroes of the new argument for a bourgeois alternative. In contrast, it was private entrepreneurs in small and middle-size firms who were thought by many Western economists to be the driving force of Taiwanese capitalism. Would the practice of an economic theory that celebrated big business produce a Chinese economy more like Brazil's, with its unsurpassed inequalities and injustices, than like Taiwan's? I think that in the form it took, the new Shanghai argument was unable to answer such piercing questions, and they were questions that almost certainly would have been asked sooner or later, particularly because by the late 1980s the "Taiwan experience" (*Taiwan jingyan*) was drawing the attention of more and more social scientists and even party leaders in China. Again, the frank Wu Tianming expressed quite clearly what was surely on the minds of many Chinese:

[When] I think of Taiwan as it was in 1949, I think of how the Guomindang fled with an army of defeated troops to a small barren island. Yet, how has Taiwan been able to do what it has in the 30-odd years since? Its reserves of foreign exchange are only less than Japan's, ranking second in the world. Everywhere we Chinese are, we are discriminated against. Yet, the Taiwanese are loaded with money and do not hesitate to speak out.[109]

Finally, there was the all-important, all-consuming question of politics. Even if the Chinese had accepted the implicit view that it was the party-state's extirpation of the capitalist seeds from civil society that had caused China to remain poor, they still might have wondered about the Shanghai argument's breathtaking lack of political sense. Who in the party-state was supposed to have the will and power to put the Shanghai alternative into full practice? Was this potentially revolutionary movement to be championed first by local governments in such places as Shanghai, thus presenting Beijing with a fait accompli? Or was Beijing itself expected to mandate the nationwide adoption of the Shanghai alternative? In civil society, who would be the supporters of the alternative? Who would be its enemies? To such questions of politics, Shanghai writers offered no enlightenment. Indeed, for all its basic simplicity, their argument could also be highly abstract and scholastic and removed from the realities of politics, especially to readers who had learned about the hard choices of politics under Chinese communism.

In fact, just like its forerunner in the 1920s, the new Shanghai argument really had nothing practical to say about politics other than to conclude that good politics make for good business. For all its awareness of the party-state, it offered no insight into how to reconcile its theory of entrepreneurial economics with the sobering politics of the Chinese party-state, a party-state whose power was infinitely more penetrating and awesome than that wielded by the warlords of the 1920s. It had little to suggest about how to translate theory into reality, about how to guarantee that a revival of civil society and a transition to capitalism could accompany or bring about a transition to good government. As Tsou writes, for China's rulers, the problem at hand was not one of surrendering power to society, but one of "allowing the civil society greater autonomy yet retaining the state's absolute control and leadership over it."[110]

Would it really be that easy to mix economic reforms and communist politics, especially if many of the ideas that justified the reforms were opposed by powerful individuals and groups in the party-state as being reactionary or as being bourgeois or simply as going against their own interests? Or should economics be separated from politics? Was such separation possible in China? What was the dynamic between proposed reforms that might in practice add up to a transition to some form of capitalist economy and the even more problematic transition of Chinese communist totalitarianism to what Tsou calls post-totalitarianism?[111] How enduring and effective could the introduction of capitalist methods be in a polity whose rulers were doggedly determined that it would remain socialist in one form or another, especially if those rulers should choose to define "socialism" to mean the unchallenged preservation of their power in both politics and economics? Might that not eventually create a politically explosive situation? Might it not lead to an irreconcilable contradiction between civil society and the state, between the ambitions of a new Chinese bourgeoisie and the pretensions of a party-state determined to keep its grip on power? The state might decide for a time to withdraw partially from society and the economy, but what was to prevent it from returning in full and terrifying force whenever it felt threatened, revoking its edict that economics and not politics was primary? Could it not take back with one hand what it had given with the other? Would Beijing tolerate, in places like Shanghai, the rise of potentially formidable rivals whose power would be rooted not in politics and the party but in money and civil society? Would even the most open-minded reformers be willing to accept that the reemergence of society might someday, if not today, culminate in a demand that they do more than merely liberalize the internal life of the party, that they in fact step down from power? If the problem were solved by merging the new entrepreneurial elite and the old party-state elite, might that not simply produce a hybrid of state capitalism with socialist trappings, an unholy alliance between men of power in Beijing and monied interests in bourgeois bastions like Shanghai, a grotesque Chinese form of what had been ridiculed as crony capitalism in the economically decaying and corrupt Philippines under Ferdinand Marcos? Might that not ultimately be no more efficient and no more productive than the older Chinese forms of state socialism? Might it not also widen the gap between the haves and the have-nots? If the party-state chose instead to suppress the entrepreneurs in civil society and restore a forced egalitarianism, whether it did so in the name of the "New Democracy" or the "new authoritarianism" or just plain "stability," there might no longer be a chance to carry out the ideological trick of justifying a transition to capitalism with the language of Marxism. But could the use of the gun end the crisis of faith in socialism, and would it guarantee the prosperity of the Chinese people? And if the party-state did nothing, would not the economic contradictions thus generated eventually explode in its face?

Those who forged the Shanghai argument, no less in the 1980s than in the 1920s, took it for granted that a sovereign Chinese state would naturally provide good government and would be wise in handling the economy. Perhaps they were correct in sensing that good government was desirable for good business. But was it so easy to enjoy good government in a communist China, with its history of totalitarianism? If it was true that a good government was one whose institutions, by their flexibility, their tolerance, and their pluralism, allowed and encouraged sustained growth, not just intermittent or serendipitous production of wealth, by civil society, then a powerful argument could be made that there had been few good governments in human history. Sustained economic growth had been very rare indeed. "Bad" governments, whose rigidity or intolerance had generated poverty or stagnation, had been far more common.[112] For every England and every Japan, there had been ten Polands and ten Burmas. Simply having stable politics is not enough. "Stability" can as easily reflect political rigidity as much as flexibility.

The Shanghai argument chose to ignore the prodigiously difficult problem of elaborating the kinds of relationships between politics and economics and between the state and society that would maximize the chances for prosperity, a problem that Albert Hirschman wisely reminds us has yet to be solved by modern social science,[113] and that Tsou correctly says has been a major theme of Chinese history since 1978.[114] Shanghai writers did not see that in neither theory nor practice was a transition to capitalism a simple matter of economic reform. One might add that in none of Asia's "gang of four" was the effort to build a prosperous capitalist economy complicated even further by the awful political burden of having to carry out a transition from totalitarian politics. In none of the gang of four did or could the state, as despotic, brutal, and authoritarian as it may have been at times, ever seek total and absolute political control over all of civil society and the economy. But China's rulers had succumbed to what Jean-François Revel has called "the totalitarian temptation." Could places like Shanghai, cautious Chinese may have asked, take it for granted that Beijing would rule wisely, that it could so readily exchange bad government for good? Could the primacy of politics be so easily dismissed, and the primacy of economics be so easily substituted?

If the old orthodoxies and the new interpretations of Chinese Marxism did not come up with a satisfying answer, neither did the bourgeois alternative. But it was a question that could not be ignored. The tragedy of June 4, 1989, in Tiananmen Square showed once and for all that the question of politics was not merely hypothetical. It was quite literally a matter of life and death. The lesson would seem to be that if one wanted to argue for building a prosperous capitalist economy in communist China, one could take nothing for granted, least of all that the transition from bad to good government and from totalitarian to post-totalitarian politics was inevitable and irreversible. What the Shanghai argument badly needed was not only a theory of transition from socialism to capitalism but also a feasible theory of transition from totalitarianism to post-totalitarianism.[115]

As China enters the last decade of this century, the bourgeois alternative may or may not still be a true alternative for China — true in the sense that it is a practical alternative. It may be an alternative because the crisis of faith in Chinese Marxism has not ended. After all these decades of communist rule, and after a decade of debate and reform, the Chinese still have no idea of where they are going or how they are going to get there. This, too, is a lesson of June 4. In what seems very likely to become another total crisis, all alternatives seem possible. A reborn Shanghai argument is but one of many proposed alternatives, exposing the massive scale of the ideological uncertainty in China today. Repression can hide the crisis, but cannot do away with it. Repression may even make it far worse. Yet the bourgeois alternative itself may be only illusory, because in the way it has been developed it is flawed. It overlooks the possibility of unintended consequences, ignores fundamental questions, and lacks the full power to persuade. Outside Shanghai, it is unlikely to convince the anti-capitalists or the pro-capitalists or even the intellectual eclectics. Perhaps the Shanghai argument will remain in limbo, restricted in appeal to the region that gave it birth. Perhaps the theoretical and empirical study of Shanghai's capitalist past will prove to be the key to nothing. The argument might be suppressed by the party-state, leaving its advocates nothing more than a sense of disappointment in what was, what no longer is, and what might have been. Or perhaps China's rulers will try to force the Shanghai argument into a marriage with the self-justifying politics of the "new authoritarianism." Who knows? And even if the Chinese do eventually accept some form of the Shanghai argument for capitalism, who can guarantee that the practice of its economic theories will lead to prosperity for China or even for Shanghai itself?

Yet, if nothing else, the unexpected reemergence of a bourgeois alternative, even in mutated form, does tell us that a new and fierce ideological debate over the basic truths of economics is taking place in communist China. Mao the philosopher was right. Ideas can change history for the better. But in the hands of men who have the power to misuse them, they can also be deadly. The Chinese realized that long ago. Now the forces unleashed by the great debate over economics may force the Chinese, rulers and ruled alike, to confront the very nature of their entire system, not only its economics but also its politics, in a way they never have, and perhaps have never wanted to before. The stakes are enormous. If the Chinese make the wrong choices, they may well lose their last chance for a more prosperous – and freer – future.

NOTES

1. D. K. Lieu, *The Growth and Industrialization of Shanghai* (Shanghai: China Institute of Pacific Relations, 1936).
2. Joseph Fewsmith, *Party, State, and Local Elites in Republican China* (Honolulu: University of Hawaii Press, 1985).
3. Tang Tsou, "Introduction," in *The Cultural Revolution and Post-Mao Reforms: A Historical Perspective* (Chicago: University of Chicago Press, 1986), p. xxxii.
4. Staff reporters, "Shanghai zhi jingji diwei ji qi fazhang wenti" (Shanghai's economic position and its problems of development), *Shanghai zongshanghui yuebao* (hereafter *SHZSHYB*) (Monthly Journal of the Shanghai General Chamber of Commerce), 7, no. 5 (May 1927): 10, under heading *Shuping*.
5. Tang Tsou, "Reflections on the Formation and Foundation of the Communist Party-State," in *Cultural Revolution*, p. 261.
6. Marie-Claire Bergere, "The Other China: Shanghai from 1919 to 1949," in Christopher Howe, ed., *Shanghai, Revolution and Development in an Asian Metropolis* (Cambridge University Press, 1981), pp. 12–14.
7. See Marie-Claire Bergere, "The Chinese Bourgeoisie, 1911–37," in John K. Fairbank, ed., *The Cambridge History of Modern China. Vol. 12: Republican China 1912–49, Part One* (Cambridge University Press, 1983), for a historical overview of that period.
8. See Fewsmith, *Party*, for a detailed history of the Chamber's internal conflicts.
9. Guo Binwen, "Zongshanghui yuebao chuangkan yizhounian jinian" (In commemoration of the first anniversary of the Monthly Journal of the Shanghai General Chamber of Commerce), *SHZSHYB* 2, no. 7 (July 1922): 1.
10. Wu Yingtu, "Weichi jiaotong fangfa ruhe?" (What way is there to maintain communications?), *SHZSHYB* 5, no. 3 (March 1925): 14–15, under heading *Shuping*; Hu Jingxiu, "Zhongguo gongshangye buzhen zhi zhengjie" (The crucial reasons for the lethargy of Chinese industry and commerce), *SHZSHYB* 6, no. 6 (June 1926): 11–20, under heading *Yanlun*.
11. Tong Mengzheng, "Jiaoyisuo zhi jiancha zhidu" (The system of inspection

in the exchanges), *SHZSHYB* 5, no. 2 (February 1925): 11, under heading *Zhuanlun*.

12. Min Zhishi, "Tichang guohuo shengzhong zhi chuangban shiye jihua" (The plan to create industry in the midst of calling for the promotion of national goods), *SHZSHYB* 5, no. 7 (July 1925): 15, under heading *Shuping*.

13. Nie Yuntai, "Lun shengchan jiuguo" (On saving the nation through production), *SHZSHYB* 5, no. 12 (December 1925): 4, under heading *Shuping*.

14. Ru Xuan, "Xingyinghangtuan yu jingji guafen" (The international consortium and economic division), *SHZSHYB* 1, no. 6 (December 1921): 1–12, under heading *Yanlun*.

15. Yu Qiaqing, "Duiyu Zhongri qinshan zhi yijian" (My view on Sino–Japanese friendship), *SHZSHYB* 6, no. 6 (June 1926): 4, under heading *Yanlun*.

16. Bo Chu, "Caili jiashui wenti" (The problem of reducing the Likin and increasing the tariffs), *SHZSHYB* 2, no. 8 (August 1922): 3, under heading *Yanlun*.

17. Tsou, "Reflections," p. 265.

18. Tsou offers very perceptive insights into why, in the wake of the May Fourth movement, the Marxist-Leninist version of socialism was accepted by many radical Chinese intellectuals: Tsou, "Reflections," pp. 262–263.

19. [Deng] Zhibing, "Zhongguo laogong yu ziben zhi genben de xietiao" (The basic compromise between Chinese labor and capital), *SHZSHYB* 7, no. 2 (February 1927): 2–3, under heading *Shuping*.

20. Lu Fuzhou, "Zailun Zhongguo gongye yu gongchao" (Again on China's industries and strikes), *SHZSHYB* 7, no. 3 (March 1927): 12, under heading *Shuping*.

21. [Deng] Zhibing, "Shanghuifa xiugai wenti" (Problems in revising the laws on chambers of commerce), *SHZSHYB*, 7, no. 7 (July 1927): 20.

22. Christopher Howe, "Industrialization under Conditions of Long-run Population Stability: Shanghai's Achievement and Prospect," in Howe, ed., *Shanghai*, pp. 169–170.

23. David S. Goodman, "The Shanghai Connection: Shanghai's Role in National Politics During the 1970s," in Howe, ed., *Shanghai*.

24. Peter Moller Christensen, "The Shanghai School and Its Rejection," in Stephen Feuchtwang and Athar Hussain, eds., *The Chinese Economic Reforms* (London: Croom Helm, 1983).

25. Tang Tsou, "Back from the Brink of Revolutionary-'Feudal' Totalitarianism," in *Cultural Revolution*, p. 147.

26. Tsou, "Reflections," p. 302.

27. World Bank, *China: Socialist Economic Development, the Main Report* (Washington, DC: World Bank Documents, 1981); Joan Robinson, *Economic Management in China 1972* (London: Anglo-Chinese Educational Institute, 1973); John Kenneth Galbraith, *A China Passage* (New York: Paragon House, 1989).

28. Zeng Huiyan, "Tamen yidian juewu dou meiyou – Wu Tianming de wusi jianghua" (They have learned nothing – Wu Tianming's May Fourth address), *Jiushi niandai* (The Nineties) (June 1989): 87.

29. Dorothy S. Solinger, *Chinese Business Under Socialism* (Berkeley: University of California Press, 1984), pp. 215–216.

30. Arif Dirlik, "Postsocialism? Reflections on 'Socialism with Chinese Characteristics,'" *Bulletin of Concerned Asian Scholars* 21, no. 1 (1989): 40.

31. Xu Xiaoming, "Qianyi chenggong guanggao de hengliang biaozhun" (A

simple discussion of standards of measurement for successful advertising), *Shanghai qiye* (hereafter *SHQY*) (Shanghai Enterprise), no. 4 (1987): 44.

32. Wei Guan, "Shanghai qiye tizhi gaige de fansi yu shenhua gaige de shexiang" (Reflections on Shanghai's reform of the enterprise system and some ideas for deepening the reform), *Shehui kexue* (hereafter *SHKX*) (Social Sciences) (Shanghai), no. 5, (1987): 32.

33. Tsou, "Reflections," pp. 299–302.

34. Jiang Xuemo, "Lun woguo shehuizhuyi chuji jieduan de siyouzhi" (On private ownership in the primary stage of socialism in China), *SHKX*, no. 11 (1987): 85.

35. See, for example, the outspoken Su Shaozhi's observations on the Hungarian and Yugoslav economies: "A Chinese View on the Reform of the Economic Mechanism in Hungary," in Peter Van Ness, ed., *Market Reforms in Socialist Societies, Comparing China and Hungary* (Boulder: Lynne Rienner, 1989), pp. 194–211.

36. See the collection of essays, written in Chinese, but published in English, in Arnold Chao and Lin Wei, eds., *China's Economic Reforms* (Philadelphia: University of Pennsylvania Press, 1982), for a sense of the feeling among many Chinese economists that their country was facing almost unlimited possibilities.

37. One can find some of the best and most scholarly works in that regionalist body of writing in the publications of the Shanghai Academy of Social Sciences (SASS). Also closely affiliated with the academy was the *World Economic Herald*.

38. Look, for instance, at the second issue of *Guangdong shehui kexue* (Guangdong Social Science) in 1986. It was packed with papers that had been selected from a symposium on the relationship between Guangdong and Hong Kong in the coming century.

39. Louise do Rosario, "Red Light, Green Light," *Far Eastern Economic Review*, April 21, 1988, pp. 70–73, was a representative report that showed the growing perception in the foreign press of Shanghai's economic woes.

40. Rhoads Murphey's *Shanghai, Key to Modern China* (Cambridge: Harvard University Press, 1953) was published in Chinese translation as *Shanghai – xiandai Zhongguo de yaochi* in 1986 and reprinted in 1987 by the Shanghai Academy of Social Sciences.

41. Andrew Shonfield, *Modern Capitalism* (London: Oxford University Press, 1969), p. 3.

42. Nie Yuntai, "Lun shengchan jiuguo," p. 4.

43. Yong Wenyuan, "A Probe into a Socialist Political Economy," in *SASS Papers 1986* (Shanghai: Shanghai Academy of Social Sciences, 1986), p. 6.

44. Tsou, "Reflections," p. 291.

45. Hu Jingxiu, "Zhongguo gongshangye buzhen zhi zhengjie (xu)" (The crucial reasons for the lethargy of Chinese industry and commerce, part two), *SHZSHYB* 6, no. 8 (August 1926): 15–16, under heading *Shuping*.

46. Ibid., p. 11.

47. Ming Qi, "Jingji gongkai yu zhishi tantao" (Economic openness and intellectual exploration), *SHZSHYB* 5, no. 6 (May 1926): 3, under heading *Shuping*.

48. Lu Fuzhou, "Zhongguo gongye yu gongchao" (Chinese industry and strikes), *SHZSHYB* 6, no. 4 (April 1926): 9, under heading *Shuping*.

49. Li Yunliang, "Yongren fangzhenlun" (On the guiding principles for making

proper use of people), *SHZSHYB* 6, no. 3 (March 1926): 16, under heading *Shuping*.

50. Xu Kun, "Lixiang shi zhiye daode jianshe de qiandao" (An ideal is the forerunner in building up professional ethics), *SHKX*, no. 5 (1987): 14.
51. Ma Mingbi, "Guanlizhe geti xingwei yingxiangli" (The influence of the individual behavior of managers), *Rencai kaifa* (hereafter *RCKF*) (Talent Exploitation), no. 7 (1988): 3.
52. Zhang Ruihua, "Lun qiye wenhua" (A tentative study of corporate culture), *SHKX*, no. 12 (1987): 33–36.
53. " 'Bentian' de jingji quanli" (The management and administration of Honda), *SHQY*, no. 1 (1987): 43–44; Shen Weijin, "Feifan de Mali Kai" (The extraordinary Mary Kay), *SHQY*, no. 3 (1987): 43–44; "Zenmo shide Suoni gongsi lianlian deshou" (How Sony Corporation had success after success), *SHQY*, no. 6 (1987): 43–44.
54. Qian Xiaoming, "Lun jindai Shanghai de qiyejia" (On the entrepreneurs of modern Shanghai), in *Zhongguo jindai jingjishi yanjiu ziliao* (hereafter *ZGJDJISYJZL*) (Research Materials on the Modern Economic History of China), no. 8 (1987): 109.
55. Yu Qiaqing, "Duiyu guoji jingji jingzheng zhi ganxiang" (My thoughts on international economic competition), *SHZSHYB* 5, no. 12 (December 1925): 1, under heading *Shuping*.
56. See Albert O. Hirschman, *The Passions and the Interests* (Princeton: Princeton University Press, 1978), for an enlightening study of the development of that idea in Europe.
57. Hu Jingxiu, "Zhongguo gongshangye buzhen zhi zhengjie (xu)," p. 13.
58. See, for instance, Qiao Xiaoming, "Lun jindai Shanghai de qiyejia," pp. 92–94; Huang Hanmin and Xu Weiyong, *Rongjia qiye fazhanshi* (The history of the development of the Rong family enterprises) (Beijing: Renmin chubanshe, 1985), p. 307; and Xu Dingxin, "Jindai Shanghai xinjiu liangdai minzu zibenjia shenceng jiegou de toushi" (A perspective on the deeply stratified structure of the two generations, the old and the new, of the national bourgeoisie in modern Shanghai), *Shanghai shehui kexueyuan xueshu jikan* (hereafter *SHSHKYXSJK*) (Quarterly Journal of the Shanghai Academy of Social Sciences), no. 4 (1988): 49.
59. Ding Richu, "Guanyu duiwai jingji guanxi yu Zhongguo jindaihua" (On foreign economic relations and China's modernization), *ZGJDJISYJZL*, no. 8 (1987): 30.
60. Zhen De, "Siyou caichan zhidu yanjiu" (A study of the system of private ownership), *SHZSHYB* 6, no. 8 (August 1926): 5, under heading *Zhuanlun*.
61. See Fewsmith, *Party*, pp. 101–103, for a discussion of the Guomindang's views on private property.
62. Jiang Xuemo, "Lun woguo shehuizhuyi chuji jieduan de siyouzhi," p. 14.
63. In the late 1950s and early 1960s, Chinese historians embraced a much darker vision of Shanghai's entrepreneurs, preferring to stress above all else the financial instability of Shanghai capitalism and the exploitation of the workers. See, for example, Zhongguo kexue yuan Shanghai jingji yanjiusuo, ed., *Hengfeng shachang de fasheng fazhan yu gaizao* (The birth, development, and reform of Hengfeng Cotton Mill) (Shanghai: Renmin chubanshe, 1959), and Shanghai shehui kexue yuan jingji yanjiusuo, ed., *Rongjia qiye shiliao* (Historical materials on the enterprises of the Rong family) (Shanghai: Renmin chubanshe, 1962). Compare the tone of those studies with

the much more laudatory and far less accusatory themes in the articles on the old Shanghai bourgeoisie that were published in the 1980s in such periodicals as *Shanghai Economic Science* and *Research Materials on the Modern Economic History of China*.

64. Fang Jiaobo, "Ying ruhe dizhi waihuo tichang guoho" (How to boycott foreign goods and promote native ones), *SHZSHYB* 5, no. 6 (June 1925): 2, under heading *Shuping*.
65. Zhi Hua, "Shangye yu zhengfu" (Commerce and the government), *SHZSHYB* 6, no. 5 (May 1926): 7, under heading *Jiangyan*.
66. Xu Weiyong and Huang Hanmin, *Rongjia giye fazhanshi*, p. 310.
67. Zong Han, "Laodongzhe shi guojia he qiye de zhuren" (The laborer is the master of the nation and the enterprise), *SHKX*, no. 3 (1987): 17.
68. Xu Hakuo, "Shehuizhuyi de laodongli liudong he laodongli shichang" (The flow of the socialist labor force and market), *SHKX*, no. 2 (1986): 36.
69. Zhou Wenfu, "Lun shehuizhuyi laodongli shichang he laodongli de shang-binxing" (On the socialist labor market and the commodity nature of the labor force), *SHKX*, no. 8 (1986): 37.
70. Lu Baorong and Chen Xiumei, "Shanghai siren jingji ruogan wenti tantao" (A probe into some problems in Shanghai's private economy), *SHKX*, no. 9 (1986): 42.
71. H. D. Fong, *Industrial Organization in China* (Tianjin: Nankai Institute of Economics, 1937); D. K. Lieu, *China's Industries and Finance* (Shanghai: Chinese Government Bureau of Economic Information, n.d.); Akira Nagano, *The Development of Capitalism in China* (Tokyo: Japan Council of the Institute of Pacific Relations, 1931).
72. [Deng] Zhibing, "Qiyejia yu zibenjia" (Entrepreneurs and capitalists), *SHZSHYB* 2, no. 11 (November 1922): 4, under heading *Yanlun*.
73. A good history of the early Japanese defense of capitalism is that by Byron K. Marshall, *Capitalism and Nationalism in Prewar Japan* (Stanford: Stanford University Press, 1967); a classic study of American views is Reinhard Bendix's *Work and Authority in Industry* (Berkeley: University of California Press, 1974).
74. Hu Jingxiu, "Zhongguo gongshangye buzhen zhi zhengjie (xu)."
75. Tu Lianghuai, "Ta bei shouyu 'quanguo youxiu guanlizhe' de haocheng – ji Shanghai wenti jinchukou gongsi jingli Zhang Lansan" (He has been given the title of "[one of] the nation's outstanding manager[s]" – Notes on Zhang Lansan, the director of the Sports and Recreation Import-Export Company), *SHQY*, no. 7 (1987): 19–21. Qi Hantang, "Cishi bugan, geng dai heshi – ji Shanghaigang meitie zhuangxie gongsi jingli Qin Shigeng" (If not now, when? Notes on Qin Shigeng, the director of the Shanghai Harbor Coal Loading and Unloading Company), *SHQY*, no. 11 (1987): 12–14.
76. Jia Songqing, "Qiyejia bu shi 'guanyuan jingli' " (Entrepreneurs are not state officials), *RCKF*, no. 7 (1988): 19.
77. Qian Xiaoming, "Lun jindai Shanghai de qiyejia," p. 113.
78. Yu Liangxin, "Shijie faming qishi" (A world-class inventor knight), *RCKF*, no. 8 (1988): 31.
79. Shu Qui, "Zichanjieji zhi zijue" (The self-consciousness of the bourgeoisie), *SHZSHYB* 2, no. 12 (December 1922): 14, under heading *Yanlun*.

80. [Deng] Zhibing, "Qiyejia yu zibenjia" (Entrepreneurs and capitalists), *SHZSHYB* 2, no. 11 (November 1922): 2, under heading *Yanlun*.

81. Wang Zhiwei, "Zhongguo gongshang bujiu zhi fangfa" (The method of remedying Chinese industry and commerce), *SHZSHYB* 3, no. 9 (September 1923): 20, under heading *Yanlun*.

82. Hu Jingxiu, "Zhongguo gongshangye buzhen zhi zhengjie (xu)."

83. Wang Zhiwei, "Zhongguo gongshang bujiu zhi fangfa."

84. Jiang Xuemo, "Lun woguo shehuizhuyi chuji jieduan de siyouzhi," p. 14.

85. Jia Songqing, "Qiyejia bu shi 'guanyuan jingli'," p. 19.

86. Chen Liyi and Pan Junxiang, "Shilun Shanghai jindai shangye de tedian jiqi fazhan yuanyin" (A tentative study on the characteristics and the reasons for the development of Shanghai's modern commerce), *SHSHKYXSJK*, no. 1 (1987): 70.

87. Qian Xiaoming, "Lun jindai Shanghai de qiyejia."

88. Hu Jingxiu, "Zhongguo gongshangye buzhen zhi zhengjie (xu)."

89. Chen Minzi and Yao Xitang, "Strategic Target Options for the Economic Development of Shanghai," in *SASS Papers 1986*, p. 93.

90. Dai Jin, "Jianli yi Shanghai wei zhongxin de Changjiang sanjiaozhou cheng-zhen tixi" (Building a network of cities and towns in the Yangtze River delta with Shanghai as its hub), *SHSHKYXSJK*, no. 4 (1986): 77–78.

91. For instance, Xu Dingxin, an economic historian in the Shanghai Academy of Social Sciences, was doing pioneering research on the Chamber; Yang Liqiang and She Weibin, both historians at Fudan University, were compiling a collection of primary materials on the Chamber.

92. Peter Brimelow, "Why Liberalism Is Now Obsolete, An Interview with Nobel Laureate Milton Friedman," *Forbes*, December 12, 1988, p. 162.

93. Jerry Z. Muller, "Capitalism: The Wave of the Future," *Commentary* 86, no. 6 (December 1988): 22.

94. Tsou, "Reflections," p. 262.

95. Ezra Vogel, *One Step Ahead in China, Guangdong Under Reform* (Cambridge: Harvard University Press, 1989).

96. A strong sense that the hinterland and treaty ports like Shanghai lived in two different worlds is given by Rhoads Murphey, *The Treaty Ports and China's Modernization: What Went Wrong?* (Ann Arbor: Michigan Papers in China Studies, 1970), the first draft of what eventually became his contribution on the subject to *The Cambridge History of Modern China*.

97. Tang Tsou, "The Values of the Chinese Revolution," in Michel Oksenberg, ed., *China's Development Experience* (New York: Praeger, 1973), p. 40.

98. Janusz Bufajski, "Solidarity's Second Coming," *The New Republic*, July 17 and 24, 1989, p. 36.

99. [Deng] Zhibing, "Lieqiang duiyu Zhongguo gongshangye shang zhi menhu kaifang wenti" (The problem of the industrial and commercial open door policy of the great powers), *SHZSHYB* 2, no. 2 (February 1922): 13, under heading *Yanlun*.

100. See, for instance, Jiang Enci, "On Statutory Protection and Encouragement Given to Foreign Investments in the People's Republic of China," in *SASS Papers 1986*, pp. 272–273.

101. Wang Zhiping, "A Brief Discussion of Public-Commodity Economy," in *SASS Papers 1986*, p. 85.

102. The characteristics of that relationship have long been debated by Marxist and non-Marxist scholars. See the *dependencia* view in Jose J. Villamil,

ed., *Transnational Capitalism and National Development* (Atlantic Highlands: Humanities Press, 1979), and a more orthodox approach in Raymond Vernon, *Sovereignty at Bay* (New York: Basic Books, 1971).

103. John E. Roemer, *Free to Lose* (Cambridge: Harvard University Press, 1988), pp. 63–64.

104. Alec Nove, *The Economics of Feasible Socialism* (London: Allen & Unwin, 1983).

105. Richard Smith, "Teng's Reforms, Neither Market Nor Socialism," *Against the Current*, no. 22 (1989): 32–33.

106. Robert Wade, "The Role of Government in Overcoming Market Failure," in Helen Hughes, ed., *Achieving Industrialization in East Asia* (Cambridge University Press, 1988).

107. John C. H. Fei, Gustav Ranis, and Shirley W. Y. Kuo, *Growth with Equity, The Taiwan Case* (London: Oxford University Press, 1979).

108. Gary S. Fields, "Industrialization and Employment in Hong Kong, Korea, Singapore, and Taiwan," in Walter Galenson, ed., *Foreign Trade and Investment, Economic Development in the Newly Industrializing Asian Countries* (Madison: University of Wisconsin Press, 1985), p. 351.

109. Zeng Huiyan, "Tamen yidian juewu dou meiyou – Wu Tianming de wusi jianghua," p. 87.

110. Tsou, "Totalitarianism," p. 179.

111. Tang Tsou, "Political Change and Reform: The Middle Course," in *Cultural Revolution*, pp. 221–222.

112. That view is developed by Douglass C. North and Robert Paul Thomas, *The Rise of the Western World: A New Economic History* (Cambridge University Press, 1973); and Nathan Rosenberg and L. E. Birdzell, Jr., *How the West Grew Rich* (New York: Basic Books, 1986).

113. Hirschman, *Passions*, p. 3.

114. Tsou, "Reflections," pp. 331–332.

115. See Brantly Womack's and Marc Blecher's chapters in this volume for discussions of the political transition in China.

PART II

Policy dynamics within the People's Republic of China

4

The contradictions of grass-roots participation and undemocratic statism in Maoist China and their fate

MARC BLECHER

One of the many unresolved puzzles regarding the political system of the Maoist period, resolution of which may also provide a key to understanding the Dengist transformation of it,[1] concerns the nature of grassroots political participation in the countryside and its relationship to the highly undemocratic character[2] of the larger state and state–society relations. The puzzle has three parts. First, there persist in the literature on local politics and participation some rather contradictory findings and arguments: Local politics was lively and dead, participants were active and passive, participation was spontaneous and mobilized, genuine and ritualistic. Second, if there was some significant political participation, how can that be reconciled with the highly undemocratic nature of the state edifice that rested upon it? Third, how can that fit with what appears to be the very rapid collapse of direct participatory institutions and practices following Mao Zedong's death? Resolution of these conundra may help illuminate the nature of the Dengist state and reflect upon its prospects and those of China in the current period of crisis, in which the question of popular participation in politics has once again been thrust into the foreground.

This is a revised version of a paper presented at the Conference on Contemporary Chinese Politics in Historical Perspective, celebrating Tang Tsou's seventieth birthday, held at the University of Chicago on December 16, 1988. Thanks are due to the Department of Political Science of the University of Chicago, and in particular to Chris Achen, for sponsoring that memorable event. Brantly Womack undertook the arduous work of organizing the conference, and also offered sympathetic and incisive criticisms of the first draft of this essay. Other participants in the conference – notably Ed Friedman, Hong Yung Lee, Mitch Meisner, and Suzanne Rudolph – also made most welcome suggestions. The National Endowment for the Humanities provided the funding to support me (grant FB–25930–88) during the time this chapter was being written. Probably my greatest debt is to Professor Tang Tsou, for seeing me through the dissertation to which these musings are afterthoughts, and for being a teacher and scholar of exemplary brilliance, wisdom, and sensitivity.

Marc Blecher

THE DEBATE ON VILLAGE POLITICS
AND PARTICIPATION

The first "view" concerning village politics and participation in China was actually a nonview. Scholarship during the 1950s and most of the 1960s simply did not pay attention to it. Like the sound of the tree that falls out of earshot, it did not exist. One can only lament the absence of contemporary studies of the grass-roots politics of cooperativization, the Great Leap Forward, or the Socialist Education Movement. But partly because of the ideological, analytical, and methodological paradigms of the day, and partly because of the absence of a solid empirical base, most China scholars writing in the 1950s and early 1960s paid little attention to village politics, either ignoring them or producing cursory accounts based on a few official documents concerning model units.[3] In later years, valuable retrospective accounts were published by William Hinton, based on his unique opportunity for participant observation, by Jan Myrdal, based on his field research opportunity, and by Vivienne Shue, using local newspapers of the day.[4]

Once Western scholars began to acknowledge the existence of political participation in the Chinese countryside and turn their attention to it, a second view quickly emerged: It amounted mainly to mass mobilization by the leadership around issues defined and controlled by the elites. Consequently, participants engaged in it reluctantly, passively, disinterestedly, and ritualistically. Mobilization was the major theme of James Townsend's work,[5] which set the tone for much thinking and analysis by those who actually began to look at the Chinese grass roots.[6] Martin Whyte's book on political study groups was perhaps the most fully developed and influential example of that approach.[7] It emphasized the ritualistic character of popular participation. In that view, participation had more to do with downward communication from the leadership and with the exercise of social control by the state than with expression of interest upward. Chinese participants adapted by learning to dissemble, feign interest, recite expected slogans, and put on a show of contrition and self-criticism. That conception accorded well with several major characteristics of the Chinese state, such as its manifestly undemocratic character, its high level of politicization, and its palpable orientation to rapid, fundamental transformation of its own leaders and people.

A third view emerged out of unease with the elitist theory of Chinese politics that had informed the first view (or nonview), as well as unease with much of the political theory and general analysis then dominant. It had various sources: the new social history's insistence on putting the people back into analysis; the democratic proclivities and convictions of a new generation of scholars, which found resonances in Chinese revolutionary theory and practice; the rise of the pluralist paradigm in U.S. political science; and the published work of Hinton and Myrdal, which suggested a different China in need of further study.

Tang Tsou's thinking provided indispensable tools for that work. First, and absolutely crucially, he drew a distinction between the mass line and mass mobilization, which the second view had conflated. As he has recently formulated it,

the term "Left" denotes the emphasis on Mao's new tenet of historical materialism [giving priority under certain circumstances to the superstructure over the base], revolutionary theory, revolutionary impulse, class struggle, coercive power, *mass mobilization*, and the political penetration of society. Correspondingly, the term "Right" refers to the emphasis on the notion of unity of theory and practice, the slogan of "seeking truth from facts," prudent respect for reality, the *mass line*, persuasion, the perceived interests and felt needs of social groups and individuals, and the energies flowing from civil society.[8]

In contrast to the mass line, mass movements and mobilization were merely means of waging class struggle, implementing radical policies, or fighting among Party factions. The recent reemphasis of the mass line on the one hand and abandonment of mass movements on the other enable us to see this distinction clearly.[9]

Second, he stressed that the rural origins of the Chinese Revolution imparted a definite popular streak to Chinese politics:

In trying to capture power and to make a social revolution, the CCP had to establish intimate links with the various social groups and strata ... [I]t gradually developed a satisfactory relationship with society by adopting a series of moderate policies which took adequately into account ... the perceived interests of the various groups and individuals without sacrificing its fundamental revolutionary goals.[10]

Third, Professor Tsou has always emphasized that "an outside observer must take seriously the ideas, viewpoints, perceptions and pronouncements of the participants whose actions he is studying."[11] That qualified Maoist phenomena such as the mass line and the local political practices associated with it as subjects worthy of scholarly analysis, at a time when many Western scholars were dismissing them as mere cant.[12]

The new approach posed questions about how production teams made decisions on matters that comprised the stuff of basic existence and daily life, such as production, distribution, investment, leadership selection, and planning. It raised issues about the relationship of the state to society. Did peasants have ways of communicating their views to the leadership at higher levels of state power? Could they choose their own leaders to represent them? Did the peasants or their local leaders exercise any effective influence over state policies that affected them? Did they constrain the making of such policies? Could they protect themselves against the state by blocking policy implementation? Was the posture of the state toward grass-roots society one of authoritarian or totalitarian domination, one of flexibility and receptivity, or something in between?

The findings of the new research challenged both the nonview and the dominant second view.[13] Village-level politics were found to be alive and well, full of spontaneous and often furiously contentious participation. Village politics contained both regular, institutionalized channels of popular expression (such as team and brigade meetings, "big-character posters," and mass organizations) and informal but no less important channels (such as evening "bull sessions" with cadres, grapevines, and rumor mills, and direct personal contacts with local officials). Such channels were in use broadly and actively. Even at brigade- and commune-level meetings, which might have been expected to be less participatory, "lots of people spoke out. After the . . . cadres [leading the meeting] stated their view, you could raise opinions in agreement or disagreement."[14] Popular participation was rather broad; it was uncorrelated with wealth or income, and the participatory pattern was shaped mainly by formal class background (former landlords were excluded systematically, but rich peasants were not) and gender (women participated less extensively than men, of course).[15] It could often be effective. In my own study I found that decisions in 38 percent of the cases of local political issues were made on the basis of proposals first raised by ordinary peasants, whereas in 43 percent of cases, opposition by peasants either modified or blocked proposals made by cadres or other peasants.[16] Ordinary peasants played a more significant role than team or higher-level cadres in nominating and electing team cadres, including team heads.[17] In addition, team leadership represented a range of social and political groups. Only half were party members.[18] Skilled and unskilled, literate and illiterate, educated and uneducated, male and female, rich and poor, old and young, former officeholders and political novices, former soldiers and civilians were all represented (to be sure, in varying, but in no case insignificant, degrees).[19] And where all else failed, peasants had numerous means at their disposal to protect themselves against unpopular state policies, by blocking implementation and engaging in subterfuge and even outright sabotage.[20]

Moreover, the state itself frequently adopted and even institutionalized a much more flexible and solicitous approach to grass-roots society than had previously been thought. Rather than merely waiting for the peasants to express or represent themselves, the Maoist state undertook a wide range of activities that *sought out* the peasantry's views to give local state officials a clear picture of and personal experience with the existential situations faced by the peasants.[21] Those included institutionalized practices such as "squatting on a spot" (*dun dian*), investigation (*diaocha*), the "four togethernesses" (*si tong*, in which cadres actually moved into peasants' homes for periods of time to live, eat, sleep, and work with them), "on-the-spot conferences" (*xian chang huiyi*), participation in manual labor (*canjia laodong*), and the dispatch of work teams (*gongzuo dui*). In more informal ways, too, such as by calling on those who were silent at meetings, dropping by the homes of neighbors, or chatting up peasants whom they encountered in the fields or along the road, local cadres sought out the views of their fellow villagers. Those practices often brought into the public realm opinions that were not being expressed through participatory channels. For example, they provided a way to tap the experience of former landlords and rich peasants and elicit the views of those reluctant to speak out, such as elderly peasants who still had not grown accustomed to the new participatory local politics, and members of minority lineage groups.[22] That sort of political solicitation could also set in motion a dialectic of drawing new groups into participatory politics, in ways not only mobilizational and co-optive but also democratic, spontaneous, and expressive of popular sentiments and concerns.[23] Vivienne Shue's study of cooperativization also found the state to have taken a pliable posture toward the peasantry, one that was open to and encouraging of popular views and that often was self-critical.[24]

Whereas all this evidence discredited the first nonview that local popular politics and participation did not exist, was insignificant, or was not worthy of study, its relationship to the second view of local politics as mainly mobilizational and ritualistic remains a key problem, for the second view was not wrong, though it may have been incomplete. But how did the statist elements and the participatory elements, the empty gestures and the real expressions, the dissimulation and the heartfelt fire of local politics interact? With what effects? By approaching these questions, light may be thrown on the deeper dynamics of the Chinese state and its politics in the Maoist period as they culminated in the Cultural Revolution decade and then were *aufgehoben* in the Dengist period and, in turn, its time of crisis.

THE MATERIAL BASIS OF PARTICIPATORY LOCAL POLITICS IN THE COUNTRYSIDE DURING THE REVOLUTIONARY AND MAOIST PERIODS, AND THEIR DECAY

This discussion begins with the following set of working hypotheses: First, *the formation of grass-roots institutions that unified politics with economics fostered the development of a grass-roots politics that was genuinely participatory.* To put it somewhat differently, *participation*

*flourished when the basic issues of productive, material life that affected
the Chinese peasantry were made legitimate and accessible subjects of
politics within local institutions that infused residential communities with
broad economic functions.* Second, under specific conditions, *such politics could evince a tendency toward radicalism,* at some times developing
from its own internal dynamics, and at other times arising from its relationship to a radical and popular state leadership. Third, *the degree
and radicalism of local participation withered as those institutions and
the politics of material life that they engendered were decomposed and
displaced by politics that were increasingly irrelevant and even damaging
to material life.*

The first hypothesis combines materialist and institutional approaches
to political participation. The former argues that material issues of productive and consumptive life have great salience in general, and thus the
quantity and breadth of political participation are likely to be positively
correlated with their presence in politics. The latter assumes that political
participation often requires possessing and expending resources and
overcoming obstacles, and it argues that the quantity and breadth of
political participation are positively correlated with the reduction or
equalization of required resources and the removal of obstacles.[25] In
China, those two changes went hand in hand. When the revolutionary
movement organized itself in the institutions of grass-roots politics within
the basic levels of social and economic organization, it was better able
to politicize economic life. At the same time, those institutions blossomed
because they were vessels containing politics of the basic existential concerns and problems facing the peasantry, such as, in historical sequence,
rent, interest, land ownership, and collective management of production,
and, over all those stages, income and livelihood.[26]

The second hypothesis, concerning the radical tendencies of the new
local politics and institutions, has diverse theoretical origins. From public-
policy theory it can be posited that insofar as local policy had a redistributive character,[27] politics could be expected to engender class-based
political cleavages.[28] From hegemony theory can be drawn Ira Katznelson's finding that one of the key factors undercutting class-based politics
in American cities was the separation of workplace from residence, with
the concomitant that the state and popular participation in it became
organized around the latter and not the former.[29] A modified converse
is hypothesized here for the Chinese case: The formation of local political/
economic institutions that coincided with residential communities was,
depending on the substantive content of politics and policy and on the
prevailing class relations, a structural condition for the development of
class-based politics. Organization theory would point up the suitability
of a deeply and vertically organized structure, such as prevailed in rural

China, to mobilization from above; when the leadership turned radical, it possessed a powerful organizational weapon at the Chinese grass roots. And finally, theories of peasant society and politics would emphasize the potential, under certain conditions, for an insecure or frightened peasantry to engage in radical outbursts.[30]

The third hypothesis is the converse of the first, but also partly represents its dialectical transformation by the radical forces referred to in the second hypothesis. The displacement of material issues from the center of local politics was a result of the rise of a radical politics that abstracted so much from real life that politics eventually became lost in abstruse and ill-formed theoretical discussion, rhetoric, and polemics. The latter fueled factional politics that became detached from the concrete issues of economic and political power that had informed the radical critique in the first place. But the Cultural Revolution aside, there was another factor at work as well. Grass-roots participation was also weakened by the state, which, in arrogating broad economic control to itself, tightly circumscribed and marginalized the range of material issues that local collective units could decide.[31]

These hypotheses conform with some general features of the trajectory of local politics in revolutionary and postrevolutionary China. The development of popular grass-roots politics in rural China began in the struggles for reductions in rent and interest and eventually for land reform, economic issues that the peasants could not have experienced as more basic. Those occurred in local communities, where politics required few resources. They became radical for several reasons. First, the issues of the day were almost purely redistributive. Second, the residential community where politics took place was also the locus of exploitative landlord–peasant relations. Third, once things got going, peasants often evinced extremist tendencies in order to maximize their gains and minimize the chances of an eventual return of the landlords to power. Fourth, local politics radicalized when the party's policy did, as in the radical land reform of 1946–1947.

Later, still energetic, though less radical, local politics came to revolve around the management of collective economic affairs in the mutual-aid teams, but especially the agricultural cooperatives. Their vitality was due to the fact that they took place within the basic units of rural ownership, production management, investment, and distribution. That infused local politics with a substantive content affecting every peasant member's income and livelihood. It also rendered political participation accessible and low in resource requirements. That those issues were less purely redistributive, that the exploitative nature of class relationships had already diminished, and that party policy on class conflict had moderated all helped dull their radicalism.

The first hypothesis can also explain the apparent deterioration of participatory politics during the Great Leap and their subsequent resuscitation. Though the dominant slogan of the Great Leap was "politics in command" of the lifeblood economic issues of popular concern, the politics took place at loci (such as the commune and county seats) that were far removed from most peasants' experience and that required resources of time, information, and mobility, most peasants' lack of which constrained their capacity to act. Moreover, many basic economic decisions of popular existential concern simply were not being made. For example, income distribution was not occurring during the periods of collective dining halls and the times of dire economic straits that followed, when in many localities there was nothing to distribute.

With the completion of the institutional readjustments in the countryside after the Great Leap, in the form of the high level of collectivism,[32] the locus of grass-roots politics returned in the first half of the 1960s to the basic units of collective economic organization. There, economic life provided much of the substance of the participatory local politics that occurred during the Maoist period: debates about production planning and management, collective accumulation and investment, distribution, and so forth. Politics in the villages were also more accessible, and participation required fewer resources. That helped reenliven popular participation in the production teams and brigades. Yet, as argued later, local participation began to experience obstacles that restricted and would eventually undermine it.

These hypotheses can also explain the politics during the "high" Cultural Revolution in the technical work unit that Gordon White and I studied.[33] There, passionate, spontaneous, genuine political participation was driven by the unit members' deep-seated concerns about material issues, such as job and housing assignments, work transfers to reunite spouses, grievances about personnel policies, political interference with professional work, and personal grudges against officials who controlled material life. Local politics became quite radical, partly because those issues were largely redistributive, and partly because in the unit we studied, like virtually all others in China, political and economic authority coincided, which placed production and consumption, and the specific class politics that had grown up around them, squarely on the political agenda. Thus, at first, unit members were able to adapt the rhetorical and polemical mode of ideological discourse associated with the wider national movement and its left elite leadership (the critique of "party persons in authority taking the capitalist road" and such) to express their more mundane and palpable concerns. But as that radical discourse began to supplant the existential issues that had drawn unit members into participation in the movement, as the factional politics of the movement itself began to displace the politicization of material life that had catalyzed it in the first place, and concomitantly as the locus of political action and power shifted upward and outward from that small unit to the regional networks of Red Guard organizations and then to what was left of the state itself (in the form of the armed forces and the worker propaganda teams), many participants became disheartened, disillusioned, and angry. Radicalism shifted away from its material base onto an idealist plane of rhetoric, a mystified level of intrigue and revenge. Thus, many people gradually stopped participating.

Finally, these hypotheses help explain the conundrum raised at the outset concerning grass-roots political participation in the countryside under high collectivism, its relationship to the wider state, and its subsequent fate in the Dengist period. In the last decade of the Maoist period, insofar as village politics involved meaningful control over the local economy as exercised through the collectives, popular participation was active, genuine, spontaneous, and occasionally radical. Thus, peasants regularly participated in political deliberations about labor remuneration (the establishment and implementation of work-point systems, income distribution), micro-processes of production[34] (such as establishing a division of labor, implementing it, and managing actual production), collective expenditure on investment and welfare, leadership recruitment, private plots, collective entrepreneurship (e.g., animal husbandry or the operation of sideline enterprises), and the selection of villagers for scarce and valued opportunities (such as schooling, military service, or contract labor outside the village).

But at the same time, grass-roots participation was beginning to wither, for two reasons. First, as the agendas of local politics shifted away from the basic material preoccupations of the peasants and onto issues that they regarded as unimportant, outmoded, irrelevant, or simply incomprehensible, the peasants reacted with bewilderment and disinterest and responded with dissimulation and cynicism. That process probably began during the Socialist Education Movement, but reached its fullest development during the Cultural Revolution, with the appearance of small-group political study and campaigns to criticize Lin Biao and Confucius or to "clean class ranks" (*qingli jieji duiwu*), the latter of which attacked people who were identified as "class enemies" under official criteria that many peasants were coming to regard as reifications or anachronisms.[35] That tendency had developed so far that even the 1970 campaign to "attack one and oppose three" (*yi da san fan*; to "strike counter-revolutionaries and oppose corruption, speculation, and wasteful extravagance"), the last three elements of which should have evoked significant popular reaction at the material level, could not do so.[36] In terms of those arenas, the second view described earlier – that political participation in rural China consisted of mass mobilization and ritualism – is appropriate.

Second, popular participation suffered because of the ways in which the state circumscribed the ability of the localities to exercise political control over their economic affairs, retaining such power for itself. Examples abound. Peasants and leaders in grass-roots collectives had neither understanding of nor control over the prices at which they sold their products and purchased their inputs and consumption goods, even though those prices were set politically rather than by the invisible hand of an alienated, alienating market. Strict limits were set on production teams' latitude in making decisions about distribution, accumulation, planning, cropping, and economic diversification. Macro-economic planning was never put on the agenda for public deliberation and debate. China's peasants were not given the opportunity to learn through, much less participate in, public discussion about the problematical relationship between agriculture and industry in developing the economy as a whole. They were not consulted about the ratio between consumption and accumulation in the national economy, or even instructed about its effect on the pace of economic growth. They were not engaged in a colloquy about the pros and cons of local grain self-reliance, or China's role in the world economy and the very direct ways in which that matter affected them.[37]

The third hypothesis suggests that, starting probably in the early to middle 1960s and surely developing through the 1970s, peasants became increasingly aware of the limits placed by the state on their ability to control and shape their economic affairs. It can be surmised that over the last decade of the Maoist period, which saw repeated tinkering with various payment systems and political and developmental "lines" (trying out different local leaders and approaches to leadership, engaging in movement after movement, castigating enemy after enemy, and ventilating obstreperous rhetoric about class struggle, though class enemies were difficult to discern),[38] many peasants began to understand or at least sense that the key to development and economic progress, at a historical juncture when collective institutions had already been consolidated, lay in policies that were determined far beyond the village, such as the price structure, the administrative barriers to townward migration, and the restrictions on free commerce or the shortcomings of state-run commerce. To the extent that the village – which had been the locus of the peasantry's greatest victories in the participatory politics of the land reform and had been a lively terrain for politics exercised around economic interests during cooperativization and, to a lesser and declining degree, the high collectivist period – came to be understood by the peasants as a place where politics had a declining impact on material life, it is hypothesized that they became disillusioned with and ready to withdraw from vigorous participation in its affairs.

THE ROLE OF THE CULTURAL REVOLUTION

The Cultural Revolution was a climacteric in the development and decay of grass-roots participatory politics. Its radicalism and spontaneity were based in the local institutions of combined political and economic power and the participatory politics that had developed within them. The politicization of the basic issues of material life in the communes produced participatory politics and a set of institutions that could under certain conditions, such as the radicalization of a popular and indeed charismatic leadership at the center, become extremely destabilizing. At the risk of committing a functionalist error, it is reasonable to suppose that the Dengist leadership has recognized this point, which understanding in turn underpins its early and continuous insistence on separating politics and economics. In other words, perhaps the Dengists have understood that the combination of political and economic power in small communities was in China a condition for popular radicalism. At least they act as if they have such an understanding. From the perspective of historical sociology, during the Dengist period the Chinese peasantry has been atomized institutionally (through decollectivization) and, partly in consequence, tamed politically. In the 1940s, China's peasants rose up to overthrow their landlords; in the 1960s many rose up against their local leaders; but in 1989 they roundly and sincerely condemned popular uprisings against the state.[39] Dengism may yet provide another instance of the structurally conservatizing effects that can result from creation of a smallholding peasantry with security on the land. One of Dengism's historic achievements may well turn out to be the conversion of the vociferous, obstreperous peasants of the Chinese revolution at last into potatoes in the Marxist sack.[40]

But the high Cultural Revolution was, dialectically, also itself partly responsible for the decay in the local participatory politics on which it was based and which it manifested in extremis. As the participatory politics of the Cultural Revolution, which contained at its roots issues of class relations[41] and state–society relations, collapsed in upon themselves (i.e., as politics of abstract ideology and factional disputation took center stage on the political agenda, displacing the concrete material interests and issues that had motivated those politics in the first place), the movement gained intensity but lost popular resonance and appeal. Popular participation at the local level became fierce and fearsome, but also increasingly irrelevant to the ongoing issues of material life that had helped catalyze it.[42] Radicalism lost its appeal as it lost its material basis. The Cultural Revolution thus paved the way for the Dengists' attack on local participatory politics, while also shaping their overriding orientation to material improvement that has further deflected popular interest in politics.

THE CONTRADICTIONS OF POPULAR PARTICIPATION AND STATISM IN THE MAOIST AND DENGIST PERIODS AND BEYOND

Was grass-roots participation ever significant? Did it ever transcend the level of what Sidney Verba has called pseudo-democracy, with its palliative, co-optive, and mystifying functions?[43] As it became or was finally experienced as so tightly constrained by the state, did it matter at all? One line of response could be that local participatory politics can be important even if they do not eventuate in or contribute to broader democracy, because they help build community, foster civic education and awareness, and even stake out some concrete gains for participants, such as a modicum of control over and humanization of the workplace or the local bureaucracy.[44] Dormitory democracy is better than none at all, especially for people who live in dormitories. While agreeing with that position wholeheartedly, here I wish to take another, rather different tack: Grass-roots participation proved important precisely *because* it contradicted the highly undemocratic politics of the larger state within which it was situated. That is, *the coexistence of highly participatory local politics formed around basic existential questions, on the one hand, and undemocratic regional and national politics strongly affecting those same issues, on the other, formed a deep contradiction in the Chinese political system.*

Through the middle 1950s, when the honeymoon between the Chinese people and the socialist state was still being enjoyed and material life was improving, that contradiction had not yet developed. During the first half of the 1950s, grass-roots cooperatives and their participatory politics were being consolidated on the basis of appeal to the peasants' material interests.[45] Moreover, as noted earlier, those were days when the state was alive to grass-roots problems of material life as peasants expressed them. But the contradiction between local participation and statist politics began to emerge as the Great Leap undercut local cooperatives and wrought economic havoc, thereby damaging the peasants' faith in the ability of the state to formulate policy wisely and effectively. The state's response beginning in the early 1960s and continuing through the end of the Maoist period was not to open the polity at large to broader popular expression on matters of material concern, which could have had the incidental benefit of helping to shift part of the responsibility for the formulation and effects of policy off itself. Instead, in the countryside, it placed renewed emphasis on political mobilization (which canalized and circumscribed genuine participation) during the Socialist Education and Dazhai campaigns, while continuing to insist on its prerogative to set many of the most important parameters of economic policy that affected the peasants' material lives.

This did not destroy grass-roots participation, partly because the participatory practices and habits formed during and since the period of land reform had acquired a life of their own by that time, partly because the still-powerful Mao would have opposed that, and partly because doing so was beyond the capacity of the state, at least so long as the structural bases of popular participation – collective institutions formed around residential communities in which economics and politics were merged – remained intact. But it did affect village participatory politics in several ways. First, it marginalized local politics, which came to be focused on minor issues that the state had left to local discretion, such as whether to allocate 4 or 5 percent of income to the village welfare fund. Second, it infused local politics with a defensive character. Local meetings, elections, informal political discussions, big-character posters, letters, petitions, and other modes of participation were used increasingly to express discontent with state policy and officials, and often to evade or sabotage them. Third, flowing from the prior two points, local participatory politics became highly divisive, along the state–society cleavage as well as other lines of fracture running through society. Furious arguments broke out between neighbors over tenths of a "work point." Former class enemies were scapegoated. Local leaders who were deemed ineffective, corrupt, or who had the "wrong" surname in villages with living traditions of lineage conflict were vilified. Grumbling about higher-level officials and policies became commonplace.

That prepared the way for, found expression in, and in turn was reproduced by the spontaneous and radical (left) participation of the high Cultural Revolution, which raised radical (deep) questions about the state itself. I hypothesize that *its radicalism was a product of the concatenation of developed local participatory politics, a growing frustration with the economic policies of the state and the restrictions it placed on local participation in forming those policies, and the resulting divisiveness within society that local participation came to manifest and exacerbate.* It was a time when the participatory institutions and inclinations created during the revolution and cooperativization were gradually turned

141

against the state that had been their midwife in the first place. In other words, *the Cultural Revolution was the fullest culmination of the contradiction between participatory local politics and undemocratic statism.*

That eventually has found its *Aufhebung* in the Dengist climacteric, in which there are two contrasting themes. One is fundamentally nonparticipatory. In general, political control of the economy has been criticized in the most extreme terms. Specifically, collective institutions at the grass roots have been dismantled, and associated political fora and direct participatory processes destroyed. By all accounts, the villages (*cun*) and villagers' committees (*cunmin weiyuanhui*), successors to the production brigades and teams, respectively, rarely meet. Their key task of letting contracts under the responsibility system was controversial and may have elicited significant local participation for a time, but is now basically complete and subject to little alteration. They are in theory responsible for provision of infrastructure and collective services, but the decline of water-conservancy work and local educational and medical institutions suggests that they are not discharging those duties very well. There is no evidence yet that the rural enterprises are run by the villages in a participatory manner. The basic issues of material life, whose politicization was a key to the creation of the new participatory politics during the revolutionary and early socialist transition periods, have been re-privatized.[46] So there is much less for peasants to participate in, and fewer ways for them to participate in such issues as may remain on local agendas. In Hirschman's terms, when exit from the collectives became possible, peasants made for the door, taking their voices and loyalties with them.[47] This is also part and parcel of what Tang Tsou has described as the state expanding its zone of indifference toward civil society.[48]

A second theme is the regularization, institutionalization, and buffering of local political participation. Indirect political participation – in the form of elections to local assemblies – is to replace direct popular participation. Legal rights for participants are to be created and guaranteed. The party is being urged to restrain itself in making or influencing policy.[49] Progress on this front has been slow, especially in comparison with the Soviet Union and Eastern Europe. Such movement as has taken place has been located more heavily in the cities than in the villages. And the June 1989 events surely do not augur well for any future development of rural (or urban) political participation. Thus, politics has become *passé* to most peasants, who are now busying themselves more single-mindedly than at any time since 1949 with the opportunities and problems of making a living in individuated and, under the structural and political conditions that prevailed for most of the 1980s, politically conservatizing ways.[50]

Thus, Dengism is bringing major structural changes in China's mode of production, class structure, and state – the second set within less than half a century. The fact that the post-1978 changes have been structural reflects the structural character of the revolutionary transformations that preceded them and their attendant crises, a point that Tang Tsou has emphasized and developed.[51] The Dengist leadership is engaged in nothing so innocuous as simple "reform."[52] One question worth debating as we look back on the Maoist period is whether and how it could have been reformed – how, for example, a more durable participatory rural politics could have been molded. But if the opportunity to reform the revolution ever existed, it was squandered. Looking from the past to the present, Tang Tsou has characterized the Dengist position as claiming that " 'revolution' is reform."[53] It seems more appropriate to say that "reform" is not reform at all, but actually revolution (or counter-revolution).

But the term "counter-revolution," even if used analytically and unpolemically, is misleading. There can be no return to the economic, social, or political structures of prerevolutionary or even pre-Cultural Revolution days. For example, the Dengist state is founded on an agrarian structure different from any in recent Chinese history, a structure that is in fact one of the greatest achievements of the Chinese revolution, and it may turn out to be one of the most lasting: the elimination of landlordism as a mode of production, class structure, and political formation, and the creation in its place of what might be called a socialist (or at least noncapitalist) version of a middle-peasant economy, that is, an economy dominated by peasants with secure usufruct claim (if not clear title) to land, with definite limits to its commodification.[54] This provides the materiosocial basis for what Tang Tsou has called – in a coincidence that nevertheless has real resonances – "the middle course" in state leadership, institutions, and ideology.[55]

Insofar as this material base endures, it provides the Dengist state – conceptualized as a regime structure rather than as the specific coalition of Deng Xiaoping and his "hard-line" colleagues of mid-1989 – a source for the durability that Professor Tsou has anticipated.[56] In fact, this proposition may help account for what on the surface appear to be, and ultimately may turn out to be, the destabilizing events of April–June 1989. In undertaking its June offensive, the hard-line leadership understood its social base to be in the countryside (including the armed forces, which issued therefrom). This concept of "social base" has two meanings. First, it connotes the source of actual support or acquiescence. Thus, the hard-liners probably directed their heavy barrage of deceitful propaganda mainly at the countryside, where the specific grounds for disbelieving it would be much weaker than in the cities. Second, and in the manner of Marx's *Eighteenth Brumaire*, it connotes the structural features of class relations (i.e., the palpable inability throughout the 1989 spring of any

143

urban opposition groups to mobilize support from a radicalized peasantry). In southern Hebei's Shulu County, a representative of the Beijing movement was met with derision and disgust and was shooed away by bewildered and annoyed peasants.[57] So far, the 1989 spring presages no particular structural change in the mode of production and its attendant class structure. There is every reason to think that the peasantry will remain atomized, with most workers and intellectuals being employed by the state and therefore subject to its close control.

That would enable the state to continue to maintain itself through a Bonapartist strategy of dividing town and countryside, as well as splitting urban groups from each other, thereby basing its power on its growing relative autonomy from society generally.[58] Professor Tsou has argued that the Dengist period has ushered in a new era in which *society has finally begun to achieve some limited autonomy from the state.*[59] The spring 1989 demonstrations bear this out. Dialectically, though, the flip side of this, seen in the June 1989 crackdown, is that *the state has also been acquiring new types of autonomy from civil society.*

In the Maoist period, the state was sufficiently autonomous from society to undertake major attacks against it, and had sufficient capacity to do so with tremendous effect. But it was not so autonomous (or high in capacity) as to be able to defend itself against society's attacks upon it – attacks that, it has been argued here, were results of the contradictions involved in the Maoist state's emphases on both direct popular participation and strong statism. The Dengist state has attempted to deal with this contradiction by closing off direct participation and opening up new avenues of indirect participation in the form of elections. This is one element in what Tang Tsou has referred to as a change from a politics of the masses to a politics of citizens.[60] The role of the state vis-à-vis society is also being circumscribed. In this new political formula, participation by society in the state has been the means, and political stability (read defense of the state) the end. To achieve this, Dengism has been willing to sacrifice not only society's participation in the state but also the extent of the state's control over society. *In short, compared with the Maoist state, the Dengist state has lost capacity but gained autonomy. Its bizarre attempts to reestablish draconian, totalistic social control in the wake of the spring 1989 events are partly the result of its increased autonomy, and they will ultimately fail because of its reduced capacity.*

Moreover, growing economic crisis threatens the reproduction of the Dengist state. Economic demands – complaints about miserable campus conditions and poor economic prospects from students and faculty, and condemnation of inflation from them and from the workers, clerks, and other groups who joined them – were integral to the urban protests of April and May. Peasants, many of whom were paid in scrip for their fall

1988 harvests, did not weigh in during that round of protests, but the deepening fiscal crisis of the state and shortages and inflation in essential inputs like chemical fertilizer[61] may well induce some of them to do so next time. An alliance of broadly and deeply discontented peasants with radicalized urban groups – the nightmare of Louis Bonaparte and Deng alike – cannot be ruled out. That could begin to bring down the Dengist regime.[62]

How likely are the peasants to play the role of the dynamite under the state edifice? On the one hand, the Chinese peasantry often has proved a difficult lot to mobilize politically. The active participation of "the masses" in the Chinese Revolution was brought about through the intense, protracted, and (only after many failures) ultimately adroit efforts of the Chinese Communist Party in the face of tremendous obstacles.[63] Most of those – including the scholar-official-landlord class[64] and the imperial state founded upon it – are gone, but in their place there is now the agrarian structure of smallholding peasants. In it, all the conditions that Skocpol identified as conducive to peasant insurrections[65] have been obliterated: In Dengism's first decade, local communities were deprived of whatever solidarity they may have had under high collectivism, the peasants were given relief from direct day-to-day supervision by exploiters, and state coercion was relaxed.

On the other hand, new forces relating to each of these three conditions for peasant radicalism are now at work. Villagers are more united than at any time since 1978 in their opposition to the state; they have been killing tax collectors, burning government buildings, and engaging in large-scale armed clashes with police over environmental and economic issues.[66] If state control is intensified to cope with the growing economic crisis – for example, to stamp out free or black-market outlets for commodities that the peasants will increasingly hold back from sale to the state at the low prices it offers, or to reinstitute acreage quotas[67] – peasants may experience that in ways not so different from day-to-day supervision by exploiters. And state control is increasing in other areas as well, including campaigns around propaganda, legal issues (such as criminal justice), and social policies (such as population control, land use, and cultural expression). All of these will fuel discontent that could predispose the peasantry to participate in spontaneous or even semiorganized uprisings more than they have already.

Earlier in this century, the Chinese Communist Party was able to build a revolutionary movement on peasant discontent through careful, painstaking organization and serious concern with local political participation. Decades later, the peasantry's disillusionment with direct political participation toward the end of the Maoist period militates against any early return to such politics. So does the absence of a leadership – like the party of the revolutionary years – committed to popular political participation, organized to lead it, and possessed of the opportunities presented by a collapsing state and a domestic situation destabilized by external forces.[68]

Once again China appears poised for deep and perhaps prolonged crisis. There is palpable, widespread, and potentially revolutionary discontent in most of its cities, including most prominently its major political and economic centers. Its armed forces are shot through with serious fissures. Most ominous of all is the prospect of rural protest that has already found expression in localized sparks. To follow Mao's metaphor, they could, by linking up with urban movements already under way, ignite a conflagration in the prairies as well as the cities nested in the interstices.[69] But unlike the period presaged by Mao's metaphor, this time peasant discontent is unlikely to be canalized in the service of broader goals. It took a great deal of work, intense commitment, brilliant organization, dedicated leadership, and many setbacks to forge a local participatory politics that could turn the peasants' destructive fury to a constructive purpose. Conditions for replicating that feat are not now in view.

NOTES

1. The terms "Maoist" and "Dengist" are used throughout this chapter in a structural sense to connote the regimes that emerged under those two leaders, rather than their personal characteristics, theories, or political styles.
2. Or totalitarian? Or Leninist? That debate is best elided here. Tang Tsou has, of course, devoted a great deal of his scholarly energy to producing the most sophisticated discussion in our field of totalitarianism. By limiting his conceptualization of it to the degree of politicization of society, and by separating it from another level of analysis that he terms "the structure of political power," he argues that we can "raise some interesting questions." Tang Tsou, *The Cultural Revolution and Post-Mao Reforms: A Historical Perspective* (Chicago: University of Chicago Press, 1986), pp. xxii–xxv. The relationship between popular participation and the state – which is the subject of this chapter – is one to which his approach opens the way. Recently he has articulated his position thus: "To ask a seemingly absurd question for the purpose of illustrating the extreme form of this complex relationship [between the analytical levels of state–society relations and the structure of political power], is it theoretically possible to have a 'democratic totalitarian' society in which the people or masses participate actively in the selection of their governors and express a preference for the state to penetrate all spheres of civil society or at least exhibit a spontaneous willingness to allow the state to do so?" (Tsou, *Cultural Revolution*, p. xxv.) One operative word in this passage is "seemingly." I have understood Professor Tsou to mean precisely that not only is such a question not absurd, but that in fact it describes the theoretical aspirations and actual historical practice of China in the Maoist period. This is but one example of the way in which he has opened up analytical terrain, rather than closing it over or imposing morphological models and theories.

3. John Lewis's important *Leadership in Communist China* (Ithaca: Cornell University Press, 1963) treated village politics only in a brief section concerning the famous Hebei model Xipu Brigade (pp. 204–211). James Townsend's *Political Participation in Communist China* (Berkeley: University of California Press, 1967), which for many years was the only book on the subject, contained but an eight-page section on "Rural Production Units" (pp. 165–172). Based mainly on a small number of articles from the Chinese press, it managed to paint a picture that rings quite true. Even Doak Barnett's *Cadres, Bureaucracy and Political Power in Communist China* (New York: Columbia University Press, 1967), the first study to make serious use of interviews with Chinese who had participated in local politics, treated the grass-roots level of popular participation in only a seven-page section (pp. 418–424).

4. William Hinton, *Shenfan* (New York: Vintage, 1984); Jan Myrdal, *Report from a Chinese Village* (New York: Pantheon, 1965); Vivienne Shue, *Peasant China in Transition* (Berkeley: University of California Press, 1980). William Hinton's attenuated struggle to wrest his notes back from the U.S. Government, which had confiscated them, is a poignant reminder of the political and ideological obstacles to field research in China in the 1950s and 1960s. No doubt there existed equally severe obstacles on the Chinese side at that time, though I know of no Western analyst who tested them unsuccessfully, and of one – Jan Myrdal – who overcame them.

5. Townsend, *Political Participation in Communist China*.

6. That emphasis conformed in a general way with the preoccupation in the then-current literature on comparative political development with the mobilization of popular support by political elites in nascent states.

7. Martin King Whyte, *Small Groups and Political Rituals in China* (Berkeley: University of California Press, 1974).

8. Tsou, *Cultural Revolution*, pp. xl–xli; emphasis added.

9. Tsou, *Cultural Revolution*, p. xliv.

10. Tsou, *Cultural Revolution*, p. xxxv. I would take issue here only with the ambiguous last phrase, if by "various groups and individuals" it refers to the bulk of the poor and middle peasantry. It seems indubitable that the revolutionary goals of the Chinese Communist Party (CCP) (at least as stated at the time, which included rent reduction and then land reform) were consistent with the objective interests of this vast majority of the peasantry, so there is no question of a trade-off in general. The CCP's achievement was to make the link between those objective interests and the peasantry's "perceived" or subjective interests in a situation in which many peasants could not conceive of a world without landlords or rent, in which many viewed rent and landlord power as legitimate, and in which they were frightened and coerced into submission the moment they began to strive for a new world. The party accomplished that transformation of consciousness through the mass-line techniques of political participation and solicitation that it pioneered and that in turn provided the basis for a more lasting participatory politics. I have discussed these aspects of China's revolution and socialism in "Structural Change and the Political Articulation of Social Interest in Revolutionary and Socialist China," in Arif Dirlik and Maurice Meisner, eds., *Marxism and the Chinese Experience: Issues in Contemporary Chinese Socialism* (Armonk, N.Y.: M. E. Sharpe, 1989), pp. 190–209. But if by

"various groups and individuals" Professor Tsou meant patriotic landlords and rich peasants or former rural bandits, toward whom the CCP adopted a flexible policy of compromise and co-optation at crucial moments, then I would quite agree with his formulation.

11. Tsou, *Cultural Revolution*, p. xv.
12. It also helps to explain the discernible lack of cynicism in the work of his students, even when they are being their most critical.
13. John Burns, "The Election of Team Cadres in Rural China: 1958–74," *China Quarterly* 74 (June 1978): 273–296; John Burns, "Chinese Peasant Interest Articulation: 1949–1974" (Ph.D. diss., Columbia University, 1979); John Burns, *Political Participation in Rural China* (Berkeley: University of California Press, 1988); Willem F. Wertheim and Matthias Stiefel, *Production, Equality and Participation in Rural China* (Geneva: United Nations Research Institute for Social Development, 1982); Marc Blecher, "Leader–Mass Relations in Rural Chinese Communities: Local Politics in a Revolutionary Society" (Ph.D. diss., University of Chicago, 1978); Marc Blecher, "The Mass Line and Leader–Mass Communication in Basic-Level Rural Communities," in Godwin Chu and Francis Hsu, eds., *China's New Fabric* (London: Routledge & Kegan Paul, 1983), pp. 63–88; Marc Blecher, "Consensual Politics in Rural Chinese Communities: The Mass Line in Theory and Practice," *Modern China* 5, no. 1 (January 1979): 105–126; Blecher, "Structural Change."
14. Blecher, "Leader–Mass Relations," p. 103.
15. Blecher, "Leader–Mass Relations," pp. 113–134.
16. Blecher, "Leader–Mass Relations," p. 160.
17. Blecher, "Leader–Mass Relations," pp. 78–82 (esp. Table 24). John Burns has concurred: "[T]he election of team cadres had democratic content, and is not the formalistic insignificant exercise previous accounts of post-Liberation Chinese politics have assumed." Burns, "Election of Team Cadres," pp. 295–296.
18. Party members usually were local leaders.
19. Blecher, "Leader–Mass Relations," pp. 59–78. In fact, the Cultural Revolution increased the representation of women and youth in grass-roots leadership. See Tables 11 and 13 and associated discussions.
20. Burns, *Political Participation in Rural China*, pp. 155ff.; Vivienne Shue, *The Reach of the State* (Stanford: Stanford University Press, 1988), pp. 137–147.
21. The insights that participation did not capture the full range of political expression from the peasants to their local leaders, that it needed to be supplemented by study of the ways in which the leadership sought peasant views, and that those might capture different kinds of views or those of different social groups came from Tang Tsou. With analytical agility that was insightful and that remains inspirational, he derived it from the distinction made by Sidney Verba and Norman Nie between what they called participation and polling strategies. See Sidney Verba and Norman Nie, *Participation in America: Political Democracy and Social Equality* (New York: Harper & Row, 1972), p. 268.
22. Blecher, "Leader–Mass Relations," chapter 5. The use of political solicitation to tap the views of former rich peasants and landlords was a surprise, inasmuch as it reversed the original purpose and function of political solicitation, which was to forge a communicative and political connection between cadres and members of oppressed classes who were too inexperienced, fright-

ened, or intimidated to participate in local politics. That such occurred suggests the capacity of civil society and local leaders (many of whom have one foot in it and one in the state) to be creative in adapting political techniques of the state to new purposes. In that case, the purpose was constructive: to help the collectives gain access to the productive know-how of former exploiting classes despite the general policy of keeping them in political disgrace.

23. Blecher, "Leader–Mass Relations," chapter 6; Blecher, "Structural Change."
24. Shue, *Peasant China in Transition.*
25. For just two examples of this widespread approach, see Verba and Nie, *Participation in America*; and Sidney Verba, Norman Nie, and Jae-on Kim, *Participation and Political Equality: A Seven-Nation Comparison* (Cambridge University Press, 1978).
26. I have developed this analysis more fully in "Structural Change." Of course, placing the fundamental issues of material life squarely at the center of local politics also required a leadership with a specific theoretical system linking politics and economics (such as Marxism) and a political commitment to carry out social and economic transformation, points that Tang Tsou has emphasized.
27. The dominant arena of local politics during the campaign for rent and interest reductions and land reform was redistributive. But redistributive issues were also present in the local politics of mutual aid, cooperativization, and the people's communes, as well as in decisions about property rights (e.g., individuals becoming members of cooperatives, village collective units being incorporated into communes) and income distribution.
28. Theodore Lowi, "Four Systems of Policy, Politics and Choice," *Public Administration Review* 32 (July–August 1972): 298–309.
29. Ira Katznelson, *City Trenches: Urban Politics and the Patterning of Class in the United States* (New York: Pantheon, 1981).
30. Moral economy theory has never had great explanatory power vis-à-vis China's revolution and socialism; it has required considerable theoretical adaptation for application thereto; see Ralph Thaxton, *China Turned Rightside Up* (New Haven: Yale University Press, 1983). Nor has millenarian theory, though that thesis has never been applied systematically to a study of the Great Leap, where fragmentary evidence suggests it might have some small bearing; see, in particular, Hinton, *Shenfan*, chapters 31–35. More appropriate are simpler notions of radicalism as a form of self-defense, such as the tendency of peasants to murder their landlords in order to prevent them from taking revenge.
31. Here an analogy to Marx's concept of the proletariat under capitalism may be drawn. For Marx, the proletariat was a class created and aggregated by the capitalist mode of production, but in a way that deprived it of control over the material forces it was creating. Marx thought that that contradiction would provide a major flash point for revolution. In China, the peasantry was not created by the revolution, but was organized by it into political institutions powerful enough to help topple landlordism and then to engage in the first phases of socialist construction. But those local institutions were then gradually deprived of significant control over the material forces that they had appropriated in the land reform and then created over many years of production in cooperatives and communes. One argument offered here is that such dispossession of the collectivized peasantry's economic power

by the state, occurring at the same time as the state had organized the peasantry to take and exercise that power, promoted revolutionary radicalism during the Cultural Revolution. But ultimately that led not to the peasants' recapture of it, but to their and the state's abandonment of the struggle for it.

32. This is my term for the period from the consolidation of the three-tiered commune structure in the early and middle 1960s through the end of the Maoist period in 1978. See Marc Blecher, "The Structure and Contradictions of Productive Relations in Socialist Agrarian 'Reform': A Framework for Analysis and the Chinese Case," *Journal of Development Studies* 22, no. 1 (October 1985): 106–110. Mark Selden prefers the term "mobilizational collectivism"; see his *Political Economy of Chinese Socialism* (Armonk, NY: M. E. Sharpe, 1988), pp. 11–19.

33. Marc Blecher and Gordon White, *Micropolitics in Contemporary China: A Technical Unit During and After the Cultural Revolution* (White Plains, NY: M. E. Sharpe, 1979). By "high" Cultural Revolution, I mean the early, radical years of 1967–1969, as distinguished from the Cultural Revolution decade (1966–1976).

34. For my definition of this term, see Blecher, "The Structure and Contradictions," p. 105 and passim.

35. I have discussed elsewhere the ambiguities of class in the late Maoist period: Marc Blecher, "China's Struggle for a New Hegemony," *Socialist Review* 19, no. 2 (April 1989): 5–35.

36. My thanks to Brantly Womack for pointing this out.

37. The Maoist leadership, which believed that ordinary people could grasp philosophy, dialectics, Marxism, and class theory, certainly could not have been consistent if it claimed that such matters were beyond the capacity of the peasants to understand.

38. Blecher, "China's Struggle for a New Hegemony."

39. Ed Friedman has recently argued the opposite; see his "Deng versus the Peasantry," *Problems of Communism* 39, no. 5 (September–October 1990): 30–43. As discussed later, I remain unpersuaded.

40. Cf. Karl Marx, *The Eighteenth Brumaire of Louis Bonaparte* (New York: International Publishers, 1963), p. 124. This is not to say that peasants always conform to this model – that smallholding peasants are always inert. As Suzanne Rudolph has reminded me, in India "bullock capitalists" have been extremely active in politics. But *structurally* they are not radical or destabilizing. Moreover, other conditions must obtain as well if peasants are to be a structurally conservative force. To name a few, their title to land must be secure (as mentioned earlier), macro-economic conditions (prices, markets) must be stable and able to provide a secure living that accords with peasants' expectations, and radical political leadership and social movements must be absent.

41. There are hints in *Shenfan*, for example, that in Long Bow, as in "the unit" (of *Micropolitics*), persons from former "bad" class backgrounds tended to join the more radical factions (the "Stormy Petrels" and the "Shankan Ridge Fighting Team"), and those of "good" class backgrounds tended to join the conservative faction (the "Defend Mao Zedong Thought Platoon"). See Hinton, *Shenfan*, pp. 528, 532.

42. Blecher and White, *Micropolitics*; Hinton, *Shenfan*, chapters 60–79.

150

43. Sidney Verba, *Small Groups and Political Behavior* (Princeton: Princeton University Press, 1961), pp. 219–225.
44. See Carole Pateman, *Participation and Democratic Theory* (Cambridge University Press, 1970), for a good exposition of this line of argument.
45. Shue, *Peasant China in Transition*, pp. 326–328 and passim.
46. Daniel Kelliher, "Privatization and Politics in Rural China," in Gordon White, ed., *The Developmental State in China* (London: Macmillan, 1991).
47. Albert O. Hirschman, *Exit, Voice and Loyalty* (Cambridge: Harvard University Press, 1970).
48. Tsou, *Cultural Revolution*, p. xxiv.
49. For excellent discussions of these matters, see Tsou, *Cultural Revolution*, pp. 169ff. and passim; Brantly Womack, "Modernization and Democratic Reform in China," *Journal of Asian Studies* 43, no. 3 (May 1984): 417–439; and Benedict Stavis, "Post-Mao Political Reforms in China" (paper delivered at the annual meeting of the American Political Science Association, Washington, D.C., September 1–4, 1988).
50. Perhaps the economic problems that have appeared in the late 1980s, including high inflation, severe shortages of inputs, and the general inadequacy and instability of markets, will create conditions that will de-conservatize the Chinese peasantry again. Structures have effects only in their historical contexts.
51. Tsou, *Cultural Revolution*, chapter 5.
52. Or, the reform in which it is engaged is deeply structural. On the concept of structural reform, see André Gorz, *Strategy for Labor* (Boston: Beacon Press, 1967); André Gorz, *Socialism and Revolution* (Garden City, N.Y.: Doubleday, 1973); Ira Katznelson and Mark Kesselman, *The Politics of Power* (New York: Harcourt Brace Jovanovich, 1975), pp. 486–488.
53. Tsou, *Cultural Revolution*, p. 253.
54. These limits may tend to provide even greater security for Chinese peasants, with their current usufruct claims to land, compared with those in systems in which land is more readily subject to market exchange. It might therefore be even more politically conservatizing than middle-peasant agrarian structures in settings with land markets, which always present the dangerous possibility of being used to separate peasants from their land. My earlier attempt to conceptualize the rural mode of production under Dengism is Blecher, "The Structure and Contradictions."
55. Tsou, *Cultural Revolution*, pp. 215–258.
56. Tsou, *Cultural Revolution*, chapter 7 and passim.
57. Field research, summer 1990.
58. It is no accident that a theory of "neo-authoritarianism" was attracting support during the first half of 1989.
59. Tang Tsou, "Back from the Brink of Revolutionary–'Feudal' Totalitarianism," in *Cultural Revolution*, pp. 144–188.
60. Tsou, *Cultural Revolution*, p. xx.
61. Louise do Rosario, "In Deep Difficulty," *Far Eastern Economic Review* 149, no. 21 (May 25, 1989): 69.
62. It may bear reiteration here that "Dengist regime" connotes the state structure that has been developing since 1978. It does not refer to the leadership

group around Deng Xiaoping that celebrated its bloody triumph in May and June 1989. The outer limit of the latter's power is the day of Deng's overdue death. The question here is the survivability or reproducibility of the Dengist state beyond the demise of Deng himself.

63. I have made this argument in "Structural Change" and in parts of "China's Struggle for a New Hegemony." A discussion that locates comparatively the obstacles to popular revolution in China is that by Theda Skocpol, *States and Social Revolutions* (Cambridge University Press, 1979), esp. chapters 1, 3, and 7.

64. Here is yet another important conceptualization developed by Tang Tsou: *Cultural Revolution*, p. xxiii.

65. Skocpol, *States and Social Revolutions*, p. 115.

66. See the following reports in Foreign Broadcast Information Service: July 5, 1988, p. 39; June 30–July 5, 1988, passim; July 18, 1988, p. 51. They are all cited in Ben Stavis, "Conflicts, Constraints, and Coalitions in State–Society Relations During Communist Reform: Insights from China" (unpublished manuscript).

67. This was already beginning in 1990 in Shulu County (field research notes).

68. Theda Skocpol has emphasized these factors of conduciveness to revolutionary movements and uprisings: *States and Social Revolutions*, pp. 19–24 and passim.

69. Mao Zedong, "A Single Spark Can Start a Prairie Fire," in *Selected Works of Mao Tse-tung* (Beijing: Foreign Languages Press, 1967), 1:117–128.

5

The Chinese industrial state in historical perspective: from totalitarianism to corporatism

PETER NAN-SHONG LEE

INTRODUCTION

Observers of Chinese politics often are impressed by its vast diversity and its conflicting images. These conflicting images are found not only in analyses of the Chinese communist regime of revolutionary vintage but also in studies of the party-state's endeavor to extend its control over an increasingly industrialized and modernized society in the aftermath of the revolution. According to one view, the party-state is seen as being totally dominant in the industrial sector, in view of such powerful tools as central planning and state ownership, coupled with administrative channels of material supply and the bank's supervision.[1] By the same token, at the enterprise level, the factory directors find at their disposal a vast inventory of tools of control, covering comprehensively all aspects of the worker's life, and this often creates an image of "totalitarian management."

But there is another view, in which empirical studies suggest that the party-state seems powerless when it confronts the task of modernization and economic growth in the postrevolutionary era. For instance, within the structure of the command economy, the industrial ministries at the central level and the industrial bureaus at the local level find it difficult to keep abreast of operations of the various enterprises because of weakness in the feedback system.[2] Thus, considerable material concessions must be made in order to induce compliance from the low-level units. Examples include the profit-retention system (1979–1984), the tax-for-profit system (begun in 1983), and the contractual-responsibility system (begun in 1984).

Thanks are due to the Institute of Social Studies at the Chinese University of Hong Kong for financial support for a research project leading to this chapter. Thanks are also due to Professor Brantly Womack for his helpful and enlightening comments and suggestions on several drafts of this chapter.

The two different images of the powerful and powerless state are reflected in Andrew Walder's studies of China's industrial organization. He has conducted extensive analyses of the roles of workshop and factory directors as representatives of the party-state. According to Walder, industrial workers are in a state of "organized dependency"[3] and are subject to powerful control and manipulation in social, economic, and political arenas.[4] Walder's other findings on the subject suggest a contradictory view that the factory directors often are more willing to encroach upon the state revenue sources than to offend workers, because both are in a "web of factory interests."[5] Again, in his view, the party-state has been experiencing severe limitations during the reform era in terms of "soft budget constraints" and so-called organic ties between industrial bureaus and enterprise units.[6]

This essay proposes a theoretical synthesis of the image of an exceedingly powerful state and that of a powerless state by focusing on the evolution of the corporatist state from the totalitarian state. The concept of corporatism can account for both the ideological and institutional constraints within the structure of the powerful party-state. This concept can also shed light on the built-in network of policies, laws, and regulations that permits the subsidiary existence of the constituent units and individual members within those units. The acknowledgment of subsidiary units in effect licenses them to act with a limited amount of autonomy vis-à-vis the political center, as well as to assume statelike authority vis-à-vis their membership. The segmentation of public power implicit in corporatism is antithetical to the unity of power entailed by totalitarianism, but it is also quite far from the model of equal market relationships.

On the basis of an empirical study of China's industrial sector, this essay argues that corporatism springs from an acceptance of the limitations of the state-administered economy, as well as the autonomy and interests given to the constituent units (including the government units, industrial enterprises, rural units, and so on). Focusing on the policy-making process and institutional mechanisms, it is argued further that the metamorphosis from totalitarianism to corporatism has resulted from the goal displacement by the party-state of its quest for full rationality and total control in the economic arena by the protection and maintenance of its revenue sources and its struggle for survival. The ideological image and organizational structure of the corporatist state gradually began taking shape in the People's Republic of China (PRC) in the mid-1950s, and such a tendency remains pronounced even during the current reform era that began in 1979.

In its early stages, the corporatist state was based on a variety of policy packages and legislation that gave recognition to the interests of various sectors and classes of the society (e.g., land to the tillers, employment and benefits to industrial workers and miners, and job security to the intellectuals and white-collar workers). Those segmentary interests were partly the residue of ideological fervor rooted in the social movements that began arising after the turn of the century. After the establishment of the PRC in 1949, moreover, the work units were given many social functions, in addition to economic functions, because of the lack of effective organizational forms in a relatively backward society. The autonomy and legitimate interests that were accorded to the constituent units and their members were also attributed to the organizational imperatives inherent in the structure of the command economy, such as the decentralization needed to improve effectiveness, and material concessions to enhance compliance. Nevertheless, those segmentary interests of constituent units were subordinated to the overall political objectives of the Chinese Communist Party (CCP): rapid industrialization, the endeavor to catch up with the advanced nations, and the effort to minimize China's vulnerability in the system of modern states.

Here the corporatist state is defined in both functional and ideological senses: functional in terms of the autonomy and actual roles of the constituent units in political, social, and economic life, and ideological with regard to a more or less coherent body of ideas that license the interests of the constituent units and the channels of their expression. The idea of corporatism can be historically and culturally specific, as, for instance, in what Alfred Stepan suggests as the Iberic version of corporatism, the Catholic mode, and so on.[7] One can assert in a general sense, however, that the corporatist state will come into existence in China when the subsidiary roles of the constituent units are fully established in both a functional sense and an ideological sense within the structure of the communist party-state. The principle of subsidiarity refers to the secondary but complementary roles of the constituent units within the state organization. These units are given an independent status; they have their own value and are not reducible to the state.[8]

In the Chinese context, the subsidiary role of the constituent unit is a result of interest-licensing by the party-state. This pattern of evolution is closer to "state corporatism" than to "societal corporatism," to use Philippe Schmitter's terms.[9] State corporatism, which gives greater weight to interest-licensing than to interest-representing, fits the evolutionary path of the Chinese political system. The party-state plays a pivotal role not only in political developments, such as nation-building, institution-building, governing capacity, and political participation (including political mobilization), but also in economic modernization. In fact, occupational groups, voluntary associations, and political organizations have not been given sufficient time to evolve and develop in a gradual fashion. To confront the "total crisis" of the political community and the crushing pressure from the international system of states, the CCP, a Leninist apparatus and movement-oriented organization, not only created its governmental institutions but also restructured society in the party's image. In many instances, the interests of new occupational groups were given recognition long before they could find time to articulate their needs or represent themselves.

The thesis of the metamorphosis from totalitarianism to corporatism is not restricted to the Chinese case alone; it is applicable to other socialist countries. Valerie Bunce and John Echols have found that "corporatism" is in fact more appropriate than "pluralism" to identify the major features of the Soviet political system, on the basis of their analysis of the role of the state in a number of functional areas during the Brezhnev era.[10] In fact, studies of the rise of "market socialism" and "socialist pluralism" along with economic and political reforms in the socialist countries have tended to lend more validity to the theory of corporatism than to the other formulations. For instance, the Yugoslav reforms toward "market socialism" did not result in either syndicalism or "market anarchism," but in a corporatist form featuring dispersion of the power of the centralized state in a society consisting of loosely connected, self-governing organizations.[11] Claiming to be moving toward "socialist pluralism," the "reform movements" of Czechoslovakia led to proposals to recognize a corporatist configuration of "manifold groups and interests which are generated in an industrial, communist-type society."[12]

THE HISTORICAL ROOTS OF THE TOTALITARIAN STATE

In common usage, "the totalitarian state" refers to a selection of tools intended to maximize political dominance and encroach upon all spheres of the society.[13] Placing an emphasis on instrumental rationality, that is, selection of the most appropriate means to attain a given set of goals, such a totalitarian endeavor might be guided by a genuine revolutionary ideology or perverted by other purposes, for either good or evil. Moreover, the instruments for political functions need not be suitable for economic management and control. For instance, the criminal penalties that were employed against factory managers in the 1930s during Stalin's era were found to be counterproductive.[14] Nor was the "commando approach," which was often adopted in socialist countries such as the USSR, able to produce desirable economic results.[15] Therefore, political totalitarianism should be analytically differentiated from its economic counterpart in view of the different tools required for control over the different functional arenas. Such a distinction is also warranted because of the changing role of the party-state in a postrevolutionary society.

Totalitarianism in its economic and political forms can be meaningfully treated as embodying two entirely different modes of decision making, and they can be contrasted in terms of ultimate objectives, leadership styles, organizational apparatus, and means of implementation. In my perspective, political totalitarianism can be taken to embody a preceptoral type of decision making marked by the moral ideal of class struggle, as well as charismatic leadership, a movement-oriented party, and a mobilizational approach; economic totalitarianism is represented by an administrative type of decision making, characterized by a quest for modernization, a sovereign planner, an organizational hierarchy, and the use of experts and regulatory means.[16] The former had deep historical roots dating back to the founding of the CCP or perhaps even earlier, but it came to full flower in the mid-1950s; the latter emerged during the civil-war period, when the industrial complex in Northeast China was taken over by the CCP and then reinforced further during the economic recovery period (1949–1952), the implementation of the first "five-year plan" (1953–1957), and beyond.[17]

Tang Tsou has given us one of the most articulate accounts on the origins of political totalitarianism in China. Focusing on the social-psychological origins of Chinese communism, he identified the theoretical linkage between the perceived total crisis and the rise of a coherent body of political ideas and all-embracing programs. The CCP basically followed Lenin's view of a two-stage revolution: the "national-democratic revolution" as the first stage, and "socialist revolution" as the second.[18] During the national-democratic revolution, up to 1949, the CCP aimed at building up a limited party-state on the basis of co-optation through the "united front" at the elite level and the "mass line" at the societal level. The first stage was also marked by a "minimum program," parallel to Sun Yat-sen's position of tutelage democracy and welfare state, and coupled with an anti-imperialist platform. The second stage called for a wholesale socialization of ownership, together with central planning.[19]

Political totalitarianism did not become mature until after 1949, when the second-stage program of the "socialist revolution" was implemented and when the CCP leaders did not feel the need for self-imposed restraint after the total defeat of the Guomindang (GMD).[20] During the second stage, after 1949, the entire society was absorbed into the framework of the party-state. That process consisted of "exclusionary" measures involving coercive and often violent means, such as the land-reform movement against the landed classes and the "three-anti" and "five-anti" campaigns against the capitalists in urban areas. That process also involved "inclusionary" endeavors relying heavily on the inducements of distributions of material benefits through agricultural collectivization (1952–1958) and industrial nationalization (1954–1956). Those political moves brought the PRC closer to a Soviet type of command economy that was reinforced by a siege mentality, as well as the war-readiness drives (notably including the "Third Front" defense project) that lasted for more than two decades to the late 1970s. That "socialist revolution" incorporated and in many cases transformed social strata, such as the peasantry and the workers.[21]

By 1956, the Chinese communist regime approximated a totalitarian state in both the political sense (e.g., total control and total mobilization) and the economic sense (e.g., central planning and state ownership). The party-state was all-powerful in the political realm, having gained unparalleled legitimacy and credibility because of victory in the revolution and success in socialist transformation, and it was building an experienced and dedicated political machine that reached into every village and basic unit in China. In spite of relative shortages of expertise, manpower, and resources, the framework of the command economy was erected and later expanded. It proved effective in facilitating economic recovery from the devastation of the wars, as well as in building defense capabilities.

Since the mid-1950s, corporatism has evolved from economic totalitarianism, though political totalitarianism has followed a different path of evolution. When it is removed from its original task environment of revolution, political totalitarianism tends either to become "neo-traditionalism" or to reassert itself in a perverted form: "revolutionary-feudal totalitarianism." Borrowed from Ken Jowitt, "neo-traditionalism" refers to a cultural form intended to legitimize the informal power, vested interests, and privileges that were derived from a revolutionary movement, but are no longer appropriate in a postrevolutionary society.[22] Following Tang Tsou's framework, "revolutionary-feudal totalitarianism" can be interpreted as a revival of a revolutionary utopia that has been losing its relevance, but is sustained by a charismatic leader and his personal following, as witnessed in the Cultural Revolution.[23]

Economic totalitarianism is intended to achieve total control over the economic sphere and to make full use of human and material resources for economic development. For example, Lenin's version of socialism approximated the administrative type of policy-making with a singular rational actor (represented by the Communist party or by the sovereign planner) and a planned economy. In his words, "the foundation of Socialism ... calls for absolute and strict unity of will, which directs the joint labour of hundreds, thousands and tens of thousands of people."[24] He also suggested that "all citizens become employees and workers of a single nation-wide state 'syndicate'; the whole of society will have become a single office and a single factory, with equality of labour and equality of pay."[25] As entailed in Lenin's view, the relationship between the socialist state and its constituent units should be structured in terms of the whole and parts. The value of the parts is subordinate to and is determined by that of the whole. In the Chinese version, that relationship has been described as the "whole country as a chessboard" in which the move of one piece is evaluated from the perspective of the entire situation (*chunchu*). That is to say, "the whole and parts" is a hierarchically ordered relationship, but the constituent units do not have values of their own.

In economic totalitarianism, the party-state was, by design, given monopoly over industrial production and control over industrial products, as well as the income derived therefrom. Even if economic totalitarianism cannot fulfill its promise of maximizing the utility of resources, its monopoly over industrial production and products does ensure stable sources of state revenue through profit remittance, taxation, and artificial pricing mechanisms in the industrial sector. The seed of corporatism is planted when the party-state is compelled, by the imperatives of organization, to begin to share its monopoly over industrial production, as well as its revenue, with the work units.

According to Alfred Meyer, the socialist system can be taken as "bureaucracy writ large," and therefore it can be analyzed in light of the Weberian "ideal type."[26] In fact, Max Weber suggests that socialism will bring an even higher degree of bureaucratization (for him, a higher degree of rationalization) than capitalism.[27] Neil Harding's formulation of the "organic labour state" is based on a view of a rational system of organization and coordination in the economic arena, as well as the defining features of central planning and state ownership.[28] In essence, totalitarianism is marked by instrumental rationality (i.e., means–end consistency), and that theoretically sets aside the issues pertaining to substantive rationality (i.e., choice of value premises) and economic rationality (cost of policy).[29] Totalitarianism can therefore be defined independently of the idiosyncrasies of individual leaders; there possibly would have been "totalistic" attempts without Stalin, and thus "totalitarianism without terror."[30] In short, totalitarianism, in either political or economic form, can be treated as a by-product of the incessant quest for rationalization, as well as the continuous march toward modernization.

THE METAMORPHOSIS INTO THE CORPORATIST STATE

Alfred Stepan was among the first authors to give hints about the possible metamorphosis of totalitarianism into corporatism when he tried to identify some salient features of corporatism in a socialist political system, such as a plan and a singular rational actor (or a cohesive group of actors) working toward organizing society and making public policies.[31] Several other authors have been more explicit, by tracing the origins of corporatism to the deficiencies and limitations of the totalitarian design, as well as its imperative in search of remedies. Such remedies often include "polycentrism" and the decentralizing tendency, as well as autonomy for the constituent units and democratization of the society. Among these authors are Jeremy Azrael, who has suggested "varieties of de-Stalinization,"[32] David Lane, who has identified divergent responses to the perverted form of "bureaucratic state capitalism,"[33] Maurice Meisner, who has analyzed the "socialist bureaucratic state" and its political and ideological reactions in China,[34] and Harry Harding, who has studied the "bureaucratic dilemma" as an unintended consequence of the party-state in China.[35] These views are parallel to Richard Lowenthal's view of the increasing limitations of the party-state and the corresponding development from totalitarianism to authoritarianism.[36] Also, Alec Nove has detailed remedial responses to the fundamental weaknesses of the Soviet economic system. He has attributed those weaknesses to the limited capacity of sovereign planners, the relative complexity of the decision-making situation, the overloading of the communications network, and the time lag in feedback.[37]

The analyses cited have examined how each of the socialist countries has tried to restructure itself, given that total dominance is not realistically possible, and what kind of political system tends to emerge in view of the limitations and weaknesses of the party-state. The existing works appear to suggest that if a political system cannot be fully totalitarian, it must move all the way to the other extreme, that is, to pluralism. For instance, Charles Lindblom has suggested, from a policy-making approach, that totalitarianism has its limitations, because as a policy-making model (i.e., the synoptic model), it cannot account for realistic situations, such as the fallibility of policymakers (be it sovereign planners or charismatic leaders), the difficulties of operationalizing ideology and utopian vision, the complexity of tasks and the relative scarcity of resources, and unanticipated results of policy.[38] Logically speaking, Lindblom's position entails that the actual policy-making should move toward the strategic model that characterizes a market economy as well as a democratic political system. That is to say, policy-making is increasingly dictated by "preference" rather than "theory," as well as by the interactions among the constituent units of the society and its individuals.[39] Such a pluralist thesis is similar to the incremental tendency in the Soviet policy-making system observed by Valerie Bunce and John Echols.[40]

There is a danger in the reduction of corporatism to pluralism. As an analytical tool, corporatism should be differentiated from pluralism in two respects. First, corporatist existence should be acknowledged not only at the meso-level (intermediate level) but also at the basic-unit level, where the work-unit-centered collectives form the foundation of the society, such as in the Chinese case. Second, interest-licensing can still mark the essential characteristics of the interaction between the state and the corporatist entities, short of interest-articulating and interest-representing activities. Therefore, one can still argue the case for corporatism in the Chinese context on the basis of the acknowledged limits of the state and the licensed autonomy and interests of the constituent units, in spite of the very weak and insignificant impetus toward pluralism.

Corporatism, rather than pluralism (or incrementalism), ought to be an appropriate alternative to characterize the socialist political system in the postrevolutionary era. Because economic totalitarianism is unitary and rationalistic, its process of decay hypothetically would appear to move toward a pluralistic and incremental direction. Pluralism and incrementalism are not likely end states for totalitarian systems, however, because of existing constraints. Such constraints often include the communist view of the infallibility of the ruling elite and the Leninist legacy of the one-party state, central planning, and state ownership, as well as all the sunk costs and inertia associated with the command economy.

With considerable experience of the limitations and weaknesses of their synoptic policy-making system, Chinese leaders have gradually moved in a corporatist direction. In three historical stages from the 1950s to the 1980s, Chinese leaders have come to the conclusion, as a first theoretical step, that economic totalitarianism had assigned an extremely large and in fact impossible role to the top policymakers. In the first stage, 1949–1956, the unintended consequences of the administered economy were said to have been merely the results of incorrect methods and techniques of projections and statistics. In the second stage, 1956–1976, the top policymakers believed that the weaknesses of the command economy were more than technical problems and that it would take more time and more experience to reach the perfect state of "proportional and planned development" in accordance with the supposedly existing "law of economy." The third stage in the post-Mao era has been marked by a recognition of an almost permanent "half-planned and non-planned sector" in a planned economy.[41] The very existence of such a sector in the economy testifies, in Hu Qiaomu's view, to unintended consequences and the fundamental limitations inherent in the structure of an administered economy, such as the unwieldy size of planning units, an overconcentration of policy-making power, overloaded communications channels, a separation between responsibility and authority, the problems of accounting and ownership systems, and the poor linkage between incentives and performance.[42] Understandably, from a post-Weberian

161

perspective, this sector is an epiphenomenon of an administered economy and encompasses the unregulated activities in a regulated system (i.e., a central planning system). Such a sector results from the irrational elements inherent in a rational organization and the uncontrollable influences from the environment.[43]

To face up to the irreducible areas of irrationality, inefficiency, and uncontrolled elements inherent in the system of economic totalitarianism, the top Chinese leaders have had to provide an ideological justification and put forth a variety of formulas to reckon with and to license the functional and legitimate footholds of the constituent units in their administered economy. With a corporatist flavor, Mao Zedong's formulation for the balanced relationship involving the state (including both the central and local units), the production units, and the individual producers was based not only on consideration of the needed decentralization of managerial power but also on considering the desirability of giving full play to the initiative (or activism, *jijixing*) of the constituent units in the production process. From the perspective of the distributive function, Mao also proposed a balancing of material interests among the state, the production units, and the individual producers in a two-tier system of distribution from the state to the production units, and from the production units to the individual producers.[44]

Liu Shaoqi proposed an early version of corporatism in his 1955 talk to the workers and staff members at the Shijinshan Power Station and Shijinshan Steel Corporation (later renamed the "Capital Steel Corporation"). He suggested that the production units be given a functional role, with a view to the optimal sizes of managerial and economic decision-making units, as well as creation of tangible and effective linkages between incentives and performance. On the same occasion, Liu went further to propose that production units form commune-like entities in which their members could collectively share the fruits of their labor in terms of welfare and amenities.[45] That idea of the "industrial commune" (or "*danwei* socialism," so to speak) was further articulated in Liu's talk at the Daqing oilfield, in the early 1960s, suggesting the need to bridge the gaps between agriculture and industry, intellectual and manual labor, city and countryside, within a corporatist entity such as Daqing.[46]

A study of the historical evolution toward corporatism in the PRC must focus on the two levels of distribution: one from the party-state to the constituent unit (i.e., work unit), the other from the constituent unit to the individual. To a considerable extent, corporatism is seen in the autonomous and effective role of the work unit that stands between the party-state and the individual. In a totalitarian system, the intermediate organization such as the work unit is not given much legal and institutional autonomy, and thus the party-state can directly penetrate into the society. A "naked" society, which consists of an aggregate of atomized individuals, is the other side of the same coin, namely, a totalitarian political system. The market system tends to give greater weight to the rights and obligations of individuals, and it attributes less importance to the intermediate organizations.

For illustration, the corporatist existence of the work unit can be demonstrated in the controversial case of "temporary contractual workers" in the period from the 1950s to the Cultural Revolution. Permanent job tenure was given to workers and staff members as early as the 1950s; dismissal of workers and staff was generally prohibited even in cases of closure, stoppage, transfer, or combination of enterprises for reasons of efficiency or reorganization. No temporary worker could legally be employed in a regular job.[47] In order to reduce labor costs and improve efficiency, Liu Shaoqi took the initiative to introduce the category of temporary contractual workers during the Great Leap Forward, a move that was resisted by ultraleftist leaders, who paradoxically argued from a corporatist viewpoint during the Cultural Revolution. Liu recommended the system of temporary contractual workers on the grounds that their pay would be lower than that of regular workers, no fringe benefits would have to be provided, and they could be sent back to the countryside when they were no longer needed. In the aftermath of the Cultural Revolution, the majority of temporary contractual workers were given regular posts and also corporatist rights and privileges in accordance with the prior regulations of the 1950s.[48]

In a study of China's developmental experience up to the Cultural Revolution, Tsou's observations on Chinese socialism, centering on the work unit, have implicitly pointed to the possibility of the rise of corporatism. He suggests that for ideological reasons, the status of individuals is defined and determined by their membership in a collectivity.[49] It is noteworthy that in the aftermath of the Cultural Revolution, as Deng Xiaoping returned to power in 1973–1975, his first move was to improve the corporatist benefits to workers and staff.[50] Since 1978, as the economic reforms picked up momentum, there has been increased spending not only for wages and bonuses but also for fringe benefits and collective welfare for industrial employees. Such spending policies have considerably reinforced the corporatist tendency, as discussed later.

THE EVOLUTION OF ENTERPRISE-AUTONOMY POLICY

The foregoing analysis has shown that some key features of the corporatist state have become increasingly salient in China with the coming of a postrevolutionary society since the mid-1950s. The remainder of this essay will demonstrate that industrial enterprises are given functional and legitimate autonomy because of their share of monopoly over industrial products as well as the so-called unplanned or half-planned sectors within a planned economy.

In the Soviet type of command economy, the production process is administered within a hierarchical relationship. The production targets (the indicators of the annual production-technical-financial plan) are transmitted from the top to the bottom of the planning structure, coupled with an administrative channel of material supply. In such a system, the unanticipated outcomes of control from above can be such deviations as low productivity, low efficiency, and poor economic results. Also, the feedback system tends to be weak because of continual conflicts of interest between the supervising authorities and enterprise units as well as the organizational distance from the top to the bottom. In other words, the supervising authorities are not able to obtain sufficiently accurate information to evaluate performance, to assess real production capacity, and to formulate realistic economic-technical indicators for the enterprise units. To maximize control and minimize deviations, conventional types of countermeasures include various forms of profit-sharing schemes, in which enterprise units can be rewarded for meeting or exceeding their annual production goals, as shown on the basis of extensive interviews of emigres from the Soviet Union by Joseph Berliner.[51]

There is evidence to suggest that a functional foothold was first given to the enterprise units in the form of profit retention when the Soviet type of command economy was established in Northeast China in the early 1950s. A profit-retention system was introduced throughout the country in 1955, but the bureaus, rather than enterprise units, were taken as the basic accounting units for shares of retained profit.[52] Along with other reform programs, a profit-retention system was formally introduced at the factory level during the Great Leap Forward of 1958–1960 on the basis of the "Regulations Concerning the Implementation of the Enterprise Profit-Retention System," promulgated by the State Council on May 22, 1958. That system was intended to give enterprise units more autonomy in the planning and management of production, and it involved a proportional increase in material incentives. However, its unintended consequence of "investment crisis" was aggravated by other decentralization measures in financial, banking and credit, and related areas during the period of the Great Leap Forward.[53]

In the aftermath of the Great Leap Forward, starting in 1961, the profit-retention system was suspended, and a modest incentive scheme was introduced instead, stressing economical use of production inputs such as raw materials and fuel. In addition, the meeting or surpassing of annual production goals warranted a percentage of profit for an "enterprise fund." The calculation of the percentage was based on the total wage bill for the given unit, rather than on output. The enterprise-fund system was stopped for over a decade, from 1966 to 1976, because of the Cultural Revolution, but it was officially restored in 1978, when the new programs of the profit-retention system were tried once again.[54] Since 1979, basically three modes of profit sharing have been introduced in the midst of continual changes, with considerable overlap among the three: the profit-retention system, the tax-for-profit system, and the con-tractual-responsibility system.

The profit-retention system was derived from the old model of 1958, but was reintroduced with much refinement during 1979–1984. There were two versions: One was a profit-retention system on the basis of a fixed comparison method, for example, a share of profit decided on the basis of the improvement compared with a fixed baseline calculated on the basis of either the preceding year or an average of three to five years before the implementation of the given profit-retention system. Another was based on the moving comparison method; that is, the enterprise unit was to be rewarded proportionally to the improvement over the preceding year.[55]

The tax-for-profit system (or "substitution of taxation for profit re-mittance") is a system in which the enterprise unit is required to pay a fixed percentage as tax and, in principle, to retain all remaining profit. However, as a transitional measure, the enterprise unit has to share its profit with the supervising authorities or pay an adjustment tax (which is a metamorphosed form of profit).[56] The contractual-responsibility sys-tem is another form of profit-sharing arrangement, allowing the enterprise unit to share profit based on individually devised rates, which in most cases are progressive.[57]

The change from the profit-retention system to the tax-for-profit system was motivated by a number of considerations. First, the share of profit being returned to the state treasury had been diminishing by the early 1980s. Second, the central and local governments had been locked in conflict over their respective shares of the profit in the midst of a drastic decline in the former's control over the direction of capital investment. However, after the introduction of the second step of the tax-for-profit system in 1985, the central government had to resuscitate and even ex-pand the contractual-responsibility system among large industrial enter-prises because it was seen as an assured and effective way to protect the revenue sources of the state.[58] As things stand now, the tax-for-profit system runs parallel to the contractual-responsibility system, with the latter mainly reserved for the large-scale industrial units.

The enterprise-autonomy policy has tended to trigger still another cycle of centralization and decentralization in the post-Mao era. Such a syndrome is congruent with the past experiences of reform during

1958–1960.[59] According to organization theory, a public organization cannot decentralize power to its lower echelons as easily as can its private counterpart. The former will find it more difficult than the latter to devise a new control system after decentralization, because the former does not ordinarily produce measurable outputs and thus cannot monitor the performances of the lower echelons according to output.[60] Of course, socialist industry does produce physical outputs that are measurable to a considerable extent. However, evaluation of performances of state-owned enterprises is complicated by "soft budget constraints," as well as a distorted pricing system, as suggested by János Kornai. Consequently, the "functional model,"[61] which highlights the features of an input-centered control system, appears more relevant to account for the complexity of the decentralization issues in the industrial sector, such as an unintended expansion of enterprise autonomy, as well as many cases of deviations at the enterprise level. In the Chinese context, the state-owned enterprises act more like public organizations than private ones. Therefore, the "product model," which is based on measurable output, is of limited use in studying the behavior of state-owned enterprises. This implies that the decentralization schemes tend to create a greater organizational vacuum in which corporatism may be able to reassert itself.

On the more general question of the nature of enterprise autonomy, there are two forms of relationships between state and enterprise unit. One involves a delegation of power within an administrative hierarchy; the other involves a web of rights and obligations in a legal and political sense.[62] The former has more of an authoritarian, if not totalitarian, flavor, to the extent that the value of the parts (state-owned industrial enterprises) is derived from the whole (the state); the latter clearly reflects an image of corporatism in the sense that parts can have their own intrinsic values, in spite of the fact that they are subordinate to the whole.

The Chinese policymakers certainly are aware of the foregoing distinction between administrative delegation of power and legal and political rights. For instance, in Hu Qiaomu's famous article "Observe Economic Laws, Speed Up the Four Modernizations," the state-administered economy is taken as deficient on two counts, and each indictment implies a different relationship between the state and the constituent units. One weakness is overconcentration of power, and thus a logical solution to it is decentralization of power. Another, which is taken as fundamental, is that economic activities are coordinated by arbitrary administrative means, not by the law of economic activities.[63] To overcome those deficiencies, Hu suggested that the relationship between the state and the enterprise units be totally restructured on new legal and political grounds. However, two months later, in December 1978, when the Third Plenum of the Eleventh Party Congress was convened, the deficiencies of the command economy were addressed mainly in terms of the former (i.e., overconcentration of power) rather than the latter (i.e., ideological validity of the socialist economy).[64] In other words, the CCP's official position tends to avoid the issue of whether or not the socialist economy is fundamentally faulty. That official position reflects the ideological strain in the metamorphosis from totalitarianism to corporatism, whereas in reality the concessions in terms of functional autonomy and material benefits have already been made to the enterprise units and individual producers.

The 1982 constitution of the PRC takes a cautious stand by stipulating that enterprise units be given only managerial and marketing autonomy, and no more.[65] In all the regulations and laws of the reform era, the format of enterprise autonomy appears to be that state-owned industrial enterprises can be allowed as much power as their supervising authorities are willing to give them, and such power is managerial and technical, rather than ideological and political.[66] It does not involve questions of rights and obligations in a legal and political sense, even when protections are given to enterprise units against arbitrary assignments of production targets without adequate supply of materials and against unwarranted encroachment on their property and resources.[67] Nonetheless, this very narrow definition of functional autonomy probably will not hold up well in view of the increasing assertiveness of the enterprise units regarding their corporatist interests.

THE CORPORATIST INFLUENCE
IN WAGE AND LABOR POLICIES

China's economic reforms in the industrial sector have thus far focused on distributive types of issues: first, profit sharing, taxation, and other financial arrangements in the relationship between the state and the enterprise; second, wages, bonuses, and welfare in the relationship between the enterprise and individual producers. The preceding section dealt with the former, together with some issues concerning production and management; this section concerns the latter.

As mentioned earlier, industrial producers and staff members are given lifelong job tenure, fixed wages, and welfare benefits that are sanctioned and protected by the laws, regulations, and established policies of the state. Contrary to the totalitarian image, these jobs, wages, and benefits cannot be taken away arbitrarily by the workshop director (or branch party secretary) or even the factory director. As a result, it is apparent that under this corporatist arrangement, the party-state (as represented by the workshop director or factory director) encounters considerable constraints when it attempts to achieve its objectives, such as greater control, increased efficiency, and higher productivity. In fact, the scales and standards for wages, bonuses, and benefits are centrally regulated and administered in socialist China; individual producers become eligible when they become members of the work unit.

In the Chinese case, and in other socialist countries, the work unit has gradually become recognized as an anchor for administering distributive justice within a corporatist framework. Here the concept of *"danwei* (work-unit) socialism" is employed to refer to the set of principles that define and legitimatize the corporatist role of the work unit in allocating material benefits. To fulfill its corporatist obligations and assert its rights, the work unit may even seek to frustrate the objectives of the state regarding cost accounting, labor productivity, and economic efficiency. Often the purpose of the economic reforms can be compromised because of these corporatist obligations of the state as well as those of the work units, to maintain full employment, living standards, and some measure of egalitarianism. The work unit has been given greater autonomy and a licensed and negotiated existence, owing to the failings of the state in the sphere of economic functioning.

The entire system of wage, pension, and welfare at the enterprise level was established by 1957, and it had marginal adjustments from 1957 to 1976, including the downward adjustment in salary scales during the Great Leap Forward, the substitution of "supplementary wages" for bonuses during the "socialist education movement," and the suspension of the piece-rate wage during the Great Leap Forward and the Cultural Revolution and its aftermath.[68] From 1958 to 1977 there was a wage freeze, accompanied by deteriorations in housing conditions, and perhaps welfare benefits. Before the fall of the "Gang of Four," attempts at wage adjustment were largely abortive.

Six wage increases were introduced between 1977 and 1983. From a corporatist perspective they were understood partly as compensation for the long wage freeze that began in 1958, not necessarily to improve productivity and efficiency. The controversial policies of bonuses and piece-rate wages were quickly clarified after Hua Guofeng's speech to the fifth National People's Congress in early 1978 through a series of forums and analyses in journals. Both systems were restored in 1978.[69] The reinstitution of profit-sharing schemes has enabled the enterprise units to make payments of bonuses and subsidies and to spend for amenities and housing. Therefore, the so-called excessive payments of bonuses mean that the growth in the total wage bill has exceeded any improvement in labor productivity. "Indiscriminate" payment of bonuses refers to the corporatist tendency toward equal shares for the members of the work unit, regardless of different contributions.

Reconstructing the picture on the basis of a series of interactions between the state and the enterprises, it appears that the state was able to control the increase in the standard wage, but not other forms of payment, throughout the reform era. The problematic bonus payments arose from the view that the state ought to repay "debts," that is, what the state owes workers, staff members, and officials in terms of the very slow improvements in living standards after 1958. The leaders in the enterprise units felt strongly that they ought to fulfill such corporatist obligations to their employees before they could begin to think of differentiated incentives, labor productivity, and economic efficiency. Needless to say, the profit-sharing schemes (profit-retention system, tax-for-profit system, contractual-responsibility system) all lent justification to, and provided the material basis for, bonus payments.

The problem of "indiscriminate" bonus payments became serious, and accordingly the State Council repeatedly issued regulations, policy papers, and amendments to the rules: in December 1980, May 1981, July 1982, and May 1983.[70] There have been numerous efforts to tighten up the controls over bonus payments through cost-accounting regulations, financial audits, and dispatch of tax representatives to the major enterprises.[71] It appears that the incidence of excessive and indiscriminate bonus payments was arrested from 1984 to 1987. However, since 1987, cases of subsidies and payment in kind have been reported, followed by countermeasures.[72] On the whole, the corporatist influence at the enterprise level remained quite strong throughout the reform era from 1979 to 1988. Such undesirable tendencies as excessive capital investment, violation of pricing rules to reap illegal profit, and tax evasion and illegal retention of profit can be attributed to this corporatist pressure.[73] All those deviations were organized by the work unit.

To reconcile that corporatist pressure, in 1984 the party-state finally made an unprecedented move to decentralize control over wages and bonuses to the enterprise level in accordance with a decision by the Central Committee of the CCP on economic reform. In that decision, control over wage scales was to be given to the enterprise, a total wage bill was to be tied to economic efficiency, and a progressive tax was to be levied over the total wage bill.[74] It took two years to design a bonus tax system and in the meantime to propose a wage-adjustment tax system. Thereby the enterprise unit was given, within a fixed total wage bill, adequate discretionary power to work out a compromise between its corporatist obligations to its employees and the pressure from the state for economic efficiency.

169

Peter Nan-shong Lee

CORPORATIST TENDENCIES IN THE
CHANGING EMPLOYMENT SYSTEM

In an endeavor to restructure the employment system during the reform era, three problem areas that were under corporatist influence were given special attention: first, the adoption of a job-substitution (*ding ti*) scheme so that the work unit could hire the children of retired workers; second, the introduction of contractual employment to recruit new workers, to be given wages and benefits comparable to those of regular workers hired in the permanent employment system; third, the introduction of a policy of the "optimal combination" (*yufa zouhe*) for regular workers, though with retention of the work unit's obligations to those "internally un-employed" workers.

First, the corporatist tendency had become manifest in the job-substitution scheme, through which the offspring of retired workers would be hired by their parents' former work units. Thus, retired workers were given additional security because of the tradition of family obli-gation whereby their children would provide financial support for them. It was stipulated in "The Provisional Measures for the Retirement and Termination of Duties of Workers" (1978) that "those workers who will have demonstrable difficulty in maintaining their family livelihood after retirement and termination of duty ... in principle, be allowed to have one of their qualified children, employed for work."[75] The scheme lasted for eight years, from 1978 to 1986, when it was superseded by new regulations.[76]

Prior to the reform era, such job substitution had been restricted to only those trades in which it was difficult to recruit labor.[77] However, the job-substitution scheme was then extended to cover all retiring work-ers in order to encourage those who were eligible for retirement to file their retirement applications. Up until 1978 there was a backlog of 1.6 million workers who were due for retirement but were kept working because of the Cultural Revolution.[78]

Second, some corporatist residue appears to have persisted in the change toward the contractual-employment system. The PRC had adopted an authority-oriented employment system, rather than a market-oriented employment system, in which the state had set a corporatist limit to its power by ruling out dismissal as an ordinary instrument of work-force control. That authority-oriented employment system was marked by the exercise of state authority, coordination through central planning, a corporatist orientation, and lifetime job tenure. China has basically used the authority-oriented employment system from 1949 to the present, except for the period of controversy over the temporary-

Table 1. *Industrial workers employed through contracts, 1982–1988*

Year	Workers
1982	160,000
1983	576,000
1984	1,724,000
1985	3,320,000
1986	5,180,000
1987	7,350,000
1988	10,076,000

Source: Jingji guanli chubanshe, ed., *Zhongguo jingji nianjian, 1989* (China's economic yearbook, 1989) (Hong Kong: Jingji guanli chubanshe, 1989), pp. vi–46.

worker system first raised during 1958–1960 and the period of the Cultural Revolution and its aftermath, as just noted.

During the reform era, a contractual-employment system has been readopted. In this new system, employment practices are dictated by interaction (e.g., negotiation, competition) and characterized by contracts, an individualistic orientation, and limited job tenure. Since 1980, contract-oriented employment has been expanding at a rapid pace, embracing about 7 percent of the PRC's industrial labor force in 1988. The progress of contractual employment is illustrated in Table 1.

On the basis of successful experience with contractual employment up to 1984, a package of four sets of laws was introduced by the Ministry of Personnel and Labour. They covered four areas: the contract system,[79] employment practices,[80] unemployment insurance,[81] and labor discipline.[82] The unemployment-insurance system was needed because it was anticipated that a small percentage of workers would be out in the market and would transfer to other jobs when they needed financial support. An insurance scheme would alleviate hardship during job transfer and unemployment. It is true that the legal status of industrial workers has changed because of the transformation from the fixed-employment system to the contractual-employment system. Nonetheless, the corporatist obligations of the state and the work unit to the workers remain discernible to the extent that all wage payments and fringe benefits for contractual workers have been made comparable to those for regular workers during the reform era.[83] The initial evidence suggests that the enterprise units have been able to tighten up labor discipline considerably and improve the quality of new recruits because of adoption of the contractual-employment system.[84]

Third, after the contractual-employment system was formally introduced to aid in the recruitment of new workers in 1986, the concept of the "optimal combination" was extended to the regular workers in order to rationalize the use of the labor force. The optimal combination is based on the discretionary power of the work units to design and adopt their own pay scales and to assign jobs among employees within the limits of a fixed total wage bill. The total wage bill is tied to a set of indicators of profit remittance and tax payments. Under this arrangement, employees are allowed to compete for the leading posts in given subunits of the enterprise unit and to effect any needed reorganization from one hierarchical level to another, and they are expected to fulfill the targets of production.[85]

Overall, the optimal-combination strategy has resulted in the selection and reassignment of suitable employees to appropriate posts, and redundant and less productive personnel have been "set aside." The latter have become "internally unemployed."[86] Nonetheless, lingering corporatism still exerts an influence and prevents the enterprise units from pushing those "internally unemployed" personnel into the labor market. Instead, it is still the obligation of the work unit to find or create jobs for them by starting new ventures: affiliated collectively owned enterprises and sideline businesses. Of course, the dependents of employees are given preference when applying for jobs in these affiliated units.[87]

The foregoing analysis suggests that during the reform era, a number of policies concerning wage and labor were intended to improve efficiency and productivity, but they were in fact distorted in the process of implementation because of the considerable emphasis on corporatist obligations to provide "compensation" to workers and staff for the slow improvement in living standards over recent decades. Moreover, China has had difficulty in substituting contract-oriented employment for authority-oriented employment because the state and enterprise units still are considered to have a corporatist obligation to provide jobs and job-related benefits to workers.

CONCLUSION

This essay has suggested that the party-state in the PRC is exceedingly powerful, judging from its stated intentions and its selection of instruments in attempting to impose total control over its entire society. Originating from the revolutionary context, the party-state reached its full-fledged totalitarian form by the mid-1950s. The empirical cases of industrial policies and management cited here confirm, however, that, contrary to its stated intentions, the party-state has encountered considerable obstacles involving both institutional and managerial factors in its efforts to maximize its control since the mid-1950s. In view of such constraints, the party-state appears relatively powerless, measured against its economic objectives, such as efficiency, productivity, and sustained growth. As discussed earlier, the metamorphosis of totalitarianism into corporatism has taken place because the omnipotent and omniscient image of the party-state could not be reconciled with the institutional and functional realities of the socialist economy. Consequently, the party-state has had to accept its limitations, to delegate power, and to make material concessions to the constituent units in a corporatist setting.

This chapter has examined not only legal and institutional factors but also the functional and managerial variables in order to account for the growth and legitimation of corporatism at the work-unit level in the PRC. To date, the PRC has not been able to move far toward market socialism because the reform in industrial management has had a limited objective, that is, to search only for remedies, rather than for total restructuring of the overly centralized edifice of economic totalitarianism. By the same token, the limited move toward wage and bonus reform has reinforced the corporatist tendency rather than the market mechanism in income distribution. Perhaps the introduction of contractual employment is one of the most ambitious reforms. However, the initial success in that area has been brought about only through a compromise, giving contractual workers pay and benefits comparable to those of regular workers who are remunerated within a corporatist framework.

As demonstrated, the metamorphosis from totalitarianism to corporatism has been rooted in the organizational and managerial imperative of the party-state. In short, the totalitarian state has gone through a process of goal displacement in the sense that its latent function of revenue collection has, to a considerable degree, substituted for its manifest function of full rationalization in the economic arena. To achieve its objective of revenue collection, the party-state has had to share with the enterprise unit its monopoly over industrial production and to make concessions through a variety of profit-sharing schemes, including the contractual-responsibility system. That move has been made necessary because of considerations of the fundamental inadequacy of the mechanisms of management, as well as legal and institutional tools. As a result, central control over income distribution has been decentralized further to the work-unit level. This, accordingly, has reinforced "work-unit socialism." On the whole, the work unit has been able to expand rather than to curtail its corporatist obligations, not only in wages and bonuses but also in welfare and benefits, as well as employment practices, during the reform era and up to the present.

NOTES

1. Thomas G. Rawski, *China's Transition to Industrialism: Producer Goods and Economic Development of the Twentieth Century* (Ann Arbor: University of Michigan Press, 1980), pp. 112–145; Alexander Eckstein, *China's Economic Revolution* (Cambridge University Press, 1977), pp. 92–96.

2. An observation on the limitations of the command economy was provided by Xue Muqiao, who once worked as chief of the State Statistic Bureau. Xue suggested that it was impossible to incorporate most products into the central-planning system, given their sheer number, variety, and specifications. The State Planning Commission can directly manage only several hundred products, the majority of which are amenable to only rough estimates. The category of those products that are subject to accurate calculation includes only several dozen. Adding to the complexity and variability within the central-planning system are the large numbers of enterprise units, the multiplicity of administrative agencies, the numerous echelons of the hierarchy, and the size of the country. Moreover, the lines of communication are exceedingly long. It usually takes several months to process one job, a feat that would seem to be achievable within one day. See Xue Muqiao, "Shehui zhuyi jingji de jihua guanli" (The planning management of the socialist economy), in *Shehuizhuyi: jingji zhong jihua yu shichang de guanxi, Shang* (The relationship between planning and market in the socialist economy, vol. 1) (Beijing: Zhongguo Shehuikexue chubanshe, 1979), pp. 15–43.

3. Andrew G. Walder, "Organized Dependency and Cultures of Authority in Chinese Industry," *Journal of Asian Studies* 43, no. 1 (November 1983): 51–76.

4. Andrew G. Walder, *Communist Neo-traditionalism: Work and Authority in Chinese Industry* (Berkeley: University of California Press, 1987), 1–27.

5. Andrew G. Walder, "Wage Reform and the Web of Factory Interests," *China Quarterly* 109 (March 1987): 22–41.

6. Andrew G. Walder, "The Informal Dimension of Enterprise Financial Reform," in Joint Economic Committee, U.S. Congress, ed., *China's Economy Looks Toward the Year 2000. Vol. II: Four Modernizations* (Washington, D.C.: U.S. Government Printing Office, 1986), pp. 630–645.

7. Alfred Stepan, *The State and Society: Peru in Comparative Perspective* (Princeton: Princeton University Press, 1978), pp. 26–72.

8. The principle of subsidiarity is taken as an empirical test for the corporatist state. Stepan, *State and Society: Peru*, pp. 35–40.

9. Philippe C. Schmitter, "Still the Century of Corporatism?" in Fredrick B. Pike and Thomas Stritch, eds., *The New Corporatism* (Notre Dame: University of Notre Dame Press, 1974), pp. 99–105.

10. Valerie Bunce and John M. Echols III, "Soviet Politics in the Brezhnev Era: 'Pluralism' or 'Corporatism?'" in Donald R. Kelley, ed., *Soviet Politics in the Brezhnev Era* (New York: Praeger, 1980), pp. 1–26.

11. David Lane, *The Socialist Industrial State* (London: Allen & Unwin, 1976), pp. 147–148.

12. Lane, *The Socialist Industrial State*, p. 173.

13. Juan Linz, "Totalitarian and Authoritarian Regimes," in Fred I. Greenstein and Nelson W. Polsby, eds., *Macropolitical Theory* (*Handbook of Political Science, Vol. 3*) (Reading, Mass.: Addison-Wesley, 1975), pp. 176–252.

14. Alec Nove, *Stalinism and After* (London: Allen & Unwin, 1981), pp. 52–54.
15. Barry M. Richman, *Soviet Management* (Englewood Cliffs: Prentice-Hall, 1965), p. 169.
16. Peter Nan-shong Lee, *Industrial Management and Economic Reform in China, 1949–1984* (London: Oxford University Press, 1987), pp. 12–14.
17. Lee, *Industrial Management.*
18. The radical element in the CCP's action program can be detected in reading Mao Zedong's work, for instance: Mao Tse-tung [Mao Zedong], "On New Democracy," in *Selected Works of Mao Tse-tung* (Peking: Foreign Languages Press, 1967), 2:339–430. Here the two-stage revolution is taken as radical because its action program called for drastic transformation of the society on a continuous basis. Chalmers Johnson was among the first authors to document the CCP's two-stage revolution, in "The Two Chinese Revolutions," *China Quarterly*, no. 39 (July–September, 1969): 12–29.
19. Mao, "On New Democracy," pp. 360–362.
20. Tang Tsou, *The Cultural Revolution and Post-Mao Reforms: A Historical Perspective* (Chicago: University of Chicago Press, 1986), pp. 267–279.
21. The notions of "exclusionary" and "inclusionary" corporatism are borrowed from Alfred Stepan, *State and Society*, pp. 46, 73–81. Andrew Walder argues that a new working class was created in China by the party-state after 1949 and that it was not the same class as before 1949. This notion of re-created classes is applicable to the peasantry as well. See Andrew G. Walder, "The Remaking of the Chinese Working Class, 1949–1981," *Modern China* 10, no. 1 (January 1984): 3–48.
22. Ken Jowitt, "Soviet Neotraditionalism: The Political Corruption of a Leninist Regime," *Soviet Studies* 35, no. 3 (July 1983): 275–297.
23. Tsou, *Cultural Revolution*, pp. 144–188.
24. V. I. Lenin, "The Immediate Tasks of Government," in *Selected Works*, pp. 424–425, cited from Stepan, *State and Society*, p. 36.
25. V. I. Lenin, *The State and Revolution* (Peking: Foreign Languages Press, 1976), pp. 122–123.
26. Alfred G. Meyer, "Theories of Convergence," in Chalmers Johnson, ed., *Change in Communist Systems* (Stanford: Stanford University Press, 1970), pp. 325–330.
27. Francis Hearn, "Rationality and Bureaucracy: Maoist Contributions to Marxist Theory of Bureaucracy," *Sociological Quarterly*, no. 19 (Winter 1978): p. 39.
28. Neil Harding, "Socialism, Society and the Organic Labour State," in Neil Harding, ed., *The State in Socialist Society* (London: Macmillan, 1984), pp. 1–50.
29. The conceptual distinctions concerning the types of rationality are based on the following works: Wolfgang Schluchter, "The Paradox of Rationalization: On the Relation of Ethics and World," in Guenther Roth and Wolfgang Schluchter, *Max Weber's Vision of History: Ethics and Methods* (Berkeley: University of California Press, 1979), pp. 11–64; Rogers Brubaker, *The Limits of Rationality* (London: Allen & Unwin, 1984), pp. 8–45; J. E. T. Eldridge, ed., *Max Weber* (London: Nelson, 1972), pp. 53–70.
30. Tang Tsou draws a distinction between "totalism" and totalitarianism. The former refers to an endeavor to impose total dominance over the society, but with subjectively good intentions. "Twentieth-Century Chinese Politics

and Western Political Science," *PS* (of APSA), 20, no. 2 (Spring 1987): 327–333. A. Kassof, "The Administered Society: Totalitarianism without Terror," in F. J. Fleron, Jr., ed., *Communist Studies and Social Sciences* (Chicago: Rand McNally, 1969), pp. 153–169.

31. Stepan, *State and Society,* pp. 40–45.
32. Jeremy Azrael, "Varieties of De-Stalinization," in Chalmers Johnson, ed., *Change in Communist Systems* (Stanford: Stanford University Press, 1970), pp. 135–152.
33. Lane, *The Socialist Industrial State,* pp. 19–43.
34. Maurice Meisner, *Mao's China, A History of the People's Republic* (New York: Free Press, 1977), pp. 55–63.
35. Harry Harding, *Organizing China, the Problem of Bureaucracy 1949–1976* (Stanford: Stanford University Press, 1981).
36. Richard Lowenthal, "Development vs. Utopia in Communist Policy," in Johnson, ed., *Change in Communist Systems,* pp. 33–116.
37. Alec Nove, *The Soviet Economic System* (London: Allen & Unwin, 1977), pp. 288–322.
38. This passage is based on a summary and interpretation of Charles M. Lindblom's view: *Politics and Markets: The World's Political Economic Systems* (New York: Basic Books, 1977), pp. 237–260, 276–290.
39. Lindblom, *Politics and Markets,* pp. 247–260.
40. Valerie Bunce and John M. Echols III, "Power and Policy in Communist Systems: The Problem of Incrementalism," *Journal of Politics* 40 (1978): 911–932.
41. Lee, *Industrial Management,* pp. 170–175, 212–215.
42. Hu Qiaomu, "Observe Economic Laws, Speed Up the Four Modernizations," *Beijing Review* 21, no. 45 (November 10, 1978): 13–23; 21, no. 47 (November 24, 1978): 13–21. That article was published in Hu Qiaomu's name, but it was likely the product of a writing group. The article was significant because its diagnosis was based on an analysis of organization rather than of class politics.
43. Nicos P. Mouzelis, *Organization and Bureaucracy: An Analysis of Modern Theories* (Chicago: Aldine, 1967), pp. 59–62; Anthony Downs, *Inside Bureaucracy* (Boston: Little, Brown, 1967), pp. 144–174; Michael Crozier, *The Bureaucratic Phenomenon* (Chicago: University of Chicago Press, 1964), pp. 183–194.
44. Mao Zedong, "Lun shi da guanxi" (On the ten great relationships), in *Mao Zedong xuanji* (The collected works of Mao Zedong) (Beijing: Renmin chubanshe, 1977), 5:267–288.
45. "Liu Shaoqi zai Shigang jinxing fangeming huodong de zuixing lu" (The criminal record of Liu Shaoqi's counter-revolutionary activities in Shijinshan Steel and Iron Works), *Beijing gongren* (Beijing Workers), no. 4 (May 17, 1961); *Jielu Zhongguo Heluxiaofu de yige fangeming xiuzhengzhuyi jingji gangling* (Expose a counter-revolutionary economic platform of China's Khrushchev) (Beijing: Red Guard publications, January 24, 1968); in the collection of the University of Chicago Library.
46. "Zhanduan Liu Shaoqi shenxiang Daqing de mozhua" (Chop off the demon's claws of Liu Shaoqi stretching to Daqing), *Changzheng* (Long March), no. 15 (April 19, 1967): 1–2. In fact, Liu Shaoqi's view is congruent with the reporting in early 1966; see "Daqing jianshe cheng gongnong jiehe de xinxing kuangqu" (Build Daqing into a new type of mining

community with worker peasant integration), *Jingji yanjiu* (Economic Research), no. 4 (1966): 23.

47. Lee, *Industrial Management*, pp. 32–33; Peter N. S. Lee and Irene H. S. Chow, "The Remunerative System in State-Owned Industrial Enterprises in Post-Mao China: Changes and Continuity, 1977–1984," in Joseph C. H. Chai and Chi-keung Leung, eds., *China's Economic Reform* (Hong Kong: Centre of Asian Studies, University of Hong Kong, 1987), p. 179.

48. Lee and Chow, "The Remunerative System," pp. 183–185.

49. Tang Tsou, "The Values of the Chinese Revolution," in Michel Oksenberg, ed., *China's Development Experience*, Proceedings of the Academy of Political Science, no. 31, March 1973 (New York: Praeger, 1973). pp. 27–41.

50. "Several Questions on Accelerating the Development of Industry," *Summary of the People's Republic of China Magazines*, no. 926 (May 23, 1977): 8–28.

51. Joseph S. Berliner, *Factory and Manager in the USSR* (Cambridge: Harvard University Press, 1968), pp. 75–87; Nove, *The Soviet Economic System*, pp. 83–119.

52. An earlier version of the profit-retention fund, known as "the factory director fund," was introduced in the state-owned industrial enterprises in Northeast China. See "Dongbei fangzhi guanliju, 'jingji hesuanzhi de zongjie' " (The summary of the experience in the economic accounting system), *Xinhua yuebao* (New China Monthly) 4, no. 2 (June 1951): 353–356.

53. Lee, *Industrial Management*, pp. 55–60.

54. A historical account of the evolution of the "enterprise fund" is given in "Sanshiwu nian lai caizheng gongzuo de jida chengjiu" (The great achievements of financial work for 35 years), *Caizheng* (Finance), no. 10 (1984): 3–8. The 1978 version of the enterprise fund is reported in "Guoying qiye shixing tiqu he shiyong qiye jijin" (The trial implementation of the retention and use of enterprise fund in the state-owned enterprises), *Renmin ribao* (People's Daily), December 28, 1978, p. 1.

55. For the key features and evolution of the two versions of the profit-retention system, see "Guojia jingji weiyuanhui guanyu kuoda qiye zizhuquan shidian gongzuo qingkuang he jinhou yijian de baogaoshu" (The report and opinions of the State Economic Commission concerning the situation and the future of the task of pilot programs of expanding enterprise autonomy), *Guowuyuan gongbao* (Bulletin of the State Council), no. 14 (1980): 419–427; "Guojia jingji weiyuanhui guowuyuan tizhi gaige bangongshi guanyu gongye guanli tizhi gaige zuotanhui huibao tigang" (The outline report of the State Economic Commission and Institutional Reform Office of the State Council concerning the conference on the reform of industrial management system), *Guowuyuan gongbao*, no. 9 (1981): 268–278.

56. "Caizhengbu guanyu guoying qiye ligaishui gongzuo huiyi de baogao" (The report of the Ministry of Finance concerning the national work conference on the substitution of taxation for profit remittance), *Guowuyuan gongbao*, no. 11 (1983): 475–478.

57. Lee, *Industrial Management*, p. 182.

58. Interview on July 4, 1988, at Beijing; "Peitao wanshan shenhua chengbao jingying zeren zhi" (Further development of the contractual responsibility system), *Renmin ribao*, February 14, 1988, p. 1.

59. Peter Nan-shong Lee, "Enterprise Autonomy Policy in Post-Mao China," *China Quarterly*, no. 105 (March 1986): 46–49.

60. Robert T. Golembiewski, "Civil Service and Managing Work," in Robert T. Golembiewski et al., eds., *Public Administration: Readings in Institutions, Processes, Behavior, Policy* (Chicago: Rand McNally, 1926), pp. 272–284.
61. Golembiewski, "Civil Service."
62. Jiang Yiwei, "Qiye benwei lun" (On the central place for the enterprise), in Zhongguo shehui kexueyuan gongye jingji yanjiusuo zhuzhichu, ed., *Jingji fazhan yu jingji gaige* (The economic development and economic reform) (Beijing: Jingji guanli chubanshe, 1988), pp. 266–289; originally published in *China's Social Science*, no. 1 (1980).
63. Hu, "Observe the Economic Laws," *Beijing Review* 21, no. 45 (November 10, 1978): 7–15; no. 46 (November 17, 1978): 13–23.
64. "Zhongguo gongchangdang dishiyi jie zhongyang weiyuanhui disanci quanti daibiao dahui gongbao" (The communiqué of the Third Plenum of the Eleventh Party Congress, CCP) *Hongqi* (Red Flag), no. 1 (1979): 17.
65. In contrast to the collective-owned industries, which are given autonomy to undertake independent economic activities, the state-owned industrial enterprises are given limited power, that is, in managerial and marketing functions only. See articles 16 and 17 of the 1982 constitution of the PRC.
66. "Zhonghua Renmin Gongheguo quanmin suoyouzhi gongye qiyefa" (The law of state-owned industrial enterprises of the People's Republic of China) *Guowuyuan gongbao*, no. 3 (1988): 80–88, articles 23 and 33.
67. Lee and Chow, "The Remunerative System," pp. 179–180.
68. "Several Questions on Accelerating the Development of Industry," *Summary of the People's Republic of China Magazines*, no. 926 (May 23, 1977): 8–28.
69. Zhuang Qidong, ed., *Laodong gongzi shouce* (The manual of labor and wage) (Tianjin: Tianjin renmin chubanshe, 1984), pp. 63–64.
70. Lee and Chow, "The Remunerative System," p. 192.
71. "Caizhengbu guanyu kaizao caiwu da jiancha de qingkuang he jinyibu yansu caizheng jilu de baogao" (The report of the Ministry of Finance concerning the situation of implementing major financial inspections and the further tightening of financial discipline), *Guowuyuan gongbao*, no. 11 (1984): 325–329; "Guoying qiye chengben guanli tiaoli" (The regulations on cost management in the state-owned enterprises), *Guowuyuan gongbao*, no. 6 (1984): 182–189.
72. "Caizhengbu, laodong renshibu guanyu yange kongzhi fafang gezhong butie, jintie he jiji tigao tuixiu daiyu wenti de baogao" (The report of the Ministry of Finance and Ministry of Labor and Personnel concerning the strict control over the payment of various subsidies, bonus and prohibition of unauthorized increase of retirement pension), *Guowuyuan gongbao*, no. 5 (1987): 195–197; "Shenjiju guanyu jiaqiang neibu shenji gongzuo de baogao" (The report of the Auditing Bureau concerning the strengthening of internal auditing work), *Guowuyuan gongbao*, no. 21 (1987): 707–709; "Guowuyuan guanyu zhankai 1987 nian shuishou caiwu wujia dajiancha de tongzhi" (The circular of the State Council concerning the general auditing of taxation, finance, and prices in 1987), *Guowuyuan gongbao*, no. 24 (1987): 787–789.
73. Walder, "Wage Reform," pp. 22–41.
74. "Zhonggong zhongyang guanyu jingji tizhi gaige de jueding" (The resolution of the Central Committee, the CCP, concerning the reform of the economic system), *Dagong bao* (Public Tribune), October 21, 1984, p. 6.

75. "Guanyu gongren tuixiu tuizhi de zhanxing banfa" (The provisional measures for the retirement and termination of duties of workers), in Laodong renshibu zhengce yanjiushi, ed., *Zhonghua Renmin Gongheguo laodong fagui xuanbian* (The selection of labor laws and regulations of the PRC) (Beijing: Laodong renshi chubanshe, 1986), p. 339.
76. "Guoying qiye zhao yong gongren zhanxing guiding" (Provisional regulations of the recruitment of workers in state-owned enterprises), in *Zhonghua Renmin Gongheguo fagui huibian* (The collection of laws and regulations of the PRC), January–December 1986, p. 785.
77. Guojia laodong zongju zhengce yanjiushi, ed., *Zhongguo laodong lifa ziliao huibian* (Collection of labor legislation in China) (Beijing: Gongren chubanshe 1980), p. 33.
78. Qiu Shanqi and Shi Mingcai, "Wo guo shehui baoxian de fazhan gaikuang" (A general account on the development of social security in the Chinese society), *Zhongguo laodong* (China's Labor), no. 12 (1985): 25.
79. "Guoying qiye shixing laodong hetongzhi zhanxing guiding" (The provisional regulations on the implementation of labor contracts in state-owned enterprises), *Renmin ribao*, September 10, 1986, p. 2.
80. "Guoying qiye couyong gongren zhanxing guiding" (The provisional regulations on the employment of workers in state-owned enterprises), *Renmin ribao*, September 10, 1986, p. 2.
81. "Guoying qiye zhigong daiye baoxian zhanxing guiding" (The provisional regulations of the employment insurance for the workers and staff members of state-owned enterprises), *Renmin ribao*, September 10, 1986, p. 2.
82. "Guoying qiye citui weiji zhigong zhanxing guiding" (The provisional regulations of the dismissal of the workers and staff in violation of discipline in state-owned enterprises), *Renmin ribao*, September 10, 1986, p. 2.
83. "Jiasu laodong gongzi renshi zhidu de gaige" (To accelerate the reform of labor, wage and personnel systems), *Zhongguo laodong* (China's Labor), no. 1 (1985): 4–6.
84. Dalian shi Laodongju, "Gaohao laodong gongzi baoxian zhidu peitao gaige, jiji tuixing laodong hetong zhi" (To improve the synchronized reforms in labor, wage and insurance and to implement actively the labor contract system), *Zhongguo laodong kexue* (Science of Chinese Labor), no. 6 (1986): 13–14.
85. "Renzhen zhili zhengdun jiji wentuo de tuijin laodong gongzi baoxian zhidu gaige" (Take the rectification seriously; enthusiastically and steadily promote the reform of the systems of labor, wage and insurance), *Zhongguo laodong kexue* (Science of Chinese Labor), no. 1 (1989): 6–7.
86. Ibid.
87. "Jiasu laodong gongzi renshi zhidu de gaige," pp. 2–3.

6

From revolutionary cadres
to bureaucratic technocrats

HONG YUNG LEE

Although the party-state that the Chinese Communist Party (CCP) created turned out to be the most powerful state in Chinese history and
frequently has used its coercive power ruthlessly to implement social
changes, the political process has never been institutionalized. That was
the case during the Maoist era, as well as in the past ten years of reform,
when Mao's patriarchal leadership has been publicly repudiated. The
bloody June 4 incident once again demonstrates China's failure to vest
political authority in offices and to develop a procedural rule for decision
making. Deng Xiaoping, whose only official position was to chair the
Military Affairs Commission, made the final decision to crush the students' democratic movement. Zhao Ziyang's greatest mistake during the
crisis supposedly was to reveal to Gorbachev the CCP's practice of referring all important matters to Deng Xiaoping.

These two contradictory aspects of Chinese politics – the powerful
party-state and the utter lack of institutionalization – lead one to view
the Chinese state as a political elite rather than as institutionalized sets
of offices whose incumbents are empowered to exercise the state's authority. These aspects also point to a broad hypothesis that the importance of the political elite is inversely related to the degree of
institutionalization of political offices.

Mosca's and Pareto's insights that a political elite exerts enormous
influence in shaping a political system were particularly true of traditional
China, where a well-defined ruling elite of gentry-scholar-bureaucrats
dominated not only political life but also economic and cultural life.
China's embrace of socialism reinforced the historical tradition. A socialist system, with ultimate faith in the rationality of the human mind,
replaced an allegedly chaotic system of market control with a system in
which decisions would be deliberately made by the political elite located
in a hierarchically constructed organizational setting. Because of the cen-
trality of the political elite in the socialist system, many social scientists

180

have attributed China's regime transformation to the rise of a new type of elite: the "new technocratic elite," the "managerial modernizers," or the "technically trained bureaucrats."[1]

With these general observations of the Chinese political process in mind, this essay analyzes the prolonged process by which the old revolutionaries have been replaced by the new generation of "bureaucratic technocrats."

REVOLUTIONARY CADRES

The CCP was founded by radical intellectuals who were concerned with the crises that beset China in the 1920s. The thirteen members who participated in the First Party Congress were from the best educated group in China at the time and were very young, with an average age of twenty-nine. None of them appears to have studied natural science; they had concentrated instead on the humanities and social sciences, so that they resembled Lasswell's "symbol manipulators." Although little background information is available on the fifty-seven original party members, a Chinese source has reported that all except four of them were intellectuals.[2]

Founded by intellectuals, the CCP first attempted to develop itself into a revolutionary party in the image of the Bolsheviks in the Soviet Union by recruiting industrial workers. After several abortive attempts at urban uprising, Mao shifted the focus of membership recruitment to the peasants. During the war with the Japanese, the party's strategy to unite itself with all patriotic elements, including intellectuals and rich peasants, allowed many educated people, who tended to come from economically well-to-do social groups, to join the party. By the end of World War II, membership had reached about 1.2 million.

However, the CCP's policy toward educated groups changed during the civil war. Its military confrontations with the Guomindang (GMD) led the CCP to adopt a radical land-reform policy that resulted in recruitment of many party members from the "poor peasants and hired laborers." By the time the CCP seized political power, it had accumulated thirty years of revolutionary experience and boasted almost 4.5 million seasoned party members. Most members were poorly educated young people from the most disadvantaged social groups.[3] For instance, family-background data for the 18,903 party members in Heilongjiang showed 21 percent workers, 49 percent hired laborers, and 25 percent poor peasants. Those three categories accounted for 95 percent of the party membership.[4] Fifty-one percent of the Heilongjiang party members were illiterate, and 23 percent "could barely recognize the characters," for a total of 74 percent with little education. Those who had attended primary

181

schools totaled 23.4 percent, whereas only a mere 2.4 percent had attended middle schools.[5]

Heilongjiang may have been an extreme case. However, in every sense, the party members were from the least well educated and most disadvantaged social groups in the rural areas. They served the party well when its main task was fighting a guerrilla war. The type of leader needed by the party at that time was the heroic, selfless guerrilla fighter dedicated to the cause, not some educated professional with specialized knowledge or administrative skills. An effective guerrilla commander had to take care of all the needs of a given base area's members by mobilizing support from the available sources. The peasant youth could readily provide those leadership qualities.[6]

Most of the members who joined the party before 1949 landed cadre positions when the People's Republic of China (PRC) was founded. Most of them stayed in their politically influential positions, dominating the Chinese political process for almost thirty years. The founders' mentality, experiences, and understanding of Marxism-Leninism had profound implications, particularly for the personnel management of cadres and the structure of the party-state.

The founders continued the practice of selecting cadre leaders from special-interest political movements, as they had before 1949. When some pragmatic leaders attempted to turn the focus of the regime to economic development, which would require the recruitment of intellectuals, the former guerrilla fighters resisted. Instead, each political movement (e.g., land reform, collectivization, the antirightist campaign, the Great Leap Forward, the "socialist education movement," the Cultural Revolution) produced activists who eventually joined the party and became cadre leaders.

The personnel-management system during the Maoist era reinforced the image of officials as heroic revolutionary leaders. Political loyalty ("virtue") became increasingly important, whereas the relative weight of achievement and expertise ("ability") declined in personnel management to such an extent that some called it a "virtuocracy."[7] Political loyalty, frequently inferred from one's class background, was first defined in terms of party membership, but as the party ranks swelled with new recruits from the most disadvantaged social groups, the criterion changed to one's enthusiasm in supporting Mao's thought. Although universally applicable to every Chinese – except those with undesirable family backgrounds, of course – the political criteria tended to become subjective, allowing the evaluators wide discretionary power, while encouraging "faked" activism. Consequently, as was the case with the former revolutionaries, those who became cadre leaders after 1949 owed their official positions to their political loyalty, as demonstrated in their political activism and inferred from their good class backgrounds. Despite their low levels of education, they gradually moved up the bureaucratic hierarchy, becoming the leading officials at all levels of the bureaucracy.

The regime failed to educate its incumbent officials. The regime's cadre educational program came to an end with the Great Leap Forward. In reflecting on what went wrong with the Chinese political system that he had helped build, Lu Dingyi, former director of the Propaganda Department, candidly attributed the Maoist radicalism to the low educational level among the cadres:

[At the beginning of the liberation, we] should have sent some Party members [from peasant and worker backgrounds] to receive an education – not short term training, but a regular college education. If [we had followed] that way for 10 years or 20 years, it would have been very good for our construction. Not pushing for that idea was largely my responsibility. That was a big mistake.

If a mistake has been made, it is better to recognize it. I am a graduate of Jiaotong University, but I have worked for a long time in propaganda, education and cultural fields, and have not paid special attention to the importance of intellectuals. That was a great mistake! Any army without culture [wenhua] is a stupid army. Without culture, how can one know what a democratic legal system is, and thereby avoid promoting feudalistic [policies], such as promoting backyard furnaces to the extent of cutting down trees, and stressing grain to the extent of eliminating sideline farming? [The lack of culture] led to blind commandism at the top level and to blind compliance at the lower level; both of them are equally ignorant. Ignorance led to the persecution of the intellectuals.[8]

The party-state not only jealously guarded its prerogative over personnel management of cadres but also exercised that authority in a highly centralized fashion, without developing any meaningful classification scheme for the gigantic cadre corps. Superior organs two levels above a cadre's level controlled its personnel authority. The party committees and organizational departments managed all the cadre corps using political criteria. The personnel dossier system gave the superior organizations tight control over cadres under their jurisdiction, further reducing the individual's job mobility and undermining effective use of scarce manpower resources, in addition to increasing the organization's grip on its people. Because of the politicization of management criteria, people lived in fear of what was contained in their dossiers, and anyone with access to dossiers could gain considerable leverage over others.

At the same time, party members were expected to play conflicting roles: not only revolutionaries but also administrators, politicians, and bureaucrats.[9] The cadres were hierarchically organized, with grades, official positions, and salaries all specified by rules and regulations. They were subject to the personnel decisions of superiors. As the subtle balance in the Leninist principle of "democratic centralism" shifted in favor of greater centralization, it became only a justification for a quasi-military command structure, with authority flowing from the Politburo down to the secretary of each party cell. As agents of the state, the cadres were expected to carry out faithfully every policy, regardless of its popularity with the masses or its accordance with the perceived interests of the masses. As revolutionaries, they were expected to represent "working-class interests" through the "mass line," but the top leaders largely pre-determined what those interests were, ignoring input from lower-level cadres.

Like politicians, cadres were required to energize the policy-making process by mobilizing and inspiring the masses through propaganda, education, and personal example. But unlike politicians in the Western democracies, they were not allowed to represent sectarian interests or to work as arbitrators of conflicting sectarian interests. Cadres were in-structed to investigate realistically the conditions in China's polity, but the findings in such investigations were not allowed to affect the general policy direction adopted by the top leaders according to ideological cri-teria. To perform those conflicting roles of revolutionaries and bureau-crats, the cadres needed the support of the masses, but they were not allowed to represent the interests of the units they led. Consequently, the Chinese bureaucratic system was a strange mixture, much different from Max Weber's ideal type. It was hierarchically organized, with full-time cadres, but it lacked such other characteristics as impersonality, technical expertise, and political neutrality.

In brief, the Maoist version of socialism reflected the system of cadre recruitment and promotion adopted during and after the revolution, and the people recruited under that system further reinforced the Maoist version of socialism.

STRUCTURE OF THE PARTY-STATE

The party-state structure that gradually evolved in the 1950s and 1960s reflected the experiences of the founders, including "their own pre-1949 experience in conducting revolutionary struggle and administering 'lib-erated areas'."[10] Other factors such as "the theoretical Leninist model of 'democratic centralism,' the post-Leninist model of Soviet society," and "China's centuries old tradition of authoritarianism, elitism, ideo-logical orthodoxy, and bureaucratic administration" also helped shape the organizational structure of the PRC. Those factors, however, were filtered through the founders' rural orientation: They stressed subsistence and self-sufficiency, as well as a moral approach to politics; they dis-trusted exchange through a market mechanism and were ignorant of the functional prerequisites for a modern society. Several observations can be made regarding the Chinese party-state.

First, the range of activities directly regulated by the Maoist party-state was all-inclusive.[11] In the name of the socialist revolution and transformation, the party-state gradually expanded its control over all governmental and coercive instruments, as well as all economic and human resources, goods, and services that the Chinese people needed in their daily lives.[12] Second, despite the comprehensive scope of the affairs regulated by the party-state, structural differentiation within it and society was minimal during Mao's era, largely because of Mao's concern that functional specialization would foster a new social stratification. Third, the party's "monistic leadership" further precluded any structural differentiation. Although initially introduced in 1942 as "a means of resolving the lack of coordination between the various organizations of the party, government, and military that were scattered all over the guerilla base areas," the party committees and the party core-group (*dangzu*) system came to dominate every organization, political, economic, or otherwise.[13] Fourth, the official ideology, although not fully internalized by cadres, operated as a structure in the Althusserian sense by limiting the policy choices of the political elite.[14]

The increase in the scope of political activities, without accompanying structural differentiation and functional specialization, resulted in enormous discretionary powers for the leaders of each governing unit. The absence of a market exchange and the low level of functional interdependence meant that any horizontal coordination and communication between two units had to be achieved through the top leaders of each unit or through the higher echelon that had jurisdiction over the two units. Because each unit was organized to be self-sufficient in providing most if not all, the services needed by its members, its leaders had authority over a wide range of matters directly affecting the daily lives of its members. There existed no institutional mechanism to check cadres' abuses of authority, despite the emphasis given to the mass line. The inability of the masses to air their opinions of the leadership largely accounted for the violent attacks on political leaders during the socialist education movement and the Cultural Revolution.[15] During normal periods, when no political campaign was in progress, any complaints about cadre leaders often went directly to those very leaders, and they in turn would retaliate against their critics.

Effective operation of the Maoist system depended heavily on the quality and ideological commitment of the cadres. Therefore, Mao subjected them to continual ideological campaigns, refusing to grant any legitimacy to their personal interests. His approach, however, did not work, because his expectations for the cadres were too high, and as such campaigns were repeated, the process became mere ritual. According to the ideal vision of the Maoists, the cadres were supposed to have forfeited their personal interests to the higher cause of the revolution, but in reality they frequently resorted to what Walder calls "principled particularism" in order to protect their personal interests, as well as to try to adjust to the conflicting pressures on them.[16]

Although many of the revolutionary heroes had been amply qualified to lead specific political movements, they were not suited for building institutions or for leading China in the task of economic development. Because usually they represented the first generation in their families to obtain official positions with prestige and a regular salary, they owed their positions, power, income, and prestige to the party-state. As beneficiaries of the new order, they were loyal to the top party leaders and eager to defend the new order. Moreover, some of them were genuine believers in the party, not exclusively because of career considerations, but also because of a certain amount of idealism and commitment to the cause of the CCP.[17]

For those reasons, revolutionary cadres enthusiastically subscribed to the official ideology of Mao Zedong's thought, which largely reflected their own successful experience of mobilizing the masses for such specific tasks as fighting guerrilla wars and promoting land reform, collectivization, and other political campaigns. They accepted uncritically Mao's version of socialism and his approach to building socialism, carrying out "whatever the party told [them] to do" as far as the commands were transmitted through the organizational channel. The Maoist method of mass mobilization and political campaigns, which stressed ideological incentives over material concerns, was congruent with their own personal experiences. In the eyes of the revolutionary cadres, when selecting or evaluating candidates for membership, dedication to the cause, obedience, diligence, conscientiousness, and correct intention were more important than ability, efficiency, ingenuity, and achievement of results.[18] In other words, the revolutionary cadres tended to stress political criteria rather than achievement-oriented criteria.

Cadre members' lack of education and narrow outlook tended to make them submissive to their superiors, carrying out irrational orders blindly. Although incumbents claimed to have "rich practical experience and familiarity with [their] work," their lack of formal schooling made it impossible for them to raise their "practical experience to the level of scientific knowledge."

Their reliance on experience, and their inability to comprehend the internal logic of matters often produced undesirable and unintended consequences. For example, the Linzhou district has a large number of mountains, and its forest is big, and that is our advantage. But because the cadres did not understand the interdependency of forestry and agriculture which promoted dialectically each other, and we did not understand the scientific notion of equilibrium in ecology, they carried out a policy of "taking grain as the key" for a long time. The result was the destruction of forests without any rise in grain production. Thus, an advantage was turned into a disadvantage, and weakness replaced strength. At the same time, the low educational level, the limited amount of knowledge, and the narrow views of some cadres made them slow to accept new things and move away from their ossified ideology. The same conditions made them comfortable with the old work style of issuing an administrative order and then "cutting everything with one knife" in violation of the laws of nature.[19]

In that respect, the communist elite were quite different from the traditional elite, who had come mainly from the landlord class and wealthy families and had their own social and economic interests to defend. At the same time, as scholar-officials appointed by the imperial court after passing the civil-service examination, the traditional elite also represented the state's authority. Their dual role helped maintain the balance between society and state.[20]

IMPETUS FOR THE CHANGES

Because of its rigidity and overconcentration of power, the Maoist system developed a number of problems. The expansion of the party-state's control over the people's activities and the elimination of resistance from civil society did not end social conflicts and tension. Instead, they were brought into the interparty struggle.[21] Replacing an impersonal and erratic market mechanism with a political authority that supposedly would make rational decisions might be ideal in a purely logical sense, but in reality the command economy turned out to have only a "strong thumb, [but] no fingers," enhancing the power of the well-entrenched cadre corps.[22] Mao's attempt to lend moral authority to the cadres' power through ideological education only politicized morality and ethics, rather than humanizing power relations, thus adding only ideological legitimacy to the cadres' domination. Mao's effort to resolve those intrinsic dilemmas by mobilizing the masses in the Cultural Revolution paradoxically further strengthened the party-state's domination, instead of democratizing the rigid system.

The Cultural Revolution symbolized the profound crisis for the first generation of revolutionaries concerning the issue of revolution versus economic development, and the concomitant issue of cadre recruitment.[23] Bureaucratic modernizers such as Liu Shaoqi and Zhou Enlai wanted to improve the overall quality of the cadre corps by co-opting the intellectuals from the "undesirable" classes into the power structure. They also tried to develop functionally specialized governmental organs and to secularize the official ideology. Mao viewed the co-optation of intellectuals as a betrayal of the Chinese revolution at the expense of disadvantaged social groups. Worried about the possibility that the cadre corps might emerge as a new ruling class, Mao insisted that the cadres continue to act as selfless heroic revolutionaries, willing to submit themselves to the masses. In addition to that ideological issue, political considerations entered into the complex maneuvering and countermaneuvering at the top level of the ruling elite. After the failure of the Great Leap Forward, some of Mao's former colleagues questioned the validity of his approach to economic development, and his popularity with the bureaucracy declined.

When Mao ended the party's control over society, allowing free mobilization of the masses, all of the social conflicts that the powerful party-state had previously managed to suppress began to erupt, throwing China into chaos. Although the official targets of the Cultural Revolution were the "power-holders taking the capitalist road," the factionalized mass organizations expanded the range of targets to include all the power-holders. Following purges of a large number of cadre leaders, who in effect symbolized formal authority, the entire authority structure of the party-state began to collapse.

When the mass-mobilization phase of the Cultural Revolution ended in 1968, the basic cleavages among the elite ran along the lines of the situational groups that had arisen during the preceding two years of mass mobilization: the initiators, the beneficiaries, the survivors, and the victims of the Cultural Revolution. Those four groups, each with its own distinctive support base, held disparate views on the Cultural Revolution and its policy agenda. Among the initiators, Lin Biao's power base, as a military man, was limited to a few military officers. The "Gang of Four" resorted to the revolutionary method of mobilizing discontented social groups against the establishment. In order to strengthen their power base, they recruited and promoted into the bureaucracy young rebels spawned by the Cultural Revolution, while resisting the rehabilitation of the purged cadre leaders. The beneficiaries of the Cultural Revolution approved of some rehabilitation, but they resisted the return of Deng Xiaoping. The survivors of the Cultural Revolution advocated large-scale rehabilitation. The maneuvers and countermaneuvers, coalitions and conflicts, of those four groups ended with the victory of the rehabilitated cadre corps after Mao's death.

The impetus for reforms can therefore be traced back to the senior leaders' personal experiences of having suffered humiliation, purge, and imprisonment. As victims of the very system they had helped to create prior to 1966, they had finally seen its flaws. When they were forced to live with peasants and labor with workers, they had the opportunity to witness the prevalent poverty. That experience changed their perception of China's reality and the masses' desires. Moreover, by the time they regained political power, the rehabilitated cadre leaders had realized that the system's legitimacy had been so undermined in the eyes of the Chinese people that drastic measures would have to be taken in order to restore people's confidence in the CCP. Consequently, the one-time victims, having been rehabilitated, became born-again reformers, shifting the regime's main task from revolutionary change to economic development, a task that would require sweeping reforms of the system.

Once the CCP had taken on economic reconstruction as its main task, it soon became clear that the existing cadre corps was ill-equipped for the new task of economic development. Because of the practice of recruiting cadres from political movements, the absence of a regular retirement system, the emphasis on seniority in the promotion system, and finally large-scale rehabilitation, the Chinese bureaucracy grew enormously. The year in which one joined the revolutionary movement generally was predictive of one's bureaucratic ranking.

As for the educational backgrounds of the 21 million cadre leaders, official Chinese sources reported that 19 percent of them (4 million, which was equal to the total number of college graduates that China had produced since 1949) were college graduates, and 40 percent had progressed no further than junior high school.[24] On the whole, the existing cadre corps were "too old, too poorly educated, and too ossified in their thinking." Higher-ranking officials and political officers tended to be older and to have had less education than lower-ranking officials and functional cadre leaders. For instance, "there is not a single college graduate among the first secretaries in some provinces, districts, and counties. In some provinces and counties a large number of the top leaders have a cultural level equivalent only to primary school."[25]

The overall educational level for party members was also rather low. Only 4 percent of party members had received college-level educations. The majority of members had only primary-school educations (42.2 percent), and about 10.1 percent were illiterate. Surprisingly, 9.4 percent of all primary-school graduates were party members, whereas only 8.8 percent of all junior-high-school graduates were represented in the party. The overall educational level for CCP members in 1985 was similar to that for the Soviet Communist party in 1937.[26]

Because it was not feasible to expel those cadre leaders and party members with little education, as the Gang of Four had done, the party therefore opted for "selective recruitment" as a means for improving the quality of membership over a long period. The party had planned to recruit approximately 2 million specialists by 1990 so as to increase the percentage of members with college or specialized middle-school educations.[27]

In order to clear the way for a new cadre corps, the regime developed a special retirement system (*lixiu*) that allowed the old leaders to retire with all their perquisites intact. Consequently, the majority of the senior political leaders – those who had joined the revolution as guerrilla fighters, then founded the new regime, occupied the leading positions of the huge bureaucratic machine they created, sustained the revolutionary momentum, experienced the purges as the "power-holders taking the capitalist road," and finally regained power as rehabilitated leaders – were finally retired. The regime proceeded to promote a new breed of cadre leader, "better educated, younger in age, professionally competent, and revolutionized," while purging the former Cultural Revolution rebels-turned-cadre leaders as the "three types of people." Because of its pragmatic and incremental strategy of changing the cadre corps step by step, level by level, and group by group, a new generation of bureaucratic technocrats has finally replaced the revolutionary cadres as China's political elite. The key component of the CCP's cadre reform was to utilize its existing educated members.

NEW POLICY TOWARD INTELLECTUALS

"Intellectuals," in China, refers to those with a certain level of education, in contrast to those with no formal education. Initially, all those with a middle-school education were called intellectuals. But as the number of educated people increased, the term came to refer to those with a college-level education. Because of the limited number of college graduates in China, the term "intellectual" is also used to refer to those in certain professions – usually those with professional careers.

Although intellectuals do not constitute an independent class, they tend to be politically active in any society.[28] They were more so in traditional China, where officials were largely recruited through the civil-service examination. The question as to what extent economic wealth affected educational opportunities is debatable, but the possession of economic resources certainly was an advantage in preparing for the examination. Moreover, becoming an imperial bureaucrat had been one way of becoming a landlord. Thus, as the term "gentry-scholar-officials" implies, the close association of wealth, knowledge, and power in the hands of the ruling elite helped the traditional system survive for a long time. It is therefore not surprising to see that the traditional system came to an end with the Qing dynasty's abolition of the examination system, and thereafter "the violence specialists" ruled China during the chaotic warlord period. In socialist China, the type of the political elite changed from the gentry-scholar-officials to the revolutionary cadres, but the elitist tradition continued, probably reinforced by the basic nature of socialism.

Intellectuals can be divided into critical intellectuals and technocrats, according to their types of knowledge. The former has knowledge of tradition, values, norms, or ideology, as well as other subject matter related to understanding the current system and developing a new vision for the future. The technocrat has the technical knowledge necessary for solving problems and dealing with formal rationality – choosing the best means of implementation once the basic goals of society have been agreed upon.[29] The first type of knowledge can lead its possessors to act as defenders of the existing system, to rationalize and justify the status quo, or to act as critics, suggesting alternative visions for the future. In fact, Gouldner makes a distinction between intellectuals and the intelligentsia.[30] Intellectuals are the discoverers of new knowledge, which provides the basis for critiques of the existing system. That is, they are critical intellectuals. In contrast, the intelligentsia are the technocrats, who, by virtue of possessing narrowly defined specialized knowledge, see their task as elaborating on the existing knowledge and using it to improve the existing system. This dichotomy roughly parallels the differences between those trained in the social sciences and humanities, on the one hand, and those trained in natural sciences and technology, on the other.

As noted, the CCP was founded by the best educated group, but it then developed a bias against the educated sectors of the Chinese population for the reasons that, first, most of them came from the exploiting classes and, second, the educated tended to develop their own views independent of the official orthodoxy. In addition, the CCP leaders, including Mao, believed that they knew best about China's conditions and had a better vision for China's future. The success of the CCP in capturing political power after the prolonged civil struggle reinforced their self-confidence.

Being symbol manipulators themselves, the senior revolutionary leaders tended to regard intellectuals as ideologues and propagandists who could be used to mobilize the masses toward socialist goals, rather than as technocratic specialists. Consequently, during the Maoist era, assessments of intellectuals placed emphasis on their political views rather than their technical knowledge and their potential as problem-solvers. Mao even compared intellectuals to peacocks with shimmering political colors, suggesting that the party should control them firmly: not too tightly, lest they suffocate, and not too loosely, lest they fly away. As a result, only those intellectuals willing to collaborate with the official orthodoxy were allowed to flourish; the critical intellectuals were suppressed without mercy. Most such specialists remained in functional positions, having no political influence within the bureaucracy, and working under the supervision of revolutionary leaders who had no professional knowledge, as exemplified by Mao's slogan that "outsiders [nonspecialists] lead insiders [specialists]."

Mao's anti-intellectual attitude reflected the opinion of the majority of the largely uneducated cadre corps, who could be easily mobilized any time the intellectuals challenged the party's cadre line favoring peasants and hired laborers. During the land reform in 1947, the peasant cadres in some party organizations spontaneously seized the leadership from the intellectuals. When some intellectuals questioned the new order during the "Hundred Flowers" campaign, the top political leaders easily mobilized the newly recruited peasant party members and ruthlessly suppressed the challengers. By the time of the "antirightist campaign," 10 percent of the most outspoken intellectuals had been silenced by the party. Poor peasants constituted the majority of the party members, and because of their mentality, outlook, and dedicated approach to carrying out political programs, they could be easily exploited by the party leaders to crush the demands of the intellectuals.

During the Cultural Revolution, the powerless intellectuals were made scapegoats in the struggle between the power-holders and the Maoist radicals. The Gang of Four, although themselves ideologues – or petty intellectuals, according to their adversaries – stepped up the discrimination against intellectuals and technocrats to the extent of making them the "stinking ninth category," after the landlords, rich peasants, counterrevolutionaries, bad elements, rightists, renegades, enemy agents, and capitalist-roaders.[31] At one point the radical ideologues rounded up the professors in Beijing's universities and subjected them to a test on Mao's thought and other ideological questions. Many of the professors failed the test, which the radicals offered as evidence of their "parasite nature."[32]

During the chaotic period of the Cultural Revolution, many scientific research institutions were shut down, and scientific and technical personnel were sent to the countryside to "reform themselves through labor" or to work in factories on a permanent basis. Large numbers of college graduates were assigned to jobs that had nothing to do with their academic training. For instance, "those specializing in rocketry were assigned as doorkeepers, remote control specialists were turned into butchers, those trained in computer science were employed in distilleries, entomologists were engaged in industrial design, mathematicians and foreign language specialists became fuel sellers or bakers."[33] Other specialists languished as buyers, salespeople, custodians, typists, cooks, and other menial workers. Most seriously affected were the scientists and technicians in the fields of agriculture, forestry, and livestock breeding; more than half of them worked as laborers, salespeople, and so forth.

That misuse of trained manpower resources further aggravated China's shortage of competent workers. Although the absolute numbers of technical personnel had risen since 1960, as a percentage of the total number of workers employed, they had decreased.

When China shifted its primary goal from revolution to economic development, giving priority to increased production rather than distribution of income, the regime's attitude toward its intellectuals also changed. The rehabilitated senior leaders for the first time publicly conceded that modernization would be impossible without knowledge, and therefore it would be necessary to "respect knowledge, and talents."[34] They also stressed possession of technical knowledge, rather than the ability to manipulate symbols, as the most important characteristic of the intellectual. For instance, Deng Xiaoping, who had been the architect of the 1958 antirightist campaign, publicly declared that because engineers and technicians were directly participating in the creation of surplus value, they were "a part of the working class."[35]

The starting point for the new policy toward the educated groups was to survey their employment conditions. In 1978, the central and provincial authorities conducted a comprehensive nationwide survey of scientific and technical personnel to determine their numbers, specialties, distribution by sector, and types of jobs held.[36]

After collecting that information on the utilization of the educated groups, the regime took several measures to improve the intellectuals' working and living conditions. First, it began to reassign scientific and technical people whose jobs did not match their specialties, giving them appropriate jobs.[37] Second, the regime tried to resolve the problems of about 320,000 couples who were living separately and about 400,000 couples in which one spouse was living in the rural areas. Third, Hu Yaobang, the director of the Organization Department, initiated measures to rehabilitate the intellectuals victimized during the Cultural Revolution.[38] For instance, on November 3, 1978, the Central Organization Department issued "Several Points of Opinion of the Central Organization Department with Regard to Intellectuals," which specified various measures to be taken for the rehabilitated, such as reinstatement to previous positions, bringing back those who had been forced to retire, providing monetary aid to those in financial difficulties, returning seized property, and restoring their party status. Those rehabilitation terms later became the standard package for rehabilitation of other types of Cultural Revolution victims.

Fourth, the regime took several measures to raise the incomes of schoolteachers, scientific personnel, athletes, and public-health workers. Special attention was given to the intellectuals' housing difficulties.

Fifth, once the intellectuals' potential to make contributions was recognized, it became obvious that there was an appalling shortage of qualified specialists. Under specific instructions from Deng Xiaoping, the cadre bureau of the State Council issued "Temporary Measures for Recruiting Scientific and Technical Personnel" and "Temporary Measures Regarding the Exchange of Scientific and Technical Personnel." Those regulations relaxed the state's tight control over personnel management through "unified recruitment and unified allocation," while allowing the specialists to hold several positions concurrently and to collaborate with people from other units.[39] Shanghai set up a "talent bank" that operated much like an employment agency.[40] The regime even contemplated introducing some kind of labor market, at least for those with the knowledge and skills needed for economic development.[41] In the labor market that had been planned, the technocrats with marketable skills would have been able to do much better than the critical intellectuals, whose social role had been declining.[42] The limited labor market for those with talent resulted in "drainage of talent" from economically backward provinces.[43] As the bidding for experts intensified, the State Scientific Commission had to issue a guideline limiting the maximum wage that any unit could offer to technical personnel.

Sixth, in order to boost morale and raise professional prestige, the regime created technical titles for its specialists. The specialists were first grouped according to their professions (e.g., engineers, teachers, medical doctors), and each of those categories contained three or four rankings (e.g., general engineer, senior engineer, associate engineer, assistant engineer). By 1981, more than a million specialists had received technical titles; in that process, many of them were promoted (e.g., from assistant professor to full professor).

BUREAUCRATIC TECHNOCRATS

In a series of bureaucratic reforms carried out from 1982 to 1986, the regime improved the working conditions for its technically trained personnel and promoted the better qualified people to leadership positions at various levels in the government departments. Consequently, by the time of the Thirteenth Party Congress in 1987, bureaucratic technocrats occupied leadership positions not only in the party but also in the government departments, industrial enterprises, and business units. For instance, among seventy-five ministers, secretaries, and governors of provinces in 1987, the average age was fifty-seven, and 45 percent of the ministers, 25 percent of the secretaries, and 33 percent of the governors were engineers. If we include those with work experience in economics and management, the numbers of those whose specialties were related to production increase to 70 percent of the ministers, 32 percent of the secretaries, and 50 percent of the governors. In contrast, there were only a few with experience in overall political leadership – 5 percent of the ministers, 36 percent of the secretaries, and 30 percent of the governors. Only one individual had had any in-depth work experience in the propaganda field. These data reveal an enormous change from the Maoist era: the decreasing importance of a political career as the necessary background for promotion to top leadership positions. Only one person among the top-level leaders of 1987 had the background of a military career: Zhang Aiping, the minister of defense. In the coming years, the new leaders probably will face difficulties in dealing with the military.

The promotion of technocrats to leadership positions was not limited to the top echelon of the ruling structure. Fragmentary information indicates that large numbers of technocrats were promoted to political leadership positions. By 1981, for instance, 92,200 intellectuals had been promoted to various leadership positions in the central government. By March 1983, some 31 percent of all high-level intellectuals working in central-government departments had assumed leadership positions. Even 41 percent of the delegates to the sixth National People's Congress reportedly were specialists in various fields.[44] The province of Ningxia reported that about 26.1 percent of the intellectuals it surveyed (total sample of 3,544) held leadership positions at various levels. Among them, 35 percent were engineers, whereas only 3 percent were specialists in cultural fields.

The bureaucratic technocrats are, by and large, of the post-liberation generation, which came of age in the new socialist China, the generation known as the third generation – after the first generation, which joined the revolution before the Long March, and the second generation, which participated in the war against Japan. Selected on the basis of functional expertise rather than political loyalty, they represent the best educated segment of the Chinese population. Most of them have studied natural sciences in college and have worked as specialists in production-related fields. Some of them have studied in the Soviet Union or in other Eastern European countries.

No data are available regarding their ideological orientations. However, it seems a fair assumption that their commitment to any political ideology – whether it be a broadly defined socialism or Mao Zedong's discredited thought – is minimal. Although some of them come from a background of the lowest social class in pre-liberation China, their experiences with past political turmoil have reduced their gratitude to the party. Many of them served at one time in technical positions without influence, watching uneducated political leaders make arbitrary decisions. Many of them have experienced condemnation as "bourgeois experts." Consequently, they have few ties with the old system, viewing the Maoist system with a critical eye. Some older revolutionaries have openly expressed their concern that the new leaders' understanding of "the basic principles of Marxism" and of "the good party tradition and work style" is so limited that they are not inclined to "use the Marxist perspective to solve present problems."

If they have any ideology, it probably is the pragmatism necessary to get the job done. Free of "the party's fine tradition of the Yanan period," they are more willing to look to the West for new ideas and new things. More concerned with raising levels of production than with equalizing distribution, they will follow Deng Xiaoping's dictum that whether it be white or black, any cat that catches mice is a good cat. For them, socialist methods and political ideology are merely means for increasing economic efficiency.

The functional necessities of industrialization require performance-related achievement criteria. Accordingly, the criteria for recruitment and promotion in the cadres have shifted from virtue and seniority to ability, which frequently is inferred from one's educational level. However, achievement is not the only consideration in personal advancement. Because there are so many people who meet the official requirements, such as age and educational level, personal connections (*guanxi*) also become a factor. The Chinese elite have been well known for their particularistic application of universal criteria.

The rise of bureaucratic technocrats to the highest positions will have profound political implications for China's future. This change indicates the CCP's commitment to modernization and economic development; at the same time it reinforces the direction of change. Although the bureaucratic technocrats' attitudes toward the Dengist reforms are unknown, it seems certain that on the whole they are more supportive of reforms than are the retiring revolutionary leaders. Owing their offices to the functional expertise they can contribute to economic development, they well know that their personal and career interests are tied to that development; they cannot base their legitimacy on any claim to represent the working class, as their predecessors did. They benefited from the reforms that promoted them to the top level, expecting to help China's economic development. Unless they deliver the economic benefits that the reform movement has promised the Chinese people, they will not be able to maintain their elite status. And unless there are continuing reforms, they will not be able to lead China to economic development. As the Maoist system reflected the old revolutionaries' experiences, goals, and understanding of the needs of China at that time, so the newly emerging system will reflect the bureaucratic technocrats' background, training, work experience, and ideological outlook.

The replacement of the revolutionary leaders by bureaucratic technocrats marks an end to the revolutionary era in modern China, an era that was shaped by the revolutionaries' background, personal experiences, and career pursuits.

CHALLENGES TO THE BUREAUCRATIC TECHNOCRATS

The historic transformation in the makeup of the ruling political elite had been accompanied by limited changes in the party-state's structure, its relation to society, and its mode of operation, or at least that seemed the case prior to the Tiananmen tragedy. The party-state had retreated from society, granting more decision-making space to various social groups, organizations, and individuals. Chinese society had undergone increasing structural differentiation and functional specialization as a result of shifting its priority from distribution to production in its economic thinking, and it had adopted the principle of one's reward according to one's contribution, in addition to allowing individuals to become rich.

The rapidly changing social environment had affected the very nature of the Leninist party. With the recognition that the party had to improve the educational level of its members if it was to succeed in leading China to economic development, the regime stepped up its effort to co-opt educated specialists and professionals.[45] Each year the Central Organization Department would assign specific targets for the number of intellectuals to be recruited in each province, and the province in turn would break down the quota into specific numbers for its lower units.[46] In addition, the party changed its recruitment policy: In order to join, a worker must have finished senior high school, and a peasant must have finished junior high school.

The party has even relinquished some of its direct control over the state apparatus, while making serious efforts to separate the party from the government and the business units. Certain state institutions, such as the state councils, were upgraded. A management responsibility system delegated to the party secretaries the function of supervising and ensuring their managers' work. In addition, the regime endeavored to rationalize its organizational structure and operation by stressing functional specialization, information flow, and pragmatic procedures for policy-making. State agencies in charge of the economy were encouraged to learn the techniques of macro-management and economic leverage – such as taxes and prices – rather than rely on administrative authority.

However, the effects of such structural and institutional changes were quite limited, largely because the regime was not prepared to abandon its monopoly of political power. The resistance to emasculating the Leninist party is still strong: The party has 47 million members, and although its legitimacy was undermined by the Cultural Revolution, it still wields enormous power and has a huge stake in continuing the existing system. Many of the remaining revolutionary leaders still insist that the party should continue to be a heroic revolutionary organization with "socially combating tasks" as its major mission.[47] The regime wants economic development, but without giving up its planned economy; instead, it hopes to develop a "planned commodity economy," that is, to combine the socialist planned economy with market mechanisms, which may not be feasible. The party also wants to extract itself from the administrative work of the government, but it wants to do so without weakening its control over the government.

The new problems that were bound to arise in the process of reform confounded some already complex theoretical and ideological questions. The decentralization of political and economic authority, although originally designed to give flexibility to the system, produced the unintended consequence of fragmenting the bureaucracy. The ministries and departments of the government and the party at the various levels used their newly gained authority in budgeting, banking, capital investment, planning, and materials allocation to pursue their own narrowly defined interests, investing heavily in such areas as consumer goods and hotels, where the profit margin was high.

Inflation is almost inevitable in the process of reforming a socialist economy characterized by permanent shortages of goods and heavy state subsidies for the basic necessities for its urban dwellers. In addition, the Chinese regime's policy of pursuing a high growth rate, supplying money faster than the total increase in material output, and regulating those goods in short supply through price increases further contributed to the extremely high rate of inflation. Of course, the rising expectations of the Chinese people posed another problem. In turn, the inflation undermined the price stability that in the past had enabled urban dwellers to survive on low wages (the only advantage of the Maoist system), hurting particularly intellectuals, who were mostly employed in the units that generated no profit.

Corruption among the cadre leaders aggravated the social and economic problems. In transitional China, the boundary between legal and illegal ways of making money has never been clear. The dual price system – one fixed by the state, and the other by the market – and the close tie between political clout and economic power provided ample opportunities for the children of high-ranking officials to make large profits. The senior revolutionary leaders apparently had learned that they could not pass on political power to their children, but wealth was another matter. Moreover, helping their children get rich was one way of accumulating the capital that China needed for economic development.

On the question of how to solve China's economic difficulties, the newly promoted bureaucratic technocrats had split into two groups even before the Tiananmen tragedy: Zhao Ziyang's liberal reformers, and Li Peng's more conservative bureaucratic technocrats. Zhao's group advocated speedy price reform, elimination of the dual price system, and further marketization and privatization of ownership. Such reformers implicitly believed that the socialist ideology should not operate so as to constrain policy choices, and they regarded a certain amount of corruption as the price China had to pay in the transitional period, not something to be eliminated through reintroduction of "political education."

In contrast, the more conservative bureaucratic technocrats, represented by Li Peng, advocated recentralization of economic authority, a tight monetary policy, and a program to perfect the enterprise contract system. Understandably, the semi-retired senior political leaders preferred Li Peng's view, or it may have been the case that those old leaders dictated the policy to Li Peng. Regardless of who led the way, Li Peng's preference resembled Chen Yun's conceptualization: that reform means expanding the bird cage so that the bird will have more space, rather than letting the bird out of the cage to fly at will. In other words, the hard-liners believed that the state's planned economy should remain the central feature, while allowing the market mechanism to play only a supplementary role.

Their disagreement on economic strategy reflected a deeper divergence on the fundamental question of how to view the relationship between political reform and economic reform. The reformers argued that without political reform the economic reform could not proceed further, and without further liberalization of the economy China could not resolve its problems of inflation, corruption, regional differences, and unequal distribution of wealth. In contrast, the hard-liners argued that because Chinese society had no capability to resolve all the problems arising from the process of reform, a strong and stable central authority was critical at that juncture in the reform. Without a strong central authority, the economic reform could not be carried out in an orderly fashion. Therefore, the party, which had a hierarchy more centralized than that of the government, would have to exercise strong political leadership. Deng Xiaoping and other senior political leaders viewed political reform as a means to strengthen the state's effectiveness and efficiency in maintaining social order and providing a minimum economic base for all social groups. In that battle for policy and power, Zhao Ziyang was losing even before the students' democratic movement.

The problems that arose from economic reforms – inflation, corruption, fragmentation of the bureaucracy, and rising demands for political democracy and an expanded ideological space for intellectuals – provided the impetus for the 1989 student movement. In addition, the students skillfully exploited such fortuitous events as the funeral for Hu Yaobang, the seventieth anniversary of the May Fourth movement, and Gorbachev's visit to China, with Western news media in tow, thereby preventing the political elite, already split among themselves, from taking well-defined, coherent measures. As the protests dragged on, the students' demands changed from rehabilitation for Hu Yaobang and elimination of corruption to the call for Deng Xiaoping and Li Peng to step down, a demand that the CCP considered a frontal challenge to its existence.

The disagreement between the reformers and conservatives in government was exacerbated by the issue of how to handle the student movement. Zhao Ziyang tended to be conciliatory toward the protesting students. According to the official news media, he had originally approved the *Renmin ribao* editorial condemning the student demonstration, but after his return to Beijing, he withdrew his support for the editorial. When he met with the students who were on hunger strike, he said, with tears in his eyes, "I came too late. I don't care about myself, but I am worried about you, the young people."[48] Public knowledge that the top leadership had split over the student demonstration emboldened the Beijing citizenry to publicly support the student movement.

Even if the casualties of the June 4 massacre did not reach several thousands, as reported in the Western news media, the incident was a great tragedy for China, casting a pall of uncertainty over China's political stability and the future of the Dengist reforms. That the regime was able to come up with no better solution than reckless, brutal use of force against its own people indicates its moral and ideological bankruptcy. The primary responsibility for that tragedy must be borne by the old political leaders, who still operate with the revolutionary mentality of "all or nothing." But the students shared in the responsibility, because they, too, were operating with the all-or-nothing revolutionary mentality, and they pushed their movement to a final confrontation. If the students had unilaterally declared a victory and disbanded before June 4, they would have made a real contribution to China's democratization.

After the June 4 incident, the technocratic hard-liners, with the support of the senior political leaders, strengthened their grip on power. But they face an almost impossible task: consolidating their power base, which will be increasingly difficult as their political patrons pass away, and leading China toward economic development, without which they will not be able to gain legitimacy.

The series of measures taken after the Tiananmen incident are not promising. The liberalization trend in official policy seems to have ended. The current hard-liners are trying to revitalize the party through ideological education and use it to strengthen central control. They apparently have given up any effort to extract the party from the government organizations: The current official position is that the party and the government will merely divide functions, while remaining structurally merged. Political education has been reintroduced for college students and workers. In the economic arena, the regime hopes to continue its open-door policy and reforms, but most of the intellectuals, whose continuing support would be crucial for economic development, have lost confidence in the regime.

It is difficult to see how the current effort to revitalize the Leninist party could work. The regime tried to unify the ideology of the party members during the three years of the party rectification campaign (from 1984 to 1986), but it failed. Furthermore, the current official ideology is too far removed from the reality in China, and Marxism-Leninism has been too thoroughly discredited worldwide for political education to be an effective control mechanism.[49] Nonetheless, what the regime seeks to achieve through reimposition of the official orthodoxy is less ambitious than the goals of the Maoist era. The Maoists were able to use political education to generate genuine commitment to socialism and a positive loyalty to the party, whereas the current leadership is using it to discourage the people from mounting frontal challenges to the regime. In other words, the current brand of political education is defensive, in the sense that its aim is to stabilize a potentially explosive political situation and gain breathing space so that the party leadership can try to develop more effective means to restore people's confidence in the party. Consequently, the party's effort to regulate all political activities has shrunk to an effort to defend the dominant role of the Leninist party, whereas during the Maoist era almost all activities were regarded as political and hence subject to control by the official ideology. The content of official ideology has also receded from a class perspective to a nation-state perspective.

The immediate future for reform and political stability in China is uncertain. It seems probable that the political lives of Li Peng and Jiang Zemin (who succeeded Zhao Ziyang as the party's general secretary) will last only as long as the corporeal lives of Deng Xiaoping and other elderly leaders. It seems likely that many of the victims of the current persecution will eventually be rehabilitated, and the leaders of the student movement, who now are condemned as counter-revolutionaries, may become heroes in the near future. If such a reversal takes place, one consolation will be that more enlightened technocrats, with a better understanding of the democratic aspirations of the Chinese population and the importance of a market economy, will replace the current hard-line technocrats.

Given the sweeping changes taking place in the Eastern European countries and the Soviet Union, a Leninist party still insisting on socialist

201

ideology appears to be incompatible with market mechanisms. Despite the current leaders' wishful thinking about combining state planning with a market mechanism, it will take time for the CCP to modify its commitment to socialism. However, allowing an ideological vacuum to occur in China is not a practical solution, where a well-defined and widely accepted official ideology has traditionally proved to be the most economical way of governing the massive Chinese population. The only feasible way for the CCP to resolve its dilemma – the need to preserve its politically dominant position and the need for a well-defined official ideology, on the one hand, and the need to develop China's economy by removing the ideological straightjacket, on the other – would seem to be to allow the official orthodoxy to incorporate divergent social interests, while diluting its cohesiveness. In other words, the official ideology will become what Juan Linz calls "mentality." According to Linz, "mentality," defined as a "way of thinking, attitude, or psychic disposition," is sufficiently vague and formless to enable diverse elite groups to work together, while retaining the loyalty of the masses.[50]

As for the democratization of its authoritarian regime, many scholars emphasize the three steps necessary for the transformation from authoritarianism to democracy. The first step involves the fragmentation of the political elite, because "political democracy is produced by stalemate and dissensus rather than prior unity and consensus [among the political elite]."[51] The second step is for one group to go outside the ruling circle and mobilize the masses for its political agenda. The third step is for the political elite to agree to an institutional arrangement through which policy will be determined. This agreement on procedural rules for decision making will increase the uncertainty about which policies will be adopted.

Applying these three steps to China, one sees that China has reached the stage where only leaders at the top level articulate the interests of their constituencies. But the Leninist party system still prohibits a leader from mobilizing his constituent group in order to bring pressure on his colleagues in the policy-making process. Besides the lingering legacy of democratic centralism, the historically conditioned fear of political chaos and civil war will tend to make Chinese leaders intolerant of the uncertainty that inevitably will arise from the crucial stage of the democratization process. The bureaucratic technocrats are not liberals advocating democracy, and their memories of Mao, who mobilized the masses against his adversaries, are still quite vivid.

However, the cases of Taiwan and South Korea demonstrate that an authoritarian political regime with a strong one-party system can be compatible with private ownership. If the Leninist party wishes to survive as the dominant political force, it should accept the erosion of its Marxist-Leninist ideology, abandon its claim of being a class-based dictatorial party, and transform itself into a hegemonic party, serving as the intermediary between civil society and the state, that makes authoritative and binding decisions. In accordance with this plan, some Chinese scholars argue that the party's task is to aggregate the diverse demands coming from the civil society and forward them to the state as "guidance inputs (*zhidaoxing*)" that the state will then use to make authoritative decisions for the civil society.[52]

As the Leninist party undergoes transformation, the role of the bureaucratic technocrats in the party offices will change. They will become what Jowitt calls "political managers," coordinating a multitude of functionally specialized organizations that are bound to arise as China experiences structural differentiation. In the case of China, coordination will involve not only the mechanical process of directing the information flow but also the political process of reconciling the conflicting interests and demands of diverse social groups. The "mixed" nature of the Chinese economic system – neither totally controlled by the state planners nor a perfectly free market – will make such coordination absolutely imperative. In fact, many Chinese leaders have already suggested that party cadres will play the roles of coordinators "among the various parts of the power organs of the state, the economic organizations, and the cultural organizations," as well as among the managers, labor unions, the Communist Youth League, and the workers' congresses.[53] This type of broadly defined coordination requires that political managers be more receptive to the wishes of the various groups and rely on their leadership skills of manipulation (particularly of perceived needs and symbols). It seems that the new generation of cadre leaders, most with technical backgrounds, are better prepared than the former revolutionary leaders, even for this mixed type of political and technical coordination.[54]

NOTES

1. M. H. Lowenthal, "Development vs. Utopia in Communist Policy," in Chalmers Johnson, ed., *Change in Communist Systems* (Stanford: Stanford University Press, 1970); W. A. Welsh, "Toward a Multi-Strategy Approach to Research on Contemporary Communist Political Elite: Empirical and Quantitative Problems," in F. J. Feron, ed., *Communist Studies and Social Science* (Chicago: Rand McNally, 1969); Peter Ludz, *The Changing Party Elite in East Germany* (Cambridge: MIT Press, 1972).
2. *Dangshi yanjiu*, no. 2 (1981): 65; *Zhonggong dangshi cankao zailiao 5* (1982): 163. Another Chinese source reports that the CCP had fifty-three members when it was founded. The occupations of forty-seven of them were as follows: seven professors and teachers, seven editors and reporters, one lawyer, one leftist GMD member, six primary schoolteachers, thirteen college students, five middle-school students, and two workers. Zhu Chengjia, ed., *Zhonggong dangshi yanjiu lunwen xuan* (Changsha: Hunan renmin chubanshe, 1963), 1:212.

3. Among all the party members in Heilongjiang, 37 percent were in the age group from eighteen to twenty-five, and 54.4 percent were between the ages of twenty-five and forty. *Jiandang* (Harbin: Heilongjiang danganshi, 1984), p. 119.

4. Ibid.

5. Ibid.

6. James Scott identifies geographical isolation, pervasive personal ties, the absence of a division of labor, self-reliance, millenarian idealism, and egalitarianism as prominent features of the peasant society: "Hegemony and the Peasantry," *Politics and Society*, no. 3 (1977): 267–296.

7. Susan Shirk, *Competitive Comrades: Career Incentives and Student Strategy in China* (Berkeley: University of California Press, 1982).

8. *Minzu yu fazhi*, no. 4 (1983).

9. For the distinction between politicians and bureaucrats, see Joel D. Aberbach, Robert D. Putnam, and Bert A. Rockman, *Bureaucrats and Politicians in Western Democracies* (Cambridge: Harvard University Press, 1981).

10. A. Doak Barnett, *Cadres, Bureaucracy, and Political Power in Communist China* (New York: Columbia University Press, 1967), p. 427.

11. For the characteristics of the Maoist system and its transformation by 1982, see Michel Oksenberg and Richard Bush, "China's Political Evolution; 1972–82," *Problems of Communism* (September–October 1982): 1–19.

12. For the evolution of the powerful party-state in China, see Tang Tsou, "Reflections on the Formation and Foundation of the Communist Party-state in China," in his *The Cultural Revolution and Post-Mao Reforms: A Historical Perspective* (Chicago: University of Chicago Press, 1986), pp. 219–258

13. *Xinhua wenzhi*, no. 11 (1987): 1–5; *Zhongguo shehui kexue* (June 1987): 3–22.

14. Louis Althusser and Etienne Balibar, *Reading Capital* (London: New Left Books, 1970).

15. For the latest book explaining the Cultural Revolution in terms of the unit system and the tension it created, see Lyn White, *Policies of Chaos: The Organizational Cause of Violence in China's Cultural Revolution* (Princeton: Princeton University Press, 1988).

16. Andrew G. Walder, *Communist Neo-traditionalism: Work and Authority in Chinese Industry* (Berkeley: University of California Press, 1987).

17. *Dangde shenghuo*, no. 12 (1983): 32–39.

18. *Weidingkao* (July 1986): 25–28.

19. Ibid.

20. Siu-kai Lau, "Monism, Pluralism, and Segmental Coordination: Toward Alternative Theory of Elite, Power and Social Stability," *Journal of the Chinese University of Hong Kong* 3, no. 1 (1982): 187–206.

21. For this point, see James Townsend, "Intra-Party Conflict in China: Disintegration of an Established Party System," in Samuel Huntington and Clement H. Moore, eds., *Authoritarian Politics in Modern Society* (New York: Basic Books, 1970), pp. 284–310.

22. Charles Lindblom, *Politics and Markets* (New York: Basic Books, 1977).

23. For the issues on which the old revolutionaries split, see Tsou, *Cultural Revolution*, pp. 77–78.

24. That 4 million in the cadres are college graduates theoretically may be correct,

because all college graduates are allocated by the party-state and start their jobs as low-level cadre members.

25. *Renmin ribao*, September 24, 1980.
26. Jerry Hough, *Soviet Leadership in Transition* (Washington, D.C.: Brookings Institution, 1980), p. 28.
27. Zhonggong Zhongyang Zushibu, ed., *Zuohao zai zhishifenzi zhong fazhan dangyuan gongzuo* (Beijing: Xinhua chubanshe, 1985), p. 76.
28. Sidney Verba, Normal Nie, and Jae-on Kim, *Participation and Political Equality* (Cambridge University Press, 1978).
29. Antonio Gramsci also makes a distinction between those doing technical and ideological specialized work.
30. Alvin Gouldner, *The Future of Intellectuals and the Rise of the New Class* (New York: Seabury Press, 1979).
31. The reasons for the Gang of Four's persecution of intellectuals included their one-sided emphasis on correct ideology at the expense of other knowledge, their commitment to Mao's simple notion that the intellectuals had to learn from toiling with the masses, their leftist idea of using class origin as the main criterion for determining who was revolutionary and who was not, and their commitment to egalitarianism. *Beijing Review*, March 31, 1980, p. 19.
32. *Zhonggong dangshi jiaoxue cankao ziliao; wenhua dageming shiqi* (Beijing: Zhongguo renin zhengzhi xueyuan, 1983), 4:4.
33. *Ming bao*, May 15, 1978.
34. *Jiaodang cankao* (Anhui), May 15, 1983.
35. *Wuhan daxue xuebao*, no. 2 (1985): 63–66.
36. *Daily Report*, June 26, 1978, p. E11; *Hebei xuekan*, no. 1 (1985): 1.
37. *Shehui kexue janjiu cankao ziliao* (Sichuna), July 21, 1985.
38. In some cultural units, intellectuals, specialists, and experts constituted 60 percent of all those purged during the Cultural Revolution. *Jaoxue cankao* (Hebei Construction Institute), no. 203.
39. On December 1, 1982, Deng said that "at the moment when the shortage of scientific and technical personnel is very keen, the waste in managing them is huge; the [specialists] are not used, and using them in the area where one has no major is very serious." He stressed the need to remove the boundaries of units and localities and to use them efficiently and to develop a twenty-year plan.
40. *Liaowang*, January 21, 1985.
41. For a discussion of introducing a labor market, see *Renmin ribao*, December 23, 1987, December 15, 1987.
42. For the distinction between intelligentsia and intellectuals, see Gouldner, *Future of Intellectuals*.
43. *Renmin ribao*, May 24, 1985.
44. *Shehui kexue janjiu cankao ziliao* (Sichuna), July 21, 1985.
45. There are two different methods of co-optation. The first is to bring the specialists into the framework of the party. The second shares power by granting specialists the status of consultants. Both attempts are being used in China. For the two methods, see Philip Selznick, "Cooperation: A Mechanism and Organizational Stability," in Robert K. Merton, ed., *Reader in Bureaucracy* (New York: Free Press, 1967), pp. 135–139.
46. Ibid.
47. *Ziliao yuekan*, no. 4 (1988): 3–11.

48. *Daily Report*, June 9, 1989, pp. 22–31.
49. For demoralization in the former political infrastructure, see W. J. E. Jenner and Delia Davis, *Chinese Lives* (New York: Pantheon, 1987), pp. 276–277.
50. Juan Linz, "Totalitarianism and Authoritarian Regime," in Fred Greestein and Nelson Polsby, eds., *Handbook of Political Science* (Reading, Mass.: Addison-Wesley, 1975), 3:175–357.
51. Adam Przeworski, "Some Problems in the Study of the Transition to Democracy," in Guillermo O'Donnell, Phillipe C. Schmitter, and Lawrence Whitehead, eds., *Transition from Authoritarian Rule* (Baltimore: Johns Hopkins University Press, 1986), 3:47–63.
52. Nie Gaomin, Li Ilzhou, and Wang Zhongtian, eds., *Dangzheng fenkai lilun tantao* (Beijing: Chunqiu chubanshe, 1988).
53. For instance, Zhao Ziyang also stressed the party's coordinating roles. *Renmin ribao*, November 26, 1987; *Sixiang zhengzhi gongzuo yanjiu*, no. 10 (1985): 12–14; Zhonggong hunanshengwi dangxiao dangjian yanjiushi, ed., *Zhizhengdangde lingdao wenti gailun* (Beijing: Zhonggong zhongyang dangxiao chubanshe, 1986), pp. 59–60.
54. Ezra Suleiman, *Politics, Power, and Bureaucracy* (Princeton: Princeton University Press, 1974), p. 380.

PART III

China's evolving world role

7

China's search for its place in the world

LOWELL DITTMER

The premise of this chapter is that at least one of the factors affecting China's (often unpredictable) foreign-policy behavior since the Chinese Communist Party (CCP) seized power in 1949 has been an attempt to find a suitable place for itself in the modern world, a national identity. Approaching the modern international system with memories of a glorious traditional status as regional hegemon, followed by the humiliation of defeat and parcelization at the hands of perceived inferiors, China was accustomed to a position of international leadership that it could not sustain in the face of its political decay and scientific-economic backwardness. That sense of sudden degradation of national status gave rise to an ambiguous attitude of admiration and indignation vis-à-vis the *arriviste* Western powers, in addition to inhibiting adaptation to the hard rules of raison d'être qua realpolitik that had come to apply to the post-Westphalian "international system." For much of the first half of the twentieth century, China was "in" but not really "of" the world.

The communist victory made it possible for China to "stand up," as Mao put it in 1949. Denouncing the past century of national humiliation in the Marxist vocabulary of imperialism, the evils of China's own regional hegemony could also be forsworn under the rubric of feudalism. Yet that left a conceptual hiatus. Although the communists in fact tapped the animus of nationalism by mobilizing the Chinese people against Japan (and then against America, in Korea), any serious discussion of China's national interests and role or mission in the world was inhibited by the Marxist denial of nationalism's theoretical legitimacy – and by a leadership posture of dogmatic certitude. Instead of publicly debating their options, the new leadership fell into the ingrained cultural practice of patterning their behavior on external role models.

I wish to thank Samuel Kim, Suzanne H. Rudolph, and Brantly Womack for their helpful comments on an earlier draft of this chapter.

To orient themselves in the modern world, Chinese leaders affiliated with two international "reference groups," identifying on the one hand with the communist bloc, and on the other with the Third World. From the CCP perspective, the bloc represented ideological legitimacy, a sense of community with the elect, a promise of collective historical vindication. Identification with the Third World provided not only a chance to associate with countries that shared China's developmental status and difficulties but also an opportunity to exercise international leadership – an opportunity not at hand within the communist bloc. As the largest and most populous of the new nations, it seemed quite plausible for China to claim a "leading role."

Thus, the People's Republic of China (PRC) identified with both groups, without apparently being aware initially that any contradiction was involved. After all, the communist world represented the Third World's future, as mediated through the Chinese model of peasant revolution, followed by high-speed industrialization. In the course of time, however, as the relationship between the second and third worlds came to seem less straightforward, the dialectical interplay between those two reference groups grew exceedingly complex. We shall first examine China's evolving role within the communist bloc, then turn to the PRC relationship with the Third World. For those countries (other than the PRC itself) that might be subsumed by either category (e.g., Vietnam, Albania), bloc affiliation is assumed to take precedence.

CHINA AND INTERNATIONAL COMMUNISM

The communist bloc first became a geopolitical reality in the post-World War II period, when the Soviet Union seized the opportunity to install communist parties in the power vacuum left by the retreating Axis forces in Eastern Europe, and the CCP seized power from the tottering Guomindang (GMD) in China. Altogether, that constituted a rather impressive international empire. The CCP had consistently adhered to the discipline of international democratic centralism, despite occasional misgivings during the revolutionary era (e.g., agreeing, at Moscow's behest, to release Chiang Kai-shek from house arrest when he fell into their hands at Xian), and after the revolution had triumphed, the PRC submerged its national identity relatively completely in the socialist community.

During the depths of the cold war (and American nuclear first-strike capability), tight bloc alignment was deemed de rigueur by most bloc members, and discipline was taut. The Eastern European countries, having been devastated by the Nazi invasion and the Soviet counterattack, presented a temporary power vacuum, into which the Communist Party of the Soviet Union (CPSU) quickly inserted emigre communist leaderships more beholden to Moscow than to indigenous constituencies. The highly centralized power structure within the Soviet Union during the late Stalinist period thus found its echo in similar relationships among "fraternal" parties within the bloc. The CCP leadership, having come to power on the strength of its own resources, with little indebtedness to outside aid, nevertheless accepted and even reinforced such an asymmetric distribution of power. The CCP fully endorsed the excommunication of Tito, for example, and party theorist Liu Shaoqi devoted a long article to the rationalization of that decision as early as 1948.[1] Sino–Yugoslav relations were to remain strained for many years thereafter (much longer than Soviet–Yugoslav relations); Beijing and Belgrade did not even exchange ambassadors until January 1955, and by fall 1957 party-to-party relations had been severed, not to be restored until 1980.

Once Stalin's initial suspicions had been overcome, the CCP was thus accorded special deference within the bloc as its largest constituent party, with jurisdiction over the world's biggest population and third-largest land mass. Stalin's death in March 1953 enhanced China's status, as symbolized by a doctored photograph appearing in *Pravda* just five days after his death, showing Malenkov with Stalin and Mao.[2] Indeed, during the period from October 1954 to the first half of 1956, the Soviets began to regard the PRC not so much as a satellite but as a relatively equal partner.[3] The Soviets frequently cited with pride Lenin's several references to the importance of China, such as the following passage from an article first published in 1923:

In the last analysis, the outcome of the struggle will be determined by the fact that Russia, India, and China, etc., constitute the overwhelming majority of the population of the globe. And it is precisely this majority of the population that during the past few years, has been drawn into the struggle for its emancipation with extraordinary rapidity, so that in this respect there cannot be the slightest shadow of doubt what the final outcome of the world struggle will be. In this sense, the final victory of socialism is fully and absolutely assured.[4]

By the latter half of the decade, however, China's sense of having its identity securely anchored in the socialist community and value system had become unhinged. The seeds for that alienation were sown in the famous "secret speech" that Khrushchev delivered to the CPSU Twentieth Congress in February 1956. Although Khrushchev recalled that Mao's initial reaction was favorable – that Mao, too, began to criticize Stalin[5] – in the long run the Maoist leadership found that Khrushchev's bold departures took international communism in a direction inimical to Chinese interests. Khrushchev introduced three important ideological innovations at that conference that were to set the parameters for the conflict that would rage for the next twenty years. Those innovations

211

signaled what Zagoria has termed a shift from *continental* to *global* strategy: Rather than focusing on consolidation of the bloc countries in the Eurasian heartland, Moscow turned its attention outward toward the rest of the world, attempting to foster détente with the developed countries and to solicit clients among the developing nations in Asia and Africa, whose decolonization struggles had given rise to a certain sympathy for anti-imperialist, anti-capitalist perspectives.[6]

First, Khrushchev introduced the theoretical possibility of establishing "peaceful coexistence" with the capitalist world, particularly the United States. (At the CPSU Twenty-second Congress in 1961, he would extend that doctrine further, saying not only that "capitalist encirclement" was at an end but also that the danger of global wars would cease within a generation.) Ideologically, that entailed what Chinese polemicists would deride as the "extinction of class struggle": Because of the development of nuclear weapons, war between blocs would annihilate people of every class background, making no distinction whether a country was socialist or imperialist.

Second, Khrushchev supported nationalist struggles among the decolonizing new nations that were not yet under the control of communist parties but had evinced a certain sympathy for Soviet foreign-policy objectives and/or some inclination toward a Soviet pattern of domestic economic development.

Third, Khrushchev liberalized socialist authority relationships, both among member parties of the bloc (by endorsing "many roads to socialism") and between masses and party elites domestically (by renouncing the "cult of personality"). In the same context, he endorsed a "transition to socialism by parliamentary means," in an evident play for nonruling communist parties endeavoring to compete in democratic electoral contests.

So far as China's attempt to resolve problems of national identity via identification with the international communist movement is concerned, this theoretical reorientation posed both short-run tactical difficulties and long-term systemic problems. The tactical difficulty was that the leader with whom Mao had personally identified in order to bolster his ascendancy within the CCP had been shorn of his legitimacy. The central thrust of Khrushchev's speech, explicitly in point three, but implicitly in points one and two as well, was to repudiate the Stalinist personality cult. Although that served Khrushchev's immediate interest in discrediting his (Stalinist) rivals within the Soviet Politburo, it also had the troublesome side effect of splitting all the satellite leaderships between those who had identified with (thereby benefiting from) Stalin's personal ascendancy and those who had suffered under Stalin or his local surrogates. In Eastern Europe, that led to the rehabilitation of leaders who had been victims of Stalinism and to demands for political and economic reforms of Stalinism as a system.[7] In China, it undermined the leadership of Mao Zedong. At the CCP's Eighth Congress (held only a few months after the CPSU Twentieth Congress), not only were all references to "Mao Zedong thought" deleted from the party constitution (at the motion of Peng Dehuai, promptly endorsed by Liu Shaoqi), but also a new position of "honorary chairman" (for which there could be but one conceivable candidate) was created. The provision contained in the 1945 (Seventh Congress) constitution permitting the party chairman to hold concurrently the post of chairman of the Secretariat was rescinded, and a separate Secretariat was created under a new secretary general named Deng Xiaoping, who was authorized not only to handle the daily work of the Central Committee but also to convene Central Work Conferences – ad hoc convocations with the functional competence to displace Central Committee plenums (which could be convened only by the chairman) during the 1962–1966 period.[8] That cleavage would endure at least a decade, emerging clearly in the purge pattern of the Cultural Revolution. Its mimetic pattern illustrates one of the perils of such intense identification with another national leadership.[9]

The systemic problem with Khrushchev's doctrinal innovations, together with the dissolution of the Cominform in April and his meeting with Tito in June, unleashed fissiparous tendencies throughout the bloc: The community into which the PRC was trying to integrate began to disintegrate. In March 1956, one month after the secret speech, riots erupted in Soviet Georgia, Stalin's birthplace; in June, civil unrest broke out in both Poland and Hungary; by October, a much more sweeping insurrection had swept through Hungary, the suppression of which would require Soviet military intervention.

The CCP leadership seems to have played an equivocal role in those developments. Susceptible to the same nationalist impulses that roiled Eastern Europe, the Chinese initially welcomed a more loosely integrated bloc, maintaining through the end of 1956 that "a serious consequence of Stalin's errors was the development of dogmatism."[10] Mao advocated that the relationships among socialist countries be regulated on the basis of his own theory of contradictions among the people and the "five principles of peaceful coexistence," rather than the principles of proletarian internationalism emphasized by the CPSU, even going so far as to urge Khrushchev to withdraw all Soviet troops from Eastern Europe.[11] Then an uprising broke out in Poznan, Poland, resulting in election of a new Politburo, from which all Stalinists were excluded, and the release from prison and meteoric rise (to the position of party first secretary, without Soviet approval) of reformer Wladyslaw Gomulka. Rubbing salt in the wound, the Poles further demanded the removal of Marshal Konstantin Rokossovsky, a Russian who had been installed as Poland's defense minister in 1949. Zhou Enlai intervened to mediate Polish–Soviet tensions, helping to prevent armed Soviet intervention or ideological ostracism à la Tito. During Edward Ochab's visit to Beijing for the CCP Eighth Congress in September 1956, Mao expressed sympathy for the liberal faction of the Polish Communist Party (rechristened the Polish United Workers' Party, PUWP), advising Moscow against intervention in a personal letter early the following month.[12] A Polish observer reported that during the tense Polish–Soviet negotiations of October 19 (when Khrushchev flew to Warsaw, with Soviet troops ringing the city), CCP support during and after its Eighth Congress helped the Poles sustain their will and not make concessions under duress.[13]

The Chinese also at first opposed the intervention into Hungary, hoping that the Polish compromise had definitively solved the "many roads" problem – the Chinese press hailed the October 18 Polish–Soviet agreement with the prediction that it also would correct "whatever was wrong with relations between the Soviet Union and Hungary."[14] The CCP leadership hesitated so long to condemn the reformers that the rumor flourished in Budapest that "the Chinese are with us."[15] When the situation in Hungary nonetheless got out of hand, the Chinese changed course 180 degrees and actively advocated intervention, even adjuring an allegedly uncertain and vacillating Khrushchev to "go to the defense of the Hungarian revolution."[16] The deciding factor for the CCP seems to have been Imre Nagy's announcement on November 1 of Hungary's unilateral withdrawal from the Warsaw Pact, declaration of bloc neutrality, and endorsement of multiparty democracy. All mention of Hungary was removed from an October 31 Chinese government commentary when it was published in *People's Daily* on November 2, and an editorial the following day roundly denounced the rebellion.[17] In early 1957, Zhou Enlai visited the Soviet Union, Poland, and Hungary in an effort to restore bloc unity. (Those broad shifts of "line" at the intrabloc level would have their subsequent domestic echo in the CCP's decision in the spring of 1957 to "let a hundred flowers bloom, let a hundred schools of thought contend," followed shortly by the repressive "anti-Rightist movement.")[18]

Those experiments with liberalization seem to have frightened the leaderships of both countries, while at the same time unveiling the unpopularity of unreconstructed Stalinism.[19] However abortive, they were not to prove politically fatal to either Khrushchev or Mao, though the two reacted quite differently to their failure. In the case of the former, the uprisings in Poland and Hungary gave birth to an opposing coalition of strange bedfellows, ranging from unreconstructed Stalinists such as Molotov and Kaganovich to erstwhile liberals such as Malenkov, in the face of which Khrushchev at first had to give ground, declaring in December 1956 that "we are all Stalinists now."[20] It is even conceivable that Khrushchev's opponents had been encouraged to challenge him by Mao's increasingly leftist stance, as Medvedev has surmised, though no conspiratorial contact has been established.[21] Having, however, disarmed his opposition by firmly repressing the Hungarian uprising and restoring bloc unity under Soviet leadership, Khrushchev was able to purge the "anti-Party group" (viz., Malenkov, Molotov, Kaganovich, and Marshal Zhukov) in the summer of 1957 and seize the premiership (while retaining the position of party first secretary) by March 1958. He then proceeded to sanctify his reforms by rewriting the official history, in three documents – "Fundamentals of Marxism-Leninism" (October 1959), the "Declaration of 81 Communist Parties" (December 1960), and the new "Soviet Party Program" (the first new program since 1919), endorsed by the CPSU Twenty-second Congress (October 1961) – thereby, however, also formalizing his doctrinal differences with the CCP.

To Mao Zedong, on the other hand, the emergence of a rightist opposition critical of his radical policies and his somewhat autocratic leadership style had hardened his conviction that the need for "class struggle" still existed (contrary to some prematurely optimistic observations by Mao and other CCP leaders at the Eighth Party Congress in 1956), and he turned sharply to the left (the right had in any case been discredited by the Hundred Flowers campaign). Despite his previous (privately expressed) misgivings about Stalin and Stalinism, Mao publicly came to Stalin's defense, reflexively shifting to the critique of "revisionism" that would preoccupy him for the next two decades.[22] In that context he introduced the theory of "continuing the revolution under the dictatorship of the proletariat," developing the notion that the seizure of power marked the beginning rather than the end of the revolution and that the superstructure tended to lag behind the base, the relations of production behind the forces of production, rather than the other way round. Those class enemies still extant after socialization of the means of production had been completed were labeled "rightist," "bourgeois," or "revisionist," not necessarily because they had a bourgeois class background but because they opposed Mao's "socialist revolutionary line," making them "objectively" bourgeois. That (plus the discrediting of the right in the Hundred Flowers episode) freed him to undertake far more radical domestic programs – notably the "Three Red Flags" of 1958–1959 (the "Great Leap Forward," the "people's commune," and the "general line"). When early opposition to that utopian experiment surfaced under the leadership of Peng Dehuai, Mao denounced (and purged) it under the ideological epitaph of rightist revisionism.

The CCP's post-Hundred Flowers turn leftward would put it on an eventual collision course with Khrushchev's CPSU, but for the moment, China's rejection of "revisionism" propelled it toward reintegration of the bloc under strong Soviet leadership. The CCP became during that brief hiatus puritanically orthodox, endorsing a laager mentality that would subordinate the interests of contending bloc members to those of the bloc as a whole. Thus, during what would be his last visit to Moscow (to attend the fortieth anniversary of the October Revolution, November 14–16, 1957, followed by a conference of leaders from socialist countries and an international conference of communist parties, the reports of which have not been published), Mao declared not only that the Soviet Union was head of the bloc but also that it was absolutely imperative to "strengthen international proletarian solidarity with the Soviet Union as its center."

Our camp must have a head, because even the snake has a head. I would not agree that China should be called head of the camp, because we do not merit this honor and cannot maintain this role, we are still poor. We haven't even a quarter of a satellite, while the Soviet Union has two.[23]

"Bourgeois influence constitutes the domestic cause of revisionism," he inscribed into the text of the conference declaration, "and capitulation to external imperialist pressure constitutes the external cause."[24] Gomulka, to whom support had been extended only the previous year, was criticized for being "too weak" vis-à-vis revisionism; Yugoslav revisionists were denounced in a series of widely publicized articles for having refused to sign the 1957 Moscow declaration of the communist parties of the socialist countries, for "following the imperialist reactionaries," and for "venomously" attacking the "proletarian dictatorship in the Soviet Union and other socialist countries."[25] Criticism of the Yugoslav League of Communists (YLC) intensified following its publication of an April 1958 congress program forecasting a world "evolution" to socialism. Whereas the crisis in Hungary previously had been attributed to the failings of the Hungarian Socialist Workers' Party (HSWP) leadership, it had recently become possible to attribute it to the pernicious influence of Yugoslav revisionism. That new Chinese line was not well taken by fraternal parties in either Eastern or Western Europe, where it stultified an incipient freedom of movement.[26]

The moment when Beijing and Moscow could stand together on a platform of unquestioned Soviet bloc hegemony was to prove fleeting, however. When Mao's strategy for the realization of national identity premised on rapid, simultaneous achievement of nationalist and communist aspirations ran aground — efforts toward completion of national unification were frustrated by the U.S. Seventh Fleet in the Taiwan Straits, and the Great Leap Forward foundered on organizational disarray and inclement weather – he refused to relinquish his dream, reasserting its essential correctness in the teeth of adversity, blaming failure on class enemies foreign and domestic.[27] As if abruptly thrown back by those losses to an earlier stage of development, PRC politics underwent re-radicalization. Diplomatic overtures to the West (cf. Zhou Enlai's polished performance at Geneva in 1954) gave way to provocative challenges, as in the repudiation of Soviet–American talks on nuclear-arms limitation, support for the reviving Vietnamese insurgency, and public derision for Khrushchev's embarrassing setback in the Cuban missile crisis. Revisionist tendencies were found to be ubiquitous; deviation from orthodoxy was soon discovered in the sanctum sanctorum itself (first in Moscow, then even in Beijing). Meanwhile, Khrushchev took Soviet foreign policy precisely in the direction most apt to excite Chinese apprehensions: toward détente with the West. Just two years after restoring unity to the bloc at the 1957 Moscow conference, Khrushchev became the first communist leader to visit the United States, amid considerable fanfare.

That fateful parting of ways was partly attributable to the different menu of opportunities and dangers posed by the international system at the time, and partly to the different developmental backgrounds from which the two states were emerging. The Soviets, having precariously consolidated their power over forty tempestuous years, despite the sacrifice of some 9 million lives in the revolutionary civil war and more than 20 million in the Great Patriotic War (not to mention millions more in self-inflicted catastrophes such as collectivization, forced-draft industrialization, and the great purge), had finally arrived at the status (symbolized by *Sputnik*) of a leading world power. Proudly looking back on an economic growth rate that averaged 7.1 percent per year between 1950 and 1958 (a growth rate nearly 50 percent higher than that of the United States during the same period), and sitting on a (somewhat illusory) lead in the arms race, they had every reason to be confident in their economic future and, by the same token, chary of risking conflict with a still-formidable military adversary.[28] Increasingly they turned their attention to the United States, not only as principal adversary but also as a role referent for the USSR's emerging national identity as a global "superpower."[29] Khrushchev's 1959 trip to Camp David was in that sense a turning point in Soviet history, visible recognition that the USSR ranked with the United States as a joint arbiter of world affairs. The Chinese, on the other hand, despite an impressive beginning at socializing and modernizing their country, still saw the world very much from the perspective of a "have-not power" (whereas the Soviets had a multiethnic empire and a host of satellites, the PRC had not yet recovered its former territories), with less to lose and more to gain from provoking strategically superior opponents. That its strategic and economic inferiority was accompanied not by humility and patience but by militant self-confidence and even occasional rhetorical bravado may perhaps be attributed to the unlikely victory of CCP arms over vastly superior forces during China's revolution.

The CCP's deviation had the effect of obliging the CPSU to pay more attention to the bloc over the next several years, which became the audience before which an increasingly vitriolic polemic was played out. Following dissolution of the Comintern (1943) and Cominform (1956), the Soviet Union began to try to coordinate and control world communism by organizing conferences of the international communist movement (ICM). They were intended to function analogously to national party conferences: The CPSU would act as the leading party among leading parties, setting the agenda, selecting participants, prefiguring policy outcomes. There were, altogether, three world conferences of the ICM, held in Moscow in 1957, 1960, and 1969. Their final documents are still accorded the status of binding agreements by the CPSU and its loyal followers. But the CPSU's ability to control the agenda diminished over time, as we shall see. Indeed, the ideological controversy became so effervescent that it tended to overspill the designated forum, as member parties availed themselves of courtesy invitations to various national conferences to attend and rejoin the fray. The CPSU Twenty-first Congress (January 27 to February 5, 1959) was still relatively civil; though Zhou Enlai made no mention in his address of Khrushchev's innovative proposal for a nuclear-free zone in the Far East and Pacific, no outward sign of tension appeared. In retrospect it seems clear that an ideological cleavage had already emerged, though it was successfully veiled by goodwill on both sides.

The first visible break emerged at a meeting held in June 1960 in conjunction with the Romanian Communist Party Congress, where Khrushchev (fresh from the failure of the Paris summit) clashed with the Chinese delegation (led by Liu Shaoqi) concerning the inevitability of war. The Soviets (promptly rebutted by the Chinese) had already breached etiquette by sending documentation to all communist parties outlining their ideological positions on the eve of the conference. Practically all the attending communist parties took the side of the CPSU. (That conference was immediately followed by the unilateral Soviet decision to withdraw all 1,600 Soviet advisors from China.) The dispute resumed at the second conference of representatives of all communist parties (except the Yugoslavs) held in November 1960. Although the Soviet perspective prevailed on most issues, Khrushchev's attempt to isolate China was frustrated, as Albania supported China to the hilt, while the Indonesian, North Korean, and North Vietnamese delegates remained neutral, inclined toward the Chinese point of view. The final declaration bore the stigmata of the dispute, awkwardly combining divergent positions on peaceful versus nonpeaceful paths to socialism, peaceful coexistence versus class war, and other central issues. In October 1961, at the CPSU Twenty-second Congress, to which the Albanians had not been invited, Khrushchev attacked Albania (read: China) for opposing the line agreed upon by all at the Twentieth Party Congress. Zhou Enlai objected vociferously, walked out, laid a wreath on the tomb of Stalin (whose body was removed a few days later from the Lenin mausoleum), and left Moscow.[30] Only two-thirds of the parties represented at the congress endorsed the attack on Albania; all the Asian parties remained mute.

Until the end of 1962, each side refrained from attacking the other directly, instead "pointing at the mulberry bush while cursing the locust" (to use a Chinese expression): The CCP directed its thrusts against "revisionism" in general and Yugoslavia in particular, sometimes also assailing the Italian Communist Party (at that time led by Palmiro Togliatti). The Soviets attacked "dogmatists" in general and (after the breach with the Albanian Communist Party in 1961) the Albanians in particular. The issues remained basically those defined in Khrushchev's 1956 speech: the question of war or peace (with the Chinese still insisting on the inevitability of international class war), the approach to the Third World (with the Chinese espousing national-liberation war, the Soviets urging communist parties in the developing countries to form a united front with the postcolonial "national bourgeoisie," as they had once urged the CCP to form a coalition government with the GMD), and the possibility of a "parliamentary road" to socialism (the Soviets in support, the Chinese remaining firmly opposed).

The heat of the ideological exchanges at these interparty forums, combined with the inability of the dominant side to prevail conclusively and ostracize the defeated minority, eventually led to paralysis. Proposals for a new international conference were put forth at the beginning of 1962 by the communist parties of Indonesia, North Vietnam, Great Britain, Sweden, and New Zealand (with Soviet endorsement), but the CCP killed the motion by proposing numerous preconditions: the cessation of public polemics, the holding of bilateral talks between parties, and the restoration of normal relations between the Soviet and Albanian parties (which had been broken off in 1961). During the fall and winter of 1963–1964 Khrushchev called for an end to public polemics and convocation of a "world communist conference"; if there were still differences between the Soviet and Chinese parties, "let us allow time [for each] to have its say as to which viewpoint is more correct" – implicitly suggesting (in Chinese eyes) an imminent showdown, in which the CPSU was confident of a majority.[31] After protracted stalling, resumed polemics, and a futile Romanian attempt at mediation, that meeting also had to be abandoned (in 1965) because of Chinese rejection and the consequent inability to reach preliminary consensus.

Not until June 1969 did the Soviet Union finally succeed in holding the long-deferred third international conference, in the shadow of the invasion of Czechoslovakia. By that time the nonparticipation of China could be assumed. Moreover, there were no representatives from Albania, Japan, Indonesia, North Korea, or indeed from any East or Southeast Asian communist party, and some of the delegations that did attend defended the Chinese/Czech right to dissent.[32] Although Brezhnev attacked Mao by name for violating the principles of scientific communism and struggling to gain hegemony within the world communist movement, there were no critical references to the CCP in the basic joint document issued by the conference.[33] As of this writing, that remains the final meeting of the "communist world movement": Moscow proposed a fourth conference in 1981, but that idea was rejected by the Chinese, Yugoslav, Vietnamese, North Korean, Italian, Spanish, Japanese, and other communist parties. Beijing rejected a CPSU call for a world conference of communist parties in January 1985, and in June 1986 Jaruzelski (presumably acting for Gorbachev) revived a proposal to convene a conference on the themes of "peace and disarmament," but it has gone nowhere.

Given the paralysis of world communist party conferences, the CPSU turned to the international organizations of the bloc that it still controlled, the Warsaw Treaty Organization (WTO) and the Council of Mutual Economic Assistance (CMEA, or COMECON), as well as summit meetings with individual communist party leaders. That permitted a distinction to arise within international communism between Soviet-controlled and non-Soviet-controlled networks, which we shall refer to respectively as the internal and external blocs. After the CCP rejected an invitation to join, in 1961–1962 the Soviets moved to transform the CMEA into a supranational planning organization (COMECON had been dormant until roused to handle economic aid to Hungary in 1957). In 1965, they likewise reorganized the WTO to permit the coordination of foreign policies, as well as joint security planning. The comprehensive program agreed upon at the July 1971 meeting of the CMEA, with its stress on voluntary coordination of national economic plans and joint economic forecasting, was an important step down the road toward economic integration. Gorbachev initially endeavored to continue or even accelerate that movement, as indicated in the "Comprehensive Program for Scientific and Technical Progress" adopted in December 1985, which attempted to include scientific as well as economic and cultural integration. He also dramatically increased the number of CMEA and WTO meetings convened, as well as summit meetings with various party leaders; since his succession, he has visited every one of the Eastern European states, some more than once. Finally, on April 26, 1985, the WTO was extended for another twenty years, plus a further ten after that unless notice of withdrawal is given a year before expiry.[34] (Of course, the apparent end of communist party hegemony in the front-line East European states in the fall of 1989 will require a major reconceptualization of both WTO and CMEA, if they survive.)

Despite incapacitating the (external) bloc, the CCP's principled dissent may paradoxically have expanded its own influence within that bloc: "In retrospect, one may say that it was from 1960 to 1965 that China experienced the greatest influence within the socialist camp."[35] Difficult as it is to measure influence, in view of the fact that previously the CCP had subordinated national demands to international solidarity, its willingness to disagree, even to campaign for leadership of the bloc (claiming the CPSU had betrayed socialism, and indeed was no longer a socialist country), seems to have enhanced its ideological status, even among those who disapproved – meanwhile also greatly impressing both superpowers.[36] Although remaining a minority, the Maoist faction split the bloc ideologically and to some extent geographically, gaining the occasional-to-regular support of Albania, Cuba, North Korea, and North Vietnam; even Poland opposed its expulsion. While sharing the ostensible interest of the CPSU in greater intrabloc pluralism and a less confrontational approach to the noncommunist world, many smaller parties were loath to support excommunication of the second most powerful bloc member, whose unpunished assertion of dissident views eroded the ideological authority of the CPSU and tacitly enhanced their own margin for maneuver. Thus, in the early 1960s, many Soviet troops and advisors were withdrawn from Eastern Europe, leaders were no longer appointed directly from Moscow, and more balanced cultural and economic ties were developed.

The schism also had spillover effects beyond the bloc, spreading to nonruling communist parties in Europe, Japan, and the developing countries. In 1963 the CCP began to call for the formation of pro-Chinese fractions in all countries where the local party leadership supported the CPSU. Thus, for example, in their "Proposal for the General Line of the International Communist Movement" (June 1963), the CCP articulated twenty-five points to define the world movement in what it considered an ideologically correct way, challenging communist parties throughout the world to overthrow the existing leadership and avoid revisionism. In Belgium, the party was "reconstituted on a national level on the basis of Marxism-Leninism"; pro-Chinese parties or factions were also organized in Spain, Italy, Austria, France, Great Britain, West Germany, Switzerland, Holland, Ireland, Denmark, Norway, Sweden, and Finland.[37] In the Third World (e.g., Argentina, Brazil, India, Chile), pro-Chinese parties were formed to parallel and compete with pro-Soviet parties. Those "Maoist" fractions were, to be sure, of dubious diplomatic value, their radical orientations as likely as not reflecting domestic political issues rather than a conscious ideological choice between rival worldviews, and the CCP was unable to control them. It was at that time that the CCP also left most of the international communist-front organizations because they were under firm Soviet control.

By the late 1960s, China seemed in any event to have lost its bid for ideological leadership of the bloc. China's bout with foreign-policy radicalism during its Cultural Revolution reduced China's stature among all but the extreme left wing of the ICM, at the same time eviscerating the PRC's own diplomatic cadre structure. During that period, the Maoist leadership repudiated the existence of a socialist camp and depicted the Soviet Union as what Mao called a "negative model" of socialism, thus, for example, linking the highest CCP purge victims, Peng Dehuai, Liu Shaoqi, and Lin Biao, with alleged pro-Soviet conspiracies. As West Germany's *Ostpolitik* matured in the late 1960s under Brandt, the Soviets shifted the role of scapegoat and bogeyman from Germany to China in their efforts to maintain discipline within the WTO.[38] The PRC thus functioned no longer as an outer limit for permissible dissent, but as an *exemple terrible* to preclude the slightest deviation. Most important, the suppression of the Czech "socialism with a human face" experiments in August 1968, and Brezhnev's ensuing declaration of his doctrine of "limited sovereignty," had a pervasive chilling effect, and China came closer than ever before to complete excommunication. It was in response to that threat that the PRC broke out of the bloc in a search for geopolitically useful support. The ensuing attempt to build an international united front against the Soviet Union was ideologically eclectic, even promiscuous, tending to detract from China's credibility. The opening to the United States was difficult to comprehend even for those communist parties still friendly to the CCP, further reducing Chinese influence within the ICM.

As China emerged from self-imposed isolation to bid for new allies under the stimulus of Soviet nuclear threats in the early 1970s, the split came to revolve around concerns of power politics rather than ideological considerations. At the CCP Tenth Congress in 1973, the leadership announced that "the socialist camp has ceased to exist," labeling the Soviet Union a "social imperialist super-power." The CPSU's forcible reassertion of hegemony in Eastern Europe in 1968 brought out the geopolitical dimension of the schism: By the end of the 1960s, aside from Albania and Romania,[39] most supporters of the CCP line (the Cambodian, Thai, Malaysian, Indonesian, and New Zealand communist parties) were in

East Asia. The CCP's 1974 inauguration of its "Three Worlds" schema exacerbated that regionalizing tendency by, in effect, dissolving the socialist "camp" (an ideologically based category) in favor of the Third World (a more regionally based, ideological catch-all category) as the main revolutionary axis in the struggle against the superpowers. It was over that reconceptualization that the Albanians chose to split with the "revisionist" CCP, though they did not announce their disagreement until several years later.[40] Seven further parties took advantage of the dispute to declare their neutrality, including, in addition to the Yugoslavian, the North Korean, Japanese, Vietnamese, and Laotian parties – the regional trend is also noticeable here.

While attempting to preserve their regional hegemony over the Asian communist movement, the Chinese adopted a policy toward Eastern Europe analogous to that of the Americans, encouraging any tendency toward greater autonomy in foreign policy regardless of its ideological thrust. Between 1968 and 1971, Sino–Yugoslav relations gradually improved, though not until Mao's death could that bitter enmity be fully reconciled; in August 1977, Tito visited Beijing, and in March 1978 party-to-party relations were restored (further exacerbating Sino–Albanian difficulties). In 1971 it was revealed that Romania had functioned as a diplomatic channel for contacts leading to the Nixon visit (at American, rather than Chinese, initiative), and in June 1971 Ceauşescu himself became the first Warsaw Pact member to visit the PRC since the Sino–Soviet rift.[41]

While the Chinese were thus nurturing their garden of Asian socialism and cultivating outposts of resistance in the Soviet backyard, the Soviets were no less assiduous in courting defectors on the Chinese periphery. Geopolitically considered, the growing warmth between China and the Western capitalist countries (particularly the United States) had placed the smaller socialist countries on the Asian rimland (viz., North Korea, Vietnam) in a tenuous position. Already exposed to American naval and air power from the Pacific, they suddenly felt their continental rear area being undermined. The Vietnamese were first to experience that type of geopolitical squeeze in the early 1970s – indeed, that was one of Nixon's major goals in his opening to China. As far as China's support of Vietnam was concerned, his efforts were not without impact, having an alienating effect on Sino–Vietnamese relations. In the case of North Korea, the PRC's growing involvement in sub-rosa trade with South Korea in the 1970s and 1980s (by 1989, Chinese trade with South Korea amounted to more than U.S. $3 billion, ten times more than that with North Korea) was acutely resented by North Korea, as was the waning of Chinese military support (moral or material) since the Rangoon attentat against Doo Hwan Chun. In both cases the political impact was a shift of patronage from Beijing to Moscow – emphatic and public in the case of Hanoi, more subtle and tentative in the case of Pyongyang.

The CCP discovered Eurocommunism toward the end of the 1970s, its own incipient domestic reform program helping to arouse mutual interest, again, however, focused primarily toward outflanking the CPSU, rather than any deep ideological affinity. The first representative of Eurocommunism to visit Beijing was Jírí Pelikan, a Czech dissident and member of the European Parliament. That visit took place shortly after the invasion of Afghanistan and the Vietnamese occupation of Cambodia (October 1979), when Chinese sensitivities about encirclement had been aroused. It was at about the same time that Chinese news media began to refer more neutrally to the communist parties of Italy (PCI) and Spain (PCE) and to suspend their polemic against "revisionism." A major benchmark was the visit of Enrico Berlinguer in April 1980, who was warmly received and had numerous meetings with Hua Guofeng, Deng Xiaoping, and Hu Yaobang. In his April 16 speech at Peking University, Berlinguer denied the existence of a unique model for all communist parties; each had to find its own individual road, based on different historical backgrounds; nonetheless, certain ideals were shared by all communist parties, the most important of which were peace and justice. The renewal of interparty relations between the CCP and PCI, Berlinguer insisted, should not be directed against any third party. Hu Yao-bang, an advocate of Marxist renewal who took his doctrine seriously, could not entirely agree at the time, insisting on the need to "mobilize the working class in the struggle against the hegemonists." Echoing Mao's original critique of "revisionism," the Chinese also professed their belief in the inevitability of war and their reservations about the "parliamentary road." Whereas Berlinguer (along with most Eurocommunists) had abandoned the concept of the "dictatorship of the proletariat" in favor of "structural reform," the CCP still deemed the former indispensable.

Since the beginning of the Sino–Soviet "thaw" (particularly since the cooling of Sino–American relations in 1981–1982), the PRC has accelerated efforts to make new friends in the international socialist movement. The major innovation has been that the search for coalition partners no longer so obviously pivots on an anti-Soviet axis – indeed, the Sino–Soviet rapprochement now often opens the door to reconciliation. Although China has no further illusions of driving a wedge between Eastern Europe and the Soviet Union, Beijing is not above taking advantage of the nationalism of these countries to score some points, particularly regarding Cambodia and Afghanistan, pointing out that "socialist fraternal assistance" to these countries entails opportunity costs for their own economies. Santiago Carrillo and B. Drakopoulos, general secretaries of the Spanish and Greek parties, visited Beijing in November 1980 and restored party relations. A French Communist Party delegation visited in 1982, followed by Georges Marchais six months later, restoring the party relations that were broken in 1965; the (likewise pro-Soviet) Dutch party restored relations the same year. The following year the CCP established relations with the Belgian, Swiss, Mexican (Socialist Unity Party), and Swedish parties, delegations traveling in both directions to formalize ties. In April 1983 relations were established with the Communist Party of India (Marxist), when its general secretary, E. M. S. Namboodiripad, visited the PRC, followed by the parties of Australia, Norway, Portugal, Austria, and Finland. China refrained from condemning Jaruzelski's December 13, 1981, imposition of martial law in Poland; instead of joining the West in imposing sanctions, China signed a trade agreement with Poland in early February 1982 (in 1987 Deng Xiaoping made clear his support for Jaruzelski's crackdown, when faced with an analogous situation in China). Since the Sino–Soviet trade agreement was signed in July 1985, each Eastern European country has signed a similar long-term trade agreement with the PRC, together with intergovernmental commissions and agreements for exchanges of films, cultural shows, scientific/technological cooperation, and reciprocal opening of consulates. It was at that point that Sino–East European trade first began to revive after its long hiatus. Though the USSR remains the principal communist trade partner, PRC trade with the bloc countries since that time has also waxed, maintaining a consistently favorable balance.

Broadening its ambit beyond those East European states that had pursued an independent foreign policy, China normalized relations with Hungary in 1984 for the sake of "exchange of experience in the construction of socialism."[42] With the visits of Honecker and Jaruzelski to Beijing in the fall of 1986, and the visits of several vice-premiers from Hungary, Poland, Czechoslovakia, and Bulgaria, China resumed official contacts with the East German and Czechoslovak parties and official relations with the Polish United Workers Party (PUWP), thereby moving decisively toward normalization of political relations with even the most loyal satellites – still insisting that that had "no direct links" with Sino–Soviet relations.[43] In 1987 the PRC received Czechoslovakian premier Lubomir Strougal, Hungarian party secretary Janos Kadar, and Bulgarian party secretary Todor Zhivkov; Premier (and acting party secretary) Zhao Ziyang reciprocated in June with a tour of Poland, East Germany, Czechoslovakia, Hungary, and Bulgaria. China remains closest to its earliest and hence "special" friends Yugoslavia and Romania, but has shown keen interest in Hungary, East Germany, and Poland – Hungary because of its reform experience, East Germany because of its economic efficiency, and Poland because its economy is perceived to be complementary to that of the Chinese (and perhaps its experience with riot control and martial law).

As a theoretical criterion for establishing party-to-party relations, the leadership has replaced anti-hegemonism with the "Four Principles," first set forth in the section on interparty relations in Hu Yaobang's report to the CCP Twelfth Congress in 1982, and reiterated in the new party constitution: (1) independence of each party, (2) complete equality among parties, (3) mutual respect, and (4) noninterference in each other's internal affairs.[44] Their basic assumption is that the tendency toward independence among communist parties has become the mainstream in the international communist movement (Marx and Engels were retrospectively found to have opposed attempts by German social democrats or French socialists to impose their views on other parties). Not only was the Brezhnev doctrine thereby repudiated; Deng Xiaoping even went so far as to disavow the universality of the Chinese "model." The Chinese revolution had succeeded by applying universally valid principles of Marxism-Leninism to the concrete reality of China, but that should not lead to the expectation that "other developing countries should follow our model in making revolution, even less should we demand that developed capitalist countries do the same."[45] Socialism has no unified pattern; each nation must determine its own road of development.[46] The value of socialism is in practice, as Hu Yaobang put it in a speech to a PCI conference in June 1986 in Rome, and thus it is necessary to respect and learn from one another's practical experience.[47]

This latitudinarian Chinese redefinition of socialist internationalism also permits the opening of relations with all types of "worker parties," spanning the ideological spectrum. The CCP has established relations with some 80 communist parties and with more than 200 vaguely leftist parties and organizations in other countries, including socialist, social-democratic, and labor parties, and various associations in the Third World (political parties and national liberation movements). Relations have been taken up with the French Socialist Party, the German SPD, the British Labour Party, and the Italian Socialist Party. During Willy Brandt's May 1984 visit to China, he was asked (and agreed) to give the CCP observer status at meetings of the Socialist International. The CCP has begun to send delegations to selected meetings of international front organizations, as observers. Former Maoist splinter groups were not forsaken in that eclectic reconciliation: The French Communist Party (Marxist-Leninist) received notice two months after the Marchais visit that they, too, were invited to Beijing, and a half year later (July 1983) a delegation of the French Revolutionary Communist Party was received in Beijing by Hu Yaobang. In March 1988, the CCP's relations with the

Communist Party of India were restored after a twenty-five-year break. Only the Japanese Communist Party has remained in the cold, largely because it has shown no interest in reviving relations (for doctrinal reasons); the CCP, however, does have good relations with the Japanese Socialist Party.

In Southeast Asia, the CCP continued to balance its relations with the nonruling parties there against its diplomatic ties with the indigenous governments, as well as competing bids for control by the CPSU or the Communist Party of Vietnam (CPV). In 1974 the PRC normalized relations with Malaysia, and in 1975 with the Philippines and Thailand – without, however, renouncing support for the (illegal) communist parties in those countries. In his 1978 tour through Southeast Asia, Deng Xiaoping, while refusing to abandon relations with the local communist parties, nonetheless made a slight concession in declaring that China would not allow party-to-party relations to interfere with improvement of state-to-state relations.[48] Zhao Ziyang went somewhat further during his August 1981 visit, emphasizing that his concern was with strengthening state relations and that China's relationship with local communist parties was only "political and moral." The Chinese have, however, been loath to sever all ties to the Burmese, Malaysian, and Thai communist parties, no doubt anxious lest they shift allegiance to Hanoi/Moscow. Thus, for example, the PRC-based Voice of People's Thailand and Voice of the Malayan Revolution radio stations, longtime supporters of guerrilla insurgencies in those countries, were shut down in July 1979 and June 1981, respectively, only to be succeeded by new, albeit less powerful, transmitters no longer on Chinese soil.

In sum, the CCP has provided a model for an alternative form of cooperation within the world communist movement, a "new unity" that acknowledges differences as unavoidable and even useful and denies the concept of a "center of leadership" or "leading party," thereby minimizing the possibility of hegemonism and even making "joint action" problematic. The paradoxical consequence is that the more the CCP integrates itself into the bloc, the more its inclusion tends to dissolve the bloc. In fact, the CCP, unlike the CPSU, no longer attributes priority to cooperation or solidarity between communist parties as a privileged group. Whereas Hu Yaobang had reaffirmed (in his 1982 report to the Twelfth Party Congress) the CCP's "adherence to proletarian internationalism," that concept is now extended to all forces that advocate national independence and progressive change on the basis of equal rights. "We no longer use the term of fraternal party relations in reference to other communist parties," party spokesman Wu Xingtang told a news conference in October 1986. "Our relationship with the other communist parties is one of moral relationship."[49]

227

This notion of proletarian internationalism tends to disregard the nature of the social and class structures in other countries, but is rather (like the recent practice of the CPSU) a function of Beijing's national interests and objectives. The bloc and its meaning are interactive with China's foreign-policy behavior. While retaining the term "international communist movement," the Chinese avoided any organizational solidarity on the international or regional levels, limiting relations with other parties to a series of bilateral ties. On questions involving previous debates within the world communist movement, the CCP has only seldom and quite vaguely taken a position – partly, no doubt, in order to avoid publicly contradicting (and thereby calling attention to) previous positions that have come to be embarrassing.

This new Chinese bloc policy has many points of tangency with that of other communist parties that have sought autonomy from Soviet guidelines – though there are also differences among them. The Romanians join the Chinese in placing the main emphasis not on class relations but on defense of the national interest. The Yugoslav and Italian communist parties are like the CCP in attempting to articulate a conception of international relations that goes beyond the confines of the international communist movement, in fact tending to negate that movement.[50] The French Communist Party, although tending to gear its foreign policy relatively closely to Moscow's line, nevertheless has come out in favor of a "new internationalism," the essence of which it sees in each party's right to self-determination.[51] All of these tendencies objectively undermine Moscow's attempts to enforce a stricter alignment of the ICM with the CPSU, but the CCP line is perhaps more vexing than those of other dissidents because of its size (with some 43 million members, the largest in the world). The CCP maintains a distinction between internal and external bloc policies, and within the former it distinguishes between Soviet and Eastern European policies – sometimes inciting Soviet accusations of pursuing a "differentiated policy," like the United States, in order to undermine the unity of the bloc.

Although the Soviets have chosen to take no official notice of recent Chinese ideological pronouncements and activities in the field of interparty relations, since the accession of Gorbachev there have been efforts to permit greater leeway within the bloc in the hope of reactivating the involvement of the CCP and other apostate parties. By replacing Comintern veteran Ponomarev with the diplomat Dobrynin as head of the International Department, Gorbachev first signaled his intention to rely on diplomacy and avoid sterile ideological disputes about first principles. The program of the Twenty-seventh Congress (February 1986) attempts to preserve an "international communist movement," but makes no claim that the CPSU is the center of orthodoxy in world communism. Although initially most concerned with halting tendencies toward bloc fragmentation and promoting further integration in economic, cultural, and scientific/technological spheres, since the spring of 1987 Gorbachev has emphasized intrabloc tolerance: "Each individual country can act independently," as Yegor Ligachev put it during an April visit to Hungary. In April and November 1987, Gorbachev endorsed "unconditional and full equality" among communist parties and claimed that there was "no 'model' of socialism to be emulated by everyone."[52] The latest edition of Deng Xiaoping's *Selected Works* (published in late 1987 and immediately translated into Russian) was reviewed favorably and at considerable length in Soviet journals. The reformist newspaper *Moscow News* carried a particularly laudatory review praising Deng's effort to combine the universal truths of Marxism with "China's specific features" and implicitly criticizing the (previous Soviet) effort to hold up the experience of a particular country as universally relevant.[53] Finally, in a March 1988 visit by Gorbachev to Yugoslavia, the two countries issued a formal document enjoining the USSR from undertaking the kinds of invasions it conducted in Hungary in 1956 and Czechoslovakia in 1968.[54]

Though leery of Western reactions, the CCP had begun to evince a cautious interest in international communist gatherings in the middle and late 1980s. True, the CCP declined to send a delegation to the CPSU Twenty-seventh Congress on grounds that "there are no interparty links between the Soviet and Chinese communist parties."[55] When Mongolia invited China and other Asian communist parties and working-class parties to a meeting in Ulan Bator in 1987, the CCP again declined, explaining that they deemed any multilateral meetings among communist parties inappropriate at that time. But the CCP did send a delegation to the celebration of the seventieth anniversary of the October Revolution in 1987, and when Gorbachev invited the delegation to an informal meeting, promising that "the meeting will be attended by communists as well as the representatives of other political parties. The meeting will not pass any document and will draw no conclusion," the CCP delegation accepted and attended.[56] When the CPSU sent a message of congratulations to the CCP on the occasion of the Thirteenth Congress (November 1987) – the first such message since the CCP Eighth Congress in 1956 – it received honorable notice in *People's Daily*.

This brief review of the vicissitudes in China's relationships with the socialist community leads one to doubt that anything about it is fixed. What is needed to reintegrate the bloc (if indeed it can now be reintegrated) in view of the declining credibility of authoritative command by a self-appointed bloc leader is a revival of its collective mission that would inspire categorical identification. Only then might closer affiliation with the international communist movement regain the domestic legitimating

229

function it once provided. The socialist reform movement may offer such a common program, once it becomes clear that it can succeed and what policies and consequences it entails. At present, the CCP's affiliation with international communism is so loose that it is questionable to what extent it serves its function of legitimizing the "leading role" of the party domestically.[57]

Since Tiananmen, complete fulfillment of China's stated preferences for Soviet noninterference in the domestic affairs of fraternal communist party-states has ironically redounded adversely to perceived CCP political interests, bringing China's relations with bloc countries to a temporary crisis point. As the masses in various Eastern European countries took to the streets in protest (in part reflecting the impact of China's democracy movement), Gorbachev replaced the Brezhnev doctrine with his own "Sinatra doctrine" (Gerasimov's term), not only refusing to intercede with Soviet troops but implicitly encouraging the demonstrators by telling incumbent leaders that they had to reform. The resulting upheavals in Poland, East Germany, Czechoslovakia, Hungary, Bulgaria, and especially Romania excited alarm and consternation in CCP leadership circles, as the dramatic political changes they unleashed proved that what had been sanguinarily prohibited in China was not impossible per se. If Tiananmen was the future of reform, Gorbachev wanted nothing to do with it; if Eastern Europe is the terminus of reform, the CCP would prefer to bail out. Each represented the other's worst nightmare. Thus, the initial impulse of the hard-line faction that had achieved primacy in Beijing was to launch another polemical assault against Moscow for "subversion of socialism" and allowing "peaceful evolution"; indeed, intraparty documents were circulated to that effect. In the end, however, cooler heads prevailed. Notwithstanding the repudiation of the leading role of the communist parties by the former Eastern European "satellites," followed by elections in many of them in which the communist parties dwindled to minority status, Beijing retained amicable diplomatic relations with all – perhaps inspired by fear that otherwise they would recognize Taiwan, as they had just recognized South Korea. And although the Chinese made it clear that they differed with Gorbachev's "new thinking," Beijing has returned to its modus vivendi with Moscow.

CHINA AND THE THIRD WORLD

From the very beginning, the CCP has considered itself especially well qualified to promote the cause of socialism in the developing countries. Emerging from a background of relatively egregious imperialist depredations ranging from the Opium War through Japanese invasion, a party that miraculously snatched victory from the jaws of annihilation with relatively little outside aid, the CCP was proud of having achieved victory via "people's war," a form of guerrilla warfare based on indigenous martial traditions. The Chinese revolution did not immediately lead to a proletarian dictatorship, but to "New Democracy," implying completion of the bourgeois-democratic revolution under communist leadership. The CCP took that to be a relevant model for the phased but uninterrupted transition of other pre-capitalist, pre-industrial societies from colonialism to socialism. In adjacent countries with strong indigenous communist movements, the CCP thus adopted a posture of militant activism, sending "volunteers" to fight "American imperialism" in Korea and also providing crucial moral and material support to the Viet Minh in their national liberation war against the French.

Even in countries with relatively weak communist parties, the Chinese enthusiastically propagated their own "model" of revolution. In the report to the Seventh Congress in 1945 in which he so lavishly praised Mao's contributions to the Chinese revolution, Liu Shaoqi contended that "Mao's thought" had relevance for the emancipation of people everywhere, "particularly the peoples of the East."[58] Marx and Lenin were Europeans, who wrote about European problems and seldom took China or Asia into account, Liu observed in the spring of 1946, whereas Mao was an Asian who had transformed Marxism "from a European to an Asian form."[59] And it was also Liu Shaoqi who made a famous statement in November 1949 outlining the CCP claim that "the path taken by the Chinese people in defeating imperialism and its lackeys and in founding the People's Republic is the path that should be taken by the people of various colonial and semi-colonial countries in their fight for national independence and people's democracy."[60]

Nor did the CCP's claims to relevance go unheeded by communist parties in neighboring new nations. In India, the pro-Soviet communist leadership was overthrown in early 1948 by a pro-Chinese faction led by B. T. Ranadive, and the Maoist strategy of a multiclass (united front) alliance for a two-stage revolution (New Democracy, followed by a transition to socialism) was accepted.[61] The Malayan Communist Party praised the Chinese revolutionary strategy, and the Indonesian, Japanese, Burmese, and Thai communist parties were also influenced to some degree by the Chinese model. The Soviets, however, were loath to accept such an abridgment of the relevance of the classic Leninist model of proletarian revolution to the developing countries. Ranadive was obliged to recant in 1949, and in 1950 an editorial in the Cominform journal, while conceding the relevance of the Chinese revolution, advised the CPI to formulate a strategy that would "draw on the experience of the national liberation model of China and other countries."[62] That November, at a conference at the Soviet Institute of Oriental Studies, the principal speaker, one Y. Zhukov, said that "it would be risky to regard the Chinese revolution as some kind of 'stereotype' for people's democratic revolutions in other parts of Asia."[63]

Over the next several years, after the Chinese intervened in the Korean War and subsequently became domestically engaged in socialization of the means of production and simultaneous economic reconstruction, all of which sorely taxed domestic resources and required Soviet assistance, the CCP became less outspoken concerning the special form Marxism must take to deal with the problems of Asia and the Third World. All discussions of "Mao's road" ceased by late 1951, and the flow of Soviet arms aid rose markedly thereafter.[64] To be sure, that retreat may have been merely tactical, as Khrushchev suggested in writing about his first encounter with Mao in 1954:

Ever since I first met Mao I have always known – and also said to colleagues – that he would never reconcile himself to another Communist Party being superior to his within the Communist world movement. He would never be in the position to tolerate that.[65]

Following the cease-fire in the Korean War (July 1953), the CCP soon reasserted its special calling to lead the Third World. However, the Chinese opening to the Third World shifted from emphasis on propagating its revolutionary model to united-front-style diplomacy. Actually, as early as 1946, Mao had made a seminal contribution to the Marxist conceptualization of the Third World, referring to the developing countries as a nonhostile buffer zone rather than a part of the capitalist encirclement.[66] At that time, he introduced the notion of an "intermediate zone" between the two camps, characterizing it as a "vast zone which includes many capitalist, colonialist and semi-colonial countries in Europe, Asia and Africa."[67] He said that the United States would first have to subjugate that zone before threatening the Soviet Union, implying that the zone's current status was undecided, not necessarily anti-communist. China dropped that line of interpretation in 1947 in the light of Zhdanov's more militant "two-camps" worldview, but returned to it after Zhdanov's (and Stalin's) departure from the scene.

The Korean War ended in July 1953, only a few months after Stalin's death. The PRC, exhausted and drained by some thirty years of virtually incessant strife, subdued its emphasis on people's war in favor of a more discreet approach to the prospect of revolution in the "intermediate zone." Zhou Enlai's evident objective was to establish a "neutral belt of states as the 'zone of peace' between the Western coalition and China,"[68] accordingly endeavoring to redefine "neutrality" as opposition to U.S. influence and rejection of anti-Chinese alliances, rather than anti-communism. Lenin's phrase "peaceful coexistence" was first revived not by Khrushchev but by Zhou Enlai in his political report to the national committee of the Chinese People's Political Consultative Conference (CPPCC) in February 1953. Having finally negotiated a cease-fire at Panmunjon, the PRC also sought truce in Indochina, which was achieved in April 1954 at Geneva, the first time the PRC was represented in an international conference. Thanks largely to the diplomatic efforts of Zhou Enlai, the Viet Minh (whom the PRC had previously aided in their insurgency) acceded to a compromise settlement in Geneva that it would subsequently regret.

Following the close of the Geneva meeting in June, the PRC delegation visited India and Burma on its way home. (India had been the first "capitalist" country to recognize China, in April 1950, the leading non-bloc proponent of immediate seating for the PRC in the United Nations, and China's only available channel to Washington and other Western powers during and after the Korean War; relations were at that time quite cordial.) As a result of Zhou's talks with Nehru and Burmese prime minister U Nu, joint communiqués were issued emphasizing that relations between the PRC and those two countries would be based on the "Five Principles of Peaceful Coexistence": mutual respect for territorial sovereignty, mutual non-aggression, mutual non-intervention in internal affairs, equality and mutual benefit, and peaceful coexistence. Those principles were further propagated at the April 1955 Conference of Asian Countries in New Delhi, followed by the Conference of Asian and African States at Bandung, Indonesia. On his June 1954 journey to New Delhi to sign the understanding, Zhou appealed to Nehru to exclude the United States and the Soviet Union from Asian affairs; Chinese leaders also successfully opposed Soviet participation in the Bandung Conference. At Bandung, Zhou called upon all overseas Chinese to adopt the citizenship of their resident countries (which was particularly appreciated by Djakarta), pledged peaceful coexistence with Laos and Cambodia, and offered direct negotiations with the United States (which began at the ambassadorial level in August 1955 in Warsaw). From November 1956 through January 1957, Zhou visited eight Asian states, further extolling the Five Principles. The Third World, Asian states in particular, greeted "new China's" bid to seek peaceful solutions to common problems (rather than sponsoring revolution) with great relief.

Alert at that time for promising innovations to distinguish his leadership from the Stalinist policies to which his Politburo rivals remained wedded, Khrushchev moved quickly to co-opt that Chinese initiative, not only generalizing the principle of peaceful coexistence to the United States and other developed capitalist countries, but adopting non-militant, gradualist tactics to promote (Soviet) communism among developing nations. As a result of the emergence of the communist camp and the weakening of colonialism, he maintained (borrowing Mao's concept of an "intermediate zone") that "a vast 'zone of peace,' including both socialist and nonsocialist peace-loving states in Europe and Asia, has emerged in the world arena," which might play a "progressive" role in weakening "imperialism" and strengthening the communist world. Thus, the neutralist, even capitalist, nations on the periphery of the communist bloc were not to be treated as objects of fear and suspicion, but as opportunities to be exploited by a more flexible foreign policy. Beginning in 1955, Soviet theorists began to redefine Soviet doctrine on the role of the bourgeoisie in "bourgeois nationalist" revolutions and the possibility of nonalignment in states without communist governments.[69] To be sure, the CCP was duly credited for its contribution to that reorientation of socialist policy toward the Third World.[70] In one section of his report to the CPSU Twentieth Congress, Khrushchev said that:

the great historical significance of the famous Five Principles, put forward by the PRC and the Republic of India and supported by the Bandung conference and world consensus, lies in that they have provided the best form of relations among nations with different social systems under the present situation. Why should not these principles become the basis of peaceful relations among all nations in all parts of the world? If all nations accept these five Principles, it would be in the self-interest and at the desire of the people of every nation.[71]

And in November 1957, the Five Principles were formally endorsed by the Conference of Twelve Nations' Communist and Workers Parties, which convened in Moscow. At that meeting, Khrushchev recalled,

I think during the Moscow conference... we suggested that the task of the international communist movement would be more readily accomplished if we adopted some kind of division of labor. Since the Chinese Communist Party had won a great revolutionary victory in Asia, we thought it would be a good idea for the Chinese to concentrate on establishing closer contacts with the other Asian countries and Africa. We were primarily concerned about India, Pakistan, and Indonesia – three nations with economic conditions similar to China's. As for our own Party, it seemed to make more sense for us to be responsible for keeping touch with the revolutionary movements in Western Europe and the Americas.

Yet according to Khrushchev, Mao just as graciously declined that invitation:

When we presented this idea to the Chinese comrades, Mao Tse-tung said, "No, it's out of the question. The leading role in Africa and Asia should belong to the Soviet Union. The Communist Party of the Soviet Union is the Party of Lenin; its cadres understand Marxism-Leninism more profoundly than anyone else. We of the Chinese Communist Party look to the Soviet Union for guidance. Therefore

I think the CPSU should be the one and only center of the international communist movement, and the rest of us should be united around that center."[72]

Apparently taking Mao at his word, Khrushchev resumed what seemed at the time to be a highly promising Soviet demarche toward the Third World. Soviet theoreticians went beyond Mao's Five Principles in hypothesizing that pre-industrial societies not only offered favorable conditions for socialist inroads but also might become socialist without having to pass through the successive stages prescribed by orthodox Marxist stage theory. Such an evolution was feasible if the countries in question first opted for a "noncapitalist" route of development, moderately socialist and nationalist in character.[73] Not foreseeing the divisive impact it would have on the Soviet empire, nationalism was coming to be deemed "progressive," in the hope that it might undermine the Western alliance structure (à la de Gaulle's withdrawal from NATO).

Under the protective cover of a policy of détente with the West, Soviet diplomatic and technical advisors of various types fanned out into the Third World, focusing on those regimes that seemed to offer the best prospects for "noncapitalist" development. Did they practice land reform? Were they "progressive"? The visits Khrushchev and Bulganin made to India, Burma, and Afghanistan in 1954–1955, where they repeatedly emphasized Soviet friendship with those nations that took a neutral position in world affairs, marked the beginning of both the Soviet foreign-aid program and the Soviet Union's special relationship with India. The arms deal with Egypt the same year was the first to be concluded as part of a new policy of military aid to noncommunist countries.[74] By the end of 1956, no fewer than fourteen economic and military assistance agreements had been signed with various new developing nations, often on terms more generous than those granted the PRC. Thus, by 1961 Soviet non-military loans to India amounted to more than twice the total amount given China from 1949 to 1961.[75] It has been estimated that by the time of Khrushchev's fall in 1964, about $3 billion (U.S.) worth of arms had been delivered to thirteen noncommunist developing countries in the preceding decade, amounting to nearly half of total Soviet aid during that period.[76] Several Third World regimes (e.g., Egypt, Algeria) declared themselves to be socialist, welcoming Soviet advisors (e.g., the engineers who constructed the Aswan Dam), along with arms and developmental aid.

Although the CCP might thus be said to have originated the first concerted communist campaign to win the allegiance of the Third World, Chinese support for the program did not survive the radicalization of "Mao's thought" that followed the abortive Hundred Flowers campaign. From Mao's impatient perspective, Bandung had not borne fruit: Only four nations established relations with China between 1955 and 1957, the most important of which was Egypt; meanwhile, the United Nations embargo ensuing from the Korean War remained intact. In its newly discovered concern for the perils of revisionism, the CCP suddenly began attaching much more stringent criteria to underwriting proto-socialist regimes, groups, or tendencies in the Third World. Instead of concerting foreign policy with moderate leaders such as Nasser or Nehru, the PRC began promoting violent national liberation movements and supporting radical programs for international reorganization (e.g., following Sukarno's indignant 1965 withdrawal from the United Nations, Foreign Minister Chen Yi called for a "revolutionary United Nations"). There are at least three conceivable reasons for that shift.

First, according to the "theory of uninterrupted revolution" adopted in that more radical phase of "Mao Zedong thought," revolutions were expected to move more quickly from the national democratic to the socialist phase than previously assumed, while under the leadership of a communist party. That meant that bourgeois nationalist regimes such as the United Arab Republic (UAR, then including Egypt and Iraq, under Nasser and Kassem, respectively) were unworthy of assistance, not to be trusted. The China-India-Egypt alignment was soon replaced by the so-called Beijing-Djakarta-Hanoi-Pyongyang axis, as the PRC shifted from a policy it had come to scorn as "class collaboration" to a policy of internationalized class war. It was also at that time that China articulated its "intermediate-zone theory,"[77] according to which imperialist attacks would not be directed against the formidable socialist camp ("The East Wind prevails over the West Wind."), but concentrated against the vulnerable "intermediate zone." It was hence incumbent upon socialist countries to support anti-imperialist, anti-colonial struggles in the "intermediate zone."

Second, although Nehru was first to endorse PRC entry to the United Nations, even in the context of the Korean War, India's surge to the forefront of the nonaligned bloc and emergence as China's main rival for Soviet patronage in Asia seems to have awakened a Sino–Indian rivalry and perhaps a competitive differentiation of platforms in a campaign for leadership of the nonaligned bloc, with the CCP perforce advocating the more militant strategy, while the Indians maintained their insistence on nonviolent resistance. As early as 1958 Beijing was annoyed to find that when Khrushchev proposed a five-power summit to devise ways of relieving international tension, China was not included.[78] That rivalry was exacerbated by Indian support for Tibet in its 1959 insurrection against Chinese occupation forces, and its granting of sanctuary to the Dalai Lama and his followers when the PRC crushed that uprising; that, in turn, precipitated intense border friction.

Third, there seems to have been a serious disagreement over the likely imperialist response to the instigation of relatively low level violence in the Third World. Although the Chinese flaunted their endorsement of class war to an exaggerated degree, reaching an eventual rhetorical zenith with Lin Biao's extrapolation of the Chinese civil war to the entire world,[79] experience proved them to be correct in assuming that socialist states could venture more support for national-liberation wars without touching off massive and instant nuclear retaliation. China thus supported the Democratic Republic of Vietnam with large amounts of military and economic assistance, also offering rhetorical support and smaller amounts of material aid to communist movements in Thailand, Burma, Indonesia, Malaya, and the Philippines. Beyond Asia, the PRC supported liberation struggles in Guinea-Bissau, Angola (UNITA during the 1960s, then to the FNLA through 1975), Mozambique (FRELIMO), Zimbabwe (ZANU), and southwest Africa (SWAPO), as well as the PLO in the Middle East and the Naxalite movement in India. In Algeria, Beijing was the first to extend official recognition to Ben Bella's insurgency. Khrushchev had warned against that line, arguing that such brushfires might escalate into nuclear conflagration devastating the East as well as the West (not to mention inhibiting neutralism and leading to the polarization of the Third World).[80]

The militant revolutionary phase of Chinese Third World policy, which lasted, with some variations, from the late 1950s through the late 1960s, had mixed results. It certainly seems to have impressed both superpowers, leading the United States to overestimate the Chinese military threat, and causing the USSR gradually to shift its own Third World policy in the direction of tendering military aid to national-liberation wars.[81] In Africa, the PRC managed to establish diplomatic relations with about ten new nations, the most important of which were Ghana, Guinea, Mali, Algeria, the UAR, the Congo (Brazzaville), and Somalia – cultural agreements were signed, trade developed, and economic assistance was given (the Chinese showed skill in allocating their limited funds and technicians to maximum public-relations advantage). Zanzibar, Tanzania, and Zambia turned increasingly to Beijing for support and assistance, and the construction of a few high-profile projects, such as the Tan-Zam railway, paid high dividends in goodwill. In Latin America, the PRC established relations with Castro on September 2, 1960, also setting up a Xinhua press office (with branch offices in Argentina, Brazil, Colombia, Ecuador, Peru, and Venezuela).

The adverse consequences of the Chinese pursuit of international class struggle began to become apparent just before the outbreak of the Cultural Revolution, just when that line had become most radicalized. Zhou Enlai undertook a tour of Africa in 1964, which seemed to be proceeding successfully until he declared that "revolutionary prospects" were "excellent" in Africa, whereupon he began to encounter such a frosty reception that his travels had to be prematurely concluded.[82] A number of African countries decried China's policies, including Niger, the Ivory Coast, Upper Volta, and Madagascar, while some even broke diplomatic relations (e.g., Ghana, Burundi), reducing the total number of African states with which China maintained ties from eighteen in 1964–1965 to thirteen in 1969. The second Conference of Nonaligned States in Algeria had to be canceled in 1965 because of an irresolvable rivalry between China and the USSR (each of which wished to attend, but the PRC only if the USSR were excluded – which India resisted). In Latin America, China's stock declined when Castro opted to side with the USSR in the Sino-Soviet dispute. Even in Asia, China suffered a setback when the Indonesian Communist Party (PKI) was brutally suppressed following an ill-advised and abortive coup attempt (in which the CCP may have been implicated), decimating what had been the largest party outside the bloc and poisoning Indonesian–Chinese relations for the next two decades. Even the three contiguous socialist states (Outer Mongolia, North Korea, and North Vietnam) began to lean, more or less, toward Moscow rather than Beijing.

Nevertheless, the initial phase of the Cultural Revolution (1966–1968) was characterized by a heightening rather than a curtailment of radical tendencies: Beijing increased its support for a variety of Maoist groups and organizations seeking revolution in various parts of the world, also engaging in vicious assaults on various Third World countries previously deemed special friends, such as Burma; there were also more concerted attempts to manipulate overseas Chinese communities on behalf of revolutionary objectives (as in Hong Kong). By late 1967, China had become entangled in controversy with more than thirty countries.[83]

Soon after the Red Guard phase of the Cultural Revolution had been terminated in 1969 and the foreign-policy apparatus reconsolidated, China hastened to establish relations with the Third World on a more ecumenical basis – greatly encouraged in that effort by border fighting and nuclear blackmail from the Soviet Union. Its efforts were again greeted with great relief, and rewarded by prompt diplomatic recognition from a veritable wave of Third World countries. China's successes were facilitated by the decline of American prestige among the new nations of Asia and Africa due to its involvement in Vietnam, as well as the unease among many smaller Third World states about the USSR's expansionist proclivities (e.g., Soviet advisers were expelled from the Sudan in 1971, from Egypt in 1972) – all of which fostered a certain mistrust of both superpowers. Also, China was the first Third World country to acquire a nuclear deterrent, and whereas many were frightened and repelled by the Cultural Revolution, it should not be forgotten that many were also impressed at the time – the claims of Chinese propagandists to have eradicated poverty, corruption, and inequality received widespread credence.[84]

Thus, when China opened the door, the response was surprisingly forthcoming. Dropping all ideological prerequisites to political normalization except "anti-hegemonism," skillfully using banquets and tourism as well as conventional diplomacy, the PRC achieved almost universal diplomatic recognition in the early 1970s – but the real breakthrough was achieved in the Third World, with which China reaffirmed its identification as never before.[85] In addition to renouncing most ideological prerequisites for normalization, the PRC at least nominally abandoned its pretensions to lead the Third World toward revolution, claiming only fellowship in that group. "Like the overwhelming majority of the Asian, African and Latin American countries, China belongs to the Third World," announced Qiao Guanhua, head of the Chinese delegation to the twenty-sixth session of the United Nations General Assembly on November 15, 1971. Mao confirmed (on June 22, 1973) that "we all belong to the Third World, and are developing countries."[86]

To ascribe greater significance to the Third World, China also reconceptualized the theoretical context in which it was embedded. During the 1950s and 1960s, the Third World had been a mere "intermediate zone," characterized by its nonmembership in either of the two "camps," rather than by any positive attributes. A slight modification was introduced in late 1964, when, apparently encouraged by Gaullist France's recognition of the PRC in January, that intermediate zone was perceived to be subdivided into two. "At the present time, there exist two intermediate zones in the world," Mao maintained to an audience of Japanese socialists. "Asia, Africa and Latin America constitute the first intermediate zone. Europe, North America and Oceania constitute the second. Japanese monopoly capital belongs to the second intermediate zone, but even it is discontented with the United States, and some of its representatives are openly rising against the US."[87] Because the "second intermediate zone" was "subjected to US control, interference and bullying," it had something in common with the socialist countries and the peoples of various countries.[88] The definitive reformulation of that worldview was articulated in Deng Xiaoping's speech to the United Nations General Assembly in 1974, which perceived not one world but three: The two superpowers composed the First World, having in common their attempts to seek world hegemony, bring the developing countries under their control, and "bully" the other developed countries. The superpowers were the "biggest international exploiters and oppressors of today," sharing a form of "monopoly capitalism" as the basis of their respective social systems. Developing countries were adjured to maintain "equidistance" from the two superpowers.[89] The Second World consisted of the other developed countries of both the East and the West, which exploited the developing countries but were in turn exploited and bullied by the two superpowers. The Third World, consisting of the developing nations of Asia, Africa, and Latin America, was exploited and oppressed by both of the other groups, but nevertheless held the key to the future.[90] With three-fourths of the world's population, three-fifths of its area, and a large share of its natural resources, markets, and investment opportunities, the Third World was Mao's "blank sheet of paper," on which the most beautiful characters could be written.

That was the first time that the Third World had been recognized for its own distinctive properties, rather than as an intermediary zone or hotbed for socialism. Aside from permitting a harsher critique of the Soviet Union than before (as not only nonsocialist but also "capitalist-roaders" and "social imperialists"), that formulation permitted the theodicy and eschatology of Marxist salvationism to be projected internationally, to China's symbolic advantage.[91]

Since the launching of China's reform program in late 1978 and the commencement of Sino–Soviet normalization talks soon afterward, China's overtures to the Third World have continued, but with three modifications. First, the PRC has suspended or at least drastically curtailed its own foreign-aid program: Chinese aid commitments dropped from $366 million in 1975 to less than $200 million for 1976, 1977, and 1978, declining further since then.[92] There has been a limited revival of Chinese military and developmental assistance to Africa since 1982–1984, focusing particularly on Zambia, Tanzania, and Zaire.[93] Second, Deng's market reforms have facilitated China's integration into the international trading and financial systems, a tendency that has continued even after the early enthusiasm for the American connection cooled. In its role as active participant in the international (Western-dominated) economic system, the PRC has tactfully opted to play down the three-worlds theory, with its implications of international class war. That has been particularly true since proclamation of China's "independent" foreign policy at the Twelfth Party Congress in 1982, which brought with it a revival of appeals to the Five Principles of Peaceful Coexistence. Third, Sino–Soviet normalization talks have permitted China to drop anti-hegemonism as a prerequisite for normalization with various socialist Third World countries. The functional extinction of the anti-hegemony plank was confirmed by its mention in the communiqué of the May 1989 Sino–Soviet summit – if the Soviet Union also agrees, the epithet has no empirical referent.

China's continued identification with the Third World has now shifted to the international legislative forums. Analysis of China's roll-call votes in the United Nations General Assembly shows the PRC to have voted much more frequently against the U.S. position than in favor, probably in deference to its Third World reference group, which now holds a clear majority in the General Assembly.[94] In 1983, China voted for the draft resolution of the General Assembly condemning the invasion of Grenada, for example, and abstained on the U.S.-sponsored draft resolution condemning the Soviet downing of the KAL airliner (in the other nineteen Security Council resolutions of 1983, China voted with the United States). In 1983, China voted against the United States almost 80 percent of the time; in 1989, China voted with the United States only 11.1 percent of the time (contrasted with 98.4 percent agreement with the Soviet Union), just below Burkina Faso.[95] In October 1981 at the Cancun conference, Zhao Ziyang proposed an ambitious plan for the creation of a new world economic order, according to which the developing countries should have full access to Western markets without protectionist barriers or disadvantageous terms of trade; indeed, the distinction between North and South in the international division of labor should be eliminated altogether, and the developing countries given "full and eternal sovereignty" over their own natural resources. In 1982, China publicly associated itself with the basic principles espoused by the "Group of 77." (China has not, however, joined the group, nor has it joined the nonaligned movement, determined as it is to adhere to its "independent" – not merely neutral – foreign policy.)[96] Nor has it chosen a significant leadership role in any of the international governmental organizations (IGOs) that service Third World demands and needs. It has, rather, sought to join those IGOs still assumed to be under the control of the First World. By 1983, the PRC had joined some 340 international organizations, tacitly underlining its commitment to the international organizational status quo.[97] From 1977 to 1988 China's membership in nongovernmental international organizations increased nearly eightfold, from 71 to 574.[98]

The leadership's apparent purpose in becoming such an avid "joiner" has been to facilitate access to credit, capital, and technology markets. China's memberships in, and applications for aid and concessionary loans from, various international eleemosynary institutions have placed the PRC in direct competition with other members of the Third World. Like many developing countries, China is a net exporter of primary products, including cotton, rubber, and wood. Indonesian oil has been squeezed out of Japan by Chinese oil exports, for example, because of Beijing's pressure on Tokyo to maintain a balance of trade. Growing concern (particularly in regions on China's periphery) about Chinese competition in traditional markets has thus to some extent qualified general Third World approval of China's self-appointed role as their advocate:

241

As China modernizes, there is a growing tendency throughout the Third World to view Beijing in South–South terms as an economic competitor and ascendant great power. In North–South terms, however, China is increasingly viewed as a champion of Third World views on economic and financial issues. Moreover, the success of its economic reforms, in the face of many Third World economic failures, makes China something of a role model.[99]

By dint of its size and market potential, China receives better credit and terms of trade than do many developing countries, and its call for capital investment and technology in the early 1980s soon attracted more offers than the Chinese bureaucracy could process expeditiously.

Throughout the 1960s, Cultural Revolution China had criticized the World Bank and the International Monetary Fund (IMF), while the country's relationship with the United Nations per se (from which it had been excluded) remained generally hostile. In 1971, making skillful use of a compromised American position,[100] China gained entrée to the United Nations General Assembly, whereupon it automatically acquired permanent membership on the Security Council and gained entrée to other UN or UN-affiliated organizations, including exclusive (i.e., excluding Taiwan) seats on the World Bank's board of governors and the IMF's board of executive directors; more recently, China has also joined the BRD, IDA, IFC, the Multi-Fibre Agreement, and the Asian Development Bank; it has applied for membership in GATT (had it not been for Tiananmen, membership probably would have been granted in 1990). Less than six months after China had been officially granted seats on the governing boards of these leading financial organizations, China succeeded in doubling its own quotas (which determine borrowing rights and voting power) in both institutions, therewith abandoning in practice its traditional advocacy of international financial self-reliance (e.g., in 1976, Maoist China had in principle refused all aid from foreign governments and international organizations in the wake of the devastating Tangshan earthquake). By releasing for the first time its "complete national income statistics" to the UN Committee on Contributions in 1979 and to the World Bank in 1980, China reduced its assessment rate (and required contribution to the United Nations) from 5.5 percent before 1979 to 1.62 percent in 1983 and finally to 0.88 percent by 1989 – based on what many believed to be a deflated per capita gross national product (GNP) of only $152 (U.S.) (the World Bank's own estimates placed China's 1978 per capita GNP at $460).[101] China has since 1979 requested long-term low-interest loans from Japan's Overseas Economic Cooperation Fund (which really amounts to foreign aid, correspondingly alarming South Korea and others) and has garnered small amounts of technical aid from West Germany and Belgium, as well as substantial assistance from the World Bank (becoming by the mid-1980s its largest borrower).[102] As with private investment, however, Tiananmen and the associated Chinese misgivings about political reform seem to have had at least a temporary chilling effect on governmental grants and subsidized loans.

Inasmuch as China's economic relationship with the Third World is now an economically competitive one, it has been argued that its real interests lie with the First World, with the industrially developed countries, rather than with the Third World. China's trade with advanced industrialized countries rose from 46 percent in 1966 to 64 percent in 1975 and over 70 percent in 1979. Its large merchant marine gives Beijing a common interest with the United States and Japan in defending freedom of the seas. Its offshore oil deposits give China an interest in extended territorial limits, rather than an internationalized seabed.[103] According to the Chinese timetable, the PRC's sojourn in the Third World is in any case only temporary, as China is scheduled for arrival in the developed world by 2050 at the latest. Whereas the composition of China's trade with the First World parallels that of other developing nations, the composition of its growing trade with the Third World is analogous to that of other First World countries. The latter trade balance has consistently been favorable to the PRC, averaging some $5.9 billion (U.S.) per year through the 1980s. Among other things, the PRC has become the world's fourth leading arms merchant (in contrast, during the Maoist period China would only give, never sell, weapons – and only to ideologically "correct" beneficiaries), plying this trade almost entirely with other developing countries.[104] Beijing has also begun to send tens of thousands of contract workers abroad, especially to Iraq and other oil countries, where remuneration for their services helps generate needed foreign exchange.[105] China also seeks to attract investment capital from the more prosperous Third World countries – Kuwait, the United Arab Emirates – to prospect and drill for oil in China and on its continental shelf, for instance. According to incomplete data, more than ninety economic-cooperation projects involving capital from Singapore, Thailand, the Philippines, and Malaysia had been built by the mid-1980s, including both jointly operated enterprises and those wholly owned by Third World businessmen.[106]

China's growing integration into world markets is justified à la neo-functionalist theory in terms of its positive political spillover effects. This functionalist perspective on the international system is inconsistent with the class struggle still implicit in the three-worlds model, and accordingly the latter has fallen into desuetude. The PRC has, since 1983, descried a "new era" in world affairs in which countries with "various social forms" become increasingly interdependent within "one world market," improving the prospects for peace.[107] In place of the (not yet explicitly repudiated) theory of three worlds, a "peace-and-development line" has emerged, according to which all nations may rise to full development according to their merits.[108] In this connection it is interesting to note that since 1984, the PRC has taken a more favorable view of the "Pacific Basin" concept, which it had in 1982 dismissed as a mask for North–South exploitation.

China's relationship with the developed First World is one of would-be exporter to import markets, precisely analogous to the relationship between the other successful East Asian developing countries ("NICs") and the West over the past two decades or so – but at a time when there is enhanced concern in the developed countries (particularly in the United States) about a structural trade deficit with the NICs. The PRC's ambition is to follow the trail blazed by the NICs toward wealth and power, at a time when that trail has become crowded and perhaps more difficult to traverse. Under the circumstances, future relations with the advanced industrialized countries seem apt to be delicate, necessitating occasional-to-frequent political negotiation. The Chinese have tended to inject the same nationalist intensity into mundane economic matters such as the balance of trade or tariff barriers that are more typically associated with symbolic issues.

By embarking on its long march toward normalization with the USSR, the PRC has suffered no real losses in the Third World (where only one or two ideological confreres had been able to seize and retain power anyhow), while in effect disarming the gatekeeper to the harem of socialist or proto-socialist developing nations. During his December 1982–January 1983 visit to eleven African countries, Zhao Ziyang thus announced that the PRC no longer necessarily opposed Soviet policy on that continent; he also met with PLO chief Yasir Arafat, with representatives of SWAPO, and with leaders of the African National Congress (ANC) and the Pan-African Congress, thereby demonstrating China's continuing support for those liberation movements enjoying wide support in the region. In May 1983, Zhao withdrew Chinese support for the National Liberation Front guerrilla movement of Holden Roberto in Angola and officially recognized the (Moscow-backed) MPLA government of that country. In January 1983, China established diplomatic relations with Luanda, and in October 1983 Beijing even received the foreign minister of Cuba, the first time since the days of "Che" Guevara that a high Cuban official had been received in China – the Chinese later explained that "Cuba has gradually readjusted its foreign policy" and was no longer deemed a dangerous accomplice of "social imperialism."[109] In 1986, the PRC established diplomatic relations (in return for diplomatic recognition) with the Sandinista government in Nicaragua. The way seems clear to improved relations with various other previously shunned Soviet clients, such as Libya, Mozambique, South Yemen, Syria, and Ethiopia – perhaps subtly offering those countries an alternative "road to socialism." Traces of the old rivalry are also visible in Chinese support for Somalia (which opposes Soviet-backed Ethiopia) and the Sudan (dating from Nimeiri's survival of a Soviet-sponsored coup in 1971).

Whereas this opening to the socialist developing countries may serve to bolster the coalition China seems intent on building in the UN General Assembly, no African leftist regime can yet be expected to turn to China as a serious alternative to the USSR as a source of military support.[110] Any serious Chinese attempt to compete with the USSR for the patronage of socialist developing nations is likely to founder on the same philanthropical incapacity that has crippled such efforts in the past. On the other hand, China's interests in the Third World may coincide with those of the Soviet Union to a greater extent now than when the Sino–Soviet dispute was in full flower – at least outside of East Asia, where the two still compete for geopolitical spheres of interest.

In sum, the PRC's identification with the Third World reflects China's sense of being unjustly oppressed and exploited by those more powerful, bespeaking a deep underlying sense of vulnerability and grievance.[111] This identification is not the assumption of a negative identity, for the Third World has remained a positive reference point, but rather identification with the victim, as a way of rekindling the moral indignation and revolutionary ardor of the Chinese masses.[112] That identity as helpless victim was internalized early in the history of China's debut in the modern international system and has survived as a *Doppelgänger* to the nation's positive image as a highly self-confident, world-transforming revolutionary/modernizing force. While determined to transcend their "victim" identity as soon as possible, the CCP leadership has balanced that ambition with recurrent assurances of its determination to continue to identify with those in this category even after their material interests diverge and "never [to] become a superpower" – by which it seems to mean, never a *victimizer*. Whether that vow will be kept remains to be seen, but in any case it is worth noting that identification with the less developed has always been a marked feature of PRC foreign policy, and it remains at this writing a relatively focal theme in an admittedly much more pragmatic and multifaceted, less rhetorically exuberant approach to world affairs. It has become a vestige of Marxist eschatological assumptions that the "meek [and numerous!] shall inherit the earth," whereby the PRC continues to see itself as a member of an unjustly maligned vanguard and thus a legitimate claimant to material compensation as well as international leadership; this gains increasing relevance in the wake of declining faith in orthodox stage theory.

Since June 1989, China has intensified its rhetorical identification with the Third World in the context of growing alienation from both super-powers – from the United States because of its public sympathy for the democracy demonstrators suppressed at Tiananmen, from the USSR because of its refusal to crack down on analogous tendencies in Eastern Europe and the breakaway Soviet republics. Identification with developing countries (few of which joined in the condemnations of Tiananmen) was far less threatening than was the opening to the West in terms of the political-cultural demonstration effect and the problem of "spiritual pollution." Li Peng thus made his first official visits after Tiananmen to Nepal, Bangladesh, and Pakistan, promising new aid; President Yang Shangkun visited Egypt and other Arab countries. China has even taken a more flexible stance toward Third World countries with which it has no formal relations, such as Israel (in 1990 the PRC opened a tourism office in Tel Aviv, and Israel opened an "academic liaison office" in Beijing). The Thai prime minister made an official visit in 1989, and Saudi Arabia, Indonesia, and Singapore established diplomatic ties in 1990 (alleviating the impact of Taiwan's recognition by six small Third World countries the previous year). The Chinese militant defense of Third World countries against superpower intervention is obviously intended to prime the latter to support China's appeals for support against Western meddling in the name of "human rights"; for instance, a condemnation of the U.S. invasion of Panama was lauded as an expression of Third World unity. In Chinese eyes, that admirable solidarity was also exemplified in a November 1989 UN General Assembly vote (with strong Third World support) defeating a Western resolution on freedom of the press, which the Chinese claim was "designed to interfere in the internal affairs of Third World countries."[113] That sort of united-front rhetoric has been accompanied by a revival of propaganda themes from the 1960s – anti-imperialism, protests against foreign interference in China's domestic affairs, reassertions that "socialism will save China" (wittily transposed on the grapevine to "China will save socialism"). Thus, a recent article criticized the Soviet Union for abandoning its ties to the Third World and siding with the United States on such issues as the need for democratic elections. "Meanwhile, the US and Western countries are now considering diverting UN aid from traditional Third World recipients [no doubt including China] to the Soviet bloc."[114]

CONCLUSION

Unlike the politics of many new nations (or more developed ones, for that matter), Chinese politics has, since the communist seizure of power in 1949, been characterized by very strong leadership, in the value-neutral sense that national priorities have been resolutely decided upon, suitable means to achieve them have been arranged, and their execution has generally been carried through with dispatch and efficiency.[115] The PRC has never been afflicted by splits between executive and legislature, deadlock between central and provincial/local governments, irresolvable civil–military strife, or sabotage or crippling cryptopolitical resistance on the part of bureaucrats. Only when the mortality or identity of the supreme leader himself has seemed at issue (as in a succession crisis) has China's leadership exhibited any symptoms of weakness.[116]

The reasons for this particular strength are not hard to find. Official histories blame errant leadership for the many disasters that befell the CCP during its fledgling years, and strong leadership has been systematically cultivated since then. In a series of writings since raised to canonical status, the architects of the political-military organization that was ultimately to prevail over such long odds set forth the qualities of skill, tactics, and personal character that should distinguish a good leader.[117] Those qualities and values were articulated and cultivated in a network of cadre schools, for which candidates were recruited on the basis of the most careful scrutiny and selection in campaign settings where leadership qualities were clearly visible. Those who exhibited such qualities were lauded as superior human beings, worthy of awe and "unquestioning obedience" from more ordinary mortals. To further enforce such obedience, the organizational qua socialization devices of democratic centralism, criticism and self-criticism, and "study" were systematically applied. Marxist-Leninist ideology provided a legitimating formula and spelled out the goals of the movement toward which all should strive. That combination of abstract ideological legitimacy and its dramatically effective application to millions of people's lives was so potent that all rival foci of organizational loyalty could be pulverized. Thus, the errors of domestic politics came not from leadership weakness but from its excessive strength, capable of precipitating enormous damage before it could be checked. In the case of perhaps the two biggest blunders, the Great Leap Forward and the Cultural Revolution, it may be argued that the strength and tenacity of the Maoist leadership were such that the latter indeed unwittingly recapitulated many of the errors of the former.

Foreign policy is another matter. True, China dared attack the world's mightiest superpower in Korea, later broke with and eventually initiated border conflict with the mightiest socialist superpower, courting nuclear retaliation in both cases. China can claim patent rights for the spate of national-liberation wars that made the Third World an arena of international conflict in the 1960s and 1970s. Those policies certainly demonstrated courage and resourcefulness, disproportionately magnifying the international influence of what was still, after all, a large underdeveloped country. And yet, beneath a good deal of rhetorical bluster, China's management of foreign affairs has been characterized by an unusual amount of ideologically incomprehensible zigging and zagging, bobbing and weaving (from pro- to anti- to guardedly pro-Soviet, from anti- to pro-U.S. to ambivalence), vastly ambitious programmatic schemes without systematic follow-through (cf. Lin Biao, or Mao, for that matter, on the international implications of "people's war"). In short, while Chinese foreign policy demonstrates the derring-do associated with strong leadership, it has also been afflicted by an unusual amount of vacillation and self-contradiction – qualities one associates not with strong leadership but with weakness. In foreign affairs, China has been like a boat with a powerful motor but no rudder.

We have attempted to argue in this essay that at least one of the reasons for this disorientation is conceptual. The starring role in foreign affairs is, after all, played by the nation-state, an entity about which the Marxist theoretical tradition has had very little to say: The nation-state has been seen as essentially illusory or "ideological," having no apparent positive functions – the state being the executive committee of the ruling class, nationalism the result of false consciousness. It is classes that have respectable Marxist ontological status, and classes are trans-national; the party, which is derivative from the class (as its "vanguard"), also supersedes the state.

Although Chinese Marxists have made some progress toward infusing meaning into this theoretically specious yet still operational category, metaphorically equating the nation-state with the class (as in "national liberation," or the designation of "bourgeois" and "proletarian" national actors), such generalizations provide no concrete guidelines for policy. For these, Chinese leaders have reverted to emulation of traditional models, adopting two national reference groups to guide them through the international miasma: the bloc of fraternal communist party-states, and the Third World. The former depicted their future, the latter their past; the two groups fit together on either end of an inexorable developmental continuum.

Unfortunately, there still has been sufficient ambiguity in an international system reduced to two positive reference groups and one adversarial role (alternately capitalism and hegemonism) to permit a good deal of lurching about. On the one hand there has been a tendency to oscillate between active involvement in international affairs and isolation, and on the other there has been alternation between reference groups, as the divergence between them has increased. Initially the bloc was the main point of reference, while the Third World provided some ambit for ego expansion. When threatened by the imperialist adversary, as in Korea or the two Taiwan Straits crises, China would identify with international communism; when the security threat ebbed, China could pursue a more vigorous leadership role in the Third World.

When neither identification seemed to work, China lapsed into isolation. The 1960s marked the low-water mark in Sino–bloc relations, as the Soviet Union reverted to Stalinist control tactics and nuclear blackmail, and China acquired its own nuclear deterrent, ultimately breaking out of the bloc to ensure national survival. At the same time, although Chinese leadership efforts in the Third World continued apace, the heroic defiance of both superpowers expected of PRC clients was not politically realistic and won few adherents. In the late 1970s China's hitherto limited dalliance with the United States seemed for a time to blossom into a more fully fledged alliance, a multifaceted relationship that might not only check the Soviet security threat but also eclipse ongoing relations with the Third World. Since the late 1980s, however, the opening to the West has cooled, while relations with both customary reference groups have experienced a revival.

Altogether, Chinese foreign policy has been characterized by sudden reversals and contradictions of considerable range and magnitude. Yet a few generalizations can be hazarded. First, Chinese foreign policy might be said to approximate, asymptotically as it were, a learning curve. Brash self-confidence, as evinced in China's early Korean adventure (not even the USSR would commit itself once the United States was fully engaged), gave way over time to artillery bombardments across the Taiwan Straits, followed eventually by the Warsaw talks; sharp border clashes at the Sino–Soviet border in 1969 and the Sino–Vietnamese border in 1979 were not repeated with those adversaries. China has been willing to learn from experience and has thus become prudent, gradually shedding more extreme or high-risk ventures.

Second, the communist bloc and the Third World have functioned as reference groups around which much PRC international behavior has rather consistently been organized. China has not remained anchored to these powers, as Germany and Japan remained anchored to the West following their defeat (a rather impressive learning experience!), but they have remained meaningful points of reference to which the Chinese have repeatedly returned – despite growing economic and security reliance on the West. Identification with the tattered remnants of the bloc is still deemed to offer ideological reinforcement for CCP legitimacy claims; the Third World, however heterogeneous, continues to provide a basis for the identification with the poor and afflicted that has been so consistently emphasized in Chinese Marxism, as well as a forum for the PRC to exercise international leadership.

The major difference in the most recent period is that China's approach to both reference groups is cooler, more detached, more imbued by the PRC's own specific economic and security interests. Why? China's domestic program of pell-mell economic modernization by whatever means seems to have created a perhaps not fully articulate sense of bad conscience about both reference groups. The Third World is increasingly seen as a collection of impoverished and inefficient competitors, many of which will ultimately be left behind, while the communist bloc is in great disarray at the moment, without a clear or convincing vision of its future. Neither seems to offer the key to China's most pressing needs. Recognition of the irrelevance of wanted external reference groups has led to increasing emphasis on China's unique traditions as a basis for national self-definition.[118] Socialism itself has not escaped this nationalistic imprimatur; it is "socialism with Chinese characteristics." The ideological self-portrait of a country at "the primary stage of socialism" that was unveiled at the Thirteenth Party Congress in October–November 1987 was even disarmingly modest, fitting more comfortably with the traditional self-image than with Mao's rather grandiloquent sloganeering.

In the wake of the radical attempt to repudiate China's historical legacy across the board, this search for "roots" (as in the "cultural fever" of the late 1980s), may portend the maturation of a distinctively Chinese national identity. This maturity was even reflected, if not in the regime response to democracy demonstrations at Tiananmen, certainly in its carefully modulated responses to Western tendencies toward ostracism and to the subsequent Eastern European upheavals. Despite speculation that an obviously weakened authority would require an external enemy to justify the suppression of internal dissent, the regime has on the whole adhered to its policy of cordial relations at all azimuths – perhaps the most successful foreign policy in and for itself in the PRC's brief history.

NOTES

1. "Lun guojizhuyi yu minzuzhuyi" (On nationalism and internationalism), in *Liu Shaoqi wenti ziliao zhuanji* (A special collection of materials on Liu Shaoqi) (Taibei: Zhonggong wenti yanjiusuo, 1970), pp. 189–199. Though written in January 1948, Liu's article was not published until 1949.
2. Robert Conquest, *Power and Policy in the USSR: The Struggle for Stalin's Succession, 1945–1960* (New York: Harper & Row, 1967), pp. 202–203.
3. During Khrushchev's October 1954 visit to Beijing, he said that "the victory of the Chinese people's revolution is the most outstanding event in world history since the great October socialist revolution." *Renmin ribao*, October 3, 1954. This signified that the PRC should rank second in the bloc. As Molotov put it in a February 1955 foreign-policy report to the Supreme Soviet, "there has been formed in the world a socialist and democratic camp headed by the Soviet Union, or to be more exact, headed by the Soviet Union and the People's Republic of China." *Renmin ribao*, February 10, 1955.

4. "Better Fewer, but Better," in V. I. Lenin, *Selected Works* (New York: International Publishers, 1943), 9:400

5. Strobe Talbott, ed., *Khrushchev Remembers* (Boston: Little, Brown, 1970), pp. 250–251.

6. Donald Zagoria, *The Sino–Soviet Conflict, 1956–1961* (Princeton: Princeton University Press, 1962).

7. Cf. Paul Keal, *Unspoken Rules and Superpower Dominance* (London: Macmillan, 1983).

8. See Parris Chang, "Research Notes on the Changing Loci of Decision in the CCP," *China Quarterly* 44 (October–December 1970): 169–195.

9. This type of mimesis was perhaps not exclusively one-way. Thus, Medvedev states that "it is clear that it was the certainty of firm support from Peking that prompted Molotov, Malenkov, Kaganovich and their supporters to come out against Khrushchev in June 1957." Roy Medvedev, *China and the Superpowers* (New York: Blackwell, 1986), p. 30.

10. Cf. "On Historical Experience Concerning the Dictatorship of the Proletariat," *Renmin ribao*, April 5, 1956, trans. in *Current Background*, no. 403 (July 25, 1956): 1.

11. According to a 1985 interview with a member of the Institute of Soviet and Eastern European Studies of the Chinese Academy of Social Sciences in Beijing.

12. "It seems that Poland and China understand one another very well, for some time, without knowing it," he said to Ochab. "The Poles are good company for us, and we welcome them." Flora Lewis, *A Case History of Hope* (New York: Doubleday, 1965), pp. 183–184, as quoted by Jacques Levesque, *Le conflit sino–sovietique et l'Europe de l'Est: Ses Incidences sur les Conflits Sovieto-Polonais et Sovieto-Roumain* (Montreal: Les Presse de L'Université de Montreal, 1970), p. 30.

13. K. S. Karol, *Visa pour la Pologne* (Paris: Gallimard, 1958), p. 37.

14. *Renmin ribao*, November 21, 1956, as quoted by Zbigniew Brzezinski, *The Soviet Bloc: Unity and Conflict*, rev. ed. (New York: Praeger, 1961), pp. 277, 502.

15. G. V. Astafiev et al., *The PRC's Foreign Policy and International Relations, 1949–1973*, 2 vols. (Moscow: Misli, 1974), 1:64. Indeed, the Chinese press did not at first refer to the rebels as counterrevolutionaries (merely as rioters) and did not blame the rising on Western instigation. Nor did it carry any report on the actions of the Soviet forces, except the announcement of the Hungarian defense minister that they would be withdrawn by October 31.

16. *China and the Soviet Union*, compiled by Peter Jones and Sian Kevill (New York: Facts on File, 1985), p. 8.

17. Levesque, *Conflit*, pp. 45–47. On November 3, *People's Daily* gave a full account of the Hungarian incident in an editorial, accusing the Nagy government of "leaning to the imperialist side and betraying the national interests of Hungary by scrapping the Warsaw Pact." The following day, the paper urged the Hungarian people to "defend socialism and defeat the insurrection of counterrevolutionaries." On November 5, in an editorial entitled "Celebrate the Great Victory of the Hungarian People," the paper emphasized the correctness of the Soviet decision to suppress the uprising.

18. These events have been most fully described by Roderick MacFarquhar in

Origins of the Cultural Revolution: I. Contradictions Among the People, 1956–1957 (London: Oxford University Press, 1974).

19. It was during the Hundred Flowers movement that the first criticisms of the Soviet model publicly emerged. General Lung Yun, vice-chairman of the National Defense Council, said that since China was fighting in Korea for the sake of socialism, it was unfair to have to shoulder the burden of all its war expenditures; although the Soviets granted a loan, it had to be paid back in a relatively short period of only ten years, plus interest. Moreover, during the Soviet occupation of Manchuria at the close of World War II, the Soviets had dismantled and removed to the USSR large quantities of machinery and industrial equipment, without indemnification. *Dagong bao* (Tianjing), July 14, 1957. Others complained about having to learn everything from the Soviet Union, calling that dogmatism. *Harbin ribao* (Harbin), August 13, 1957. Anti-Soviet utterances reported by the Chinese press during the Hundred Flowers movement came from all parts of the country, but particularly Manchuria.

20. In the spring of 1957, the temporary rehabilitation of Stalin reached its zenith. An article in late March stated that "great credit is due to Stalin for what he has done for our Party, the working class and the international workers' movement.... Marxism does not deny the role of outstanding personalities in history, nor does it deny the role of the leaders of the working people in leading the revolutionary liberation movement and in building a society." "Why the Cult of the Individual Is Against the Spirit of Marxism-Leninism," *Pravda*, March 28, 1957. The resolutions adopted by the CPSU Central Committee and published in *Pravda* on July 2 gave an even higher appraisal of Stalin's contributions, holding (with the Chinese) that Stalin had more merits than faults.

21. Medvedev, *China*, p. 30.

22. In December, opposition to dogmatism and opposition to revisionism were accorded the same priority: "While we are strengthening the opposition to dogmatism, we must simultaneously firmly oppose revisionism." *Renmin ribao*, December 29, 1956, as quoted by Yang Junshi, *Xiandaihua yu Zhongguo gongchanzhuyi* (Modernization and Chinese communism) (Hong Kong: Chinese University Press, 1987), p. 150, fn. 4. Then, at a propaganda work conference in March 1957, it was decided that "in the current situation, revisionism is even more dangerous than dogmatism." Mao Zedong, in Ting Wang, ed., *Mao Zedong xuanji buyi* (Supplement to Mao Zedong's selected works) (Hong Kong: Ming Pao Yuekan she, 1971), 3:140. The same accent is visible in Mao's essay, "On the Correct Handling of Contradictions among the People," published three months later.

23. Quoted by Hoxha, in Jon Halliday, ed., *The Artful Albanian: Memoirs of Enver Hoxha* (London: Chatto & Windus, 1986), p. 215. Mao insisted that the phrase "the socialist camp is headed by the USSR" be included in the conference declaration, but Khrushchev caviled at the term "head." Khrushchev later revealed in conversation that it was not at his initiative that the leading role of the CPSU was explicitly set forth in the declaration. *Pravda*, July 12, 1958; *New York Times* (hereafter cited as *NYT*), June 15, July 15, 1958.

24. As quoted in Levesque, *Conflit*, p. 26. The fortieth anniversary conference, which included representatives of the ruling parties of all thirteen socialist countries (excluding only Yugoslavia), was one of the last to meet under

relatively normal circumstances. Khrushchev displayed great cordiality toward the Chinese delegation, whose support he needed to consolidate his own still-precarious ascendancy. The Chinese delegation, under the leadership of Mao himself, enthusiastically championed Soviet primacy, grateful as they were for Khrushchev's promises of strategic military assistance. The final declaration incorporated significant concessions on which the CCP had insisted in a compromise formulation that both reaffirmed the principle of peaceful coexistence and the possibility of "non-peaceful" transition to socialism, and condemned both "revisionism" and "dogmatism."

25. See the polemic *In Refutation of Modern* (Beijing: Foreign Languages Press, 1958), p. 45.
26. Participants later reported that Mao's pro-Moscow role in 1957 particularly annoyed the Polish Workers' Party and the Italian Communist Party. See P. Ingrao (PCI Standing Committee member), "Mao a Mosca nel 1957," *Rinascita* (Rome), no. 37 (September 17, 1976): 10ff., as cited by Heinz Timmermann, "Peking's 'eurokommunistische' Wende: Zur Wiedereinschaltung der Kommunistische Partei Chinas in das internationale kommunistische Parteiensystem," Berichte des Bundesinstituts für ostwissenschaftliche und internationale Studien, no. 25, 1983.
27. Incidentally, the Great Leap also had repercussions in Eastern Europe, particularly Bulgaria, which conducted some Maoist-inspired experimentation in agriculture. See Nissan Oren, *Revolution Administered* (Baltimore: Johns Hopkins University Press, 1973).
28. See Walter Lafeber, *America, Russia, and the Cold War, 1945–1980* (New York: Wiley, 1980), p. 37.
29. See Christer Joensson, *Superpower: Comparing American and Soviet Foreign Policy* (New York: St. Martin's Press, 1987).
30. Robin Edmonds, *Soviet Foreign Policy, 1962–1973: The Paradox of Super Power* (London: Oxford University Press, 1975), p. 17.
31. *China and the Soviet Union*, p. 48.
32. On the eve of the Moscow conference, 39 of the 88 communist parties in the world were pro-Soviet, 5 pro-Chinese, 30 split, and 14 independent or neutral, according to U.S. government calculations. "The World's Communist Parties," *Time*, June 13, 1969, p. 28.
33. Yung-hwan Jo and Ying-hsien Pi, *Russia Versus China and What Next?* (Lanham, Md.: University Press of America, 1980), p. 63.
34. Zdenek Kavan, "Gorbachev and the World – the Political Side," in David A. Dyker, ed., *The Soviet Union under Gorbachev: Prospects for Reform* (London: Croom Helm, 1987), pp. 164–204.
35. Levesque, *Conflit*, p. 105.
36. Cf. Albert Hirschman's analysis of the power of the threat of boycott, in his *Exit, Voice and Loyalty: Responses to Decline in Firms, Organizations, and States* (Cambridge: Harvard University Press, 1970).
37. Kevin Devlin, "Schism and Secession," *Survey* (January 1965): 38; and "Lonely Revolutionaries: The Pro-Chinese Groups of Western Europe," Radio Free Europe report, February 25, 1970, as quoted in Barbara Barnouin, "Dissonant Voice in International Communism," in H. Kapur, ed., *The End of an Isolation: China After Mao* (Dordrecht: Martinus Nijhoff, 1985), pp. 202–233, quotation on p. 213.
38. The resolution of World War II boundary issues (between West Germany and the USSR and Poland in 1970, between West and East Germany in

1973) lowered the threat of German revanchism. In 1969, the Soviets linked Chinese and German territorial aggression, and the Bulgarians and even the East Germans invoked the threat of Nazism by referring to an alleged Bonn–Peking axis. By 1972, the West Germans were disappearing from such nightmare scenarios. Jeffrey Simon, *Cohesion and Dissension in Eastern Europe: Six Crises* (New York: Praeger, 1983), p. 126.

39. Military intervention into Czechoslovakia forced the Romanians to recognize that it was the Warsaw Treaty Organization (WTO) that posed the principal threat to its independence. They denounced the use of force against a fraternal ally, adopted the Yugoslav policy of territorial defense, developed a credible "Patriotic Guard," and broadened economic, political, and military ties with the West, the PRC, and the nonaligned Third World. Simon, *Cohesion and Dissension*, p. 222.

40. The Albanians blamed China for proposing that the socialist camp had disappeared and for putting itself and Albania in an indiscriminate Third World, alongside Mobutu's Zaire and Pinochet's Chile, and for erasing all "class differences" among states. See Elez Biberaj, *Albania and China: A Study of an Unequal Alliance* (Boulder, Colo.: Westview Press, 1986), pp. 95–96, 126–138.

41. Richard Nixon went to Romania August 2–3, 1969 (the first such visit to a communist state since Roosevelt went to Yalta in 1945), where he discussed with Ceauşescu the need for a new Sino–American relationship. The Romanians conveyed that message to Beijing. In his October 26, 1970, meeting with Ceauşescu in Washington, Nixon proposed an exchange of high-level representatives short of the reestablishment of diplomatic relations, and that message was relayed to Beijing in a visit by Vice-Premier Corneliu Bogdan. Zhou Enlai responded with a message to Nixon to the effect that the PRC was prepared to receive a special envoy in Beijing and that in view of Nixon's pioneering visits to Bucharest in 1969 and Belgrade in 1970, Nixon himself would be welcome in Beijing. Romania was the only Warsaw Pact member to react favorably to Nixon's July 15, 1971, public acceptance of Zhou's invitation.

42. Jacques Levesque, "Les 'trois obstacles' dans un monde changeant," *Le Monde diplomatique* 31, no. 361 (April 1984): 1, 6–7.

43. *Renmin ribao*, May 7, 1987, p. 4, as cited by Chi Su, "Sino–Soviet Relations in the 1980s: From Confrontation to Conciliation," in Samuel Kim, ed., *China and the World*, 2nd ed. (Boulder, Colo.: Westview Press, 1989), p. 115.

44. "Constitution of the Communist Party of China," adopted by the Twelfth National Congress (September 1982); "Principles Governing Relations with Foreign Communist Parties," *Beijing Review* 17 (1983).

45. Deng Xiaoping, "An Important Principle for Handling Relations Among Fraternal Parties" (May 31, 1982), *Beijing Review*, May 22, 1983, p. 15.

46. Dong Fusheng, "Theoreticians in Yugoslavia, Romania, Poland, and Hungary Explore Questions of Socialist Theory," *Renmin ribao*, August 1, 1986, p. 7.

47. Radio Beijing, June 25, 1986.

48. Xinhua, November 1978, as cited by Barnouin, "Dissonant Voice."

49. Pierre-Antoine Donnet, Hong Kong Agence France Presse, October 17, 1986, trans. Foreign Broadcast Information Service (*FBIS-China*), October 17, 1986, p. C1.

50. The PCI remains the most advanced in this regard, though the CCP is not far behind. One of the theses adopted at its Seventeenth Party Congress in April 1986 states that the PCI sees itself "as a part neither of a given ideological camp nor of an organized movement on a European or global level."

51. Timmermann, "Peking's 'eurokommunistische' Wende," 41–43; see also Timmermann, *The Decline of the World Communist Movement* (Boulder, Colo.: Westview Press, 1987), p. 109.

52. *The Times* (London), April 11, 1987; *NYT*, November 5, 1987, pp. 1, 6.

53. Gavriil Popov, in *Moscow News*, no. 4 (January 24, 1988): 4, as cited by Gail W. Lapidus, "The Making of Russia's China Policy: Domestic/Foreign Linkages in Sino–Soviet Relations," in Roman Kolkowicz, ed., *The Roots of Soviet Power: Domestic Sources of Foreign and Defense Policy* (Boulder, Colo.: Westview Press, 1991).

54. *NYT*, March 19, 1988, p. 1. Though this would certainly seem to nullify the Brezhnev doctrine, it is worth noting that a similar document was issued in 1955, just one year before Soviet troops crushed the Hungarian uprising.

55. *NYT*, November 1, 1988.

56. *Pravda*, May 20, 1987.

57. That is, by claiming that no communist party has the universally correct "line," the CCP is implicitly endorsing a pluralistic conception of doctrine at odds with its claim to exclusive domestic ideological hegemony. Moreover, by broadening the ambit of bloc relations to include democratic-socialist parties as well as communist parties, the CCP risks including alternative models for political reform. "Our Party will continue to strengthen its friendly relations with socialist parties and social democratic parties in various countries," as one wary article put it. "However, we cannot deny the principled differences between the Communist Party and the Social Democratic Party in the ideological field and between scientific socialism and 'democratic socialism.'" Educational Work Department of Beijing Municipal CPC Committee, "Who Represents the Mainstream and Direction of the Socialist Movement? Analyzing and Commenting on 'Democratic Socialism,'" *Guangming ribao*, April 21, 1987, p. 3.

58. Liu Shao-ch'i, *On the Party* (Beijing: Foreign Languages Press, 1951), p. 31.

59. Mao Zedong interview with Anna Louise Strong, as quoted in Zagoria, *The Sino–Soviet Conflict*, pp. 25ff.

60. Xinhua, November 23, 1949; see also Robert C. North, "Two Revolutionary Models: Russian and Chinese," in A. Doak Barnett, ed., *Communist Strategies in Asia* (London: Pall Mall, 1963).

61. At the CPI's Second Congress, Ranadive remarked, without Soviet approval, on the "international significance" of the Chinese revolution. Throughout 1948, reports and articles appeared in *People's Age* (the central CPI organ) hailing the victories of the CCP and predicting that "the final victory of the Chinese revolution will decisively shift the balance of forces in favor of the fighting people of Asia against the imperialist-bourgeois axis." *People's Age*, September 9, October 12, November 11, December 5, 1948, as cited in Heman Ray, *The Sino–Soviet Conflict over India* (New Delhi: Ablinav, 1986), pp. 7–8.

62. Ranadive was chosen to deliver the first public repudiation of Mao, calling him a "heretic" and "deviator" from "Marxist, Leninist, and Stalinist teachings" and emphasizing (in a 35,000-word article in the CPI's theoretical

journal) the validity of the "experience of the Russian revolution" for other communist parties. *The Communist* 2, no. 4 (June–July 1949): 9–89; Barnouin, "Dissonant Voice."

63. David Allen Mayers, *Cracking the Monolith*: *US Policy Against the Sino–Soviet Alliance, 1949–1955* (Baton Rouge: Louisiana State University Press, 1986), p. 117.

64. Harvey Nelsen, *Power and Insecurity: Beijing, Moscow, and Washington, 1949–1988* (Boulder: Lynne Rienner, 1989), p. 10.

65. Talbott, *Khrushchev Remembers*, p. 464. Khrushchev's account was constructed retrospectively, but circumstantial evidence confirms his account of Soviet mistrust preceding the break. A Chinese informant recounted that Khrushchev asked Adenauer during a state visit in the early 1950s what he should do about his Chinese threat, implying that he hoped the Germans might in some way offset the PRC.

66. In late 1945 to early 1946, the CPSU and other communist parties still praised nationalist movements and their leaders in Asia, advocating a united front "from above." Evgenii Varga was a leading exponent of that viewpoint. However, it came under attack in 1947, when Zhdanov, in his speech to the inaugural session of the Cominform, called for a more aggressive policy in the colonies consistent with his world strategy of struggle between "two camps," repudiating bourgeois nationalism. The attitude toward the newly independent states thus became one of nonrecognition and subversion. Roger E. Kanet, "The Soviet Union and the Colonial Question, 1917–1953," in R. E. Kanet, ed., *The Soviet Union and the Developing Nations* (Baltimore: Johns Hopkins University Press, 1974), pp. 1–27.

67. Mao Zedong, "Talk with the American Correspondent Anna Louise Strong" (August 1946), *Selected Works* (Beijing: Foreign Languages Press, 1967), 4:98.

68. Kuo-Kang Shao, "Chou En-lai's Diplomatic Approach to Nonaligned States in Asia: 1953–60," *China Quarterly*, no. 78 (June 1979): 324.

69. Roger Kanet, "Soviet Attitudes toward Developing Nations Since Stalin," in Kanet, *Soviet Union and Developing Nations*, pp. 27–51.

70. In Molotov's foreign-policy report to the Supreme Soviet in February 1955, he noted that the Five Principles announced in the Sino–Indian and Sino–Burmese communiqués should be respected – the first time those principles were mentioned in official documents issued by the highest Soviet authorities. *Renmin ribao*, March 11, 1955. (Yet his support may have been nominal, for when Molotov was purged on charges of anti-party activities in April 1957, one of his alleged crimes was his opposition to peaceful coexistence.)

71. *Renmin ribao*, February 18, 1956, as quoted in Chin Szu-k'ai, *Communist China's Relations with the Soviet Union, 1949–1957* (Kowloon: Union Research Institute, 1961).

72. Talbott, *Khrushchev Remembers*, pp. 254–255.

73. See V. Solodnovikov and V. Boslovisky, *Non-Capitalist Development*: *An Historical Outline* (Moscow: Progress Publishers, 1975); also Zhukov et al., *The Third World: Problems and Prospects* (Moscow: Progress Publishers, 1974).

74. Edmonds, *Soviet Foreign Policy*, p. 12.

75. Robert O. Freedman, *Economic Warfare in the Communist Bloc: A Study*

of *Soviet Economic Pressure Against Yugoslavia, Albania, and Communist China* (New York: Praeger, 1970), pp. 119, 139.

76. Thomas W. Wolfe, *Soviet Power and Europe, 1945–70* (Baltimore: Johns Hopkins University Press, 1970), p. 130.

77. *Renmin ribao*, February 28, 1958.

78. On July 19, 1958, Khrushchev proposed that the Soviet Union, United States, Great Britain, France, and India meet to discuss "removing threats to peace." Beijing's reaction was quite hostile, viewing that as a Soviet attempt to anoint India leader of the Asian and African countries. After his visit to Beijing later that summer, Khrushchev dropped the proposal. *Pravda*, July 20, 1958; for the Chinese reaction, see *Renmin ribao*, August 4, 1958.

79. Lin Biao, "Long Live the Victory of People's War," *Renmin ribao*, September 2, 1965; trans. in *Peking Review*, September 3, 1965, pp. 9–30.

80. *Pravda*, June 22, 1960. The Soviet assumption at the time was that the United States would not tolerate the loss of a strategic spot anywhere on the globe without putting up a fight, utilizing local incidents to realize global strategies in a nuclear exchange. Writing Eisenhower in 1957, Premier Bulganin conveyed the impression that the polarization of the world had virtually precluded the possibility of limited hostilities anywhere. "Poslanie Predsedatelya Soveta Ministrov SSSR, N. A. Bulganina, Prezidentu Soedinnenykh Shtatov Ameriki, Duaitu D. Eizenkhauery" (A letter from the chairman of the Council of Ministers of the USSR, N. A. Bulganin, to the president of the US, Dwight D. Eisenhower), *Pravda*, December 12, 1957, as cited in John Yin, *Sino–Soviet Dialogue on the Problem of War* (The Hague: Martinus Nijhoff, 1971), pp. 135–140. Khrushchev expressed the same idea in talks with the British Labour Party in October 1957. Interviewed by a group of Brazilian journalists, he said that in the present epoch "small wars" could not remain small for long and would ultimately involve other nations and even coalitions of nations. *Mezhdunarodnye zhizn'* (International Life) 12 (December 1957): 6, as cited by Yin, *Sino–Soviet Dialogue*, pp. 138–139.

81. Moscow was initially less willing to concede the necessity for violent transition to socialism because that would have stultified its own peace policy. But in the face of Chinese pressure (and apparent success in some cases), Khrushchev was ultimately persuaded to relent. At the CPSU Twenty-second Congress in early 1961, he said that national-liberation wars were just and ought to be supported by the bloc, endorsing such struggles in Algeria, Vietnam, West Irian, and the Congo. Later, after coming to the brink of war with the United States over Cuba in the fall of 1962, he reverted again to a more prudential policy. Under Brezhnev, the Soviets of course became major backers of guerrilla wars in Vietnam and elsewhere. Although it is difficult to generalize in view of such tactical vicissitudes, it would seem that (1) the Soviets have always been less rhetorically exuberant than the Chinese in their endorsement of national-liberation wars, and (2) the Soviets have also been more wary of any direct confrontation with the United States.

82. See Harry Harding, "China's Changing Roles in the Contemporary World," in Harding, ed., *China's Foreign Relations in the 1980s* (New Haven: Yale University Press, 1984), pp. 181–193.

83. Lillian Craig Harris, *China's Foreign Policy Toward the Third World* (New York: Praeger, 1985), pp. 30–40.
84. Marie-Luise Naeth, *Strategie und Taktik der chinesischen Aussenpolitik* (Hannover: Niedersaechsischen Landeszentrale für politische Bildung, 1978).
85. The recognition of the PRC took place in three phases. During the first phase, 1970–1971, China established diplomatic relations with nineteen countries, only four of which were from the West (Canada, Iceland, Italy, Austria), the other fifteen being developing countries. During the second phase, 1972–1973, those nations that had withheld recognition out of deference to the United States, taking a new cue from the Nixon visit and Chinese entry into the United Nations, established relations with the PRC. Twenty were in that grouping, including the United Kingdom (which upgraded relations to the ambassadorial level, having recognized the PRC in 1950), West Germany, Japan, Australia, and New Zealand – most of them anti-communist. During the third phase, 1974–1976, an additional seven states, all of them staunchly anti-communist, recognized the PRC, including Malaysia, Thailand, Brazil, and the Philippines. Finally, in January 1979, the United States formally established ties.
86. *Peking Review* 47 (1971); also 26 (1972): 3.
87. Translation in Franz Schurmann and Orville Schell, eds., *China Readings. Vol. 3: Communist China* (Middlesex: Penguin, 1967), p. 368.
88. *Renmin ribao*, January 21, 1964; trans. in *Peking Review*, no. 4 (January 24, 1964): 7.
89. *Renmin ribao*, September 1, 3, 1986, as quoted in *Beijing Review*, no. 37 (1986): 10–11.
90. Deng's speech was translated in *Peking Review*, special supplement to no. 15 (April 12, 1974).
91. The Chinese scenario is that the strong will progressively decay, and the weak correspondingly grow stronger, resulting in an emerging multipolarity. Thus, they argue that the 1970s marked the beginning of a shift in the balance of economic power from the First World to the Second and Third.
92. Robert G. Sutter, *Chinese Foreign Policy: Developments After Mao* (New York: Praeger, 1986), p. 46.
93. The PRC also has occasionally written off Third World debt (as they did in 1983 vis-à-vis Zaire, Zambia, and Tanzania) or extended it when the creditor has appeared to be having difficulty (as in the case of Kinshasa). *Africa*, 138 (February 1983): 34; *Far Eastern Economic Review (FEER)* 119 (February 3, 1985): 25.
94. Detailed analysis of China's General Assembly voting record during its first decade in the United Nations shows that its positions were more favorable to the Third World than to the West, though it seems to have had little impact in the UN program area. See Trong R. Chai, "Chinese Policy Toward the Third World and the Superpowers in the UN General Assembly, 1971–1977: A Voting Analysis," *International Organizations* 33; no. 3 (Summer 1979): 392; see also Samuel Kim, *China, the United Nations, and World Order* (Princeton: Princeton University Press, 1979), pp. 280, 329–330, 402.
95. Chai, "Chinese Policy." China's alignment with the Third World is by no means automatic, however. For example, China has continued its friendship with the Pinochet regime in Chile, seeing the relationship as strategically

and economically useful, and has refused to join Third World-sponsored resolutions at the United Nations condemning the Pinochet regime's violations of human rights, despite considerable criticism.

96. See Gerald Chan, *China and International Organization: Participation in Non-Governmental Organizations Since 1971* (London: Oxford University Press, 1989).

97. Robert L. Worden, "International Organizations: China's Third World Policy in Practice," in Lillian Craig Harris and Robert Worden, eds., *China and the Third World: Champion or Challenger?* (Dover, Mass.: Auburn House, 1986), pp. 75–100.

98. Union of International Associations, *Yearbook of International Organizations, 1988/1989*, 6th ed. (Munich: K. G. Saur, 1988); vol. 2, Table 3; as cited by Samuel Kim, "Chinese Foreign Policy in the Shadows of Tiananmen: The Challenge of Legitimation" (paper presented at the Sino–American Conference on Mainland China, Taipei, June 12–14, 1990).

99. Robert Manning, "The Third World Looks at China," in Harris and Worden, eds., *China and the Third World*, pp. 139–156, quotation on p. 154.

100. The American delegation, placed in an awkward position by public announcement of Nixon's forthcoming trip to China, opted for the first time not to define China's admission to the United Nations as an "important question," as a result of which the issue could be decided on the basis of a simple majority, rather than a two-thirds-majority vote. Thus, when the draft Albanian resolution was introduced to award all of "China's" rights to the PRC and exclude the GMD regime, the most strenuous U.S. efforts to defeat it proved of no avail.

101. Samuel S. Kim, "Chinese World Policy in Transition," *World Policy Journal* (Spring 1984): 603–633. Thus, in 1986, China paid $6.5 million (U.S.) into the United Nations and received back $27.7 million from the UN Developmental Program in technical assistance and $1.2 billion from the World Bank in loans and credits. In 1982, China contributed $300,000 (0.23 percent of the total) to UNFPA funds, receiving in return $11 million in aid. At the same time, China criticizes the industrialized countries for inadequate magnanimity.

102. When A. W. Clausen visited China in May 1983, he indicated that the World Bank had already provided loans and aid amounting to $870 million (U.S.) and would give $2.4 billion (U.S.) in loans in 1984 and 1985 for the construction of twenty projects in agriculture, energy, education, industry, and communications. In 1986, China received another $1.2 billion from the World Bank to help fund ten projects, and it was anticipated that loans given to China during the "Seventh Five-Year Plan" period (1986–1990) would double or triple the amount given in the previous five years.

103. Bruce Reynolds, "China in the International Economy," in Harding, *China's Foreign Relations*, pp. 93–104. China has nonetheless consistently supported the Third World position on law-of-the-sea matters, championing the 200-nautical-mile territorial sea for reasons of solidarity, as well as in order to protect its own wealthy coastal area.

104. Although the PRC cannot compete in the market for sophisticated weaponry, it does produce an extensive line of conventional arms, and Chinese arms sales are up several times over what they were in 1980. The Congressional Research Service estimates that China sold $5.3 billion worth of arms between 1983 and 1986; exports of "aerospace products" reached

$2.1 billion (U.S.) in 1989, an increase of 60 percent over 1988. While the top three sold far more – the USSR almost $60 billion, the United States $25.5 billion, and France $16.5 billion during that period – the rapidity of China's emergence in this market is striking, representing a 167 percent increase in sales over the previous three-year period. The Chinese estimate that arms sales bring in more money (about $1.34 billion per year) than the Chinese military spends on arms (the best foreign-exchange earners are the missiles). China's sales policy seems to be relatively indiscriminate, oriented around earning foreign exchange rather than promoting any particular ideological cause; see, for example, the lucrative recent sales of arms to both Iran and Iraq (between 1980 and 1987 nearly 70 percent of China's exports went to those two belligerents, accounting for nearly a third of the money Iran spent on weapons from abroad, and about 10 percent of Iraq's arms imports – all running athwart Beijing's declared policy of promoting a negotiated settlement). When it was discovered in 1988 that China had sold CSS–2 (1,600-mile range) IRBMs to Saudi Arabia, the United States exerted pressure to discontinue such sales; but future prospects for limiting arms traffic are not bright, as Western leverage has diminished in the wake of Tiananmen. A diplomatically isolated PRC increasingly holds the key to arms proliferation. See Wei-chin Lee, "The Birth of a Salesman: China as Arms Supplier," *Journal of Asian Studies* 6; no. 4 (Winter 1987–1988): 32–47; *FEER* (September 22, 1988): 42.

105. The total number of Chinese experts and workers sent abroad under such contracts increased from about 18,000 in 1979–1981 to 31,000 in 1983, and to 59,000 by the end of 1985. From 1979 through 1985, the total value of labor-service contracts was $5.1 billion (U.S.). Samuel S. Kim, *The Third World in Chinese World Policy* (Princeton: Center of International Studies, Woodrow Wilson School, January 1989), pp, 37–39.

106. *Liaowang*, no. 12 (1986): 30–31.

107. See Carol Lee Hamrin, "Domestic Components of China's Evolving Three Worlds Theory," in Harris and Worden, eds., *China and the Third World*, pp. 34–53.

108. In this connection, Chinese writing about Third World schemes for economic redistribution have begun to assume a more critical tone. "Factors such as failed policies and improper management can be held responsible to varying degrees in particular countries," wrote one author. "It is not practical to blame the North for all the South's troubles, though exploitation is truly a root cause of the situation." Tong Dalin and Liu Ji, "North–South Cooperation for Mutual Prosperity," *Beijing Review*, no. 26 (July 1, 1986): 19, as quoted by Samuel S. Kim, "China and the Third World," in Kim, ed., *China and the World*, 2nd ed. (Boulder, Colo.: Westview Press, 1989); pp. 148–180.

109. Levesque, "Les 'trois obstacles'," p. 6; Qi Yan, "New Trends in Cuba's Foreign Relations," *Shijie zhishi* (World News) (Beijing), no. 9 (May 1, 1985): 7–8, trans. *FBIS-PRC*, May 15, 1985, p. J1.

110. Lawrence Freedman, *The West and the Modernization of China* (London: Royal Institute of International Affairs, Chatham House, 1979), p. 19.

111. See Lucian W. Pye, *Spirit of Chinese Politics: A Psychocultural Study of the Authority Crisis in Political Development* (Cambridge: MIT Press, 1968). Pye seems to enjoy satirizing and to some extent even mocking Chinese feelings of righteous indignation. Still, it seems inescapable that

such feelings do play a prominent role in the makeup of the modern Chinese national identity.

112. I owe this point to Susanne Hoeber Rudolph, in a very perceptive commentary.
113. Chen Jiabao, "Third World's Role in International Affairs," *Beijing Review* 33; no. 4 (January 22–28, 1990): 14–16.
114. Commentator article in *Liaowang*, January 8, 1990.
115. For a thoughtful discussion of the implications and problems of political leadership, see Robert Eden, *Political Leadership and Nihilism: A Study of Weber and Nietzsche* (Tampa: University of South Florida Press, 1983).
116. See Lowell Dittmer, "Patterns of Elite Strife and Succession in Chinese Politics," *China Quarterly* (Fall 1990).
117. E.g., cf. Mao Zedong's "On Correcting Mistaken Ideas in the Party," "The Chinese Revolution and the Chinese Communist Party," "On New Democracy," or "On the People's Dictatorship," or Liu Shaoqi's "On the Self-Cultivation of Communist Party Members," or "On Inner-Party Struggle."
118. For contrasting perspectives on this development, see Allen S. Whiting, "Assertive Nationalism in Chinese Foreign Policy," *Asian Survey* 23; no. 8 (August 1983): 918–939; and Michel C. Oksenberg, "China's Confident Nationalism," *Foreign Affairs* 65; no. 3 (1987): 501–524.

PART IV

Tiananmen

8

The Tiananmen tragedy: the state–society relationship, choices, and mechanisms in historical perspective

TANG TSOU

THE WORST-CASE SCENARIO
AND "HOPE AGAINST HOPE"

Let me begin this afterword with a sentence from Brantly Womack's Introduction: "It is unclear how long [the current regime] will last, what might succeed it, and how it will attempt to resolve its contradictory commitments to repressive recentralization and to continuing moderni- zation and 'openness'." He may be understood as raising this question about the political-economic-social-cultural system in its configurational uniqueness as an entity, though not about all its parts. There are, in China and abroad, those who expect an almost imminent collapse of the regime, who foresee an impending revolution, nonviolent or otherwise, and who fix their gaze on a miraculous transformation of China into its opposite. Of course, there are also those who still celebrate the victory of the June 4 crackdown and who believe that the current system will

This chapter will carry no acknowledgment except to Brantly Womack, who urged me to put something down on paper, and to Edmond Lee, who turned my messy handwritten pages into a draft and transliterated the Chinese characters into pinyin. Those who taught me about Chinese politics and those who gave me valuable suggestions after reading a preliminary draft will recognize with knowing smiles their contributions. Here they shall remain nameless.

I have put my thoughts in the following pages as the record of a person analyzing the tragedy from afar soon after the event. I hope to raise questions that need to be answered. My judgments, right or wrong, may be useful to future historians. In writing this essay I have violated all the rules that previously I had followed. I repeat myself here and there, sometimes for emphasis, sometimes to get at a slightly different formulation of the same idea in a different context, and sometimes unconsciously. On rereading, I have allowed these repetitions to stand.

This chapter was completed in July 1990. Before the final draft was submitted to the publisher in November 1990 some revisions were made to highlight the relationship between the Tiananmen tragedy and the basic pattern of twentieth-century Chinese politics. At the time of copyediting in March 1991 some minor revisions and additions were made.

survive that tragic blunder, as well as other grave errors and serious acts of misrule in the past.

These two groups of political actors, some in the limelight and others still relatively unknown to the public, occupy the two extremities of a new and deadly form of polarization produced by the events of June 3 and 4, 1989, which were presented to us in the outside world in bloody and macabre scenes on our color televisions in our living rooms day after day for weeks on end. They not only were the latest personification of the tendency toward eventual polarization in twentieth-century Chinese politics but also remind us in some way of a basic pattern that can be seen not only in the intraparty struggles in the Chinese Communist Party (CCP) but also in the historic conflict between the Nationalist party, (the Guomindang, GMD) and the CCP in the period 1927 to 1949 on the mainland. This pattern of conflict resolution at the highest macropolitical level can be stated in broad strokes as follows: Serious conflicts over the inseparable questions of power and policy lead to confrontations and, sooner or later, to an outcome in which one side wins, retaining all real power to make decisions, whereas the other side is totally defeated. This basic pattern does not preclude the co-optation of defeated leaders as individuals by the winning side, and along the way to the final confrontation there will be tactical compromises and temporary cooperation, as well as partial victories, partial defeats, and indeterminate periods of stalemate.¹ None of these confrontations has thus far resulted in any institutional structures and social expectations that would enable the Chinese on the mainland to resolve their conflicts through negotiations, bargaining, and an unending series of compromises and accommodations that would in turn strengthen such institutional structures and expectations. Whether or not the two groups of political actors at the polar extremes realize it, there is the danger that they may perpetuate this calamitous tendency, this repeatedly observed pattern of interaction and, perhaps even more important, the underlying expectations, perceptions, and assumptions.

As of July 1991, the victorious group in Beijing has reimposed its political, ideological, and social control on the students, intellectuals, and employees in the various types of enterprises. The workers shy from active political participation. The peasants in the vast countryside are indifferent to or even ignorant about the events in the large cities. But the message of the voices that were silenced in China has been magnified in volume and reach by prominent intellectuals in exile and tens of thousands of Chinese students supported by well-funded organizations abroad. The dissidents occupy a position of moral strength. They brilliantly use democratic, liberal slogans. They have triumphed in the news media in the Western world. They find thunderous echoes in the U.S. Congress. They are heard with sympathy and not unexpectedly touch the right chord for the man on the street and for us in the living rooms of our homes. Within China, they find silent but quite widespread support among intellectuals and students who have the same goals. Their presence abroad is one of the many factors that help the more moderate intellectuals inside China and make life more difficult for those with more radical views. Although they are divided in their strategies and tactics and come from diverse occupational groups, they are united in opposing the current system. Many small networks and groups, each in its own way, work to prepare for new alternatives in every area of policy, institutional life, and leadership. But getting their message to the broad Chinese masses, particularly to the peasants, is a difficult task. By themselves, they cannot pull down the regime and provide an alternative. If there is to be an alternative, it must emerge inside China, not from outside. But there is no conceivable way that the Beijing regime can defeat these vocal opposition forces abroad or eliminate by force the silent dissent at home.

Thus, a stalemate has developed. The Beijing regime has achieved a victory only in the sense that it has been able to maintain itself in power, however poor its prospects for economic development, however uncertain its political future, however adverse its international circumstances. Although by November 1990 the overseas forces of opposition were on the ebb, they can be said to have won an important campaign in 1989 and early 1990 in the sense that by taking advantage of the regime's blunders and mistakes, they have inflicted serious damage (perhaps even what will eventually be a fatal wound) on the regime by imposing a series of inescapable dilemmas regarding its choices in domestic and foreign policies and can continue to do so for many years to come.

If the regime desires international economic aid in the form of loans, long-term credit, expansion of joint ventures, foreign investment on a large scale, and technology transfer, it will have to take some steps to satisfy the outside world's concern on the question of human rights, and that will risk a renewal of opposition activities in China. If the regime seeks scientific exchange and advanced training abroad for its students and technical personnel, it will risk an irreversible "brain drain," raising basic questions about the function of Chinese universities in China's development and the problem of their role in China's relationship with the outside world in cultural, economic, and political spheres. These new dilemmas are now added to a number of old unresolved problems, all of which will come to a head in the next few years: the succession crisis, the change in political generations, the increasing sense of relative deprivation, the trend of rising expectations, the crest of the population increase, and the deterioration of the environment. Superimposed on all these new dilemmas and old problems is a drastic but seldom-discussed decline in China's international position, quite apart from the repercussions of the American–Soviet rapprochement and the changes in Eastern Europe. China was accorded increased international status in the 1970s because of its direct or indirect use of military power in Korea and Vietnam. Now, however, economic strength, not military power, is the immediate determinant of international status and of success or failure in foreign policy; today, China's use of military force would be counterproductive in its part of the world, quite aside from its backwardness in military technology. Any mistake committed by the regime, any unexpected change in the international realm unfavorable to China, any failure to communicate its policy accurately and rapidly to the outside world, and, in particular, any serious, disruptive struggle for power would be skillfully exploited by the forces of opposition abroad, with both open and covert support from many sources. Some still want a violent revolution; others envisage a Romanian-type upheaval.

But it is unrealistic to think that China's leaders and their longtime followers, who won total power in a protracted revolution of twenty-eight years and have governed the country for another forty years, will give up their power without a last-ditch struggle, even if such a fight involves the high risk of a headlong march to the brink of collapse or even beyond. Having in mind the sheer size of China's population, its appalling poverty, the dead weight of its past, and its cultural distance from the West, one wonders if any rescue attempt launched at that time of crisis from inside and/or outside could be successful except over a period of decades, even if one assumes the availability of an alternative group of farsighted and wise leaders inside China and an outpouring of international goodwill from every corner of the globe.

This is admittedly the worst-case scenario. But we should not flatly exclude its possibility. If in the years from 1977 to 1986 Chinese leaders still had the confidence necessary to search for ways out of the deep crises created by the Cultural Revolution, after the bloody crackdown of June 4, which graphically revealed that the Cultural Revolution had eroded the foundations of the system even more deeply than we had thought, our only "hope against hope" is that China still can avoid the worst outcome over the next ten years by accomplishing the almost impossible feat of learning and applying the fundamentals necessary for a process of state–society reconciliation. Through that process, they themselves can proceed once more to restructure their state and their society in whatever forms they wish to adopt as a result of a prolonged period of building trust, negotiating, bargaining, and reaching compromises. All of this implies a reversal of their philosophy, mode of thought, and attitudes developed over a period of more than half a century. This

268

process must also be accompanied by attempts at reconciliation between China and world opinion.

THE TRADITIONAL RULING CLASS AND THE NEW STATE–SOCIETY RELATIONSHIP

The reason we should not hastily exclude the worst-case scenario from our consideration is that the tragedy of Tiananmen cannot be understood merely as the product of factional struggle and popular disaffection. In their specific Chinese forms, and in the way in which they have interacted to produce ripple effects around the world, these two factors have been shaped by the CCP political system as it has gradually developed since 1921 and by the political tradition in twentieth-century China that this system has intensified and disseminated to the whole society. We have to take into account the operation of the rules and norms governing the political behavior of party members, the political structure, the system of communications within the party and between the party-state and society, the philosophy of revolution, and the "art of struggle" of the political actors both within the party and in the society as a whole. Once we step back from our preoccupation with spectacular events, we can understand that Tiananmen signified nothing less than the latest in a series of failures in the twentieth century to rebuild the Chinese state, to restructure its society, and to establish a viable state–society relationship – this time in a wider, international environment that the Chinese leaders have not been able to understand.

Those attempts were made after the destruction of a unique socio-political system that, in its essential features, had endured for hundreds of years. In that system, the absolute rule of the emperor was supported and enforced by an organic ruling class composed of the most powerful elements in three spheres of social life – the landowners in the economic system, the scholars in the cultural sphere, and the officials in the political realm. Those three elements, quite powerful in themselves, were linked together by effective mechanisms. Landownership was the source of wealth that allowed the sons, relatives, and protégés of landowners the time to study and become scholars. The scholars then became government officials by selection through an examination system that stressed ideological and cultural orthodoxy. The officials were organized into a centralized bureaucracy that managed the examination system that selected its new personnel. The wealth accumulated by officials through both legitimate and corrupt means was reinvested in land. It is probable that more land was acquired by landowning families after their members had become officials than was acquired by these families through income accrued by the cultivation of their land. As the saying goes, land does not breed land. That ruling class controlled the state, achieved ideological and cultural hegemony in society, and dominated the economy.

In that system, the state allowed the economy a very large measure of freedom to operate, exercising its control only at key points. The formal bureaucracy of the imperial government stopped at the *xian* level, and below it the local society had a definite role to play. The agricultural economy was what one might call a "precapitalist free-enterprise system," to borrow a term from an economic historian.[2] Nevertheless, the state and its officials, with long-established authority to raise taxes and an army, were extremely powerful, and the state and the ruling class faced few countervailing forces, such as the social institutions and organizations embodied in the church and the estates that had confronted monarchs in Europe. At times, the state was sufficiently strong and rational enough to restrain the power of the large landowners and to implement a policy of class accommodation justified in the name of Confucian virtues.

External pressure from the Western powers, in addition to the example provided by the wealth of their societies, the internal pressure from China's population, and the dead weight of China's past traditions, ultimately led to the collapse of that imperial system. The reformers and revolutionaries were the instruments of history to dismantle it piece by piece: the examination system in 1905–1906, the monarchy in 1911, and the ideological system of Confucianism during the May Fourth period (1915–1921). It was during the May Fourth period that forces in society, particularly the intellectuals who had been freed from the examination system and formally dissociated from the bureaucracy, led the process of change. Society, as personified by the intellectuals, students, factory workers, and other city dwellers, could play that role not because it had a strong institutional base or a long-established organizational structure but because the state had degenerated into warlordism and lost its legitimacy: The bureaucracy was paralyzed, the economy had developed too slowly, and the traditional, organic ruling class no longer existed. The state had to be rebuilt, the economy modernized, the society restructured; the relationships among the state, society, and the economy had to be reestablished on a new foundation.

The state that emerged after twenty-eight years of protracted civil and foreign wars was based on a Leninist party in which all power was concentrated in the party center; no factions were to be allowed legitimacy. At its inception, the CCP adopted an ideology – Marxism – that embodied a distorted view of the state–society relationship: Capitalist society was viewed as one in which a single economic class totally dominated the state. In contrast, the utopia at the end of human development would be one in which civil society would administer everything, and the state would wither away. We do not know to what extent that theory of the state–society relationship influenced Chinese communist practices, but what cannot be doubted is that in the process in which the cities were surrounded and eventually captured by socio-political forces organized in the countryside, the intellectuals turned themselves into party leaders, military strategists, ideologues, politicians, and bureaucrats. At various times they mobilized, organized, and led the peasants, "patriotic landlords," petite bourgeoisie, free-floating in-tellectuals, and students into powerful social movements and mass organizations. They occupied pieces of territory, established govern-ments, built up armies, and constituted themselves into states within a state in which they further strengthened their control over the various segments of society.

By means of such interactive processes the party-state penetrated deep into society. Indeed, after 1949, the party re-created the entire society in its own image, to the extent that was possible. It established mass or-ganizations in most of the important functional spheres and territorial bodies, ostensibly to represent the people, but in practice to govern them as well. An entirely new pattern for a state–society relationship was created. After the socialist transformation of industry and commerce of 1956 and the cooperativization and collectivization movement of 1955–1958, the relationship between the state and the economy changed drast-ically. In other words, the party-state, through various instrumentalities, occupied most of the social spaces. Society had no institutions or orga-nizations that spoke for it freely and authentically. One can safely come to the conclusion that civil society as such did not exist. That new pattern could be labeled "totalitarianism" or, perhaps more accurately in the case of China, "totalism." We use this term to mean a sociopolitical system in which there are no moral or ideological limits to the extension of state functions into any sphere of social life, except such limits as its top leaders adopt and hence can change at any moment. But we also recognize that the state is subject to many practical and even political constraints in its plans, policies, and actions to expand or, alternatively, to contract state functions. Thus, the actual reach of the state is not totally without bounds. Indeed, in real life we can speak of "degrees of totalitarianism" or "totalitarianness," just as we can conceive of the state as a conceptual variable and speak of degrees of stateness, only in this case the state is a party-state. As many scholars have pointed out, the reach of the state may vary at different times and for different functional areas, territorial jurisdictions, and ethnic groups, even within a single totalitarian or totalistic party-state.

Not too long ago, and perhaps as part of the effort to reform the party-state, an extremely revealing lead article was published in the house journal of the Chinese Academy of Social Sciences that can be used to further substantiate our analysis. Its authors were extraordinarily clear that in 1942 the party had adopted "the party's monistic leadership" (*dang de yiyuanhua lingdao*) as an important principle for organizing the whole society during the period of "democratic revolution."[3] That principle was retained and reaffirmed after 1949 in view of the need for a command center in which power could be concentrated. Beginning in 1957, emphasis was placed on the frequently repeated principle that in seven spheres – industry, agriculture, commerce, education, military affairs, governmental affairs, and party affairs – the party leads everything. During the Cultural Revolution, in spite of the "total destruction" of the structure of the "leadership system," the inference was made that "all political, economic, and cultural organizations must obey the so-called 'Party's absolute leadership'," although in reality the highest authority was in the hands of Mao Zedong as "an individual" and the Cultural Revolution "Small Group."[4] Those authors advocated separation between the party and the government as the key to reform of the leadership structure. For the purpose of our discussion, that article gives us an excellent summary of the origins and the development of the totalistic party-state. It also tells us that from 1942 onward, the "party groups" in all of the people's organizations (*renmin tuanti*) were supposed to implement unconditionally the decisions of the local party committees and their higher-level organs. That principle and the fact that subsequently the various social spheres in many localities came to be controlled by a single officially sponsored and recognized organization responsible to the party were to play vital roles in preventing the party from making a slight concession to the students' demands in the period from late April to May 13, one that would have eased the tension before the students escalated the conflict by staging a hunger strike, in effect setting a deadline for meeting their demands.

A separation between the party and the government, which would relax the hold of the party over the government and give the government a larger role in managing the affairs of the state and society, undoubtedly would lessen the control of the party-state over society, because the reach of the government, due to its structural limitation, is not as far and deep as that of the party, which was built even before 1942 to mobilize the masses, recruit an army, establish a government, and make sweeping, fundamental changes in society – in short, to make a total revolution. But even if the party were separated from the government, the problem of the scope and depth of government control over the economy and civil society would remain, and that problem should now be addressed in depth by scholars and analysts both inside and outside of China.

The Tiananmen tragedy

THE RECESSION OF STATE PENETRATION,
THE SPLIT WITHIN THE PARTY,
AND THE INFLUENCE OF THE OUTSIDE WORLD:
QUESTIONS TO BE PONDERED

In retrospect, it is clear (indeed, it may have been clear during the Cultural Revolution or even the Great Leap Forward to those who had been the principal builders of the powerful party-state) that the almost unlimited expansion of state power into the economy and society was counter-productive, that it hindered economic growth, that it was detrimental to the authority of the party-state (the state becoming incapable of discharging its self-assumed functions, and the party being blamed for any failure in society), that it led to stagnation and even retrogression in the spheres of literature, art, culture, and intellectual life (the party-state's strict control and deep penetration impeding the development of initiative and creativity among individuals and social groups). The relationship between the party-state, on the one hand, and the economy and society, on the other, had to be redefined, and the boundary between the public and the private redrawn. Whatever their motives and intentions, Deng Xiaoping and his followers pushed forward, step by step, a series of ideological positions and practical reforms that reversed that long-term trend. The Third Plenum of 1978 remains the symbol of that historic turning point, whatever the eventual fallout from the Tiananmen repression may be – whether it be a total collapse accompanied by a revolution or, alternatively, a fundamental change in the system initiated, sponsored, and carefully controlled and calibrated from above.

The pragmatic orientations and practical policies adopted since then have been labeled "reforms and openness" (*gaige yu kaifang*). Paradoxically, it was the mixture of successes and failures of such policies that had created the conditions leading to the Tiananmen tragedy, which intensified the series of dilemmas confronting the regime, while enabling the regime to stay in power.

The retreat of the party-state in the area of agricultural production has produced the most striking and successful results, because the adoption of a "system of responsibility" in agricultural production has meant, in many respects, though not all, a return to a system of practices that had been in place for hundreds of years before cooperativization and collectivization. The loosening of the state's control over agricultural production has entailed a relaxation of the state's control over rural society as a whole. The latter has made the lives of the peasants easier than before, but also has revived old problems that the extension of state power into society was supposed to resolve – problems that have found expression

273

in the failure to control the birthrate, as well as some deterioration in the systems for education, health care, and even water management. These and other frequently noted phenomena, such as the reappearance of superstitious practices, traditional customs, and local cults, are some of the signs of revival of the old society, at a time when a new one has not yet been established to solve the new problems or incorporate the old customs into a new framework. State and society coexist peacefully, if not without tensions. Party cadres at the lowest levels remain natives of their villages. Some of them are in good positions to take advantage of the new policies. The peasants can now engage in many sideline occupations or work in local collective enterprises. The peasants have not had sufficient reason to take actions that would put their recent gains at risk. Nor do they have enough political power to demand greater changes toward unencumbered landownership. Concerning policies toward the rural areas, the party has been able to come to a consensus relatively easily. The ideological and cultural influences of the West have yet to penetrate the countryside to such an extent and in such a way as to produce difficult political problems.

By contrast, the party-state's retreat from involvement in society created an extremely complex situation in the urban areas, almost without precedent in twentieth-century Chinese history. Immediately before the Tiananmen tragedy, we witnessed a series of spectacular, contradictory, and puzzling phenomena that no one had expected, which now we must seek to put into proper perspective: First, not since the May Fourth period had the intellectuals qua intellectuals exercised such profound influence over the ideological orientations of the students and general public, and yet they were unable to provide the latter with guidance in political actions. Second, the leadership of the student movement shifted time and again: from those who took a more moderate position, to those who were more radical, and ultimately to a very small minority who insisted on continued occupation of Tiananmen Square. They were daring and politically sophisticated, but at the decisive moments their lack of prudence and their hubris were factors contributing to the tragedy. Third, office employees took an active part in the demonstrations, particularly after the differences in opinion within the party had become public on May 4, and that public display of differences was perceived as a split in the party. Fourth, there was little organized participation on the part of workers in factories, but *getihu* (self-employed persons and entrepreneurs in the private sector) and ordinary city dwellers played active and sometimes spectacular roles. Fifth, in early May, some journalists suddenly abandoned their traditional role of reporting only on official views and writing from the official perspective. Sixth, there were numerous small networks among the activists, and their cacophony of slogans was bewildering. Seventh, the spontaneous, nonviolent, orderly demonstrations on a large scale suggested a groundswell of disaffection and resentment toward the regime, some of which undoubtedly was a response to the failure of price reform in 1988. Eighth, numerous organizations sprang up after May 17, and an overall organization claiming to represent people of "all circles" in Beijing was belatedly established. Ninth, all of those factors added up to what Andrew Walder called an "unprecedented popular rebellion" or "a massive, non-violent rebellion."[5]

That unexpected concatenation of events raised high hopes for a giant leap toward freedom and democracy, only to have them crushed under the tread of tanks. But what do those phenomena tell us about the relationship between the state and society during that period of time? Did they mean that a regenerated society began to assert itself? Did the retreat of the party-state create a new civil society? Or was a new civil society stillborn? We shall make some observations on these questions later. But before we can do that, we must mention briefly two other factors that were inextricably intertwined with the party-state's retreat from society.

The first was the split within the party, and it has been the primary focus of most reports and articles on Chinese politics. We tend to use factional struggle as a primary explanation for everything else in Chinese politics or, to use our jargon, as the independent variable to explain all other variables. But in examining the Tiananmen Square tragedy, we must keep clearly in mind that it was the student movement, with its own independent momentum, that focused the preexisting differences within the party and turned them into an open split between the reformers and the hard-liners. The policies of the reformers had created an ideological and cultural atmosphere in which students could become socially active and politically oppose the hard-liners, and they soon grew to be a powerful social force in Chinese society, with widespread mass support. In other words, they became a new social force or, more precisely, a vast collection of new political actors. Thus, the following questions relating to the state–society relationship and political strategy occur to us: If the students and the reformers within the party had coordinated their strategies and tactics, could they have overcome the influence of "the old comrades" by alternately exerting and relaxing political pressure, while avoiding a direct military confrontation? What prevented the reformers within the party from initiating a coalition with moderate elements among the students from the very beginning, or from building up their strength while checking the influence of the more radical students? In other words, what were the mechanisms of control by the party that prevented the reformers from reaching out to the students and joining with them in an alliance, thus giving them the leadership they needed? Alternatively, what prevented the party-state from making some small concessions, such as granting recognition and formal status to the autonomously formed student organizations in a public gesture of generosity and magnanimity? Why did the old comrades, in charge of what had once been an all-powerful state, controlling all social spheres, suddenly find themselves with no other recourse than to resort to brutal repression to save their regime? Can we shed some light on these questions by looking at the structure of power, the rules of the game governing factional struggle, and the systems of communication within the party and between the party and the people? We should look at the mechanisms of communication and control in the party and the effects of those mechanisms on the relationship between the students and the party, and in a broader sense the relationship between the party-state and society.

The second factor that affected the outcome of the party-state's retreat from society was the influence of the world outside the mainland, particularly Hong Kong and Taiwan and the noncommunist West, as one of the primary meanings of "openness" in China was openness to the capitalist countries and societies.[6] What is not apparent to us is to what extent the various Chinese leaders, all of them skillful in realpolitik, understood the deep currents in Western societies and the rapidity of the changes there. Did they grossly underestimate the strong attraction of the West for Chinese people in urban areas? Did the presence of the West in China — cultural contacts, trade, the open door to the West for travel, study, and residence — alter the structure of alternatives for many Chinese? Did the old comrades' memory of old China, their recollection of the past successes of their revolution, and their own propaganda and ideological blinders lead them to see their new China in too favorable a light? What have been the political consequences of those deficiencies in understanding and knowledge? But what is of most interest to us, What were the structural characteristics of the regime that facilitated and magnified the influence of the outside world?

IDEOLOGICAL HEGEMONY, PUBLIC SPACES, AND THE OFFICIAL SYSTEM OF COMMUNICATION

The answers to the questions raised in the preceding section are obvious to all in retrospect. To make our answers more explicit, to give them more substance, and particularly to show how the three dimensions (i.e., the changes in the state–society relationship, the split within the party, and the influence of the outside world) interacted to produce the tragedy, we have to repeat some generally known facts, call attention to other events not officially stressed, and put all of these into our framework of the state–society relationship.

There is no doubt that in the 1970s and even the early 1980s, the party leaders realized that they were confronted with a crisis and that there was a possibility of "the extinction of the party and the state" (*wangdang wangguo*). But apparently they thought that they could preserve the communist system by making reforms within the system, by maintaining intact the basic structural and ideological elements (i.e., Deng's four cardinal principles, though allowing some leeway in interpreting those principles and some modifications of the structures so as to strengthen them), and by adopting the policies of reform and openness. But all of those changes had to be made under the auspices of the party's leadership and by people and forces that the party could ultimately control. In undertaking to reform that system, Deng was to pursue a middle course, balancing two sets of potentially contradictory principles. He was to play a decisive role, for better or for worse. But the three factors – the party's retreat from society, the split within the party, and the impact of the outside world – interacted so as to produce tremendous social forces for reform and openness that Deng could not control. In the end, Deng himself and the system he represented were directly challenged by forces that he had unintentionally unleashed.

First, over the years 1978–1988 the party had increasingly lost its hegemony over society in the fields of ideology, culture, literature, and art. Deng was "a strong disciplinarian" who clearly placed more emphasis on maintaining ideological orthodoxy in the political sphere than did many of his liberal followers. He wanted the party to uphold Marxism-Leninism and "Mao Zedong thought." But up until 1986, Deng had acquiesced in General Secretary Hu Yaobang's liberal policy of allowing some intellectuals to "develop" Marxism, to reinterpret it, and even to call for new breakthroughs in individual parts of Marxist theory. The "Institute of Marxism-Leninism and Mao Zedong Thought" was the spearhead and symbol of that development. The ideas of Euro-communism, the ideas of neo-Marxism, and the ideas behind the policies and practices adopted in Eastern Europe and Yugoslavia were introduced to China. Bold agendas for understanding Marxism anew were publicized. In searching for some large framework to replace Marxism, which they rejected silently or simply put aside, young scholars snatched many theories from the West. The so-called three theories – systems theory, cybernetics, and the theory of communication – achieved sudden popularity in the late 1970s and early 1980s. The theory of postindustrial development, "the third wave," and the theory of scientific decision making all had their exponents. The "new Confucianism" was brought back to China from the United States by China-born scholars who drew huge audiences.

In philosophy, perhaps because of the endemic Chinese need to grasp the whole before understanding the particular, and perhaps because of the habit of mind cultivated by study of Marx and Hegel, continental European traditions dominated. Heidegger was considered a great master, but John Rawls's *Theory of Justice* was also translated. In the social sciences, young scholars had begun to find Weber more interesting than Marx. Western political common sense and political science had wide impact; nearly all students talked about checks and balances, freedom and rights, and the rule of law. Progressive professors who were critical of the party drew huge audiences, whereas orthodox "Leftist" teachers found few students in their classes. The "public courses" required for many students were caricatured; the course on Marxist philosophy was labeled a course of empty talk; the course on Marxist political economy, a course of boasting; the course on party history, a course on telling lies. Clearly, the party's ideology was rejected by the students and held in contempt.

Innumerable new short stories, novellas, novels, and memoirs were being published, breaking with revolutionary realism and destroying old taboos with a vengeance. New techniques and new idioms were given more attention than substance. Those new writings were supported by a group of new literary critics who soundly routed their old-fashioned opponents in the debate over the merits of the substance and style of the new literature and the art of literary criticism itself. Kant and Nietzsche were echoed in those writings. There is no doubt at all that the vitality, seriousness, high standards, novelty, variety, and relevance to life of Western ideology and culture contrasted sharply with the poverty, lifelessness, monotony, and emptiness of the old literature under party guidance. All of those developments were supported by the reformers. Such support was symbolized by the appointment of Wang Meng (who had introduced techniques of the stream of consciousness to Chinese literature) to the post of minister of culture. It was also the deliberate policy of Zhao Ziyang that the party should interfere as little as possible with the writing of literary works. With such policy initiatives, the party created new ideological and cultural spaces that were quickly filled by writers and writings inspired by Western ideas.

The party had no adequate response to the challenge posed by the influx of Western ideas. After all, philosophy, the social sciences, and the humanities had developed with extraordinary speed in the capitalist and social-democratic West since the days of Marx and Lenin. In contrast, the party could not find in its inherited ideology any fundamental axioms or postulates on which it could rebuild, from the ground up, a new theoretical edifice. It was too heavily influenced by orthodox Marxism-Leninism to rediscover, to fasten on, and to develop the humanist ideals in the works of the early Marx. Its collective mind was not innovative enough to see in Marx's writings the antecedents to new ideas formulated by Western social scientists, humanists, and philosophers. Mao Zedong thought had emerged out of practical actions and policy decisions undertaken in the past; it consisted essentially of the rationale behind those undertakings and of their justifications. It gained its legitimacy and appeal because it proved effective as a means to gain power during the revolutionary struggle. After 1957, it lost its legitimacy because of the failures of the policies supposedly derived from it, and certainly rationalized by it. It was discredited by Mao himself through his actions during the Cultural Revolution. To repeat, the party has lost its ideological hegemony over society in many aspects of social life.

The party's retreat from society, its relaxation of control, and its policies of "reform and openness" made available a number of public spaces that previously had been occupied by the party-state or unoccupied by anyone. Society can maintain a life of its own even when it is submerged under state control. Small networks of such people had always existed, even during the Cultural Revolution. With the new reforms, they multiplied and extended their scope, and the content of mutual exchange became richer, increasingly including large measures of political information, opinion, and gossip. By 1986 there were many "salons" in Beijing, though it is unknown whether the Chinese transliteration for that famous institution that preceded the French Revolution was being deliberately or unknowingly used. Many new journals were being published, and their editorial boards provided a nucleus for shaping and disseminating intellectual opinions, cultural views, and artistic orientations. *Dushu* (*Reading*) was one of the most influential of those journals in the fields of philosophy, the social sciences, and the humanities. It sponsored meetings to discuss a variety of issues, and they were eagerly attended by the best young minds. The Western practice of publishing series of books by writers of similar intellectual orientations was adopted. *The Series of Studies on Advancing Toward the Future (Zou xiang weilai congshu)* was one of the best known; *The Series on Translations of Well Known Works in the West* was also planned. The *Great Encyclopedia*, reminiscent of the eighteenth-century French work and the writings of the *philosophes*, was another vital focus for intellectual activities. Its editors and its writers met regularly to discuss a wide range of subjects. *Guangming ribao*, the official party newspaper, with intellectuals as its intended readers, had an ideological orientation slightly different from that of the *People's Daily*. It published informative, candid articles by the courageous Dai Qing, who often broke new ground in discussing political and theoretical issues. New newspapers, such as the *World Economic Herald (Shijie jingji daobao)* in Shanghai and *Science and Technology Daily (Keji ribao)* in Beijing, were published and given tacit support by reformist leaders at the top level. Those were some of the networks and organizations on the borderline between state and society from which the buds of a hundred flowers and the sprouts of a hundred schools began to emerge for a period of a few years.

As new ideological spaces were opened up, there was an accompaniment of expanding choices, widespread hopes, enlargement of the political arena, and experimentation with new ideas and new forms of political participation. In order to help them find the right policies to push forward their reforms, the party and the government established many new research organizations. The Chinese Academy of Social Sciences, developed out of the former Department of Philosophy and Social Sciences of the Academy of Sciences, housed three of the most important reformist research institutions: the Institute for Literature, the Institute of Marxism-Leninism and Mao Zedong Thought, and the Institute for Political Science. Those official organs and many others like them at once reflected and shaped opinion in society. They existed at the outer limit of the boundary of the state, touching on society in many ways.

The extremely complex relationship between state and society, the channels through which society can influence the state, the creation of new official organs to reflect the needs and demands of society, and finally the attempts of those organizations to become autonomous, independent voices for society can best be illustrated by mentioning briefly the informative case of the origins and development of the Institute for the Study of the Development of Agricultural Economy *(Guowuyuan nong-cun jingji fazhan yanjiusuo)* and the Institute for the Study of Reforms in Economic Structure *(Zhongguo jingji tizhi gaige yanjiusuo)*: During the Cultural Revolution, a group of young men found themselves, for one reason or another, working in the countryside and thus learning something about the problems of the rural area and the peasantry. Both by accident and through personal connections, they met each other and organized themselves into a group. Later, they were given official recognition when the party realized the necessity of making fundamental changes in the system of agricultural production. Under the sponsorship of certain leaders, and with a push from below by peasants in Anhui province, that group became one of the most important forces in shaping the "responsibility system" and modifying the system of *tonggou tong-xiao* (the centralized purchase and sale of the most important agricultural products, such as grain). Some of the leading members of that group later split off to form the Institute for the Study of Reforms in Economic Structure, which had a larger purview. Two other organizations played important, but at the time relatively obscure, roles, the Beijing Institute of Research on Social and Economic Sciences and the *Economic Studies Weekly*. The two persons responsible for these were to receive in 1991 sentences of thirteen years of imprisonment, the heaviest punishment inflicted thus far on intellectuals.

On May 19, 1989, two days after the decision to declare martial law had been made, a joint declaration issued by *Tigaisuo, Fazhan Yanjiusuo,* the CITIC's Research Center for the Study of International Problems (*Zhongxin gongsi guoji wenti yanjiusuo*), and the Association of Young Chinese Economists (*Zhongguo qingnian jingji xuehui*), praised the "patriotic democratic movement" of the students and the masses and denounced the party and the government for their errors and delays that had created the crisis. That step undoubtedly was related to the final split in the party, which had occurred on May 17 when Zhao Ziyang refused to implement martial law. But it can be interpreted as a sign that the two official research institutes, together with the research center for China's largest corporation for international investment and the economists' voluntary association, had shaken off their official links and sought to become the voice for an emergent civil society. In other words, the student movement magnified the split within the party, which in turn led some actors on the border areas between the state and society to break with the party and assert their separate identities as spokesmen for society. For a few days, until June 4, that appeared to be one of the signs that a new civil society was being born.

At this point we should also note the role played by one of the most prominent organizations in civil society and the economic sphere: the Beijing Stone Group Corporation (*Shitong jituan gongsi*). That conglomerate had begun as a small company organized by a few individuals to import and to develop new technology. During the hectic days of April and May, it provided much of the student demonstrators' electronic equipment, and a not insignificant sum of money. Its president and its officers played salient political roles. We mention such individuals and groups as examples of new actors in the state and society as a preliminary step to an attempt to construct a more complete account and topology at another time. One of the most difficult problems in research, analysis, and interpretation is to understand the actions and attitudes of the amorphous collection of the multifarious individuals known as *getihu* and the ordinary residents of the city.

In spite of the decline in the party's hegemony over urban society, the opening up of new public spaces, and the emergence of new political actors, the political actions that have been called "a public rebellion" might not have taken place if the people's perceptions of events in the preceding years, and particularly during the decisive period from mid-May to June 4, had not been so totally different from those of the political leadership, and the party leadership might not have reacted as it did if it had realized the extent to which the public's perception of events was so different from its own. The perceptions on both sides might have been different if there had been a better system of communication within the party and between the party and the public. But it probably was impossible for the system of communication to have been different, because the system was totally determined by the structure of power and the rules and norms governing intraparty politics, as we shall see.

Despite their earlier reputation as great propagandists, the Chinese communists had for a long period of time been using a rigid official system of communicating information about policies, the background to policies, the decision-making processes, and the real reasons for adopting particular policies in which one's position in the hierarchy determined the amount of information one was given. When information was communicated downward through official channels, it became increasingly more general and less specific, more vague and less concrete, more about ideological principles and less about practical considerations. There were different categories of documents classified according to their political importance and sensitivity. In the most important cases, it would be specified that a document would be sent down to a certain hierarchical level, or that a certain document should be read only by leaders at a certain level, with its message then being transmitted orally to those at lower levels.

The intraparty, intragovernment system of communicating information about policy would have been less pernicious had it not been for the fact that it was the central structure in the general system of communication and that it shaped the latter. The amount of information about policies and about the policy-making processes leading to particular policies that was communicated to the public through official newspapers and periodicals was limited by rules imposed by the intraparty, intragovernment system. Any news or analysis published in the official media had to be approved by editors who knew more about high-level decisions than did the writers, and those editors would try to anticipate the reactions of their leaders as they performed their daily tasks of censorship and self-censorship. The official news media did little to enlighten the public about the substance of a policy or its rationale, apparently for fear that they would make statements contrary to official policy or to the thinking of some party leaders who may have agreed to some specific policy but entertained widely different views about the larger issues surrounding it, such as the fundamental course being pursued in China. As a result, the Chinese system of communication gave one the impression that it was built on the idea that the less said, the better, concerning the regime's policies, the considerations underlying them, the policy debates, and the policy-making process in any particular case – virtually a *mechanism* for controlling information based on the idea that "less is more." Although that system underwent some changes during the eleven years of reform, although official control was relaxed a bit, although a few newspapers, such as *Science and Technology Daily*, the *World Economic Journal*, and *Guangming ribao*, dared to break the rules, the system as a whole remained basically the same in 1989. That general system of communication was intended to be the day-to-day mechanism for control of the less powerful by the more powerful at every level of the hierarchy. But it had perverse effects and was counterproductive. The Chinese official media of communication were barren of news. Party journals were scarcely read. What little news was provided was ignored or misinterpreted. The situation was described at the time as a massive "failure of public relations."

In that situation, the general public, particularly the intellectuals, the students, and other "concerned persons," tried to fill in the gaps in information by seeking news and analysis elsewhere. The most reliable sources were friends and former colleagues who had moved on to serve at higher levels. The more irresponsible sources were the children of higher-level leaders. But the most widely used sources were Chinese journals published in Hong Kong, which somehow found their way into China and were read by many opinion-makers, intellectuals, and students. One of the most influential was *Cheng ming*, which carried simple, short, gossipy reports, supposedly by correspondents traveling to Beijing. Once printed, the "alley news," or information about intraparty struggles, political instability in China, maneuvers over succession, infighting over control of the army, and so forth, supposedly leaked by high-level leaders or members of their families, was "imported" back into China. Credibility assessments for such journals were quite high; they were taken seriously by Chinese intellectuals, some of whom believed that news carried by the two or three top journals published in Hong Kong was 80–90 percent reliable. The *Nineties* was the best Chinese monthly on mainland Chinese affairs published outside of China after the decline of *Ming Pao Monthly* and before the inauguration of *The Twenty-First Century*. It sought to play the role of the relentless but responsible critic of the regime and the system itself. Its posture coincided with the views of many Chinese intellectuals and students. Such journals provided much of the missing information that the Chinese public wanted. Worst of all, most of the sensitive documents sent down to lower levels, as well as other important information leaked from high levels, quickly found their way abroad, to be reported in the media outside of China, which presented such revelations in contexts quite different from those the party had intended, thus shaping a popular image of the regime diametrically opposed to the image the party wanted the public to have. All of those kinds of information, misinformation, and disinformation were transmitted downward through a variety of small networks, shaping the common perceptions of the intellectuals, students, and citizens and providing the basis for their common actions.

For day-to-day events, the Voice of America and BBC broadcasts in Chinese, as well as major news media in Hong Kong, were the principal sources of information. Both Western journalists and Beijing propagandists agreed that the Western communications media played a principal role in the student demonstrations. In some instances, they provided the information on which the various groups of students planned their actions. In a few instances they even served as a stimulant to the behavior of students; occasionally the students may have looked to them for cues.

Worst of all, distortion of information also occurs in the process of upward transmission. The senior leaders at the top rely on their lieutenants' reports for an understanding of rapidly evolving situations and the perceptions and sentiments of the people at lower levels. The lieutenants have their own axes to grind, while the senior leaders make decisions on the basis of those pieces of information that fit their personal interests, their ideological biases, and their own past experiences. In short, the nonstate actors and the actors in the border zones between the state and civil society perceived the political situation in an entirely different light than did the state actors at the top. Hence, they misjudged each other. The many misjudgments and miscalculations contributed significantly to the ultimate tragedy.

For the sake of simplicity, and with some exaggeration, the foregoing verbal description is represented in Figure 1. It is hoped that this simple figure will help readers visualize the widening political cleavage between the party leaders, on the one hand, and the intellectuals, students, and citizens, on the other. As the system for transmitting information about policies and the reverse process of upward distortion concerning popular sentiments shape the general communications system and have indirect effects on ideological and cultural matters, they also played a role in the party's loss of ideological and cultural hegemony, allowing Western ideas to enter the ideological and cultural vacuum. That paved the way to a situation in which naked political and military power directly confronted a vast array of enthusiastically espoused but disembodied ideas.

PROCESSES, THE CONCENTRIC CIRCLES OF POWER, AND THE RULES AND NORMS OF POLITICAL CONDUCT OF PARTY MEMBERS

The loss of the ideological and cultural hegemony of the party-state over society, the opening up of political spaces, the development of public,

The pyramid of power
The core

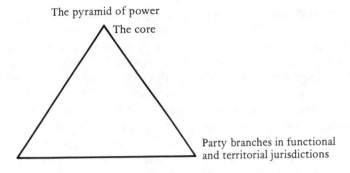

Party branches in functional
and territorial jurisdictions

The reverse pyramid of information about policy

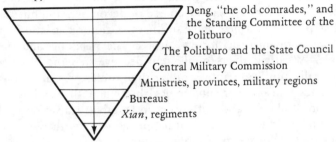

Deng, "the old comrades," and
the Standing Committee of the
Politburo

The Politburo and the State Council

Central Military Commission

Ministries, provinces, military regions

Bureaus

Xian, regiments

The information bulge of the intellectuals and students

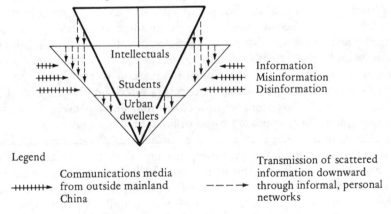

Intellectuals

Students

Urban
dwellers

Information
Misinformation
Disinformation

Legend

++++++++► Communications media
from outside mainland
China

- - - ► Transmission of scattered
information downward
through informal, personal
networks

Figure 1. A schematic representation of the system of communications about
policies in China.

semi-official, voluntary, or private organizations in the border area between the state and society, the progressive multiplication of nonstate
actors in public life, the influence of reformist ideas developed by the
intellectual-activists in society or transmitted through cultural contact,
and the increasing vulnerability of the official system of communication
to penetration by messages, information, misinformation, and disinformation sent by media outside continental China – all of those changes
presaged some sort of fundamental political change, either abruptly
through revolution or incrementally through evolution. Those of us who
wished China well, who found the intellectual and political atmosphere
increasingly hospitable to new ideas, and who had encountered some
leaders open to suggestions, wanted to see the party-state not only continue to move forward on the course of decompression but also take the
first step to enter a new stage of liberalization by strictly implementing
its constitutional provisions to protect the freedoms and rights of the
people.[7] We urged them to take that decisive step and begin the process
of liberalization from above, rather than under pressure, so as to regain
legitimacy and popular support for the regime. It was hoped that after
a period of liberalization of uncertain length, a transition to democracy
would take place. Instead, what happened was another sequence of processes that followed the decompression of the preceding eleven years:
mobilization, radicalization, polarization, confrontation, military crackdown, and recompression.

Although the individual processes that could have occurred in those
two alternative schematic sequences are familiar to us, the Tiananmen
tragedy revealed some distinctive features of interest to both Chinese
analysts and social scientists. In less than seven weeks, from April 15 to
June 4, events in China went from mobilization to repression and recompression, with each of those processes intertwined with what had
gone before and what came next. At each momentary pause, and at each
turning point, there appeared to be opportunities to make choices. Yet
the momentum of the rush toward a miraculously transformed China
confronted a pyramid of power that, though full of cracks, could not be
pushed down like a wall. From the hopeful beginning, when both the
students and the CCP leaders showed restraint, to the tragic outcome,
when the stubborn will of the old comrades brutally crushed the heroic
innocence and fatalistic determination of the young people, history
seemed to both sides to move with an inevitability defying human will.
To an analyst looking back, every tragic error has an explanation, and
every missed opportunity offers a lesson that can be learned if we are
prepared to look at the political game using assumptions fundamentally
different from those of the old comrades and the extremist students.

Because all those processes were interactions between the party and society, because the students and intellectuals were conditioned both negatively and positively in their actions by the political system, and because both the party reformers and the old comrades had to act within the framework of the rules and norms of the party and the political system, we must examine what is generally known about the structure and the operative rules and norms of the party and see how those constraints affected the attitudes, choices, and behaviors of the actors in those crucial seven weeks.[8]

In the preceding section we used the image of a pyramid of power to describe the structure of the CCP in order to bring out another image to represent the official system of communication (i.e., the reverse pyramid of information about policy), in the hope that the contrast between the two images will enable us to visualize clearly one of the fundamental structural defects of the political system that led to the regime's loss of credibility. These two images, plus a third – the information bulge of the intellectuals and students, as well as the distortion in the reverse process of the upward flow of information – will give us part of the explanation as to why the perceptions of the party elders and those of the intellectuals and students were totally different, or at least why the sets of information on which the two sides acted were sufficiently different to produce a political confrontation.

Now, if we should look downward from the sky directly above the top of the pyramid of power, we would see what I call a concentric-circle structure of power: the party's congress, the Central Committee, the Politburo, and the standing committee of the latter.[9] In the eleven years of reform after 1978, the crucial question was whether or not that concentric-circle structure had a one-man center. The center of the concentric circle was loosening up. Hu Yaobang and later Zhao Ziyang were increasingly given more authority to make decisions over a wide range of affairs, but depending on what was considered the most important question at a particular moment, it was still true that Deng had "the ultimate decision-making authority over the most important questions but does not concern himself with other problems."[10]

The events immediately before and after the Tiananmen tragedy once more confirmed that well-known fact. But they added one metaphor that will bring to completion our image of the concentric circles of power. Furthermore, they illustrate vividly how the official system of communication tried to conceal a most vital piece of information from the public, and how a public admission of a piece of generally known information is a political act, sometimes with extremely serious consequences, intended or unintended. The last point will be clarified in a later section when we discuss the China News Agency's report on General Secretary Zhao's remark to General Secretary Gorbachev when they met on May 16.

Suffice it here to say that General Secretary Zhao's substantially correct remark about Deng's role as the helmsman was reaffirmed in dramatic fashion in a talk by Deng with eight of his most powerful colleagues on June 16, 1989, just a week before the Fourth Plenum of the Thirteenth Central Committee was to meet on June 23–24 to dismiss Zhao from all his posts and elect Jiang Zemin general secretary. According to what purports to be an official summary of the talk, Deng said to the group that "any collective leadership must have a core. A leadership without a core is unreliable. The core of the collective leadership of the first generation was Chairman Mao. In the second generation, I am in reality the core. Because there is this core, even the removal of two leaders [i.e., Hu and Zhao] has not affected the leadership of the party. The party's leadership has been stable from the beginning to the end."[11] At a time when a new standing committee and a new general secretary remained to be formally elected, Deng asked the prospective members of the new standing committee to foster and protect the new "collective" and its "core" (i.e., the prospective general secretary, Jiang Zemin). If those statements should be further confirmed, one will have to examine the meaning of the formal rule of "collective leadership" even more carefully than before.

Thus, from the point of view of our analysis of the power structure of the party, the concentric circles of power have always had a center of one person since Mao established his authority, with the possible exception of a brief period in 1976 and 1977 when Hua Guofeng attempted to claim Mao's mantle, but failed. In the case of Mao, the core was institutionalized in the party's constitution of 1945, ten years after the Zunyi conference. In the case of Deng, the actual locus of power was not congruent with the formal system, in which the party was successively headed by Hua Guofeng, Hu Yaobang, and Zhao Ziyang. That was one of the major issues raised by the dissident intellectuals.

Under the real structure of power, once a decision was made by the core leader, it could not be changed unless he could be persuaded to do so, and there were not many ways to make him change his mind. Between 1956 and June 1957, Mao in effect reversed his own decision to let "a hundred flowers bloom and a hundred schools contend." He did so because some intellectuals had attacked the CCP itself rather than its policies, and some wanted it to abandon its monopoly of power. In 1960–1962, he acquiesced to attempts by his leading colleagues to discard the policy of the Great Leap Forward and modified the most unrealistic aspects of the commune system, while retaining its nominal structure. In

1966 he unleashed the Red Guards, but in 1968 he curbed them because they fought each other rather than pursuing his goals. In 1973, a year and a half after the defection of Lin Biao, he was persuaded by Zhou Enlai to rehabilitate Deng, and then he dismissed Deng once again after the first Tiananmen Square demonstration in April 1976. Deng also vacillated several times over policies (e.g., in the case of Bai Hua in 1981, the issue of spiritual pollution in 1983, and the question of price reform over a period of several years). But in many of those cases, Hu and Zhao, singly or in combination, and with the support of many other party leaders, worked behind the scenes and strictly within the limits of party rules and norms to persuade Deng to follow their advice, and Deng's involvement was not publicized. His authority was not openly challenged. There were no demonstrations in the streets and no hint about his loss of popularity. The situation leading to the Tiananmen Square tragedy was just the opposite of the previous occasions when Deng or Mao had changed course, with the possible exception of the 1957 episode, which seems minor when compared with the Tiananmen tragedy. As we shall see, the structure of power sharply limited the alternatives available to Zhao.

That structure of power with a core leader developed side by side with a series of intraparty struggles, each of which ended in a final confrontation in which one side won and retained real power to make decisions and the other side sooner or later lost it. Many of those struggles began with attempts at cooperation, in the course of which differences in viewpoints developed, magnified by the crisis situations confronting the protagonists; usually, after many deescalations and escalations, they would end in a winner-take-all contest, with few fixed institutional or practical constraints.

Shortly before Lin Biao's defection and death in September 1971, Mao told high military and political officials, in preparation for a final confrontation with Lin Biao, that there had been "ten major line struggles" (confrontations over the party line) in the past fifty years. The antagonists involved had been (1) Chen Duxiu, (2) Qu Qiubai, (3) Li Lisan, (4) Luo Zhanglong, (5) Wang Ming, (6) Zhang Guotao, (7) the "Gao Gang–Rao Shushi antiparty group," (8) Peng Dehuai, (9) Liu Shaoqi, and (10) Lin Biao.[12] Many observers have noted that most of those conflicts actually had not been party-line struggles.[13] In the first four struggles, the Comintern was the dominant force on one side, and the corresponding four Chinese protagonists were the scapegoats and victims. The fifth struggle was the last one in which the Comintern played a dominant role. It was an amazing testimony to the authority and influence of the party center and the Comintern that the Chinese leaders installed by the latter had succeeded in gradually reducing Mao's power and authority from 1931 to 1934 in the base area that Mao had established and in taking over command of the military units he had organized or controlled. On the eve of the Long March, in October 1934, he was not even consulted when the plan to evacuate the regional base at Jiangxi was adopted.

The process by which Mao won total power from Wang Ming and Bo Gu, the leaders of what was called the "returned students group" or "the 28 1/2 Bolsheviks," was prolonged and complicated. But that story has been frequently told. Suffice it to say that he began by regaining control over military affairs, then acquired political control, and finally achieved ideological hegemony. By June 1945, his total victory was formalized and institutionalized in a party constitution and the new party structure, in which he was the chairman of the Central Committee and concurrently the chairman of the Politburo and Secretariat. In the process, he won over some of his former antagonists, principally Wang Jiaxiang and Zhang Wentian, to be his allies and then turned them into his lieutenants. When they crossed him again, he deprived them of all real powers and influence, leaving them as decorations for his rule. After his victory in the sixth struggle with Zhang Guotao, Mao made Zhang a figurehead in his regional government. Within two years Zhang had defected to the GMD.

The last four struggles occurred after the CCP had driven the GMD from the mainland. The outcomes were the same. Gao Gang committed suicide; Liu Shaoqi died in confinement for lack of medical care; Lin fled for his life when he saw that Mao was tightening the noose around him. There was a twist in the case of Peng Dehuai. Mao dismissed him in September 1959 from his posts in the area of national defense, but in 1965 he reappointed Peng to a much less important post to undertake military-industrial construction in southwest China when Mao felt threatened by the American forces in Vietnam. When Mao launched the Cultural Revolution and unleashed the Red Guards in 1966, Peng was arrested by the Red Guards and brought back to Beijing as an object of "mass struggle" and a "special-case investigation."

In his talk on the ten major party-line struggles, Mao apparently wanted to impress upon the party members that dissent could have only one outcome, no matter who the players were and what actions they took. He summarized the lessons of those struggles with three basic principles: "Practice Marxism, do not practice revisionism. Unite and don't split [the party]. Be open and aboveboard and don't engage in intrigue and conspiracy."[14] Those principles became known as the "three do's" and "three don'ts." They were meant to be both operative rules sanctioned by party discipline and internalized norms acquired through "living an organizational life," the practice of "criticism and self-criticism," "thought remolding," and "rectification campaigns."

Those seemingly obvious rules and norms call for some comments. When the word "revisionism" is replaced by terms like "anarchism," "right-wing opportunism," "adventurism," "Trotskyism," "Li Lisan-ism," "dogmatism and subjectism," "two whateverism," and "bourgeois liberalization," the first set of do's and don'ts holds for the whole period of party history.[15] "Unite and don't split [the party]" means obey the party center, accept party discipline, and put the preservation of the unity of the party above the desire to express one's dissenting views about party policies and above one's political and personal interests. "Be open and aboveboard and don't engage in intrigue and conspiracy" means that everything must be done and views must be expressed through the proper party channels and in accordance with proper procedures.[16] One should not conspire with people outside the party against the party center. One should not form "small organizations" within the party that we refer to as "factions."

The three do's and don'ts are powerful instruments in the hands of the top leader to prevent any party members from challenging his views and policies, no matter how obviously wrong the leader may be and however correct the challengers. If a party member, particularly a leader near the top who is considered to be a potential rival, expresses views that the top leader believes, rightly or wrongly, to be a public challenge to his authority either inside or outside the party, the top leader can invoke these rules and norms to turn back the challenge, even if his policies are clearly headed for disaster. For the other party members, these rules and norms are enforced by party discipline, backed ultimately by the top leader, who can resort to the use or threat of military power for enforcement. When he thought that he had been publicly challenged by Peng Dehuai, who as defense minister enjoyed a high reputation in the People's Liberation Army, Mao declared ominously that if the regime should collapse and be replaced by another, "I would go immediately to the villages to lead the peasants to overthrow the [new] government. If you, the People's Liberation Army, would not follow me, I would find the Red Army [obviously referring to a hypothetical peasant guerrilla force that he would raise]. [But] I believe that the People's Liberation Army will follow me."[17]

The three do's and three don'ts also help the top leader once he makes his position clear; at least they did in the case of Mao. Mao could interpret Marxism "authoritatively." He could and did bypass regular party channels and procedures, as in the case of organizing in late 1965 the writing of the famous article on Hai Rui that was the prelude to the Cultural

Revolution. In capturing total power over the party from 1934 to 1945, his actions were legitimized by his successes in saving the party from destruction and in greatly expanding its military power and political influence. After 1945, he dominated the party center, and his actions could not be challenged by the accusation that he was causing a "split," even when he almost destroyed the party in the Cultural Revolution. Thus, after he had become the core, the do's and don'ts were rules for others to obey and norms for others to internalize, but not for him. For him, there was no third-party enforcer; injured parties could do nothing against him, at least not for a long time to come. Daring to challenge heaven and sinicize Marxism, he feared nothing, with the possible exception of the judgment of history.

But many of the top party leaders did obey the rules and internalize the norms. As early as 1929, Chen Duxiu and others, who had just been purged, observed that "the biggest weapon with which the bureaucrats of the party's ruling organizations control the party members is 'iron discipline'; party members bind themselves because of their superstitious belief in this weapon."[18] We must assume that this "superstitious belief" continues to exist among party leaders. In the period from 1949 to the Cultural Revolution, there was, in addition, a fear of Mao's political skills and his control over the military forces. Thus, at the Lushan meeting in 1959, when Mao made his position clear, many important party leaders tried to persuade Peng to acquiesce to Mao's false accusations and voice self-criticism in order to preserve party unity and minimize the split. Peng ultimately admitted his "mistakes," except the charge that he had organized a "military club" to carry out his intrigues. Under "persuasion" by other leading officials, including Liu Shaoqi and Zhou Enlai, the chief of staff, Huang Kecheng, was forced to make the false confession that he had become a member of that club. Zhou Xiaozhou, the first secretary of Hunan province, admitted that he was a member of Peng's "antiparty group." Actually, there was no "military club," no "antiparty group," and no faction in the ordinary sense of the term of a formal organization with identifiable membership. Instead, there was a groundswell of opposition to the Great Leap and the commune and a widespread demand for an even more rapid reversal of direction than Mao was willing to allow. Peng took the lead in urging Mao to change his policies more drastically and in a more clearcut fashion than Mao had been willing to do. In a letter to Mao, he offered criticisms and characterizations of Mao's views that angered Mao. The victims at the Lushan meeting had close personal ties and had exchanged views informally. After having heard Mao's attack on Peng, on the fateful night of July 23 Huang, Zhou, Li Rui, and Peng, as well as a fifth person, visited together. Li Rui was already concerned that such a get-together to exchange views could be viewed as constituting "a small organization"[19] formed outside the proper party organization and channels.

During the final confrontation, in July and August 1959, all the disagreements, disputes, and personal clashes in the past were recalled, in a process generally known in China as a final settlement of accounts. The "criticism and self-criticism" looked at times like an intraparty trial, without any fixed procedures, at which the defeated leaders were almost total defenseless.[20] That process of criticism and self-criticism has two indirect, unintended, and perverse effects: On the one hand, it is disruptive of human trust, obstructive of genuine public communication, and destructive of human dignity; thus, it discourages frank discussion of controversial issues and encourages hypocrisy and lies. On the other hand, it creates an atmosphere conducive to the spread of rumors, slanders, half-truths, and gossip. Chinese, as individuals, can be brilliant; Chinese small networks are closely knit and strong; but Chinese work-unit communities have lost some of their vitality, and China as a political community is seriously ill.

That pattern of disagreement, conflict, struggle, confrontation, and outcome – as well as the rules and norms of a political game played under a structure of power with a one-man core – must be borne closely in mind in order for us to understand the Tiananmen tragedy, particularly the alternatives available to Zhao, his choices, and the final outcome. Even the use of brute force against the protesters must be seen in the light of the partly hidden but ubiquitous presence of the military factor in all important intraparty struggles. To be more specific it can be said that the fear of being accused of forming a faction or causing a split in the party is a most powerful mechanism of party control over important matters of policy and organization. Everything possible will be done to paper over differences within the party. The existence of factions is always publicly denied until the final confrontation yields an outcome, and in some cases not even at that time. There is continual admonition "to keep in step with the party center." For a leader to make a public statement that conflicts with policies adopted at the top is ipso facto a mistake. It is an established rule and norm that the party cannot have two voices or two headquarters. Under certain circumstances, even party officials at the highest level have to obtain the approval of the appropriate party organization before making official contacts with nonparty groups or individuals on important matters. This is a mechanism for control over important policy matters, and the system of communication is a control mechanism for day-to-day affairs. All these rules and mechanisms operating within the centralized structure of power put heavy constraints on the actions of an individual party leader and severely limit his set of feasible alternatives, particularly in any attempt to reach out to social forces and to enlist their support for him as an individual. All these rules and norms made it nearly impossible for the reformers to establish an early alliance with the students – the only strategy that could have prevented the Tiananmen tragedy, as we shall see.

Zhao has been said by many of his former subordinates to be a weak man. But that perception of weakness may have resulted from his understanding of his position in the structure of power and his appreciation of the rules and norms of conflict and the persistent pattern of political struggle in China. As we shall see, Zhao faced a basic dilemma. If he tried to establish open contact with the students so as to coordinate their actions with his own policies, he would violate party rules and norms. If he adhered strictly to party rules and norms, he could not build up a strong social force behind him to deal with the old comrades who controlled the armed forces.

Belatedly, he attempted to strengthen his support among the students by issuing a generally conciliatory statement, without clearing it with his colleagues, and later there was officially approved dialogue with the students undertaken by people with the proper credentials. But for him to have been able to establish an alliance with the students, while avoiding direct confrontation with Deng and the military, he would have had to have been able to persuade the students to limit their actions. But there were groups of extremist students who were determined to play the game to the bitter end. If they could not win their points, they would rather lose everything in an act of supreme sacrifice in order to "expose the true features of the regime," in the hope of contributing to its downfall as soon as possible – so the ex post facto rationalization goes. Both the extremist students and the old comrades acted according to the tradition of twentieth-century Chinese politics and philosophy: Politics is ultimately a life-and-death struggle of revolution against "autocracy," "dictatorship," "feudalism," or their remnant reactionary forces, or else it is revolution against counter-revolution. In the confrontation that sooner or later brings about an outcome in which one side wins and retains all power, and the other side loses it, no measure, however brutal and immoral, or however romantically unrealistic, is excluded, not even by the inevitability of long-term adverse consequences for the nation. Politics is either a matter of acting on good intentions or keeping power to preserve revolutionary gains. Like the perfectionist who improves himself to death, revolutionaries in China, for a period of twenty years, have revolutionized their society to economic stagnation and cultural retrogression, and reform attempts have always ended in still another attempt at revolution. Will the Tiananmen tragedy finally demonstrate to the Chinese the necessity to change their philosophy of revolution, the major assumption of their politics?

THE REJECTED OPTION AND THE INACCESSIBLE ALTERNATIVE

On April 17, two days after General Secretary Hu Yaobang had died, the students in Beijing took to the streets, and the demonstration in Tiananmen Square attracted worldwide attention. The students' actions were entirely spontaneous and unorganized, though they followed on the heels of a number of predisposing factors: the decline in the party's cultural and ideological hegemony, the loosening of political control, the opening up of public spaces, the emergence of numerous small networks of liberal thought, the general acceptance among intellectuals of the slogans of democracy and freedom, and a loss of confidence in the party. The students were the advance elements of an emerging civil society struggling to surface. Many students, workers, and small networks of a few liberals had planned to take action of some kind on the seventieth anniversary of the May Fourth movement of 1919. Hu's death provided a reason to move the date forward. The students went into the streets in large numbers, the individuals and small groups using gestures, eye signals, and brief exchanges of remarks to communicate with each other. The absence of student organizations that could have better coordinated matters on the various campuses was not accidental. Prior attempts to set up secret organizations to build student movements and lead demonstrations had been quickly discovered and broken up by the authorities. Only individuals and small groups acting without formal liaison and coordination were left to lead the students, if there was any leadership at all. They found safety in numbers, and the numbers of demonstrators grew daily, with the young undergraduates taking the first steps, and the more politically sophisticated and cynical graduate students remaining behind the scenes to coach their younger colleagues. Students and other citizens alike responded positively to the slogans honoring Hu, a symbol of political decompression and prospective liberalization, and later to the call for democracy and freedom. There was no conspiracy, except perhaps a conspiracy by small networks of a few people to use the occasion to express their grievances against the party and to demand more open space in the political and public spheres.

There is no evidence whatsoever that the party reformers instigated the students' actions. During the period before Zhao left for North Korea, on April 23, on a trip that had been scheduled some time earlier, Zhao was responsible for dealing with the student movement, with acquiescence by Deng. Zhao's attitude toward the student demonstration at the beginning is still a matter of debate. One view is that at that time he was basically opposed to the student movement. Another view is that the restraint shown by the police and public-security personnel can be taken as a sign of Zhao's sympathy for the students and a signal to the students. Still a third view is that the leaders thought that if the regime showed restraint, the student demonstrations would peter out. By coincidence, or perhaps because of subtle signaling between students and authorities, the student demonstration was relatively orderly and was kept within certain limits. The specific demands were mild, the most significant being freedom to publish their own newspapers. The student movement could have been a political boon for Zhao. For some time prior to Hu's death there had been rumors that Zhao would be forced to step down because the failure of the regime's economic policies, specifically price reform, was attributed to him. The old comrades behind the scenes were pushing for Li Peng to replace him, but the reformers hoped to see a comeback by Hu to a more responsible position, as compensation for Zhao's losing some of his influence or even being eased out. Some Chinese reformers thought at the time that the student movement would save Zhao. It seems probable that Zhao was more sympathetic to the students than were the old comrades. In an interview with Barbara Walters, televised on May 18, 1990, Jiang Zemin, the new general secretary, said that a split in the party had prevented the regime from taking strong measures, such as a ban on assembly in Tiananmen Square at the beginning of the student unrest, that could have made it unnecessary for the regime later to resort to a military crackdown with lethal weapons. Jiang was pointing his finger at Zhao without naming him.

After finding safety in numbers, acquiring a taste for their power in the street, receiving applause and indeed accolades from the sympathetic citizens of Beijing, and attracting the attention of the news media the world over, the students began to organize, first into students' autonomous associations on individual campuses; they soon formed a citywide coordinating committee and declared a boycott of classes. The leadership of the student movement began to pass into the hands of those who advocated more radical actions of one kind or another. The establishment of student organizations tended to give more power to those who played the most conspicuous roles in the demonstrations. The call for a boycott similarly boosted the influence of the radicals, leaving the moderates somewhat on the outside. The students asked for a direct dialogue with the government as a condition for their return to the campus and an end to the class boycott. But underlying that demand was the basic issue of recognition of the legitimacy of their autonomous associations, exercising the right to publish their own papers and enjoying the freedoms formally granted by the constitution.

While Zhao was out of the country, from April 23 to April 29, the standing committee was led by Li Peng, who was acting for Zhao in dealing with the student movement. On the basis of reports by top Beijing officials, it seems that Li Peng persuaded Deng that the students' demands should not be met, and the regime should take a tough stand. An editorial was drafted; it characterized the student movement as a "planned conspiracy" and "turmoil," the essence of which was "basically to repudiate the leadership of the Chinese Communist Party and to repudiate the socialist institutions." Specifically, it mentioned the establishment of "illegal organizations" in universities and colleges that had "seized power" from the official student organizations; some of them had even occupied the broadcasting stations of the universities and colleges. The text of the editorial reportedly was sent to Zhao, in North Korea, who notified the party center of his approval by telegram.

On April 25, the lower levels of the government and other public bodies were informed of the gist of the editorial and of a tough talk that had been delivered by Deng on April 24, on the basis of which the editorial was drafted.[21] On April 26, the editorial was published. Deng had drawn the line over which the confrontation would later take place. The response of the students was swift, not only in China but also on college campuses in the United States. Such quick reaction suggests that the students had been able to establish an effective system of communication with up-to-date equipment, conspiracy or no conspiracy. Organizing swiftly to defy Deng's talk and the April 26 editorial, 150,000 students and activists protested on April 27 in Tiananmen Square. The demonstration lasted fourteen hours, and more than a million people were watching them from the sidewalks. Subsequently, that demonstration was hailed by all student activists as a historic event. It is said that the democracy movement of 1989 was the most successful and historically important demonstration in Chinese history, because of its enormous scale and the popular response it evoked, if not for anything else.

When Zhao went back to Beijing on April 29, he apparently reassessed the situation in light of the demonstrations and the briefings by his confidential advisors, who had been excluded from the inner circle of officials making the decisions leading to the April 26 editorial. Zhao made a valiant attempt to change the government's policy. He had two alternatives. The first was to persuade Deng to change his mind and modify or even repudiate the April 26 editorial. According to President Yang Shangkun, Zhao, on the second day after his return to Beijing, raised the point that the April 26 editorial had made an incorrect characterization of the student movement, that the charges leveled against the students were too serious, and that the editorial was wrong.[22] If Zhao had succeeded, a slight and reasonable concession might have altered at one stroke the course of events in the next several weeks. It might even have become the first step in a new process of liberalization if it had been followed by other steps to recognize the legitimacy of the students' autonomous organizations.

But Zhao apparently had not the slightest chance of success, for what would seem to us like a small and reasonable concession meant something very different from Deng's point of view. Deng was a pragmatist in economic matters, but in politics he was a "strong disciplinarian," and he valued "the maintenance of ideological orthodoxy."[23] The rejection of the students' demands was not a mere matter of personal preference. In the CCP system of politics, once the paramount leader, the core of the collective leadership, had made a decision, that decision could not be easily reversed, particularly if he had publicly committed his authority and prestige on it. A reversal would have meant admission of a loss of authority by the leader or the entire party or, almost as bad, a split within the party, followed by a battle between the two groups, which would be followed by other confrontations leading to total victory for one group and total defeat for the other.

Most important, recognition of legal status for the students' autonomous associations would have meant the beginning of a fundamental change in the state–society relationship, an alteration of the Chinese communist system in which only one officially recognized association had jurisdiction over a specific range of affairs in a social unit, under the strict guidance of the party. It would have been regarded as a betrayal by the party of the officially recognized associations composed of loyal, longtime members of the party and the Youth Corps. Although it had been some time since those organizations had effectively performed their original function of providing leadership for the students, they still performed many routine services for the party, including surveillance of other students. For all those personal and structural reasons, even a slight concession to the students in the direction of liberalization could not be tolerated, unless Deng had the wisdom and foresight to see that fundamental change in the existing system would be inevitable and that it would be better for him and his party to sponsor, guide, and shape that change, with the hope that the party would continue to hold power even in a new political system.

But for a period of time, Deng temporized. It was said that he left Beijing to give serious thought to the forthcoming summit with Gorbachev. It seems more likely that he allowed Zhao and Li to fight it out. Perhaps equally likely, he wanted to wait and see if Zhao's more conciliatory attitude and Li's hard-nosed posture could somehow work as a carrot-and-stick combination to get the students to return to the campuses. In any case, he seems to have been confident that once he made a decision and spoke out, things would be settled.

The second alternative open to Zhao was to find a position acceptable to the students without openly repudiating the April 26 editorial. That was essentially what he did on May 4 in his conciliatory speech to a conference of representatives of the Asian Development Bank. His speech was written by his confidant, Bao Tong.[24] According to Li Peng, it was not cleared by the standing committee, nor shown to any of its members.[25] According to other sources, Zhao went to Beidaihe to see Deng, and Deng was reported to have said to Zhao that "the most important thing you should do is stabilize the situation. . . . If the situation is under control, you can implement your plans if they prove feasible, disregarding whatever I have said."[26] Perhaps Zhao did talk with Deng. But in the speech to the Asian Development Bank, and in all his subsequent public remarks, he never openly repudiated the April 26 editorial, although he substantially altered its emphasis. Specifically, he said that the students absolutely were not opposed to "our fundamental institutions and that they demanded the elimination of the defects of our work." He expressed his belief that what was needed most was a cool head, rationality, restraint, and proper procedures in order to resolve the problems along the paths of democracy and legality.

In taking that step, Zhao was running a great risk, as he surely realized. For a party leader to reach out openly, without prior agreement or even consultation with the appropriate party committee, to social forces outside the party was against the rules of the game and even party discipline. At this point, we should remind ourselves that party officials must follow the rule of "keeping in step with the party center," especially in public. That rule was needed to achieve a high degree of concentration of power within the party. It was also used to prevent an individual leader from bypassing the proper party organ to generate popular support for himself and thus achieve a certain degree of independence from the party, a development that could lead to factionalism and a split within the party, or exacerbation of any differences that already existed. The official system of communication was one of the expressions of that rule. Indeed, Premier Li Peng, the front man for the hard-liners and Zhao's nemesis, later charged that then, if not earlier, everyone could see that there were two different opinions in the party. He accused Zhao of causing a split within the party and of making it public.[27] In an official report on the Tiananmen affair, submitted on June 30, Mayor Chen Xitong declared that "there are some who said: 'The Party Center has two voices. Who's right and who's wrong?' Some others said: 'We are asked to keep in step with the Party

Center. Which Party Center should we keep in step with?' "[28] "Keeping in step with the center" is indeed a powerful mechanism for control over important activities and pronouncements by party officials, particularly in their dealings with the public. According to President Yang Shangkun, Deng personally told Zhao later that Zhao's speech had been a turning point, and that from then on the students stirred up more trouble.[29] Thus, it was, for the party leaders, a turning point from the existence of differences of opinion within the party to an open split that everyone could see. A final confrontation leading to an outcome in which one side would win and retain all power to make decisions, and the other side would lose, was taking shape, along the same course as intraparty struggles in the past. But even at that stage, it would seem that it still should have been possible to postpone a final confrontation, or if a final confrontation did occur, the contest need not have been lost so soon and so completely by Zhao, or at least should not have culminated in the most disastrous single day in Chinese internal affairs in the twentieth century.

But Zhao's breach of the rules and norms of the party was not without its potential political benefit. His speech was very well received by the students. Coincidentally or not, on that seventieth anniversary of the May Fourth movement, an estimated 50,000 students were joined by 250,000 other citizens in a march to protest the government's refusal to conduct a dialogue with the students. The next day, students at all universities and colleges except Peking University (Beida) and Beijing Normal University ended the classroom boycott. Zhao's speech had, in effect, offered a tacit alliance with the students and the intellectuals. Zhao had been able to tap an immense political resource that had been building since 1978, partly because of the direct efforts of the party reformers and partly because of societal conditions produced by their reforms. But how valuable would that resource be? Would his use of it turn out to be the cause of his downfall?

Given the party's mechanisms of control, the hard-liners were not without recourse. It was widely believed by students and intellectuals that Li Peng said, on May 5, that Zhao's speech to the Asian Development Bank represented his personal opinions, and that Deng's talk on April 24 conveyed the essence of the policy of the party center.[30] According to another source, Li said that Zhao's speech had been intended for foreign consumption.

At this point, let us distance ourselves slightly from those rapidly developing events and ask ourselves what political scientists have to say about situations of this kind, in order to speculate on the possibilities of adopting alternative actions and achieving entirely different outcomes. By greatly simplifying the conclusions of three political scientists,[31] we can say that a transition from an authoritarian regime to a democracy can be achieved under the following conditions: First, the reformers must establish an effective alliance with the moderate elements and social forces in society. Second, there must be a split within the armed forces or the security apparatus or both. In the Chinese case, there would seem to have been only minimal conditions for success in reforming the totalistic regime and keeping Zhao in power. The second condition never obtained. To be sure, there was, within the People's Liberation Army (PLA), resistance to the idea of using force against unarmed civilians, as well as hesitancy to be the first to confront and shoot them. In an uncertain number of cases there were refusals to execute the orders to move troops into specified positions. But the reports of such understandable reactions must be put into the context of the ultimate strength of military discipline and the need for the military leaders to hang together and follow the directions of the party. All the impressions about a split within the PLA before and after June 3 and 4 were based on sheer speculation, wishful thinking, misinformation, or disinformation. They were dismissed by some American experts at the time.

But the party reformers, the intellectual-activists, and the students still could have followed another course of action. They could have worked out strategies and tactics that would have involved retreats, withdrawals, and acceptance of temporary losses and admissions of defeat so as to avoid a direct confrontation with the armed forces, while preserving their strength to pursue long-term goals. That would have been simple common sense. In retrospect, such a course of action would seem to have been the best alternative, no matter what the outcome would have been over the next few years or decades. With such a strategy, the reformers, intellectuals, and students could have preserved and further built on their hard-won gains and achievements over the preceding ten years of decompression: the new ideological and cultural momentum, the relatively relaxed political atmosphere, the various small networks of liberal activism, the semi-legal organizations, and, in particular, the various professional and semi-professional bodies – in short, a civil society in the making. Unlike the countries in Eastern Europe, China had never had any experience with democracy, nor a long tradition of liberal and democratic thought, nor, in the preceding forty years, what we could call a strong, vibrant civil society. Before China can build democracy and institutions guaranteeing freedoms and rights, it must establish a tradition of strong, resilient social groups and institutions with deep roots that can manage their own affairs in the various sectors of society, that can help to define their own spheres of freedoms and responsibilities, and that can then conduct an ongoing dialogue and establish institutionalized relationships with the state. Only on such a basis can paper guarantees of freedom and rights become more than empty words.

For the reformers to have pursued such a long-term strategy success-fully, two conditions would have been required. First, a moderate group of students and activists would have had to have been the dominant element in the leadership of the social movement. Second, the reformers and the students would have had to have been able to consult with each other continually and openly to coordinate their basic views, general strategies, and short-term tactics. The second condition had been pre-cluded by the rules and norms of party politics. Indeed, those rules and norms limited the party reformers' ability to keep the public or even the rank and file of the student and democracy movements informed about the intraparty debate and conflict.[32] Whereas the reformers endeavored to make their move in light of the real power situation, sometimes the actions of the students were in response to information provided by their own small networks and by news media outside China, but sometimes they appear to have responded to their own impulses and the emotions of the crowd.

The first condition did not obtain because the party had never allowed autonomous, independent social organizations and institutions to arise and gradually develop a stable leadership and a tradition of adjusting to reality and learning from experience and history. Although at one point the students wanted to borrow "Solidarity" as the name for their au-tonomous student association, China had never had anything like Po-land's Solidarity union, with its history of pushing for labor reforms and its experience in political struggle, nor did China have anything to parallel the role of Poland's Catholic church, with its centuries of religious faith and mundane wisdom. During the period of the Cultural Revolution, once the constraints of the party organization had been broken, even Mao, who had taken the initiative in mobilizing the students, could not control the Red Guards until he sent the workers' and PLA propaganda teams into the campuses to run the universities and schools. In 1989, Zhao did not have the authority, the instruments, or the experience to control the students in a similar manner. Ironically, the revolutionary behavior of the students at once reflected the revolutionary tradition of the CCP and the normless behavior of a civil society just emerging from the totalistic control of the party-state. For better or worse, the party-State still shaped civil society even as civil society labored to reemerge from its control.

THE RADICALIZATION OF THE STUDENT MOVEMENT AND THE POLARIZATION OF CHINA

In the preceding section we simplified the views of three political scientists to consider some counterfactual situations, to lay out certain hypothetical alternatives, and to state roughly the conditions under which those alternatives could have been available or accessible. In this section we shall mention certain key events in which those inaccessible alternatives can be dimly seen. To put it more bluntly in nonacademic terms, those events suggest that certain opportunities existed and that if the students had seized those opportunities, they could have avoided the tragic outcome not only for themselves but also for the intellectuals, the Beijing citizens, and China itself.

In retrospect, it is clear that Zhao's partial support for the student movement, or what one can characterize as an attempt to establish a tacit alliance with the students, was doomed to failure unless he could persuade the students to set a limit to their actions, by offering them some concessions and reassurances, and unless they could be induced to cooperate with him in finding a settlement short of a total and explicit repudiation of the April 26 editorial and, thereby, the authority of Deng and the CCP. But the ebb and flow of the student movement, the increases and decreases in the numbers of demonstrators, soon brought about another escalation of actions in opposition to the regime and thrust into leadership positions students even more radical than their predecessors.[33] It also happened more than once that when a radical student leader took a moderate position in the spectrum of opinion at a particular moment, that leader would be replaced by a more radical leader, and then still later when the deposed leader again took up a radical position, he or she would be acclaimed and recognized as a leader once more. One's degree of radicalism was measured by one's position on repudiation of the April 26 editorial and one's determination not to withdraw from the square.

It was the radical students as a group who determined not only the fate of the student movement but also the fate of the reformers like Zhao, and their choices and actions will still be influencing the fate of China over the next few years. Their success in getting out of the university to demonstrate in the street won the leaders and the demonstrators acclaim, and it discredited those who had advocated caution. The start of the classroom boycott on April 23 brought increasingly more radical students into leadership positions, and a citywide coordinating committee was formed even before the April 26 editorial was published. On April 28, the "Federation of Students' Autonomous Associations in the Universities and Colleges in Beijing" elected the famous radical Wuerkaixi as president, replacing the more moderate Zhou Yongjun of the coordinating committee as leader of the overall organization of students. Recognition of such associations was the underlying unresolved issue in the dialogue and negotiations between the regime and the students. As noted earlier, Zhao's talk on May 4 seems to have had a calming effect on the students. On May 5, classes were resumed in all universities and colleges except

Beijing University and Beijing Normal University, and the student movement seemed to be ebbing. If the students had then gradually settled down to their normal life, Zhao's position within the party and the nation would have been greatly strengthened. Although the students had not gained legal recognition for their organizations, the organizations existed in fact and would have continued to play a role in the universities and society. But a hunger strike began on May 13, with the participation of more than 2,000 students in Tiananmen Square. That expressive act gave the student movement a focal point that brought about an unprecedented outpouring of sympathy from the citizens of Beijing, young and old, rich and poor, highly educated and semi-literate. It pushed the student movement to a new high point. In terms of tactics it was a great success, but in terms of strategy it was a serious mistake, for it meant that instead of deescalating the conflict with the government after Zhao had taken serious political risks to offer what must be considered to have been significant concessions, the students escalated it to a new level. In retrospect, the students had missed their first good opportunity to respond to Zhao's moderate statement and to accept what can be characterized as his tacit offer of an alliance with him. Furthermore, their action, in effect, set a time limit on the government's response, for the Chinese believed, rightly or wrongly, that the lives of the hunger strikers would be in danger after seven days, because they were drinking only water, not milk. Zhao, on the one hand, and the old comrades, on the other, had to find some kind of solution before May 20.

We do not know for certain if the hunger strike was staged for the purpose of increasing the number of students occupying Tiananmen Square, giving the demonstrators a shot in the arm, and bolstering their morale before the arrival of Gorbachev on May 15,[34] but there is no doubt that it raised the bargaining power of the students to new heights. The regime, particularly the reformers, redoubled their efforts to persuade the students to leave so that the welcoming ceremony for Gorbachev could take place as usual in Tiananmen Square. According to some accounts, on the night of May 14 Zhao had begun to feel that the hunger strike at the square should not drag on any longer. He made preparations to visit the students in the square on May 15 to talk to them, and even had his official automobile ready to go. But Li Peng stopped him from going by warning him that if he went, he would be "splitting the party center."[35] That invocation of party rule was effective. Zhao did not talk to the students, but rather tried to make a gesture by having his car circle the square twice. That fear of being charged with causing a split in the party is a strong mechanism for control to back up the rule that one must keep in step with the party center.

On May 16, sources in Hong Kong reported that several days earlier,

Yan Mingfu, head of the United Front Department of the CCP and a leading reformer, had told a Hong Kong member of the "People's Consultative Conference" that although he had refused to recognize the organization autonomously elected by the students, he had agreed to conduct a dialogue with the students, and he had characterized the student demonstrations as a valid way to express public opinion in a modern society. According to that report, he had promised that the regime would not retaliate against the students after the student movement had subsided (i.e., would not resort to the familiar tactic of "settling the account after the autumn harvest").[36] On May 14 there was a dialogue between Yan and the Beijing "Students' Dialogue Delegation" in the United Front Department building.

According to a big-character poster at the People's University, dated May 15, "not long after the dialogue had begun, representatives of the hunger-strike group who had come over from Tiananmen Square requested that they be allowed to read aloud a document of 'last words' that they had written for their parents. The reading of these last words took place against the sound of weeping from all sides."[37] According to Xiang Xiaoji, head of the Dialogue Delegation, a crowd of students had surrounded the building housing the United Front Department. Xiang admitted that looking at that angry crowd, he had never in his life been as frightened as he was that evening. He had to go outside several times to persuade the students to calm down so that the dialogue inside with the government leaders could go on. Each time, he had to summon up courage to make himself go. He reminisced: "There was a possibility that those students would rush at me in an uproar and beat me up, thinking I was a student scab."[38] During the dialogue, Yan said to the Dialogue Delegation that "if you think that there is a faction of reformers in the party center, then give them a little time and a chance, please."[39] It was Xiang's considered judgment that the students of the radical faction had destroyed that chance.

In retrospect, even Wuerkaixi suggested that the movement as a whole could be divided into two phases, with May 13–14 marking the turning point. Before that point, the students had been solemn and courageous, filled with grief and indignation. After that, they became arrogant. It was that arrogant force that rushed into the conference site at the United Front Department. From that time on, the movement daily became more radical as it marched determinedly toward failure.[40] The episode of May 14 shows how the hunger strike radicalized the student movement. Riding on a tidal wave of sympathy from the people of Beijing, the Hunger Strike Group captured the leadership of the student movement from the more moderate Dialogue Delegation.

Another dialogue was held on the morning of May 16,[41] while Deng was holding a much less fateful summit meeting with Gorbachev. Later, accompanied by some young scholars, Yan even went to the square to try to persuade the students to end their hunger strike and withdraw. He was the first high official to go there. It seems that on either May 14 or 16, according to Hu Ping, Yan explained to the students that it was impossible for the government to admit its mistake openly, but he offered them a guarantee that there would be no "settling of accounts after the autumn harvest."[42] The students voted against withdrawal.

By having asked two top officials, one in the party and the other in the government,[43] to conduct a dialogue with the students, the regime had given de facto recognition to the students without explicitly re-nouncing the April 26 editorial. There was at least no attempt to suppress them. But the negotiations failed because Deng had drawn his line on the April 26 editorial, and the students had drawn their line on its repudiation.

The intellectuals were more sober and much wiser than the students. On May 14, the day before Gorbachev's arrival, and in the context of the dialogue between the government and the students, twelve of the leading intellectuals, most of them moderates, issued the most noteworthy statement made during those critical seven weeks. They affirmed their belief that the student associations, elected by the majority of students using democratic procedures, were "legal organizations" and should be recognized by the government. They demanded that the party center openly declare that the student upheaval was a patriotic, democratic movement and that the government take no action against the students after the dispute was settled. They expressed their opposition to any use of violence against the students. But, wisely, they asked the students to withdraw temporarily from the square so that the Sino–Soviet summit could take place smoothly. Finally, they declared their determination to work together with the students to realize their three demands.[44] We do not know what strategic thought went into that statement. In any case, the students refused to accept the suggestion, either because they were reluctant to give up their tactical advantage of the moment or because they were so self-righteous about their moral stand that they could not condescend to consider such mundane matters as long-term strategy. On the day of Gorbachev's arrival, more than a million people were milling around Tiananmen Square. The welcoming ceremony had to be moved to the airport. China had lost face. Deng's nervousness was shown to all the world when a piece of food slipped from the chopsticks in his shaking hand, with Gorbachev sitting next to him and managing his chopsticks adroitly.

If the party had missed its best opportunity to get a settlement when it had rejected the students' demands for a genuine dialogue in the early days of the student movement, the students now missed their best opportunity to consolidate their gains in influence and power and to further the tacit alliance offered by the reformers so that the students, the intellectuals, and the reformers could continue to bargain and negotiate with the old comrades over a long period of time, when time would be on their side. If nothing else, they could have avoided for themselves, for the intellectuals, and for the reformers the disaster that was to befall them all. By insisting on continued occupation of the square, the students made the position of the reformers and the intellectuals untenable. Three days later, the reformers would be out of power completely, and the split within the party would end with total victory for one side and total defeat for the other. China would soon be polarized.

The Chinese leaders and the leading intellectual-activists fully realized what was at stake. On May 17 they made desperate, last-ditch attempts to try to persuade the students to withdraw from Tiananmen. In the early morning hours of May 17, Zhao Ziyang issued a statement (*shumian tanhua*), speaking not only for himself but also as a representative of all the other members of the standing committee of the Politburo: Li Peng, Qiao Shi, Hu Qili, Yao Yilin. Zhao said that the party center and the State Council had taken an affirmative attitude toward the students' demands for democracy, legality, and reform, but that they hoped that the students would end the hunger strike. He also said that after the students had "returned" (to the campuses), the comrades of the party center and the State Council would continue to listen to their opinions. He flatly assured them that the party and the government would not retaliate against the students afterward.[45]

There is a vivid eyewitness account by a writer, Zhang Langlang, of at least one intellectual-activist trying to send a message to the radical students whose actions at that moment would have a decisive effect on the whole situation.[46] On the morning of May 17, Dai Qing,[47] a special correspondent for *Guangming ribao* and a leading intellectual-activist, phoned Zhang and asked Zhang to serve as her representative to deliver an oral message to the student leaders at the Tiananmen Square broadcasting station. The message was that there was "now the following program": First, Zhao's talk (i.e., his written statement) in the early morning could be considered a preliminary expression of attitude on the part of the government, clearly affirming that there would be no "settling of the account after the autumn harvest" (i.e., no retaliation afterward). Second, a top government official would come to Tiananmen Square to conduct a dialogue with the students that would be broadcast "live." Then, somewhat unclearly, the message was that at "two o'clock in the afternoon the workers, peasants, and soldiers will stage a parade." After that, the students occupying the square would "return to the campus in triumph." After passing through several security lines manned by student pickets, Zhang finally reached a student leader and delivered the message. The student leader replied to Zhang solemnly that the students respected Dai as a writer, but that for Dai to play the role of mediator would hurt her image. The student leader said that "we could not agree to a measure of this kind because it was too general" and added that if the leaders of the government and the party wanted to talk to the students, they should do so directly, not through a mediator. In addition to illustrating the considerable power of a few leaders in the square to influence the fate of China, that episode vividly reveals the students' radical, maximalist ideas of a strict division into two camps ("we" and "they") and their peremptory rejection of the advice of a less radical intellectual-activist who also had good contacts with the reformers. Zhang, a longtime friend of Dai, described her as a person who managed her affairs on the basis of emotion and whose enthusiasm sometimes exceeded her thoughtful judgment. After Zhang reported to Dai the answer to her message, Zhang expressed the thought that even Dai must certainly have been surprised, wondering how people could communicate with each other. Was it possible that the numerous organizations of the radical students had the same sort of hierarchy, the same kinds of security systems, the same Manichaean worldview, the same tendency to bury their heads in the sand, the same inability to communicate with "the others," and the same revolutionary idealism as the old comrades? Perhaps they were mirror images of each other: one having new ideals, the other revolutionary memory; one having a newly acquired sense of people's power, the other crusted habit.

Still, the students' fear that the party would "settle the account after the autumn harvest" was not without ground. They continued to believe that only a repudiation of the April 26 editorial and an explicit declaration by the party to the effect that the students' movement was "a patriotic, democratic movement" would reassure them. For one reason or another, they paid more attention to the "provocations" of Li Peng than to the assurances offered by Zhao and Yan. They placed more emphasis on verbal declarations than on strategic calculations. Extracting a public declaration from the party seems to have been more important to them than preserving and strengthening the influence of the reformers in the party. Perhaps all that was irrelevant. Some of the most radical students just wanted to live one more day, one more hour, in the exhilarating and liberated world of their movement, thinking that the dream would thereby become reality.

While Zhao was preparing the statement urging the students to keep a cool head, to be rational and wise, to act with restraint, to follow procedure, to consider and to look after the whole situation, and to preserve and protect stability and unity, he must have known that in all probability he could not persuade Deng to rescind the April 26 editorial, nor could he persuade the students to withdraw. Hence, another important dispatch by the China News Agency, dated May 16, reported Zhao's meeting with Gorbachev in a manner that stressed Deng's ultimate authority in making final decisions in all important matters. Zhao told Gorbachev that according to an official but unpublished resolution adopted by the First Plenum of the Thirteenth Central Committee (when Deng resigned his posts in the standing committee and the Politburo), "we [i.e., the rest of the Chinese leaders] still need Deng at the helm on the most important questions."[48]

The factual content of the resolution and the appropriateness of re-affirming Deng's ultimate authority were not disputed by Yang Shangkun later in an internal speech made on May 22, but Yang noted that the news release had begun with that piece of information, and he charged that reporting the news in that way constituted an endeavor to shift the responsibility to Deng, to put Deng at the forefront, and to say that Deng was the source of all errors in handling the student movement.[49] The political implication was that Zhao had endeavored to make Deng the target of attack by the students and intellectuals, while hinting that Zhao himself did not agree with the April 26 editorial. It was assumed that some of Zhao's close advisors had drafted the dispatch, and Zhao had approved of it. To live by their official system of communication, even the highest officials had to be deaf and dumb most of the time on the important questions of the day, or resort to platitudes and official formulas, except when they were authorized to speak or when they were willing to risk their political careers. For our purpose, the point is that the intraparty split no longer turned on a difference in substantive policies alone, but had come to depend also on questions of personal responsibility and on how and when information about the authority structure and the policy-making process would be transmitted to the public.[50]

On May 17, the party finally acted, and Deng clearly reaffirmed his decision that no retreat from the April 26 editorial would be possible. As Li Peng explained later, further retreat would have meant giving China to the students.[51] In other words, a retreat at that time, after days of "forbearance," would, in Li's view, have led ultimately to an outcome in which one side would have won all, with the other side losing all. The problems of personal and generational succession may have contributed to a perception that the confrontation would have lasting effects. Under the strong urgings of the other old comrades, Deng, an old comrade himself, sided with Yang Shangkun and Li Peng and authorized the proclamation of martial law over part of Beijing. Zhao said that he could not implement the decision, and offered to resign. The party then split into two parts. When confronted with a choice between Zhao and the party center, few among his top-level colleagues supported Zhao, although many of them probably agreed with him in their hearts and minds. Zhao never had an organized personal following. He tried to lead on the basis of his ideas and proposals, drawn from his long experience or supplied by his advisors.

Even after Deng had made the decision to declare martial law, Premier Li Peng, on May 18, held a last official dialogue with the students, asking them to end the hunger strike and withdraw from the square. As Dai Qing's oral message to the students had informed them, the meeting was televised live. That could have been construed as de facto recognition of the students' voluntary associations, this time by the topmost official of the government, the very person said to have taken the most hard-line position against the students and to have persuaded Deng to adopt the April 26 editorial. Instead of reciprocating with even the slightest civil gesture, the radical student leader Wuerkaixi came to the meeting as if he were the victor who was coming to teach the defeated a lesson. For our purpose, two points are most important: First, he said that the students had heard about or read Zhao's statements of May 17 and that they refused to leave the square because they felt that it had not made enough concessions. Second, he haughtily told the premier that if 99.9 percent of the students should vote to leave, but 0.1 should decide to stay, all of the students would remain at their side.[52] The principle of unanimity was used to enforce the radicals' leadership of the movement, or at least its spokesman was pushed by the radical movement to adopt that principle. However impractical that was, and no matter how hypocritically it was used by Wuerkaixi, the mere fact that it was publicly announced on such an occasion said a great deal about the immaturity, the naiveté, and perhaps the fanatical idealism of the student movement.

In the wee hours of May 19, Zhao Ziyang, the victim who had been crushed between the irresistible force (the radical students) and the immovable object (Deng), went to Tiananmen Square to see the students. He apologized to the students, saying that "we come too late." He asked them to terminate the hunger strike, supporting his plea with the Chinese medical finding that after seven days a hunger strike would endanger life. Finally, he said that he was old and did not matter, but that the young people of nineteen and twenty should not lightly sacrifice their lives. He told them the situation was serious, and he begged them to think about the consequences coolly. In taking his tearful leave of the students, he also said farewell to the political stage. He never appeared in public again. In the late evening of May 19, at a huge assembly attended by party, government, and army officials, the regime announced its decision to declare martial law, but Zhao refused to take part in the meeting. The split in the party was there for all to see. Zhao's failure to attend the meeting was another charge against him. Six weeks later, on June 24, he was formally relieved of all his posts in the party by the Fourth Plenum of the Thirteenth Central Committee. The official charge against him was that "in the critical hours of the life and death of the party and the state, comrade Zhao Ziyang committed the error of supporting the turmoil and splitting the party." Finally, the mechanism of control was formally invoked.

That sequence of events suggests that Chinese politics has never been simple and straightforward. It is entirely possible that Deng was playing an extremely complicated game, balancing Zhao and Li, using them as instruments of his two alternatives up to the last moment: If Zhao's written statement of May 17 succeeded in persuading the students to withdraw from the square, Deng would move a step forward in resolving the most urgent problem confronting him without resorting to drastic measures. If Zhao's conciliatory approach failed, Deng could claim that he had been right all along in his characterization of the student movement as "turmoil." He would then implement his second alternative: to impose martial law and to use the army in a military crackdown. One can also suggest that after Deng had drawn the line on the April 26 editorial, whether Zhao or Li would win, whether the reformers or the hard-liners would win, would depend on the students' decision to withdraw or to continue the confrontation. If additional evidence later shows that this guess is not entirely incorrect, the Tiananmen tragedy will certainly be remembered as one of those cases in history where the outcome seems to have been inevitable, and yet where there also appear to have been many opportunities to avoid the seemingly inevitable outcome.

Meanwhile, the nation was also beginning to split apart. If the news dispatch of May 16 was intended as a signal, it had its effect almost immediately. On May 17, a group of thirty-five leading intellectual-activists signed a declaration condemning Deng in the strongest possible terms. It said that although the Qing dynasty had died seventy-six years earlier, China still had an emperor without the title of an emperor, a senile, fatuous dictator. After referring to Zhao's statement of May 16 that all important decisions had to go through that senile dictator, it called for the overthrow of personal dictatorship, an end to gerontocracy, and the resignation of the dictator. It noted that the students had already proclaimed through their actions that the student upheaval was a great patriotic, democratic movement to bury the dictatorship and the monarchial system at last. It was not merely an anti-Deng statement; it was a revolutionary declaration.[53] As noted in another context, the two most important research organizations, together with two other organizations, openly blamed the party for its failure to affirm the student movement as a patriotic, democratic movement. They called for the convening of special sessions of the National People's Congress and the party's congress to handle the situation.

After the declaration of martial law, there still were many attempts by the more moderate intellectual-activists to induce the radical students to withdraw from Tiananmen Square. On May 22, Wan Runnan, president of the Beijing Stone Group Corporation, proposed at a meeting with a group of almost one hundred student leaders that they "should not lose the opportune moment to withdraw from the square but should take the initiative to go back to the campuses and to persist in the struggle there."[54] But Wan said that there had been questions and demands that would accompany the withdrawal: First, "the troops would go back to where they had come from." Second, martial law would be canceled. Third, Li Peng would step down, and Deng, Yang, and other "old men" should retire with honor "according to procedure." Finally, and most important, according to Wan, Zhao should be given support. The contrast between the May 14 statement of twelve intellectuals and Wan's talk on May 22 suggests that Wan, as an intellectual-activist and a person closely connected with the reformers, had explicitly and emphatically linked the student movement to a new objective: to support Zhao and to oppose Li Peng and hence "Deng and Yang and others." That semi-public move was the logical culmination of a number of events: the news report of May 16, Zhao's remark to Gorbachev, the standing committee's decision on May 17 to proclaim martial law, Zhao's offer to resign and the statement issued on the same day by thirty-five intellectuals, and Zhao's refusal to take part in the public meeting on May 19. Wan was trying to build an alliance between the students and the reformers. Many reformers may have had that idea for a long time, but the rules and norms of the party must have imposed such strong constraints on the Chinese reformers that they could not openly or even semi-publicly espouse such a strategy from the beginning. They also could not communicate directly and explicitly with the students so that the two groups could coordinate their tactics on the specific demands to be made, the advances and retreats in their actions, and the all-important question of timing in a complicated political struggle with the hard-liners. It was only after Zhao had definitely lost out in the power struggle on May 17 that the reformers and intellectuals came out more openly, but still only in a semi-public fashion, with their political strategy. But by the time that Wan made his proposal, the student movement had been thoroughly radicalized.

Furthermore, there was a widespread view on the part of the students that their movement had been used from the very beginning by the reformers as a tool in intraparty struggle, and they feared that their movement would lose its independent nature if it should explicitly support one side or the other or if it were to coordinate its actions with those of the party reformers. That view may have been an expression of the cynical belief that the reformers were losing the fight, or indeed had already lost it, and that the students should distance themselves from the reformers and attempt to save their movement. Alternatively, their view might be interpreted as a perverse overreaction against the totalistic regime, as well as an expression of a lack of confidence and an absence of a strong sense of self-identity on the part of individuals and groups in a civil society that had just begun to emerge from totalistic control, through a program of decompression sponsored by the reformers in the party-state. In either case, it was part and parcel of the political culture created by the political system.

The probable reactions of the students to Wan's proposal might have been seen in another bizarre episode: Whether he was persuaded by Wan or by his fear of the impending military crackdown, or by sheer coincidence, on May 22 Wucrkaixi, in his capacity as chairman of the Federation of Students' Autonomous Associations in the Universities and Colleges in Beijing, asked, without consultation with other student leaders, that the students evacuate the square. He was dismissed from his post, and a collective leadership was established.

At that critical moment, a television station in Hong Kong suddenly broadcast the news that during an enlarged meeting of the Politburo Li Peng had been forced to step down. According to a postmortem by five Hong Kong correspondents who were in Beijing at the time, "part of the students and citizens of Beijing learned about the news of Li Peng's stepping down and other news [that was] circulating in Hong Kong. They made erroneous estimations of the whole political situation. They were drunk with the atmosphere of 'victory' as they stubbornly and irrationally insisted on not withdrawing from the square."[55]

At that time, there was a widespread belief that the PLA would not turn its guns on the people. It is impossible to know who first began promoting that opinion and how it became so widely accepted. But it is true that many students and Beijing residents believed that the army was "the people's army" and would not carry out any orders to harm the people. They tried to fraternize with the soldiers, in effect turning the party's propaganda against the party itself. There were many reports that armed units had refused to implement martial law and had clashed with units that were ready to follow orders. It was also said that the two remaining old marshals and several top military figures had urged the government not to use force against the students. Whatever their origins, and whether or not they were accurate, such opinions were believed, and such belief must have been a good argument against withdrawal at one time or another. Still later, there were reports of troop movements and new deployments, with the implication that civil war was imminent. These and many other pieces of information, misinformation, and disinformation will fascinate historians for a long time to come.

I mention those episodes not to set up a research agenda but to emphasize a point about the defects in the system of communication analyzed in an earlier section. That point concerns the failure of the regime, through its news media or other forms of communication, to accomplish either of the following things: first, to persuade the students to withdraw for political and moral reasons and to convince them of the sincerity of its promise that there would be no retribution, no "settling of accounts after the autumn harvest"; second, to make credible the regime's threat to use force that was implicit in the declaration of martial law. If the regime had had sufficient credibility, the students and Beijing residents would have perceived that the use of force was imminent and would be overwhelming, and that would have made withdrawal a natural response. Instead, some of the students acted on information and analysis whose origins and reliability were not always known. In fact, they may not have tried very hard to determine such matters.[56] The fact that many people believed that the party could not control the army and that its threat was not credible reveals glaringly the decline in the party's authority.

Shortly before and after the declaration of martial law, many associations representing workers, intellectuals in various professions, and other citizens were established. Two of them deserve mention. The first is the "Joint Conference of Persons of All Circles in Beijing," attended by forty-odd people, with Wang Dan as the convener. One official source said that it was composed of the "Association of Intellectuals," the "Federation of Students' Autonomous Associations in the Universities and Colleges in Beijing," the "Autonomous Association of Beijing Residents," the "Dare-to-Die Corps of Beijing Workers," the "Beijing Workers' Pickets," the "Dare-to-Die Corps of Beijing Residents," and so forth.[57] For the first time, Beijing had an overall organization not sponsored by the regime or subject to its control, but rather formed by organizations and individuals opposed to the regime in one way or another. The second was the famous "High Command of Tiananmen Square," which held the fate of the student movement in its hands for the next eleven days. For its commander in chief it selected Chai Ling, who had delivered a moving speech to urge students to join the hunger strike and who on May 15 had stood up to "maintain order" after Wuerkaixi had suggested that the hunger strikers and the students evacuate part of the square so that the ceremony to welcome Gorbachev could take place there.[58] Order was maintained. The students did not move.

On May 27, the leaders of the Joint Conference, the High Command of Tiananmen Square, the Federation of Students' Autonomous Associations in the Universities and Colleges in Beijing, the Workers' Autonomous Association, and the Beijing Residents' Autonomous Association called a joint news conference, with Chai Ling, Wang Dan, and Wuerkaixi as the principal sponsors and speakers, to announce that on May 30 all the students would withdraw from the square after a worldwide victory parade. But within two days that proposal was canceled. It was reported that the students wanted to wait until the standing committee of the National People's Congress held its scheduled meeting on June 20. According to some Hong Kong informants, Chai Ling and other leaders were supported mainly by students who had arrived in Beijing only in the past few days and were eager to see some action; if the square were vacated, they would have no place to stay in Beijing and would have to go home. The High Command of Tiananmen Square itself was not a well-organized body. Chai, at one point, said that she was tired; she left her post as commander and asked the students to support the vice commander in chief, who happened to be her husband. On June 1, Chai called a news conference to accuse another student, one of the six initiators of the hunger strike, of intending to kidnap her. At about the same time there was a dispute over how the money contributed to the students was to be shared among leaders, who could use it to escape and to save their own lives after the anticipated military crackdown occurred. But that chaotic and pathetic situation can be understood: The successive steps in the radicalization of the student movement had pushed aside the moderate elements, people with a sense of responsibility and those with a feel for strategy and tactics. The radicalism of the leaders in the square in the last days of the movement merely reflected the immaturity of a section of civil society that had just begun to emerge.

It was obvious that the student leaders could not control their followers, but it was also true that some of the leaders, principally Chai Ling and her advisors and supporters, made no attempt to restrain the most radical students and residents of Beijing. Instead, their highly emotional speeches and flamboyant actions tended to inflame popular feelings. Certainly it is not easy to attribute responsibility to any particular leaders, but that is not to say that none of them had any responsibility.

June 3 and 4 brought the expected assault by the army into the heart of Beijing. The onslaught of the tanks, armored cars, and personnel carriers and the gunfire from soldiers on forced march split China into two parts: an immovable pyramid of power and a recompressed civil society. The world was shocked and watched in disbelief, while Chinese wept voicelessly in their souls. After ten years of a slow process of decompression, with several fluctuations, China went through in a matter of seven weeks a cycle of mobilization, radicalization, polarization, bloody confrontation for two days, and recompression. The subsequent orders for arrests and the atmosphere of fear and uncertainty drove some of China's best minds into exile, and others into silence in the prisons or in their homes. The tragedy of Tiananmen left a deep divide between China and world opinion at a critical juncture in China's economic and political development, when it needed all the help that the world could give. What will happen to the good earth of yesteryear or the yellow earth of recent days?

MORAL REDEMPTION AND POLITICAL TRANSFIGURATION THROUGH RECONCILIATION

By using overwhelming force and lethal violence against unarmed people under its rule, the regime lost its moral case against the students occupying Tiananmen Square, however good a political case it had tried to develop by its restraint and patience in the preceding forty days, and however much one can sympathize with it in its humiliation at the hands of the students during Gorbachev's visit. In forty-eight hours it destroyed much, if not all, of the legitimacy it had carefully built up since the days of the revolution, as well as what remained of its political support in urban areas. Coming after its failure to countermobilize any social groups (not even the "proletariat") against the students and the city dwellers in Beijing, its use of naked force revealed the moral exhaustion of a regime that had to resort to its last remaining resource: the ultimate, brutal weapon of repression. Its loss of ideological, cultural, and moral hegemony over society was there for people all over the world to see. The regime won the battle for Tiananmen Square, as no one had doubted that it could. But in winning that battle, it lost a decisive campaign for the hearts and minds of the Chinese people and many of their foreign friends and well-wishers. That moral error cannot be glossed over; it can only be redeemed, as has happened many times throughout history for a variety of errors, or even sins, some more unforgivable, others less serious, than this one. Such moral redemption can be achieved over a period of time by reconciliation with recompressed society and by fundamental reform of the system itself.

While the Tiananmen tragedy revealed the moral exhaustion of the CCP political system, it also showed some extravagant characteristics among the student leaders who came to dominate the movement in its final phases: curious combinations of political daring, but lack of political wisdom; political sophistication in raising slogans, but naiveté in political understanding; oratorical brilliance, but an utter lack of a sense of political reality; an ability to move the hearts of millions, but a hubris seldom matched in human history. Let us affirm emphatically their ide-

316

alism and patriotism. Let us refrain from seeing any self-serving motives behind their actions, not even the ever-present selective incentives in any collective action. Let us acclaim their individual acts of heroism. Let us believe that they were ready to sacrifice their lives for the moral cause they championed so courageously. But for all that, their collective actions and their interactions with one another provided one of the two necessary components that led to utter disaster for everyone, including themselves. We now know from both theory and practice that individual acts of self-sacrifice and heroism, performed prematurely *at the beginning* of a revolutionary social movement, will expose that movement to attack, bring about social and political repression, and damage the very cause for which those acts are performed. The Tiananmen tragedy shows that individual and collective acts of self-sacrifice and heroism, carried out in disregard of strategic and political calculations at *the later stages* of a social movement, when it has won many hard-fought battles at great risk and when it involves a very large number of people, will do immensely greater damage to the cause – the more successful the movement has been, the greater will be the damage. Heroes and heroines, freshmen, sophomores, and new graduate students, who were prepared to offer their lives, may not have cared greatly to live in this world, but a social movement for a political cause has significance only if it is of this world. Many outside observers reported startling changes from cynicism to idealism in many students' attitudes over a short period of several weeks. But, in fact, fanatical idealism and radical cynicism have one thing in common: They are both irresponsible to entities larger than themselves. The fanatical idealist is responsible only to his or her ideal, and the radical cynic is responsible only to his or her narrow self-interests.

The actions of the student movement as a whole were not governed by any strategic, long-term political calculations. Obviously, some participants must have given a great deal of thought to questions of strategy and tactics; they must have had a good knowledge of political reality. But they never succeeded in playing leadership roles. Their ideas were pushed aside in a familiar process in which large numbers of radical individuals and organizations suddenly emerged and claimed the leadership of the movement, in which those with more radical ideas displaced those with a more moderate approach. Thus, one cannot detect in the actions of the students any strategic, long-term political calculations. That absence of strategic calculations and the students' infantile credulity in information and views that tended to justify their radical actions were amazing features of a movement that shook the world and is now given credit by some as an important factor leading to the revolution in Eastern Europe in the second half of 1989. But the young radicals and even the middle-aged activists can still learn many lessons from their headstrong folly if they are not pushed again by their circumstances to try to become the saviors of China and the world.

It may be argued that even without any strategic, long-term political calculations, the radical students have created a situation in which the regime will be brought down sooner than it would if they had withdrawn from the square and the military crackdown had not taken place. The validity of that argument cannot be determined, just as we cannot prove or disprove the counterargument that if the students had withdrawn, the system would have undergone fundamental change sooner. But there is no doubt that the costs inflicted by the students on themselves, on the intellectuals, on the party reformers, on the other Chinese, and on China itself have been extremely high. The first argument in effect assumes that another revolution will take place in China that will justify those costs and others still to be incurred.

Now that China is polarized, the party-state and the recompressed society must seek reconciliation with each other, for the superficial calm that prevails at this moment in China cannot hide the fact that society did little or nothing to cooperate with the party-state in its suppression of the student and democracy movements. Indeed, one can argue that large segments of society, particularly the intellectuals and the professionals, are engaging in acts of passive resistance insofar as the political repression is concerned. The accused, the arrested, and the released are given sympathy and encouragement. The calm has been maintained only because beginning in September, the regime imperceptibly shifted its emphasis from pursuing the harsh policy adopted in early June to a much more ambiguous policy that puts stress on superficial conformity in following the party's line and on the maintenance of order. The party leaders probably realized that cooperation had not been forthcoming and could not be obtained by a policy of persecution and revenge.

In March 1990, the Sixth Plenum of the Thirteenth Central Committee adopted a resolution to strengthen the linkage between the party and the masses of the people. It revived one of the best of Mao Zedong's ideas – the mass line. That decision resurrected the once-effective slogan of "from the masses and to the masses," but coupled it to the operational procedure of "democratic, scientific decision-making and implementation" and to the building up and strengthening of "socialist democracy and legality" – both of the latter ideas developed during the Dengist period. This looks at first glance like a step toward reconciliation with "the people" and society, or the silent majority in the urban areas, for the mass line that called for giving more attention and weight to public demands and wishes was historically an idea that contributed to the adoption of moderate policies and served as a counterbalance to the concept of class struggle. But masses are not citizens with distinct rights and obligations. The mass line is not the same as democracy.[59] Moreover, the idea of the mass line during the period of struggle with opposing political forces was frequently combined with the idea of "developing the progressive forces, winning over the middle forces, and combating or isolating the die-hard forces."[60] It is still nothing more than a method of leadership in a revolutionary struggle.

Most important, nothing thus far has suggested that the Chinese leaders have freed themselves from the tradition of viewing political struggle as a series of encounters leading to a final confrontation in which one side wins and retains all power to make decisions, and the other side loses. That twentieth-century tradition has guided the party's political struggles with other political forces in society, with other factions within the party when factionalism has arisen, and even with party members who have offered their criticisms of party policies in times of crisis or who have entertained fundamentally different views on the course of China's development when the power to make final decisions has been at stake. It is true that at times there were compromises, concessions, admissions of defeat, negotiations, and even cooperation with such opposing political forces, but those were tactical measures that did not lead to permanent institutions and fundamental processes according to which all political forces would have to conduct their contestations, promote their interests, and accept the results.

Instead of simply reviving Mao's ideas and adding new concepts to them, the party now must fundamentally transform them from conceptions to guide revolutionary political struggle into individual elements in a fundamentally different process of contestation, negotiation, bargaining, and compromise that will lead to a reconciliation with recompressed society. If such a process is to lead to a reconciliation, it must also be the source from which will emerge new, mutually acceptable institutions and rules of the game. For such a process to be successful, the Chinese on all sides, particularly the party, and to a lesser extent the radical dissidents, must abandon once and for all the various attitudes, ideas, and styles of political action that assume the inevitable occurrence of a final confrontation in which the winner takes all. Unless that can be done, there will be no chance of achieving historic compromises through a prolonged process of negotiation and bargaining, nor any chance that a set of solid, stable, and fundamental institutions can be built to relate society organically to the state and to make peaceful change possible.

It is beyond my ability to explain in theoretical terms why my last argument is correct or relevant. But certain historical experiences in China suggest that if even one side believes that it can win in an all-out confrontation, then no permanent and genuine reconciliation will be possible.

During the Sino–Japanese War, when the CCP was the weaker party in the conflict with the Guomindang (GMD), Mao developed the idea of waging what might be called a "limited war"[61] against the GMD to counter the latter's "limited war" against the CCP. The two sides co-operated in the war against Japan, but fought each other at the same time. They negotiated while fighting each other, and fought each other while negotiating. They fought and negotiated at different times on different political and military levels. After Mao had triumphed over Wang Ming in 1938, signals from each side to the other were clearly sent and received. Both the CCP and the GMD could be considered "unitary actors." There were no Chinese voices that could confuse the signals to such an extent that either party would act without knowing clearly what the other side intended to do.

But most important of all, both sides respected the constraints imposed upon them by the Japanese occupation of a large part of China, particularly the major cities and the lines of communication there. That situation actually created a stalemate that made what could be called a "limited war" and a "limited peace" possible in spite of the fact that both sides believed that a final, all-out confrontation would occur after the Sino–Japanese War was over.

The end of the Sino–Japanese War removed the constraints, and the perceived stalemate was over. The GMD believed that it could win an all-out war and insisted on the CCP's acceptance of what the latter clearly considered unacceptable conditions. The CCP believed that it would not lose all if it rejected the GMD's conditions and fought a protracted war. Once more, a final confrontation to win all or lose all took place, until the GMD had lost the mainland, and the outbreak of the Korean War prevented a planned communist invasion of Taiwan. The twenty-two years of conflict between the GMD and the CCP suggest that the expectation of a final confrontation is not something to be found only within the CCP, but is a fundamental aspect of twentieth-century Chinese politics.

That sequence of events suggests that if one side believes that it can win all in a final confrontation and is willing to pay the necessary price, there is nothing the other side can do to prevent that from happening. The same kind of reasoning leads to the thought that only a protracted stalemate can change an ingrained expectation of the occurrence of a final confrontation to settle all accounts and replace that expectation with an anticipation of a game of no total winner and no total loser, or even contestations that will reiterate themselves indefinitely within the same fundamental institutions. In other words, a prolonged process of repeated negotiation and bargaining leading to a strategic compromise is possible only if there is a stalemate and only if there is a common perception that neither side can inflict a quick and total defeat on the other. The mutual perception that a stalemate will continue indefinitely into the future will help to change the expectation that there will be a final confrontation and settlement of accounts. Ultimately, reconciliation between the party-state and a recompressed society will depend on a continued stalemate between the two. Paradoxically, the Tiananmen tragedy may have created such a situation. The dissidents will not be able to overthrow the system in the foreseeable future, and the party-state will continue to need the active cooperation of the intellectuals, professionals, and students, both inside and outside China, if it is to overcome the overwhelming crisis confronting it and if China is to prosper in the modern world. Beijing cannot control world opinion, but world opinion cannot govern China.

If a reconciliation does come about, it will be achieved through a prolonged process of contestation, dialogue, negotiation, threats, and counterthreats. It will eventually be possible if the Chinese leaders realize at some future time that their system, as it revealed itself during the Tiananmen tragedy, can no longer operate effectively in the new international environment. To avoid the worst-case scenario of a gradual decline and ultimate collapse, one alternative would be for the party itself to lead the changes in the political system, in the hope it can continue to play a leading role in a new system that can enable China to survive and prosper.

What the new system will be, no one can foresee. It will depend on another period of soul-searching such as occurred under Deng, for the Tiananmen tragedy exposed many fundamental defects in the system beyond those acknowledged by the Chinese leadership following the Cultural Revolution. It has now been seen how incapable the system was of relating itself to the students, the intellectuals, and the urban population, how vulnerable it was in the midst of a modern world in the new age of communication, how easy it was to lose a whole generation of the best and brightest minds. This new soul-searching should lead to reexamination of the rules, norms, and mechanisms governing intraparty politics, a realm where fundamental reform must sooner or later be made. Another area involves the structural principle under which there can be only one official mass organization in each unit for one functional area. In other words, the party-state should allow civil society to develop and strengthen itself by establishing voluntary, legal, autonomous associations that not only can help to run social affairs but also can be politically and socially responsible actors in society. Such developments would imply the eventual existence of many factions in any one party and many parties in the state. The relationships between the state and society and among the many conflicting interests would be governed by a set of institutions that would evolve over a period of time through negotiation and bargaining, cooperation and conflict. Strong, well-established organizations and associations in civil society will cause many problems for the governance of the country, but they will at least be responsible bodies, with accumulated practical political experiences and a tradition to maintain.

Such a development of civil society will be possible only if the students and intellectuals inside and outside China also do some soul-searching, a process that has already begun among some of the more sober minds. Above all, they must learn to be responsible, to act with a sense of accountability to any entity in whose name they speak to demand sacrifices from themselves and others. They also should learn that freedom and human rights include the right not to participate, to be silent, to be free from what I call the "politics of involvement." They should divest themselves of the modes of thought and political styles (including a paranoid Chinese McCarthyism) that they have subconsciously assimilated from the political system under which they have lived so long.

Perhaps such a reconciliation and reconstruction of the state and society will turn the moral blundering and ideological exhaustion of the regime into moral redemption and political renewal; perhaps the utter political irresponsibility and ineptitude in dealing with the real world shown by some of the students will become transfigured into new concepts of citizenship, loyal opposition, and ultimately responsible leadership. Reconciliation between the party-state and society will in turn foster a reconciliation between China and world opinion. As my penultimate line, I shall use the same verse with which I ended my book on post-Mao reform:

Mountains multiply, streams double back
I doubt there is even a road;
willows cluster darkly, blossoms shine –
another village ahead.

Only this time, I no longer entertain the hope that I will see that "village" with my own eyes.

NOTES

1. In other words, I am trying to describe, with a great deal of oversimplification, a historical pattern in which the players are different and the actions are different, but the outcomes are the same in all cases. These terms – "players," "actions," and "outcomes" – are borrowed from Eric Rasmusen, but do not have the technical meanings implied when he refers to them as "the rules of the games." See his *Games and Information* (Oxford: Basil Blackwell, 1990), p. 22. I hope that someone with the necessary competence will write a book or a series of volumes on twentieth-century Chinese politics from a game-theoretical perspective and provide a systematic explanation and comparative

treatment of this extraordinary, complex, and tragic experience, while linking together the macro-historical level with the various micro-levels.

2. See Chi-ming Hou's paper presented at the annual meeting of the Association of Asian Studies, March 31, 1981, p. 6.
3. Pang Song and Han Gang, "Dang he guojia lingdao tizhi de lishi kaocha yu gaige zhanwang" (A historical investigation of the party's and the state's leadership structure and the outlook on reform), *Zhongguo shehui kexue* (Chinese Social Science), no. 6 (November 10, 1987): 4.
4. Ibid., p. 6.
5. Andrew G. Walder, "The Political Sociology of the Upheaval of 1989," *Problems of Communism* 38 (September–October 1989): 30.
6. To Guillermo O'Donnell and Philippe Schmitter, the "external factor" plays an "attenuated" role in the liberalization and democratization of authoritarian regimes that involves "a critical component of mobilization and organization of large numbers of individuals." My tentative view is that the "outside factor" played an extraordinarily important role in the events leading to the Tiananmen tragedy, and indeed over the preceding ten years.
7. Zou Dang [Tang Tsou], "Zhongguo ershi shiji zhengzhi yu xifang zhengzhixue" (Twentieth-century Chinese politics and Western political science), *Zhengzhi yanjiu* (Political Studies) (Beijing) (September 1986): 1–5. For an English translation and Theodore Lowi's introduction, see *PS* 20, no. 2 (Spring 1987): 325–333.
8. I try to use the terms "rules" and "norms" consistently. The term "rule" refers to written rules in authoritative party documents. Some are operative, and some are not. "Norms" are internalized rules of conduct or notions of propriety. Most of the time, operative rules are internalized norms. But not all norms need find expression in written rules. In many cases, operative rules and internalized norms cannot be clearly distinguished. Rules and norms in this sense form part of what Rasmusen calls "the rules of the game" because they exercise constraints on the actions of the players and influence the outcome.
9. Tang Tsou, *The Cultural Revolution and Post-Mao Reforms: A Historical Perspective* (Chicago: University of Chicago Press, 1986), pp. 309, 310, 318. Actually, the concentric-circle structure of power within the party is, from a broad perspective, the innermost circle in a larger system of concentric circles encompassing the whole of Chinese society. The outer circles are successively the government, the army, the workers, the office employees, and the peasants. This image of concentric circles probably is more accurate for understanding China than is the generally used notion of parallel structures.
10. Ibid., p. 310.
11. That text was originally published by the *Orient Daily* (*Dongfang ribao*) (Hong Kong). The reports of that newspaper were not always reliable. For example, an extra issue of that newspaper announced on June 6 that Deng was dead and that the 27th Army, which had, according to an earlier report, perpetrated the massacre in Beijing, had surrendered. But some of the points in the text, republished by a Chinese newspaper in New York, seem credible. *Huaqiao ribao* (China Daily News) (New York), July 15, 1989, p. 6.
12. "A summary of the important points of Chairman Mao's remarks to responsible officials along the way in the period of his tour outside Beijing" (from the middle ten days of August to September 12, 1971). Reprinted in

Tang Tsou

Zhonggong nianbao (Yearbook on Chinese Communism) (Taiwan: Society for the Study of the Chinese Communist Party, 1973), sect. 7, pp. 5–8. This summary was enclosed in a circular to high-ranking party officials issued on March 13, 1972. For a more general discussion, see "Prolegomenon to the Study of Informal Groups in CCP Politics," in Tsou, *Cultural Revolution,* pp. 67–94.

13. Lowell Dittmer, *Liu Shao-ch'i and the Chinese Cultural Revolution* (Berkeley: University of California Press, 1974); see also Frederick Teiwes, *Politics and Purges in China* (White Plains, N.Y.: M. E. Sharpe, 1979), and his earlier papers. For Deng Xiaoping's characterization of those ten struggles, see *Deng Xiaoping wenxuan* (Selected Works of Deng Xiaoping) (Beijing: People's Publishing House, 1983), p. 257. He discouraged party officials from using the phrase "ten line struggles."

14. *Yearbook on Chinese Communism,* 1973, sect. 7, p. 5. It has been pointed out to me how amazingly Mao's statements coincide with Jon Elster's characterization of the simplest social norm: "Do *X*" or "Don't do *X*." *The Cement of Society* (Cambridge University Press, 1989), p. 98. Mao could write fairly complicated prose. He apparently chose the most simple form of expression to drive home his point for the party cadres without much education.

15. It is not correct to say that the first set of "do's" and "don'ts" is too vague to be important. When Deng challenged Hua Guofeng's authority, he first promoted the slogan "Practice is the sole criterion for testing truth," in opposition to Hua's "two whateverism."

16. In his account at the Lushan meeting in 1959 of his successful recapture of control over military affairs in 1934–1935, Mao tried to convey the impression that he had meticulously observed the rule of the minority obeying the majority, as well as the rule that a party leader does not express publicly his views that are opposed to those of the party center, unless he is authorized to do so. Talking about his public challenge of the military strategy and tactics of Bo Gu and Otto Braun in December 1934 at Liping (Guizhou province), he said that up to that time, "the vote was four to three. I obeyed [the majority] and would not talk to the fourth person. It was not until we arrived at Liping [on December 12, 1934] that I changed my strategy and tried to win over the masses and spoke out publicly and Bo Gu [the head of the party center] approved [of my speaking out]." The gist of Mao's lengthy talk was reported by Li Rui, *Lushan huiyi shilu* (The true record of the Lushan meeting) (Hunan: Chunqiu Publishing House, 1988), p. 231. Li was the fifth most important official implicated in the Peng Dehuai affair. For an account of the Politburo meeting held at Liping on December 18 and its significance, see Harrison Salisbury, *The Long March.* I use the Chinese translation of his book because I have misplaced the English version, and it is easier to identify the names of places and persons in the Chinese edition. There are two Chinese translations. The translation published by the People's Liberation Army Press is used here. See pp. 128–130 of that version.

17. Li, *Lushan huiyi shilu,* p. 172.

18. Chen Duxiu et al., "A Statement of Our Political Opinion," dated July 15, 1929; see the collection of documents distributed widely by a bookseller in Hong Kong: The Archival Office of the Party, *Selection of Documents of the Party Center of the CCP,* 5:482.

19. Li, *Lushan huiyi shilu,* pp. 178, 179, 305–306.

324

20. Ibid., pp. 226–319.
21. For the text of Deng's talk, see *Huaqiao ribao*, June 7, 1989, p. 5.
22. *Huaqiao ribao*, June 14, 1989, p. 4. Even after the decision to declare martial law had been made on May 17, Zhao telephoned Yang to express his hope that Yang would talk to Deng *again* to convince Deng to admit that the editorial was a mistake.
23. Tang Tsou, "The Historical Change in Direction and Continuity with the Past," *China Quarterly*, June 1989, p. 345.
24. Chen Xitong's official report, dated June 30, 1989, *Renmin ribao* (overseas edition), July 7, 1989, p. 4. Chen was the mayor of Beijing.
25. *Huaqiao ribao*, June 14, 1989, p. 4.
26. Lowell Dittmer took that quotation from the *South China Morning Post* and *Ming pao*. Lowell Dittmer, "The Tiananmen Massacre," *Problems of Communism* (September 7, 1989): 7.
27. *Huaqiao ribao*, June 14, 1989, p. 4. President Yang underscored the split in the party as the "root" of the student movement in his speech on May 25 to an emergency meeting of the Military Commission. *Huaqiao ribao*, May 30, 1989, p. 9.
28. Chen's official report; see note 24.
29. *Huaqiao ribao*, June 14, 1989, p. 4.
30. Article by Mu Wang, *Huaqiao ribao*, June 14, 1989, p. 8.
31. I am relying almost entirely on the works of Adam Przeworski and Guillermo O'Donnell and Philippe C. Schmitter. But I know that I am tackling a different problem. See Adam Przeworski, "How Do Transitions to Democracy Get Stuck and Where?" (unpublished paper dated September 1988). For a fuller exposition and analysis, see his forthcoming book: *Transitions and Reforms: East and South*, chap. II. Guillermo O'Donnell and Philippe C. Schmitter, *Transitions from Authoritarian Rule: Tentative Conclusions About Uncertain Democracies* (Baltimore: Johns Hopkins University Press, 1986), is also a path-breaking work.
32. One of the demands in the famous statement issued on May 19 by the "Three Research Institutes and One Association" was to make public the inside story of policy decisions and differences of opinion at the top level of leadership. Those four organizations were (1) the Research Institute on the Reform of Economic Structure, (2) the Research Institute on Agricultural Development in the state council's Center for Agricultural Research, (3) the Research Institute on International Problems of the China International Trade and Investment Corporation, and (4) the Association of Young Economists in Beijing. They constituted Zhao's brain trust and his most loyal supporters.
33. In this case, the term "radical" is used to describe an idealist who is willing to take even greater risks when the chances of achieving the desired goal decrease. Such radicals live by an ethic of conscience alone, totally ignoring the ethics of responsibility. They live in a dream world of ideals and absolute freedom. By their actions they feel liberated. Nothing else counts. They prefer to show their dedication to ideals rather than to achieve political success. To their credit, however, they do not advocate the use of violence. One wonders if they fully realize that their actions will lead to violence: sporadic and defensive use of violence on the part of people in the streets, and systematic, unnecessarily brutal, sometimes irrational use of weapons by soldiers under orders to shoot, or reacting out of fear, or in response to harmless

provocations. Most of the dead in the June 4 tragedy were ordinary residents of the city, not students.

34. The mayor of Beijing attributed to Wang Dan, one of the best known leaders of the Beijing students, the remark that "to begin the hunger strike on the thirteenth will enable us to use Gorbachev's visit to China to bring pressure on them," *Renmin ribao*, July 7, 1989, p. 4.
35. *Huaqiao ribao*, June 14, 1989, p. 8.
36. *Huaqiao ribao*, May 16, 1989, p. 1.
37. "Record of the Aborted 'May 14 Dialogue' (Big-Character Poster at People's University circa May 15, 1989)," in Han Minzhu, *Cries for Democracy* (Princeton: Princeton University Press, 1989), pp. 204–206).
38. See Qian Feng's report of a discussion among Hu Ping [editor of *Zhongguo zhi chun* (China Spring)], Xiang Xiaoji, and Wuerkaixi on the experiences of the democracy movement of 1989 and lessons to be learned. *China Spring*, no. 86 (July 1990): 7. I have taken some liberty in translating the term *xuezei* into "student scab."
39. Ibid., p. 8.
40. Ibid., pp. 9–10.
41. *Huaqiao ribao*, May 16, 1989.
42. Hu Ping, "Bajiu minyun de fansi" (Reflections on the democracy movement of 1989)," *Zhongguo zhi chun*, no. 5 (1990): 10. Hu's article and an earlier one in the 1990, no. 4, issue are undoubtedly the best of all the pieces that I have read.
43. The other official was Li Tieying, the chairman of the Commission on Education.
44. For the Chinese text, see *Huaqiao ribao*, May 15, 1989, p. 2. For a list of those who signed the statement, see Han, *Cries for Democracy*, p. 209. For an account of the origin of the statement, see Yan Jiaqi, "The Forty Days That Changed the World," *Zhongyang ribao* (Central Daily News) (international edition), June 4, 1990.
45. For the Chinese text, see *Huaqiao ribao*, May 17, 1989, p. 1. It was also published in *Renmin ribao*.
46. Zhang Langlang, "Dao Tiananmen shao ge kouxin" (To deliver an oral message to Tiananmen), *The Nineties* (Hong Kong), no. 233 (June 1989): 14–15.
47. Dai Qing also took the lead in gathering together the twelve intellectuals who signed the urgent appeal to the students on May 14. She was released from detention on May 9, 1990.
48. *Huaqiao ribao*, May 17, 1989.
49. Yang's remarks made at a meeting on May 22, 1989. Excerpts reprinted in *Huaqiao ribao*, June 14, 1989, p. 4.
50. See the earlier section "Ideological Hegemony, Public Spaces, and the Official System of Communication" for an analysis of the official system of communication.
51. *Huaqiao ribao*, June 14, 1989, p. 4.
52. For a partial text of the dialogue, see *Huaqiao ribao*, May 19, 1989, p. 4.
53. Yan Jiaqi, former head of the Institute of Political Science of the Chinese Academy of Social Science, and chairman of the Federation for a Democratic China, in 1989–1990, now says that he drafted the document alone in a moment of indignation after he noticed on that day how public sentiments had turned against Deng. He has expressed his sadness that some innocent

people were interrogated and imprisoned because of his statement. Yan, "The Forty Days That Changed the World," *Zhongyang ribao*, June 4, 1990. For Dai Qing's criticism of the recklessness and muddleheadedness of Yan and persons like him, see Dai, "My Imprisonment," *Shijie ribao*, May 20, 1990, p. 32.

54. *Renmin ribao*, August 7, 1989, reprinted in *Xinhua yuebao*, no. 9 (1989): 59.

55. Lu Yongxiong et al., "The Dirty Spots in the Brilliant Achievement of the Hong Kong Journalists," in *Renmin bu hui wangji* (People Will Not Forget), edited by sixty-four Hong Kong correspondents (Hong Kong: Association of Hong Kong Correspondents, 1989), p. 332.

56. For students of the social sciences, the following episode was astounding. It said a great deal about the student movement in its last days. Chai Ling and her husband, Feng Congde, succeeded in evading the Chinese police and escaped to the West. According to Feng, he had attempted in the wee hours of June 4 to persuade the students to leave the square. The story goes that Chai Ling said to him that Zhao Ziyang (the general secretary) and Yan Minfu (head of the United Front Department of the CCP) had sent a message to them and asked them "to persist until dawn." The quoted words are from a report appearing in *Zhongyang ribao* (international edition), May 11, 1990, p. 1. Hu Ping, editor of *China Spring*, commented on that report that it was difficult to say how accurate the message was. Yan Jiaqi expressed his doubt that Zhao and Yan Mingfu would have sent that message. Whether Chai's remark will prove to be true or false, it can be said in either case that with friends like her, one doesn't need enemies. In an interview reported June 20, 1990, in the *New York Times*, Chai Ling, invoking Buddhism, said that she had been "reborn." Let us all wish her well in her new incarnation.

57. *Xinhua yuebao*, September 1989, p. 58.

58. Li Peier, "The Passionate Commander-in-Chief Chai Ling," in *People Will Not Forget*, p. 216.

59. Tsou, *Cultural Revolution*, pp. 270–271.

60. Mao Zedong, *Selected Works* (Peking: Foreign Languages Press, 1965), 2:422, 426.

61. Mao Zedong, "Current Problems of Tactics in the Anti-Japanese United Front," and "Freely Expand the Anti-Japanese Forces and Resist the Onslaughts of the Communist Diehards," in *Selected Works*, 2:421–436. Incidentally, the translators used the phrase "tit for tat" to render the Chinese phrase *zhenfeng xiangdui*. As used by Mao, the Chinese phrase denotes only half of the meaning of tit for tat (i.e, If you defect, I will defect).

Index

Index

Cohen, Paul, 3, 38
COMECON, 220, 221
Comintern, 66, 289
communications system, 17, 282–284
communism, 65, 66
  Mao's vision of, 74
communist bloc, 14
  China's affiliation with, 210
  China's relations with, 14
Communist Party of the Soviet Union. *See*
  CPSU
conflict resolution pattern. *See* all-or-
  nothing approach
confucianism, 42, 57, 59, 270
  neo-confucianism, 41–42, 44, 277
conservatives, 81–82
Constitution, of 1982, 167
corporatism, 19, 156, 158–160
  corporatist state defined, 154–155
  differences with pluralism, 160–161
  state, 155
  three stages of Chinese, 161–163
CPSU (Communist Party of the Soviet
  Union), 210, 213, 218–221
  Twentieth Congress, 211, 234
  Twenty-first Congress, 218
  Twenty-second Congress, 212, 219
  Twenty-seventh Congress, 228, 229
criticism and self-criticism, 293
Cuba, 221
Cultural Revolution, 5, 8, 10–11, 13, 15,
  24–25, 27, 41, 65, 85–86, 136, 142,
  158, 163, 168, 185, 188, 272–273,
  292, 302
  analysis, 76–78
  impact on foreign policy, 238
  impact on grass-roots participation,
  139–140
Czechoslovakia, 156, 220

Dai Qing, 279, 307–308, 310
democracy, 6, 19, 53–54, 61, 85, 286,
  319
  new, 95, 231
  as power of people, 54–55
democratization, 6
  three steps of, 202
Deng Liqun, 40
Deng Xiaoping, 3–4, 8, 12, 15, 17–18,
  53, 59, 78–80, 84, 95, 163, 180,
  188, 196, 200, 224, 273, 277, 287–
  289, 297–298, 303, 306, 309, 311,
  321
  Dengist state, 10, 129
  era of, 5–6, 11, 23, 39, 85–86
  June 9, 1989, speech, 17
  political thought of, 82–83

Deng Zhibing, 93, 105, 107, 112
depoliticization, 24
Dewey, John, 61
Ding Richu, 102
Ding Wenjian, 38
Dirlik, Arif, 95
Dittmer, Lowell, 4, 14–15

Eastern Europe, 142, 195, 201, 213, 277
Echols, John, 156, 160
elite, 130
  activism, 28, 30–31
  political, 12–13, 180
  theory, 19, 130
  traditional, 187
employment system, 170–172
entrepreneurship, 105
Euro-communism, 224, 277

Fang Jiaobo, 90, 104
Fang Lizhi, 32–33, 39–40
Feng Shaoshan, 90
Feng Youlan, 41
Fewsmith, Joseph, 4–5, 23
"five principles of peaceful co-existence,"
  213, 233–234
"Four Cardinal Principles," 23, 79
four principles for party-to-party relations,
  226

Gang of Four, 77–78, 188
Gao Gang, 289–290
Geertz, Clifford, 65
getihu (self-employed individuals), 274,
  281
GMD (Guomindang; KMT; Kuomintang),
  7, 28, 32, 46, 64, 71, 157, 181, 210,
  219, 320
  alliance with CCP, 66–67
  GMD state, 61
Goldstein, Steven, 45
Gomulka, Wladyslaw, 213, 216
gong (public), 28–31, 46
Gorbachev, Mikhail, 15, 84, 220, 228,
  288, 298, 309
Gouldner, Alvin, 191
Great Leap Forward, 8, 11, 13, 74–76,
  136, 164, 168, 188, 217, 273, 288
guan (state), 28
Guan Guangmei, 35
Guangdong, 97–98, 111
Guomindang. *See* GMD

Habermas, 29–30, 47
  on public spere, 29
Harding, Harry, 160
Harding, Neil, 159

330

Index

Index

separation of party and government, 272

reformers, 199, 275
  position, 85–86
  strategies, 300–301
regional hegemony, 209, 223
relationship between "private" and "public," 5, 25, 28–31, 44, 46
Ren Zhongyi, 34
Revel, Jean-François, 118
revisionism, 76, 215–216
River Elegy, 5, 44
Roemer, John, 113
Rousseau, Jean Jacques, 70
Rowe, William, 28–30
ruling class, traditional, 269–270
Russell, Bertrand, 61

Sa Mengwu, 38
Schmitter, Philippe, 155
Schoppa, Keith, 28
Shanghai argument
  criticism, 112–115
  old and new, 100–109
  private property, 103
  profit, 106–107
Shonfield, Andrew, 98
Shue, Vivienne, 130, 133
si (private), 28–29
Sinatra doctrine, 230
Singapore, 42, 97
Skocpol, Theda, 145
socialism, 158–159
  Lenin's vision of, 158–159
  Mao's version, 184
  parliamentary road to, 212, 219
  primary stage theory, 25
  work-unit, 12, 162, 168
socialist camp, 216, 223
socialist transition, 71, 73
Solinger, Dorothy, 95
Song Renqiong, 40
South Korea, 42, 97, 202, 223
Soviet Union, 14–15, 72, 142, 156, 181, 195, 201, 210, 220
  anti-party group, 215
  Brezhnev era, 156
  command economy, 164
  hegemonism, 15
  relations with India, 235
  Sino-Soviet split, 216–220
  Sino-Soviet thaw, 224
stalemate, 16, 18, 266–267, 320
Stalin, Joseph, 74, 156, 211, 219
  personality cult of, 212
Stalinism, 11, 212–213
State Council, 307

state-society relationship, 4, 16, 46, 129, 270, 275–276
  polarization of, 18
  reconciliation of, 268
statism, 9–10, 140, 142
  of Dengist period, 143–146
  of Maoist period, 140–142
Stepan, Alfred, 155, 159
Strand, David, 28–31
student movement, 200, 274–275, 295
  autonomous organizations, 297–298
  characteristics of, 316
  lessons, 317–318
Sun Longji, 100
Sun Yat-sen, 6–7, 53, 60–61
  compromise approach, 63–64
Sun Zi, 58

Taiwan, 42, 65, 97, 115, 202, 276
Tang Yijie, 42
Tao Xisheng, 38–39
technocrats, 13, 180–181, 191
  challenges to, 197–203
  ideological commitment, 195–196
  promotion to leadership, 194–195
  two types of, 199
"ten major line struggles," 289–290
"theory of three worlds," 15, 239–240
Third Plenum of the Eleventh Central Committee of 1978, 23, 167, 273
third world, 4, 14, 232, 234
  China's identification with, 210, 245–246
  China's relations with, 15
Tiananmen, 8, 13, 17–18, 230
  tragedy of, 144, 180, 200, 265, 269, 273–274, 286–287, 316–317, 321
Tito, 211, 213, 223
Toffler, Alvin, 37, 40
Togliatti, Palmiro, 219
total crisis, 2, 6
totalism, 271
totalitarianism, 11, 154, 156, 159–160, 271
  economic, 11, 157–159
  limitations of, 160
  political, 11, 157–158
  revolutionary-feudal, 158
Townsend, James, 130
Tsou, Tang, 3–4, 16–17, 23, 44, 55, 79, 93–94, 111, 117–118, 131, 142–144
Tu Wei-ming, 41

United States, 15, 102, 217, 222, 277
  Congress, 267
  negotiations with China, 233
  normalization with China, 15

Index